Cyber Risk Management in Practice

Cyber Risk Management in Practice: A Guide to Real-World Solutions is your companion in the ever-changing landscape of cybersecurity. Whether you're expanding your knowledge or looking to sharpen your existing skills, this book demystifies the complexities of cyber risk management, offering clear, actionable strategies to enhance your organization's security posture. With a focus on real-world solutions, this guide balances practical application with foundational knowledge.

Key features:

- **Foundational insights:** Explore fundamental concepts, frameworks, and required skills that form the backbone of a strong and pragmatic cyber risk management program tailored to your organization's unique needs. It covers everything from basic principles and threat modeling to developing a security-first culture that drives change within your organization. You'll also learn how to align cybersecurity practices with business objectives to ensure a solid approach to risk management.
- **Practical application:** Follow a hands-on step-by-step implementation guide through the complete cyber risk management cycle, from business context analysis to developing and implementing effective treatment strategies. This book includes templates, checklists, and practical advice to execute your cyber risk management implementation, making complex processes manageable and straightforward. Real-world scenarios illustrate common pitfalls and effective solutions.
- **Advanced strategies:** Go beyond the basics to achieve cyber resilience. Explore topics like third-party risk management, integrating cybersecurity with business continuity, and managing the risks of emerging technologies like AI and quantum computing. Learn how to build a proactive defense strategy that evolves with emerging threats and keeps your organization secure.

"*Cyber Risk Management in Practice: A Guide to Real-World Solutions* by Carlos Morales serves as a beacon for professionals involved not only in IT or cybersecurity but also across executive and operational roles within organizations. This book is an invaluable resource that I highly recommend for its practical insights and clear guidance."

José Antonio Fernández Carbajal
Executive Chairman and CEO of FEMSA

Security, Audit and Leadership Series

Series Editor: Dan Swanson, Dan Swanson and Associates, Ltd., Winnipeg, Manitoba, Canada.

The ***Security, Audit and Leadership Series*** publishes leading-edge books on critical subjects facing security and audit executives as well as business leaders. Key topics addressed include Leadership, Cybersecurity, Security Leadership, Privacy, Strategic Risk Management, Auditing IT, Audit Management and Leadership

Team Intelligence: A New Method Using Swarm Intelligence for Building Successful Teams
Mohammad Nozari

The Gardener of Governance: A Call to Action for Effective Internal Auditing
Rainer Lenz and Barrie Enslin

Navigating the Cyber Maze: Insights and Humor on the Digital Frontier
Matthias Muhlert

Safeguarding the Future: Security and Privacy by Design for AI, Metaverse, Blockchain, and Beyond
Alan Tang

Security Relationship Management: Leveraging Marketing Concepts to Advance a Cybersecurity Program
Lee Parrish

A Cybersecurity Leader's Journey: Speaking the Language of the Board
Edward Marchewka

Cyber Risk Management in Practice: A Guide to Real-World Solutions
Carlos Morales

For more information about this series, please visit: https://www.routledge.com/Internal-Audit-and-IT-Audit/book-series/CRCINTAUDITA

Cyber Risk Management in Practice

A Guide to Real-World Solutions

Carlos Morales

CRC Press
Taylor & Francis Group
Boca Raton London New York

CRC Press is an imprint of the
Taylor & Francis Group, an **informa** business

Designed cover image: Shutterstock image ID 252752416

First edition published 2026
by CRC Press
2385 NW Executive Center Drive, Suite 320, Boca Raton FL 33431

and by CRC Press
4 Park Square, Milton Park, Abingdon, Oxon, OX14 4RN

CRC Press is an imprint of Taylor & Francis Group, LLC

ISBN: 978-1-032-84238-7 (hbk)
ISBN: 978-1-032-90113-8 (pbk)
ISBN: 978-1-003-54620-7 (ebk)

DOI: 10.1201/9781003546207

Typeset in Sabon
by Newgen Publishing UK

Access the Support Material: www.routledge.com/9781003546207

To my beloved wife, and my wonderful son and daughter: You are my strength, my compass, and my purpose. Your unconditional love and support always inspire me to keep learning and growing every day on this journey.

To my Mom and Dad: Your endless encouragement, wisdom, and love have been the foundation of my aspirations and achievements.

To all the people who have taught me something in my career, investing your time in me: Your trust and friendship will always be treasured.

"There is no one braver than the person who is unaware of the risks around them." – My Dad.

Contents

Foreword by José Antonio Fernández Carbajal xiii
Acknowledgments xvii
Author biography xix

Introduction 1

SECTION I
Mastering the essentials of cyber risk management **7**

1 Fundamentals of cyber risk management 9

2 Cyber risk management frameworks 16

3 Governance and cybersecurity culture 32
Aligning corporate governance and security culture 37
Connecting the dots in cyber risk management 45

4 Cyber risk management methodology and risk register 50
Cyber risk management methodology 50
Cyber risk register 65

5 Laying the groundwork 71

SECTION II
Executing cyber risk management in five steps **93**

6 Starting the process: Contexts and information gathering 95
Risk contexts 95

Limiting the scope 104
Understanding the business environment 107
Gathering essential information 110

7 Risk assessment: From identification to characterization 125
Risk assessment 125
The art of risk identification 127
Assessing the impact and likelihood of risks 134
Risk characterization: Aggregation of risks above the risk appetite 154

8 Risk treatment strategies 163
Risk treatment planning 163
Exploring risk treatment options 166
Selecting the optimal path forward 187
Treatment plans in practice 189

9 Making things happen: Communication and implementation 207
Organizing projects for treatment plans implementations 207
Risk treatment plan implementation 212
Executing risk acceptance 218

10 Risk monitoring and metrics 221
Risk monitoring 221
Ongoing monitoring practices 226
Cyber risk management metrics 229

SECTION III
Elevating beyond basics: Achieving cyber resilience 239

11 Third-party risk management 241
Understanding third-party risks in the supply chain 241
Due diligence processes 253
Assurance processes 258
Offboarding processes 262

12 Building cyber resilience 268
The core components to build cyber resilience 269
Crisis management and response 280

13 Advancing toward risk quantification **287**
The evolution of cyber risk quantification 287
Integrating quantitative and qualitative approaches 302

14 New technologies: Methods, tools, and challenges **306**
Navigating cyber risks in generative AI 306
Quantum computing and cyber risk: The next frontier 315

SECTION IV
Conclusion **321**

15 Bringing it all together **323**
A breath of time—Some advice for your career 328

Illustration credits 330
Index 331

Foreword

The technological revolution is transforming fields such as software, connectivity, immersive technology, robotics, mobility, space exploration, and many others. With the explosive advent of new and popular forms of AI in 2023, there is tremendous potential for advances in areas like energy production, agriculture, education, and health—just to name a few. However, these technological developments also pose significant threats, including disinformation, social isolation, the potential for autonomous technology, and, critically, cyber vulnerability.

Cybersecurity challenges have become a pressing issue, reshaping the political, economic, and social landscapes of the world. Effective cybersecurity management is now a core concern for all organizations, especially businesses, as any threat could impact every aspect of their operations—from supply chains to customer service.

In this complex environment, *Cyber Risk Management in Practice: A Guide to Real-World Solutions* by Carlos Morales serves as a beacon for professionals involved not only in IT or cybersecurity but also across executive and operational roles within organizations. Cybersecurity has emerged as one of the top issues in both management and corporate governance.

This book arrives at the perfect time and in the right way: it offers not only a solid theoretical foundation but, more importantly, a clear and accessible path into the intricate world of cybersecurity. Carlos uses a unique and effective method—presenting cybersecurity through a dialogue filled with real-world examples, making the complex material easy to understand and practical to implement.

Carlos Morales begins with a clear outline of the essentials in cyber risk management. He guides readers through a five-step approach to achieving cyber resilience, the highest level in cybersecurity. A cyber-resilient organization has the knowledge and ability to prevent attacks, manage incidents, and, most importantly, continue its business operations. Achieving resilience minimizes the impact of cyberattacks, which, as Morales highlights, can have far-reaching consequences—ranging from data breaches to serious financial, reputational, regulatory, and customer trust issues.

Among the many insights in this book, three stand out. First, cyber risk management is crucial for corporate governance. Second, building an organizational culture that prioritizes cybersecurity is essential. And third, cybersecurity is a continuous process, adapting alongside rapid technological advancements. Here, I'd like to share FEMSA's approach to these critical areas.

FEMSA is a 134-year-old company operating in 18 countries, with 400,000 employees who serve millions of consumers daily. We are proud of our strong corporate governance, which is vital to the responsible management of our business and ensures accountability, alignment with stakeholders, and the creation of long-term value.

Within our corporate governance framework, cybersecurity plays a major role in ensuring data privacy and information protection. Cybersecurity is not solely a technical issue; it involves social and legal considerations, as well as security awareness and behavior. We prioritize threat deterrence, detection, response planning, and recovery processes to proactively protect against potential risks.

In the event of a breach, we rely on advanced cyber intelligence tools, countermeasures, and incident response processes to maintain business continuity while managing risks to both our company and our customers swiftly and decisively.

We also require that our suppliers and third-party partners safeguard FEMSA's personal data and information assets throughout their entire life cycle—from access to deletion and destruction.

The responsibility of protecting our assets is shared by everyone at the company. That's why we've invested in building a strong culture of cybersecurity awareness and knowledge. Every employee understands the escalation process for reporting suspicious activities, and we reinforce this through seminars, courses, and specialized training. Every click, every email, and every interaction with data must be handled with care to ensure it does not compromise our organization's security. Our policy is zero tolerance for vulnerabilities, and we prioritize caution in all security matters.

As Carlos Morales wisely notes, cybersecurity is a journey, not a destination. Attacks are constantly evolving, and the threats we've encountered in recent years will be different from those we'll face in the near future. For FEMSA, this makes it essential to continually enhance our security processes, implementing robust controls and countermeasures based on risk assessments, and regular external and internal audits.

Successfully implementing an information security program is a gradual process of learning, reviewing, and adapting. As technology advances, new threats will emerge, and security incidents will inevitably increase. Therefore, organizations must adopt a proactive approach to cybersecurity governance grounded in risk management, rather than merely reacting to breaches.

At this juncture, *Cyber Risk Management in Practice: A Guide to Real-World Solutions* by Carlos Morales is an invaluable resource. I highly recommend this book for its practical insights and clear guidance.

José Antonio Fernández Carbajal
Executive Chairman of the Board of Directors and Chief Executive Officer of FEMSA

Acknowledgments

I am deeply grateful to those who generously shared their time, anecdotes, and insights for this book. Your contributions have enriched this work and made it truly meaningful. A heartfelt thank you to:

- José Antonio Fernández Carbajal, Executive Chairman of the Board and CEO of FEMSA
- Bruce Gnatowski, Managing Director, Digital Risk Management at Crumpton Global
- Ram Elboim, CEO of Sygnia
- Rick Doten, VP of Information Security at Centene
- Tyson Johnson, CIO of UNI Financial Cooperation

Your guidance and support have been invaluable.

Author biography

Carlos Morales, MBA, A. CCISO, CISM, GRCP, GRCA, CRISC, IRMP, CDPSE, IDPP, IPMP, IAPP, ICEP, is a cybersecurity professional with over 18 years of experience in risk management, privacy, and information security across diverse global landscapes. An advocate for cybersecurity as a business enabler, Carlos is recognized for developing pragmatic, risk-based models that align security initiatives with organizational objectives.

His international expertise is marked by his active participation in initiatives that bridge the gap between the private sector, public institutions, and academia. Carlos has worked with organizations of all sizes around the globe, from multinational conglomerates to startups, bringing a broad, practical perspective across industries. This experience allows him to tailor cybersecurity strategies that are effective and scalable, regardless of organizational size or sector.

He served as an advisor on cybersecurity matters to the Executive Office of the President of Mexico for the National Cybersecurity Plan and was a member of the first Cybersecurity Innovation Council led by the Organization of American States (OAS), where he fostered collaboration among participating countries. At the Instituto Tecnológico y de Estudios Superiores de Monterrey (ITESM), Carlos played an active role in shaping the design of the Cybersecurity HUB and the master's degree in cybersecurity. He continues to share his expertise as a professor in the ITESM master's program in cybersecurity, guiding the next generation of professionals.

Carlos is also an active participant in international forums, where he shares practical insights and connects with diverse audiences, bridging technical and nontechnical perspectives with clarity and impact.

Introduction

Family has always been a guiding force in my life, symbolizing support, trust, and respect. For me, family isn't just about the people at home; it also includes the teams we work with every day. If you're picking up this book, you're likely part of the cybersecurity family and on a mission to improve your cybersecurity posture, whether stepping into a new role, refining your organization's cybersecurity strategy, or simply eager to expand your understanding of cyber risk management. Whatever your motivation, you're in the right place. Welcome to *Cyber Risk Management in Practice: A Guide to Real-World Solutions*. We're about to embark on a journey that's as much about understanding the evolving landscape of cyber threats as it is about building resilient, adaptable strategies to safeguard your organization.

In today's hyper-connected world, where every click, transaction, and communication can introduce new vulnerabilities, the need for robust cyber risk management has never been more urgent. But let's be honest: the world of cybersecurity can feel overwhelming. It's full of jargon, complex frameworks, and evolving threats that can make even the most seasoned professionals feel like they're constantly playing catch-up. That's why I didn't want this book to be about throwing theories at you, but about breaking down those complexities and offering practical, actionable guidance that you can apply directly to your unique context.

I've been fortunate to spend years working in the trenches of cybersecurity, facing innumerable challenges, and learning from some of the best minds in the field. Along the way, I realized that many resources out there either over-simplify the journey or they dive so deep into technicalities that it becomes inaccessible. This book aims to strike a balance. I hope you'll find it as a conversation, a dialogue where we explore not just the "how" but also the "why" behind effective cyber risk management, sharing stories, real-world examples, and insights that bring these concepts to life.

Before we get into the details of the book, let's take a moment to talk about why cyber risk management is so important. Nowadays it's clear that cybersecurity isn't an IT issue, but a business imperative. The risks associated with cyber threats are not confined to data breaches or financial losses; they

DOI: 10.1201/9781003546207-1

extend to reputation damage, regulatory penalties, and erosion of customer trust. The challenge lies in recognizing that these risks are not static. They evolve as quickly as the technologies we use, requiring a dynamic approach that's rooted in continuous learning and adaptation.

What sets this book apart is its focus on pragmatism. Cyber risk management isn't about achieving a perfect state of security; that's an illusion. Instead, it's about being better prepared, more resilient, and continuously improving your defenses. It's about understanding that risk management is a journey, not a destination, and as we progress through this book, I encourage you to embrace a mindset of continuous improvement. Don't aim for perfection; aim for progress. Learn from every assessment, every incident, and every decision. Use these experiences to refine your strategies and build a culture of resilience within your organization. And remember, this journey requires patience and perseverance.

Building a strong cybersecurity posture doesn't happen overnight. It takes time, effort, and, sometimes, a bit of trial and error. Be prepared to face setbacks and challenges, but don't let them deter you. Instead, view them as opportunities to learn and grow. With persistence, you'll find that each step, no matter how small, brings you closer to your goal. Throughout our journey, you'll find anecdotes and real-world examples, and this isn't just for the sake of engagement but because I believe that stories have the power to transform abstract concepts into tangible lessons. I'm sure that sharing anecdotes from my experiences and those of my peers will provide you a clearer understanding of the challenges and opportunities ahead. These stories are intended to inspire critical thinking about your own practices and encourage new approaches to managing cyber risk.

I structured this book to guide you through what you have ahead, helping you build a comprehensive cyber risk management program that aligns with your organization's goals and risk appetite. We begin with the fundamentals, ensuring that you have a solid understanding of the key concepts and frameworks that reinforce effective risk management. From there, we move into practical applications, providing step-by-step guidance on implementing these strategies in real-world scenarios. Finally, we'll explore more advanced topics, building on top of the first two sections and preparing you to elevate your approach and achieve true cyber resilience. To make this journey as smooth and productive as possible, this book is divided into three main sections, each designed to build upon the last. Here's a brief overview of what to expect:

SECTION I: MASTERING THE ESSENTIALS OF CYBER RISK MANAGEMENT

In this first section, we lay the foundation for your cyber risk management journey. We start by diving into the fundamental concepts and frameworks that are essential for any cyber risk management program. If you're new to the field, this section will provide you with an in-depth preparation about the basics. You'll learn about key concepts like threat modeling, risk assessments, and the different types of controls that can be implemented to mitigate risks. But even if you're experienced, there's value here for you. We explore these foundational elements in a way that challenges you to rethink your assumptions and deepen your understanding. For instance, if you've often found yourself describing risks simply by pointing out vulnerabilities, this section will encourage you to think more holistically. We'll get into how to properly assess risks, always considering all three key components of risk: vulnerabilities, threats, and impacts. This section also emphasizes the importance of understanding your organization's unique context. Effective risk management isn't a one-size-fits-all solution; it requires a tailored approach that considers your organization's specific goals, risk appetite, and regulatory environment.

But understanding the technical side of risk management is only part of the equation; equally important is cultivating the right culture and fostering change management and people skills that will help accelerate your initiatives and make your efforts more effective. A successful cyber risk management program thrives on a culture that prioritizes security and encourages everyone to play their part, creating an environment where every employee, from top leadership to frontline staff, understands their role in safeguarding the organization. It's about more than just policies and procedures; it's about embedding cybersecurity into the fabric of your organizational culture. In this section, we'll explore how to build a security-first culture that supports your cyber risk management goals, including strategies for engaging employees, communicating the importance of cybersecurity in relatable terms, and fostering a sense of ownership and responsibility across the board. We'll also discuss the crucial role of change management in implementing and sustaining cybersecurity initiatives, as change, even when it's for the better, can be challenging. Strong change management skills are needed to guide your organization through transitions, manage resistance, and build support for new initiatives. We'll cover practical techniques for leading change, from securing buy-in from key stakeholders to effectively communicating changes and managing the human aspects of implementation. Lastly, we can't discuss cyber risk management without addressing the importance of people skills. In cybersecurity, as in many fields, the human element is often the most unpredictable and challenging to manage. This section provides insights into developing the people skills necessary to lead cybersecurity efforts effectively, including building trust, fostering collaboration, and navigating the complexities of human behavior in the context of cybersecurity. At the end of this section, you'll have a strong foundation that combines technical knowledge with a focus on culture, change management, and people skills. This foundation will give you the tools to identify and manage risks while empowering you to drive meaningful change within your organization, ensuring your cybersecurity initiatives are embraced, sustained, and successful.

SECTION II: EXECUTING CYBER RISK MANAGEMENT IN FIVE STEPS

Once we've covered the basics, we move on to the practical application of these concepts. This section is a hands-on guide to implementing a cyber risk management program in your organization. We break down the process into five manageable steps, providing clear, actionable advice at every turn. Each chapter in this section is designed to walk you through a specific phase of the risk management process, from analyzing our business contexts, identifying and assessing risks to developing and implementing risk treatment strategies. We'll explore how to prioritize risks based on their potential impact, develop a risk treatment plan, and monitor and review your program to ensure its ongoing effectiveness.

This section is about understanding the particularities and complexities involved in each step and learning how to adapt your approach to fit your organization's needs. We discuss common pitfalls and challenges you might encounter and offer practical solutions to help you overcome them. You'll also find tools, templates, and checklists that you can use to streamline your efforts and ensure you're covering all the bases.

Whether you're setting up a new risk management framework or fine-tuning an existing one, this section provides the practical tools and steps you need to effectively manage cyber risks. I'm confident it will be a resource you can refer to at any point in your journey, ensuring you have the support you need to navigate the complexities of this field.

SECTION III: ELEVATING BEYOND BASICS: ACHIEVING CYBER RESILIENCE

By the time we reach this section, you'll have a solid understanding of the essentials and practical aspects of cyber risk management. Now, it's time to take things to the next level. This section focuses on advancing your strategies toward achieving cyber resilience. Cyber resilience, along with readiness, represents the other side of the same coin and goes beyond just protecting against threats; it's about ensuring your organization can continue to operate and thrive in the face of adversity. Achieving this requires a proactive approach that emphasizes continuous improvement and adaptability. We'll explore advanced topics such as managing third-party risks, integrating cybersecurity with business continuity planning, and leveraging emerging technologies to enhance your defenses.

We'll discuss how to establish a culture of continuous improvement within your organization, encouraging your team to regularly assess and refine your cybersecurity practices. We'll also explore the importance of collaboration and communication in achieving cyber resilience. Effective cybersecurity isn't something one person or team can handle alone; it requires the collective effort of everyone in your organization. You'll learn how to foster a collaborative environment, break down silos, and ensure everyone understands their role in protecting the organization.

In this way, throughout the book, you'll find that each section builds on the last, providing a comprehensive roadmap for developing and implementing a robust cyber risk management program. But remember, this isn't a linear process. Cyber risk management is a journey, and you may find yourself revisiting certain concepts or sections as your understanding grows and your organization's needs evolve. I encourage you to approach this book with an open mind and a willingness to learn. Whether you're just starting out or looking to enhance an existing program, there's always room for improvement and that's what this book is all about, helping you continuously improve your approach to cyber risk management so you can protect your organization and thrive in today's digital world.

Thank you for choosing to embark on this journey with me. Together, we'll have fun exploring the complexities of cyber risk management, turning challenges into opportunities, and paving the way for a more secure and better future. Let's get started!

Section I

Mastering the essentials of cyber risk management

Chapter 1

Fundamentals of cyber risk management

You will find that in the field of cyber risk management, clarity and consensus on fundamental concepts are essential for effective teamwork and strategy implementation. It's critical that when we discuss risks, threats, vulnerabilities, and impacts, we are all picturing the same scenarios and understanding the terms in the same way. This common ground forms the foundation of a robust cyber risk management strategy.

Starting with the basics, let's talk about what we mean by these terms. A 'risk' in the cyber world refers to the potential for experiencing harm or loss because of a threat exploiting a vulnerability in our systems or processes. It's vital that everyone understands a risk is not just any problem; it's a specific issue that arises from the intersection of a threat with a vulnerability. To have a risk, we must find the three key components of risk: Threat, Vulnerability, and Impact.

In Figure 1.1, we see the core components that define cyber risk, represented through three overlapping circles: Threat, Vulnerability, and Impact. Each of these elements is crucial in understanding how risks manifest in the digital world.

The 'Vulnerability' circle reflects those weaknesses within our systems, software, procedures, or people that can be targeted by threats. These are the gaps in our armor and understanding them requires a detailed knowledge of our digital and physical environments. Identifying vulnerabilities is a proactive step in preventing security breaches.

The 'Threat' circle symbolizes anything that can take advantage of a weakness in our digital defenses, whether through malicious intent like a cyberattack or through accidental occurrences like a software malfunction. It's important for the team to recognize that threats can come from many sources, both external and internal, and can vary greatly in their nature and origin.

Where these two circles overlap, we find 'Potential Cyber Risk.' This highlights the specific areas where identified vulnerabilities could be exploited by threats. It's the starting point for understanding where risks are likely to emerge.

DOI: 10.1201/9781003546207-3

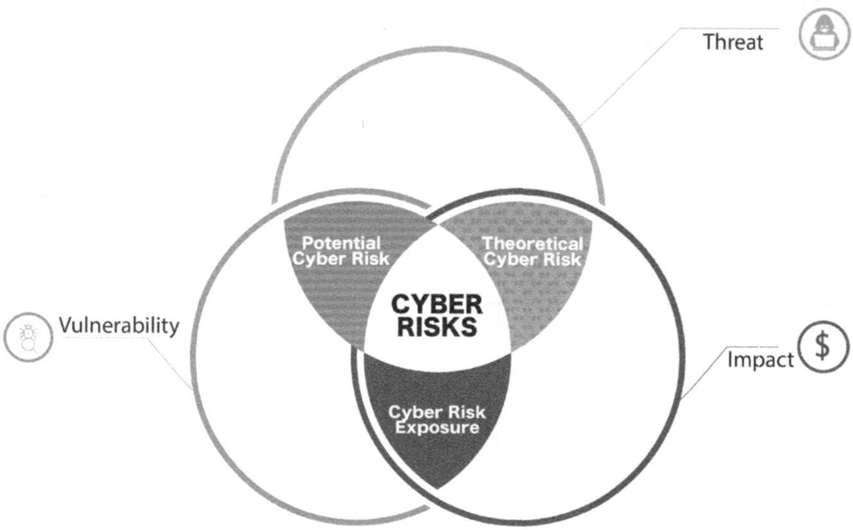

Figure 1.1 Cyber risks.

The 'Impact' circle outlines the potential consequences or effects that can result if a risk becomes reality. Impacts can be wide-ranging, affecting everything from operational capability to legal compliance and reputation. The team needs to appreciate that the impact is a measure of the severity of a risk materializing and can help prioritize which risks need immediate attention.

Where the Impact and Vulnerability circles intersect, we see 'Cyber Risk Exposure,' indicating the areas that could be affected if a threat materializes. This serves as a reminder that even if a specific threat isn't yet known, the system remains exposed and needs monitoring.

In the section labeled 'Theoretical Cyber Risk,' where Threat and Impact overlap without involving a vulnerability, we're looking at risks that could arise in theory. While the threat and potential impact are clear, the absence of a known vulnerability means there's no immediate risk. However, this doesn't mean we should overlook these areas, as vulnerabilities could emerge over time.

Finally, at the center where all three elements, Threat, Vulnerability, and Impact, intersect, we find the true 'Cyber Risk.' This is the point where all conditions for a cyber risk are present, with a specific vulnerability that a known threat could exploit, leading to an outcome beyond the organization's tolerance level. This is the area we focus on when assessing and managing risks. In cyber risk management, our goal is to continually identify, assess, and mitigate these risks, ensuring that threats, vulnerabilities, and their potential impacts are managed proactively.

Cyber risk is about recognizing the potential for things to go wrong before they actually do. It's an understanding that a vulnerability exists, a threat is out there, and the impact could be significant. The risk comes from the possibility that these elements could align, leading to a security incident. This is where we focus our proactive efforts, helping us prioritize resources effectively. By addressing vulnerabilities, deterring threats, and preparing for potential consequences, we can strengthen our defenses and protect our digital assets. This understanding allows us to view cyber risk as a whole and reinforces the importance of managing each part to reduce our overall exposure. It's not just about fixing weaknesses but also about preparing for threats and mitigating the possible outcomes. Having a clear understanding of these elements is essential when planning defense strategies, ensuring we are always one step ahead. Now, let's review a few other key concepts that are critical to keep in mind as we continue managing cyber risks effectively:

Likelihood is a term we use to describe the probability or chance that a given threat will exploit a vulnerability within our systems. It's an estimate that helps us understand how often we might expect a certain type of security incident to occur, based on experience or industry knowledge. The assessment of likelihood considers various factors, such as the level of threat activity in the cyber landscape and the attractiveness of the vulnerable asset to potential attacker.

Annual loss expectancy (ALE) is an estimate of the yearly cost your organization might face from specific risks. It's like looking ahead and trying to predict how much money you could lose over a year if certain bad things happened. You calculate ALE by figuring out how often a risk might occur in a year and then multiplying that by how much it would cost each time it happens. This gives you a ballpark figure to help decide how much you're willing to spend to prevent these losses.

Annual rate of occurrence (ARO) tells us how often we can expect a particular risk to happen within a year. Imagine predicting the chances of rain in a particular month; the ARO does the same for risks. If you know a certain type of cyberattack might happen twice a year, the ARO for that risk is two. It helps in understanding the regularity of potential threats, guiding us on how prepared we need to be.

Single loss expectancy (SLE) represents the cost of a risk materializing once. If a cyberattack occurs, SLE estimates the financial impact of that single incident. Understanding the SLE helps you measure the financial impact of individual risks, allowing you to prioritize which risks to address first based on their potential damage.

Value at risk (VaR) is a bit more complex and is used to estimate the maximum loss your organization could face over a specific period, under normal conditions, at a given confidence level. Picture setting aside an emergency fund; VaR helps decide how big that fund should be to cover potential losses from risks. It's a financial tool that says, "Given the worst expected scenario, here's the most we could lose." This helps in financial planning and ensures that unexpected losses won't completely derail your organization.

Risk in the context of cybersecurity refers to the adverse impact on an organization and how likely is that to happen. It's the intersection where all three elements (threat, vulnerability, and impact) come together, highlighting an area where attention is needed. It is important to always keep in mind that we need all three elements to call it a risk.

Inherent risk is the level of risk that exists before any safeguards, controls, or actions are taken to alter its impact or likelihood. It's the raw exposure that exists due to the environment, systems, and processes currently in place.

Risk appetite (as we can see in Figure 1.2) is the amount of risk an organization is willing to accept in pursuit of its objectives. It's a strategic choice that dictates how much risk is acceptable. For instance, a company might have a higher risk appetite for launching innovative products quickly, accepting the risk that comes with moving fast.

Risk tolerance is closely related to risk appetite but focuses more on the level of variation an organization is willing to withstand around specific risks. It's like setting boundaries on how much fluctuation you can handle in your investments before you need to act.

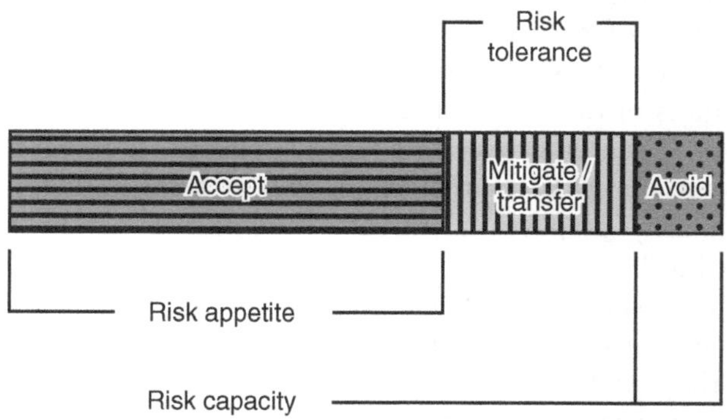

Figure 1.2 Risk appetite, tolerance, and capacity.

Risk capacity is the maximum amount of risk an organization can absorb. This is the absolute limit beyond which the organization's survival might be threatened. It's the point at which the consequences of a risk could be so severe that the organization might not recover.

Safeguards/controls are the measures put in place to mitigate risks. These can be policies, procedures, technology, training, or anything that reduces either the likelihood of a threat exploiting a vulnerability or the impact if it does.

Actual Risk is the exposure that remains after you've identified the inherent risk and applied your controls. This is the real-world risk level you're dealing with, the one that requires constant monitoring, management, and may need to be addressed by defining treatment plans if it is above your risk appetite. You can use then the reduction from your inherent risk to your actual risk as part of the equation to calculate the efficiency of your controls. The second part of that equation is the cost of your controls.

Risk Treatment Plan is our blueprint for managing actual risk. It details the methods you'll use to implement controls, aiming to reduce each risk to a level that's acceptable for your organization. This plan acts as your guide, locating exactly how to enhance our defenses at the intersection of vulnerabilities and threats to lessen their impact. Treating a risk involves several strategies: you might choose to avoid the risk entirely, take steps to mitigate it, transfer the responsibility to another party, or accept that some level of risk is inevitable. Each option is a strategic choice, reflecting your organization's approach to handling potential threats and safeguarding its operations. When defining treatment plans, it's important to remember two key aspects: first, every new control introduced into our environment will bring its own set of risks, which we also need to carefully assess. Second, the cost of implementing treatment plans should never exceed the potential loss from the risk itself. These principles ensure that our approach to risk management is both effective and economically sensible, prioritizing the protection of our assets in a balanced and strategic manner.

Residual Risk is what's left after you've implemented your risk treatment plan. Be aware that after implementation, residual risk becomes your actual risk. In other words, residual risk is the bit of risk that still exists because no system or control is ever completely foolproof. It's the chance of a security breach, even after you've locked the doors and set the alarm. This is the risk you continue to live with and monitor over time, ensuring it stays within your organization's risk appetite and tolerance levels. It is only achieved once treatment plans are fully implemented. Remember, having a plan does not make a risk go away.

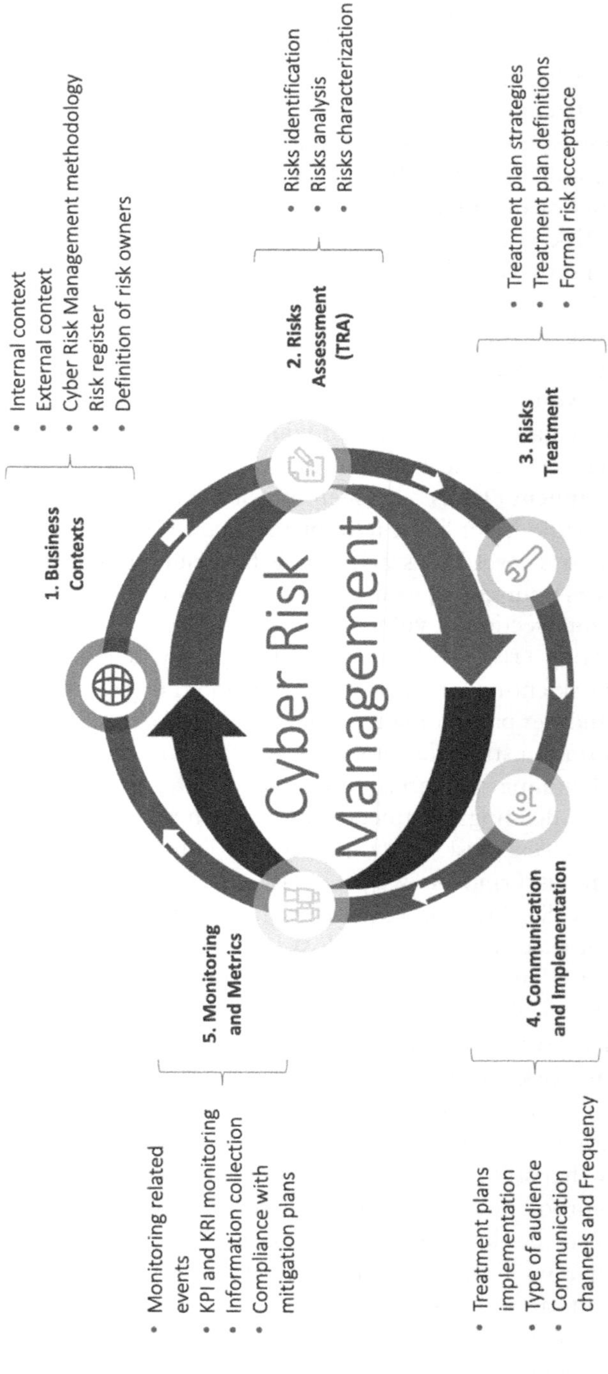

Figure 1.3 Cyber Risk Management cycle.

With all these concepts clearly established, we can now bring together the cyber risk management framework and its phases. Figure 1.3 is the visual representation that outlines each critical phase of the process, from understanding the business context to monitoring and metrics. In the following sections, we'll review each of these phases in detail and explore practical ways to implement the framework within your organization. The aim is to ensure that this methodology not only provides a structured approach but is also applied in a pragmatic and actionable way, aligned with your organization's unique risk landscape.

For cyber risk management to be effective, everyone involved, from IT specialists to top executives, must share this understanding. Misinterpretations or assumptions can create gaps in defense strategies, shift priorities in the wrong direction, and weaken responses to threats. Starting with a shared vocabulary and clear understanding of these fundamental principles ensures that discussions about risks lead to meaningful actions that protect our organization from potential cyber harm. This shared understanding is not just a technical necessity; it's a strategic advantage. It enables a unified approach to assessing, prioritizing, and mitigating risks, ensuring that every team member can contribute effectively to the organization's cyber resilience.

Chapter 2

Cyber risk management frameworks

Are you familiar with the concept of the always-evolving cybersecurity landscape? I'm sure you've heard the phrase, "Security is a journey, not a destination." This rings especially true in the field of cyber risk management. Security is also a feeling, one that evolves as we continuously improve our understanding of vulnerabilities, threats, and impacts. Because we'll never know everything, achieving perfection in protecting our organizations is impossible, much like we can't mitigate a risk 100%. As we start this journey, understanding the fundamental structures of risk management is our first critical stop. Risk frameworks are essential in this process. They provide structured guidance for identifying, assessing, and managing risks effectively. Following these frameworks allows us to systematically address threats and vulnerabilities, ensuring our risk management efforts remain comprehensive and adaptable.

There are several key frameworks out there, each with its own set of guidelines and best practices. Some frameworks are broad and can be applied to various industries, while others are more specific, tailored to particular sectors like retail, finance, or healthcare. One common goal of these frameworks is to help organizations set a structure that will work constantly and consistently. Following a framework allows businesses to systematically address risks, decide which ones need to be tackled immediately, which to monitor over time, and which to accept as part of their operations.

Implementing a risk framework will help you to have structured guidance. Also, it will help in recognizing opportunities for growth and improvement. A well-managed organization can navigate uncertainties and seize new chances for success by having a robust risk management strategy in place. A common misunderstanding in the field of cybersecurity involves confusing frameworks and their purpose. For instance, confusing security program frameworks with risk management frameworks. While both are crucial for enhancing an organization's security posture, they serve distinct purposes and operate on different levels of the security planning and implementation

DOI: 10.1201/9781003546207-4

process. Recognizing the difference between these two types of frameworks is essential for effectively managing cybersecurity risks and implementing comprehensive security measures.

In Figure 2.1 you can see the most relevant security frameworks, such as the National Institute of Standards and Technology Cybersecurity Framework (NIST CSF) or ISO/IEC 27001, primarily provide organizations with guidelines for developing, implementing, and managing their overall cybersecurity programs. These frameworks focus on identifying the best practices for establishing your cybersecurity program and protecting systems, networks, and data from cyber threats. They offer a structured approach to cybersecurity, emphasizing the identification, protection, detection, response, and recovery from cyber incidents. Following these frameworks allows you to establish a robust cybersecurity program that safeguards your organization's digital assets against a wide range of threats.

Risk Management Frameworks, such as the NIST Risk Management Framework (RMF), ISO 27005, Center for Internet Security (CIS) Risk Assessment Method (RAM), and Factor Analysis of Information Risk (FAIR), are designed to help you manage information security risks. These frameworks guide you through a systematic process to understand your organization's risk landscape, evaluate the potential impact of various threats, and identify effective strategies for addressing them. Using these frameworks allows you to prioritize your security efforts based on risk, ensuring that resources are efficiently directed toward the most critical

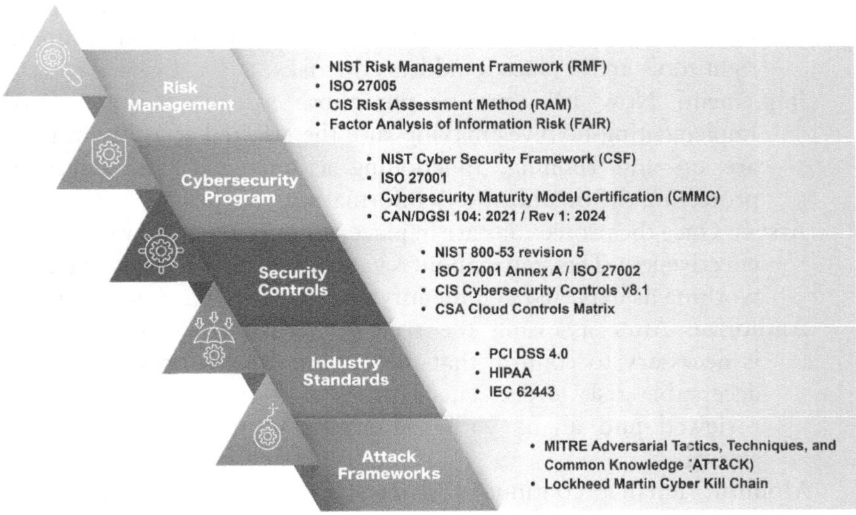

Figure 2.1 Security frameworks and standards.

vulnerabilities. Let's review the foundations of some risk management frameworks.

NIST RMF: The NIST RMF provides a broad process that integrates security and risk management activities into the system development life cycle. The RMF is designed to help organizations manage security and privacy risks, and it is structured around a seven-step process: Prepare, Categorize, Select, Implement, Assess, Authorize, and Monitor. This framework is particularly useful for organizations that work closely with the US federal government or those looking to align with its rigorous standards. The RMF emphasizes the importance of continuous monitoring and real-time risk management, making it a dynamic tool for managing cyber risks.

Let's walk through the seven steps of this framework, each offering its own insights and tools for each stage:

Prepare: Before taking action, it's essential to get everything in order. This involves understanding what information the company holds, determining which assets are most critical, and deciding how to protect them. It's about ensuring that everyone understands what's important and how to approach protecting it.

Categorize: This step is about organizing the company's information, identifying what needs the highest level of protection, and what carries less risk. The goal is to focus efforts on protecting what truly matters.

Select: With a clear understanding of what's important, it's time to choose the right security measures. This means identifying the safeguards and practices that will best protect the organization's vital information from potential threats. It's about making sure the right tools are in place to address the risks.

Implement: Now it's time to put those safeguards into action. Implementing involves making sure the selected security measures are up and running, functioning as intended, and effectively protecting the organization's information.

Assess: Once the protections are in place, it's important to evaluate their effectiveness. This step is about reviewing whether the safeguards are working as expected and identifying any gaps that need attention.

Authorize: After assessing the security measures, formal approval is necessary to confirm that the organization is operating within acceptable risk levels. This ensures that everything is properly reviewed and aligns with the organization's risk management strategy.

Monitor: Finally, continuous monitoring is crucial. This involves keeping an eye out for any changes or new threats, ensuring that the security measures are still effective and making adjustments when necessary to maintain protection over time.

For official information and detailed guidance on the NIST RMF, you should refer to the NIST's publications, specifically *NIST Special Publication 800-37: Guide for Applying the Risk Management Framework to Federal Information Systems.*[1] This publication provides an overview of the RMF, detailing its purpose, scope, and the step-by-step process for its implementation. It is designed to help federal agencies and other organizations understand how to apply the RMF to their information systems and environments of operation. The guide outlines each of the RMF steps, offering in-depth explanations and guidance for each phase. These publications and other related documents can be found on the NIST website under the Computer Security Resource Center (CSRC) section. NIST regularly updates these publications to reflect changes in cybersecurity threats, technologies, and best practices, so it's important to consult the latest versions for the most current guidance.

ISO 27005:2022[2] is an international standard that offers guidelines for information security risk management. Unlike NIST RMF, which is more prescriptive in nature, ISO 27005 provides a framework for conducting risk assessments in the context of an organization's overall information security management system (ISMS), particularly those implementing ISO/IEC 27001. It covers the entire risk management process, including risk assessment, risk treatment, risk communication, and risk monitoring and review. ISO 27005: What is truly amazing is that it's designed to be adaptable to any organization regardless of its size or industry, offering a flexible approach to identifying, analyzing, and treating information security risks.

ISO 27005 outlines a structured approach to managing information security risks, categorized into five distinct phases. This approach not only simplifies the complex landscape of information security but also ensures a thorough and systematic process to safeguard against potential threats. Let's explore each phase:

Context establishment: The journey of risk management begins with establishing a solid foundation. This initial phase is about setting the stage for all risk management activities to follow. It involves defining the scope and boundaries of the risk assessment phase, understanding the organization's objectives, and identifying the information assets that need protection. This groundwork ensures that the risk management process is aligned with the organization's overall goals and addresses the correct assets and areas of concern.

Risk assessment: The heart of the risk management process lies in risk assessment, a comprehensive phase that encompasses risk identification, risk analysis, and risk evaluation.

- Risk identification: Here, we embark on a detailed exploration to uncover potential threats to our information assets and vulnerabilities within our systems that could be exploited.

- Risk analysis: With threats and vulnerabilities in hand, we analyze them to understand the likelihood of occurrence and the potential impact on the organization. This analysis helps us measure the severity of each risk, much like assessing the difficulty of the obstacles on our way to achieve business objectives.
- Risk valuation: Finally, we valuate these risks to determine their significance in relation to our risk criteria, prioritizing them based on their potential impact on our organizational objectives. This step decides which risks need immediate attention and which can be monitored over time.

Risk treatment: Having identified and assessed our risks, we now decide on the best strategies to manage them. Risk treatment involves selecting appropriate risk management options, such as avoiding, transferring, mitigating, or accepting risks, and then implementing the chosen treatment plans. In most of the cases, a combination of treatment methods is required for addressing a risk.

Communication and consultation: Keeping everyone in the loop is a must-do in managing risks well. This step is all about making sure we talk and listen to everyone involved from the board to the project team implementing the plan, making sure the whole team knows the game plan and the decisions made. But there's more to it. Once we decide on our plan to deal with these risks and our treatment plans, they need to be put into action. It's like saying, "Risks won't pack up and leave on their own. We've got to roll up our sleeves and get to work on these security moves we've planned." This means we also need to keep an eye on how these plans are going, making sure they're really kicking those risks to the curb. And if something's not working as well as we thought, we're all about adjusting our approach. So, this phase is not just about getting everyone ready and informed but also making sure we're all staying on track and making the necessary moves to protect our organization. It's about teamwork, staying alert, and making those important updates and changes together.

Risk monitoring and review: The final phase is a continuous process of vigilance and adaptation. The risk landscape is ever-changing, with new threats emerging and old threats evolving. Regular monitoring of risks and the effectiveness of treatment measures, together with periodic reviews of the risk management process, ensures that the organization remains agile and can adapt to new information or changes in the environment.

We know that managing the cyber risks needs a clear and organized plan. ISO 27005 provides that structure to make it happen. Helping you to figure out how to spot, assess, handle, talk about, and keep an eye on security risks in a smart way.

CIS RAM[3]: The CIS RAM is a free-to-use framework, designed to help organizations implement the CIS Controls, which are a set of best practices for securing IT systems and data. CIS RAM provides a method for assessing their specific risk scenarios and determining the appropriate implementation of the CIS Controls. It emphasizes the importance of understanding the relationship between business objectives and security practices. CIS RAM is particularly useful for organizations looking for a straightforward, actionable approach to risk assessment that is directly tied to the implementation of CIS security controls. Let's walk through the key aspects of CIS RAM in an approachable and professional manner.

One of CIS RAM's key strengths is its ability to prioritize cybersecurity efforts by assessing risks. It helps organizations identify threats, using the CIS community's attack model, and directs resources toward closing the most significant security gaps first. CIS RAM also emphasizes the importance of aligning your risk management practices with legal and regulatory requirements. This ensures that your cybersecurity measures not only protect your organization but also comply with industry standards and legal obligations, much like how building codes ensure that construction projects are safe and compliant with regulations, demonstrating due care and reasonableness.

Just as it's crucial for all members of a community to understand and participate in security practices, CIS RAM encourages widespread engagement across the organization in the risk management process. This means involving stakeholders from various departments in assessing risks, deciding on controls, and understanding the rationale behind each decision. It fosters a culture of cybersecurity awareness and collective responsibility. The implementation of CIS RAM involves a detailed assessment of how each CIS Controls reduces specific risks, followed by a decision-making process on which controls to implement and how to prioritize them. This step-by-step approach ensures that every action you take contributes directly to lowering your cybersecurity risk profile.

The FAIR[4] methodology is a structured and systematic approach to understanding and analyzing information risk. It quantifies risk in financial terms, making it easier for organizations to prioritize risk management efforts based on potential impact. FAIR differentiates between threat event frequency and probable loss magnitude, enabling more accurate risk assessments. This approach helps organizations identify, assess, and address risks in a way that aligns with business objectives, enhancing decision-making processes around cybersecurity investments and mitigation strategies.

The FAIR methodology stands out by converting the abstract concept of risk into a language that resonates across all levels of an organization: financial figures. This shift from qualitative descriptors to quantitative analysis helps businesses identify where their cybersecurity measures are most needed and how to allocate resources effectively. FAIR distinguishes between the frequency of threat events and the magnitude of potential losses, offering a detailed perspective on risk. This distinction deepens understanding of how often certain types of cyber incidents might occur and the scale of their potential impact. For instance, a high-frequency, low-impact risk may require a different approach than a low-frequency, high-impact risk. This level of detail allows for tailored risk management strategies that align closely with an organization's specific risk appetite and business goals.

This is how FAIR empowers organizations to move beyond the often fear-driven, reactive posture toward cybersecurity, guiding them toward a proactive, informed approach. Quantifying risk in financial terms allows stakeholders to make reasoned decisions about where to invest in cybersecurity defenses, balancing cost with risk reduction. This means not all risks are treated equally or require immediate action; instead, decisions are made based on a clear understanding of what poses the greatest threat to the organization's financial health and operational continuity.

In practice, applying the FAIR methodology involves identifying potential risk scenarios, analyzing the likelihood of their occurrence, and estimating the financial impact of each scenario. This process requires a collaborative effort across departments, bringing together expertise from IT, security, finance, and operations to ensure a comprehensive view of risk. Such cross-functional collaboration fosters a culture of risk-aware decision-making, where cybersecurity is seen not just as an IT issue but as a strategic business imperative.

Imagine trying to communicate the importance of cybersecurity. You might talk about hackers and malware, but it's when you break down the risks into concrete scenarios and numbers that it really hits home. FAIR does just that. It encourages us to dissect cyber risk into smaller, digestible parts. Here's how this journey develops, step by step.

Starting with scope, we need to clearly define what we're focusing on. This means identifying specific assets under threat, such as data or systems, and understanding the types of risks they face. Defining the boundaries of our analysis ensures we focus our efforts where they matter most.

The next step is identifying threat events and vulnerabilities. Here, we list the ways those assets could be compromised, considering different types of attacks and areas where defenses might be weakest. This creates a detailed inventory of potential issues we need to address.

Estimating frequency involves determining how often these threats could occur. This isn't guesswork; it's based on data, trends, and industry insights. We're answering the question, 'How likely is this within a specific timeframe?'

Assessing potential impact is about calculating the damage that could result from each threat. This includes direct and indirect costs, from immediate expenses to long-term consequences, turning the abstract idea of risk into financial terms.

Evaluating risk combines the frequency and impact assessments. Understanding how often an event might happen and its potential cost gives us a clear view of the overall risk. This step helps us prioritize which risks need attention first.

Finally, analyzing risk in context means aligning these findings with your organization's risk tolerance. Every organization has its own level of acceptable risk, and this step ensures our strategies match that. It helps determine which risks require immediate action and which can be monitored over time.

Developing and implementing mitigation strategies is about taking action. Based on our analysis, we create plans to reduce the likelihood or impact of risks. This could involve enhancing security measures, implementing new policies, or increasing awareness. It's a proactive approach to managing cyber risks and quantifying the cost of controls versus the risk itself that helps to drive the conversation with senior management making decisions on what initiatives to approve when improving or adding security controls.

Monitoring and review is the final step, but it's an ongoing one. The world of cyber threats is always changing, so we continuously track the effectiveness of our measures and update our risk assessments. This ensures our approach to risk management evolves with the landscape, keeping our defenses strong.

Through the FAIR methodology, we systematically break down the complex issue of cyber risk into manageable, quantifiable parts. However, the real magic happens with quantification. Rather than vague terms like high risk, FAIR pushes us toward estimating potential losses in financial terms. How costly could a breach be? This isn't about making wild guesses. FAIR lays out a systematic approach to estimate financial impact, considering both the likelihood of an incident and its potential repercussions. This method transforms abstract anxieties into tangible concerns, grounding our strategy in reality.

Although FAIR is an amazing framework, it's important to consider there are some disadvantages to gain a balanced perspective. One notable challenge is the requirement for detailed data. FAIR relies heavily on accurate, quantitative data to estimate risk in financial terms. This can pose a significant hurdle for organizations that may not have access to extensive historical data on security incidents or those that find it difficult to quantify the impact of potential threats. As a result, the process of gathering sufficient data to make informed assessments can be time-consuming and resource intensive.

One last example of a limitation of FAIR is the complexity of the methodology itself. While FAIR provides a comprehensive framework for risk assessment, its complexity can be daunting, especially for organizations without specialized risk analysis expertise. The process requires a detailed understanding of risk factors and demands a high level of skill in data analysis and interpretation. This complexity can lead to challenges in effectively communicating risk to stakeholders who may not be familiar with the complexities of risk quantification, potentially hindering decision-making processes.

Adopting the FAIR approach requires a permanent commitment to risk management. In cybersecurity, where the landscape is perpetually shifting with new threats surfacing and existing ones evolving, the data and assumptions supporting a FAIR analysis are forced to require frequent updates to remain relevant. This dynamic nature of risk management requires organizations to engage in continuous monitoring and revising of their risk assessments. Far from being a simple problem, this requirement stresses the deeper truth about the nature of managing risks; it's a journey rather than a destination. Our reality in the world of risk management is that standing still is not an option.

FAIR demystifies the often-nebulous concept of cyber risk, translating it into actionable, quantifiable terms. This methodology empowers you to proactively manage risk, ensuring resilience and strategic advantage in the ever-evolving digital landscape. However, it's important for us to be aware of its challenges because by recognizing these disadvantages, we'll guide our organizations to be better prepared for the demands of implementing FAIR and make more informed decisions about how to integrate it into their overall risk management strategy.

Risk Management Frameworks like NIST RMF, ISO 27005, CIS RAM, and FAIR provide structured approaches to managing cybersecurity risks. Each framework has its strengths, whether it's the systematic process of NIST RMF, the adaptability of ISO 27005, the practicality of CIS RAM, or the quantitative focus of FAIR. Understanding and leveraging these frameworks will help you prioritize security efforts and allocate resources efficiently to address the most critical vulnerabilities. Also, it will help to set the course of our cybersecurity program toward the adoption of a proactive risk-based approach; however, we still need to understand that those are just part of the whole picture. It is because, in the world of cybersecurity, risk management frameworks work hand in hand with security control frameworks; they are like two sides of the same coin, working together to protect organizations from cyber threats by minimizing risk materialization. Think of risk management frameworks as the big-picture plans that guide how an organization identifies, assesses, and manages cybersecurity risks. On the flip side, security control frameworks provide the specific tools and actions needed to put those plans into action. Let's explore an overview of how risk management frameworks use security control frameworks, such as NIST 800-53, CIS Controls v8.1, and ISO 27002, to build a robust defense against cyber threats.

Security control frameworks are like the instruction manuals for cybersecurity. They list out specific actions, practices, and technologies that an organization can use to protect itself from cyberattacks. These controls are the building blocks of a secure information system, covering everything from password policies and firewalls to employee training and incident response plans.

When a risk management framework sets the course for identifying and prioritizing risks, it turns to security control frameworks to find the best solutions for those risks. Here's how it works with some of the most recognized frameworks.

NIST 800-53[5]: This is a comprehensive list of security and privacy controls developed by the NIST for federal information systems and organizations. But the truth is that it's not just for the government, but many private sector organizations use it too. NIST 800-53 controls are designed to be tailored. A risk management framework might point out that data encryption is a priority, and NIST 800-53 will provide detailed options on how to implement encryption effectively.

NIST 800-53 provides a comprehensive framework designed to help organizations protect their information. It offers an extensive set of over 1,000 controls, each addressing specific cybersecurity risks. These controls cover a wide range of areas, from physical security measures to advanced technical strategies. The framework guides organizations in selecting the right controls to mitigate identified risks and ensure that their systems and data remain secure. The controls in NIST 800-53 are organized into 20 different categories, making it easier to find exactly what you need.

1. Access control: This is about controlling who can access or view information within your organization's systems, ensuring only authorized individuals can access specific areas or data.
2. Awareness and training: This acts as an extensive training module to arm your team with the knowledge and skills needed to identify and respond to cybersecurity threats effectively.
3. Audit and accountability: This focuses on meticulously documenting actions within your systems, creating a traceable record of activities like a registry. This enables tracking of actions to understand events and identify participants.
4. Assessment, authorization, and monitoring: This serves as a health check for your cybersecurity measures, continuously evaluating their effectiveness and making necessary adjustments to uphold security standards.
5. Configuration management: This entails securely and methodically setting up your systems from the outset, ensuring everything is correctly positioned for easy management and protection.

6. Contingency planning: This prepares your organization for emergency scenarios with strategies and processes designed for rapid recovery and restoration of normal operations following incidents.
7. Identification and authentication: This guarantees system access is granted only after verifying the identity of the user.
8. Incident response: This involves having a predetermined plan for addressing and managing incidents efficiently, ensuring preparedness for unexpected situations.
9. Maintenance: This concerns the upkeep of your systems to maintain their operational integrity and security.
10. Media protection: This focuses on the security of data stored across various media types, ensuring sensitive information is safeguarded against unauthorized access.
11. Physical and environmental protection: This relates to securing the physical sites of your systems against unauthorized access or environmental threats, safeguarding the infrastructure that houses your digital assets.
12. Planning: This emphasizes the necessity of having a coherent cybersecurity strategy and action plan before launching security initiatives.
13. Program management: This overlooks the holistic management of an organization's cybersecurity efforts, ensuring all elements function in concert for effective protection.
14. Personnel security: This manages risks related to personnel access to systems, ensuring individuals are scrutinized and considered reliable before being granted access to sensitive information.
15. Personally identifiable information processing and transparency: This concerns the meticulous handling and transparent processing of personal data, respecting privacy at all stages.
16. Risk assessment: This entails a thorough analysis of potential risks to systems and data, preparing for and proactively addressing possible security concerns.
17. System and services acquisition: This ensures security considerations are integral to the procurement or development of new systems or services.
18. System and communications protection: This guards the integrity of internal and external communications, preventing unauthorized access or interference with data exchanges.
19. System and information integrity: This aims to maintain the accuracy and trustworthiness of systems and data, preventing unauthorized alterations or corruptions.
20. Supply chain risk management: This addresses the security risks presented through the supply chain, emphasizing the importance

of securing products and services used by the organization to prevent security breaches. This critical aspect highlights the growing need for diligent management and assurance process of supply chain risks, which we will explore in a dedicated chapter focusing on practical strategies for managing these extensive and complex risks.

CIS Controls v8.1[6]: The CIS Controls are a set of actionable practices for cybersecurity that focus on critical areas of attack. They're designed to be accessible and implementable, making them a favorite for organizations of all sizes. If a risk management framework identifies that protecting endpoints from malware is a key risk area, the CIS Controls offer specific, straightforward practices to secure those endpoints.

The CIS Controls v8.1, made by the CIS, acts as a master list of key actions and strategies designed to reinforce an organization's cybersecurity defenses. Picture them as the ingredients in a recipe for a secure digital environment. With cybersecurity threats becoming more sophisticated, these controls are like the fundamental spices and herbs that, when combined correctly, create a robust defense against potential attacks.

In its eighth version, the CIS Controls have been refined and categorized into 18 groups, making it easier for organizations to understand and apply them effectively. These groups are thoughtfully designed to cover various aspects of cybersecurity, from managing hardware and software to dealing with more intricate issues like data protection and incident response.

Here's a brief overview of these 18 groups, each serving a unique purpose in the cybersecurity toolbox:

1. Inventory and control of enterprise assets: This ensures you have a clear picture of all the hardware within your organization. It's crucial for understanding the scope of your digital environment and securing it effectively.
2. Inventory and control of software assets: This focuses on keeping track of all software applications in use, essential for managing licenses, updates, and security patches to maintain a secure software environment.
3. Data protection: This involves safeguarding data from unauthorized access and breaches, critical for maintaining the confidentiality and integrity of sensitive information.
4. Secure configuration of enterprise assets and software: This is about establishing and maintaining security settings for your systems and applications, a fundamental step in protecting against vulnerabilities.
5. Account management: This manages user accounts to ensure only authorized individuals have access to specific data and systems, a key aspect of controlling access rights within an organization.

6. Access control management: This regulates who can access resources in the network, crucial for preventing unauthorized entry and minimizing the risk of data breaches.
7. Continuous vulnerability management: This involves regularly scanning for and addressing vulnerabilities in your systems, an ongoing process critical for strengthening your cybersecurity posture.
8. Audit log management: This keeps comprehensive records of system activity to monitor and analyze events, essential for detecting and investigating security incidents.
9. Email and web browser protections: This protects against threats that come through email and web browsing, vital for blocking phishing attacks and other malicious activities.
10. Malware defenses: This implements measures to protect against malware infections, critical for preventing software designed to disrupt, damage, or gain unauthorized access to systems.
11. Data recovery: This ensures the ability to restore important data following a loss, crucial for business continuity and resilience in the face of data loss incidents.
12. Network infrastructure management: This involves securely managing the network infrastructure to ensure reliable and secure data transmission paths, fundamental for the integrity and availability of network services.
13. Network monitoring and defense: This keeps an eye on network activity to detect and respond to threats promptly, essential for maintaining the security of network traffic.
14. Security awareness and skills training: This educates staff on cybersecurity best practices and potential threats, vital for empowering employees to act as the first line of defense against cyberattacks.
15. Service provider management: This involves overseeing third-party vendors to ensure they adhere to security standards, which is important for managing risks associated with external services and products.
16. Application software security: This ensures that applications are developed and maintained with security in mind, key for mitigating risks in software that organizations rely on.
17. Incident response management: This prepares for and manages the response to cybersecurity incidents, crucial for minimizing damage and recovering quickly from security breaches.
18. Penetration testing: This regularly tests security measures by simulating attacks, which is important for identifying weaknesses before they can be exploited by actual attackers.

The CIS Controls v8.1 not only categorizes cybersecurity best practices into 18 groups but also introduces a practical approach to implementation through its tiered levels. These levels are designed to help organizations of various sizes, resources, and maturity stages to prioritize and focus their cybersecurity efforts effectively. These levels are the stages in a journey toward cybersecurity maturity, where each stage builds upon the previous, adding layers of security measures as the organization's capabilities and resources grow. The three levels of implementation guidelines in CIS Controls v8.1 are:

Level 1—Basic cyber hygiene: This foundational level is ideal for organizations just beginning their journey in cybersecurity. It emphasizes the implementation of basic, yet crucial controls that are straightforward and don't require advanced knowledge to apply. These initial steps are about establishing a solid foundation for your organization's cybersecurity program, much like learning the essential hygiene practices to maintain a clean and safe environment.

Level 2—Foundational cyber hygiene: As organizations progress, Level 2 builds on the initial groundwork by introducing a broader set of practices that delve into more complex aspects of cybersecurity. This level is designed for organizations ready to enhance their defenses with a slightly more sophisticated understanding of cybersecurity. It's about strengthening your organization's security posture to protect against a wider range of threats, preparing you to deal with increasingly complex cybersecurity challenges.

Level 3—Organizational: The top tier of the framework, Level 3, is tailored for organizations that have a strong foundation in cybersecurity and are poised to tackle advanced challenges. This level involves implementing complex controls that address sophisticated threats, requiring a significant investment in resources and expertise. At this stage, an organization is fully equipped to handle complex cybersecurity issues, ensuring comprehensive protection against advanced threats and vulnerabilities. The tiered approach of the CIS Controls v8.1 allows you to manage your cybersecurity journey systematically. Starting with level 1, organizations can gradually build up their cybersecurity practices as their capacity and needs evolve, moving through levels 2 and, if required, level 3.

Annex A of ISO 27001:2022[7] and ISO 27002[8]: Part of the wider ISO 27000 family, they provide guidelines for selecting, implementing, and managing information security controls, based on the information security risk environment of an organization. It's all about choosing the right controls that fit an organization's specific risk profile. For example, if the risk management process uncovers a high risk of data breaches, ISO 27002 will guide on which controls could best prevent those breaches, such as access control measures and data encryption.

Annex A of ISO 27001 standard acts as a detailed guide, offering specific measures, or controls, that help steer you through the complex world of information security. These controls provide the practical steps to complement the broader strategy outlined in ISO 27001. From managing sensitive information securely to implementing technical defenses like encryption, the controls in Annex A span a wide array of security aspects.

What truly sets Annex A apart is its adaptability to each organization's unique journey. Recognizing that every organization faces different threats, vulnerabilities, and objectives, Annex A allows you to customize the controls to meet your specific needs. This customization is crucial, as it ensures that the protective measures you implement are both effective and aligned with your organization's particular landscape.

Implementing these controls is like planning a detailed expedition. It involves identifying the safest and most efficient paths to your goal and determining the resources and equipment you'll need. This step is critical and requires input and collaboration from across your organization. It's about assembling a team where each member brings their expertise to the table, working together to carve out a path that's not only secure but also supports your organization's overarching goals.

Now, it's important to understand how Annex A relates to ISO 27002. While Annex A serves as the blueprint for selecting and implementing information security controls within the ISO 27001 framework, ISO 27002 provides the guidelines and best practices for establishing, implementing, maintaining, and continually improving an ISMS. Essentially, ISO 27002 dives deeper into the controls listed in Annex A, offering more detailed guidance on how to apply them effectively. If Annex A outlines what controls should be considered, ISO 27002 explains how to implement those controls in practice, offering insights and examples that can help organizations understand and apply the controls in the context of their ISMS.

The support of Annex A, and by extension, ISO 27002, could provide a solid path toward enhancing your organization's information security posture. This approach doesn't just offer a set of tasks to complete; it provides a strategic and customizable framework that evolves with your organization, and unlike NIST CSF, ISO 27001 is certifiable. In practice, integrating security controls is like looking into a 'toolbox'—the security control frameworks—to find the right tools (controls) for the job. This might mean choosing specific controls from NIST 800-53, CIS Controls, or ISO 27002 that directly address your assessed risks.

Security control frameworks like NIST 800-53, CIS Controls v8.1, and ISO 27002 offer detailed guidance on protecting against identified risks. NIST 800-53 provides a comprehensive list of controls for various threats, tailored to the needs of federal and private sector organizations. CIS Controls v8.1 focuses on practical, actionable practices to bolster defenses, categorized into different levels to match the organization's maturity. ISO

27002, along with Annex A of ISO 27001, offers guidelines for selecting and implementing controls based on the organization's specific risk profile.

I know this is a lot of information and takes time to digest it. However, remember this section is all about the foundations we need to build to get the right toolset for us to effectively implement pragmatic cyber risk management in our organizations. For sure, a basic step is truly understanding Risk Management Frameworks as they set the course for adopting a proactive, risk-based approach in your cybersecurity program. However, these frameworks are only part of the overall picture. In the world of information security, risk management frameworks and security control frameworks work together to protect organizations from cyber threats. Risk management frameworks guide how an organization identifies, assesses, and manages cybersecurity risks. On the other hand, security control frameworks provide the specific actions and tools needed to implement those plans.

Understanding and leveraging correctly, security program, risk management, and security control frameworks will clear our approach to cybersecurity, streamline our efforts, and ensure we're guiding our organizations to build a robust defense against cyber threats. These frameworks help prioritize security initiatives, ensuring resources are allocated efficiently to address the most critical risks. As we move forward, we'll explore how these frameworks can be practically applied to create a comprehensive and resilient cybersecurity strategy.

NOTES

1 National Institute of Standards and Technology. (2018, December 20). Risk Management Framework for Information Systems and Organizations: A System Life Cycle Approach for Security and Privacy. CSRC. https://csrc.nist.gov/pubs/sp/800/37/r2/final

2 International Organization for Standardization. (2022, October 25). ISO/IEC 27005:2022. ISO. www.iso.org/standard/80585.html

3 Center for Internet Security (October 2021). CIS RAM. https://learn.cisecurity.org/cis-ram

4 Freund, J., & Jones, J. (2014). *Measuring and Managing Information Risk: A FAIR Approach*. Butterworth-Heinemann.

5 National Institute of Standards and Technology. (2020, October 12). Security and Privacy Controls for Information Systems and Organizations. CSRC. https://nvlpubs.nist.gov/nistpubs/SpecialPublications/NIST.SP.800-53r5.pdf

6 Center for Internet Security. (2024, June 25). CIS Critical Security Controls v8.1. https://learn.cisecurity.org/cis-controls-download

7 International Organization for Standardization. (2022, October). ISO/IEC 27001:2022. ISO. www.iso.org/standard/27001

8 International Organization for Standardization. (2022, March). ISO/IEC 27002:2022. ISO. www.iso.org/standard/75652.html

Chapter 3

Governance and cybersecurity culture

Always, as we lay the foundations for a pragmatic cyber risk management program, it's indispensable to establish the pillars that will support and sustain our efforts. At the core of this foundation are two critical elements: Governance and Cybersecurity Culture. These elements are often overlooked as organizations and cybersecurity professionals jump directly to assessing risks or implementing technologies. However, Governance and Cybersecurity Culture are the bedrock upon which effective and resilient cybersecurity practices are built.

Governance, in the context of cybersecurity, stands as the guiding authority that ensures everything functions smoothly through the establishment of clear guidelines, policies, and protocols. This structure is essential for managing and overseeing information security across an organization. It's designed to align cybersecurity efforts with the organization's broader objectives, guaranteeing that every step taken not only serves the immediate goal of security but also contributes positively to overall business continuity and success. Governance is about the allocation of necessary resources, organizational structures, clarifying roles, facilitating informed decision-making, and preventing conflicts of interest.

One common debate that often sidetracks the development of effective cybersecurity strategies is the organizational placement of the Chief Information Security Officer (CISO). Should the CISO report within the IT department or directly to a higher level outside of IT? While this discussion might seem essential, it's important to recognize that the success of a CISO, and the cybersecurity posture of the organization as a whole, resides less on their reporting line and more on the establishment of robust governance mechanisms. Without a strong foundation of governance to guide decisions, set priorities, and ensure accountability, the effectiveness of the CISO and the cybersecurity initiatives they lead will be compromised, regardless of their place in the organizational chart.

However, this makes evident the importance of focusing on creating a solid governance structure as a critical step toward empowering the CISO

DOI: 10.1201/9781003546207-5

and our security program to enhance the organization's cybersecurity resilience, and by establishing a formal, well-defined governance body, an organization ensures that cybersecurity initiatives are not just reactive measures but are integrated into the fabric of organizational strategy. This strategic alignment empowers every participant within the organization to understand their role in maintaining and enhancing security, in this way fostering a more cohesive and unified approach to tackling cyber risks. Governance, then, is about creating an ecosystem where cybersecurity succeeds as a collective priority, guided by clear leadership and the commitment to safeguarding the organization's business objectives, assets, and reputation.

With the release of NIST CSF 2.0[1] on February 26, 2024, this focus on governance has become even more pronounced. As we can see in Figure 3.1, the new version introduced a dedicated function titled 'Govern,' highlighting the importance of structured oversight in cybersecurity risk management.

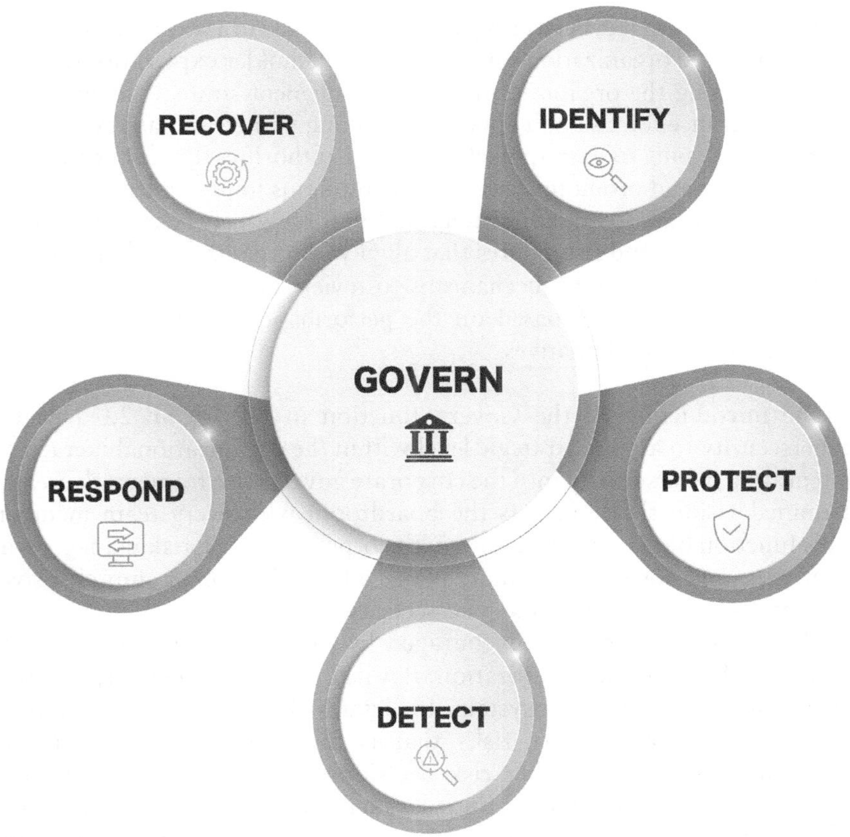

Figure 3.1 NIST CSF 2.0 functions.

This updated framework is geared toward providing a structured approach that aligns cybersecurity efforts with the organization's mission, culture, and strategic goals. The Govern function emphasizes a comprehensive understanding of the organizational context, a well-defined risk management strategy, and the establishment of roles, responsibilities, and authorities. It also emphasizes the importance of developing cybersecurity policies and processes that are communicated across the organization and enforced to ensure a risk-based approach.

The controls within the Govern function address the need for clear communication lines regarding cybersecurity risks, including those associated with the supply chain. The aim is to integrate cybersecurity considerations into every facet of organizational decision-making, thus embedding a culture of security awareness and risk management into the fabric of the organization.

Key aspects of the Govern function include:

- Ensuring that cybersecurity risks are managed in a way that is coherent with the organization's mission and stakeholder expectations.
- Defining the organization's risk management strategy, including its tolerance for risk and appetite for taking on new initiatives.
- Developing roles, responsibilities, and authorities that foster accountability and promote a culture of continuous improvement.
- Establishing, communicating, and enforcing cybersecurity policies, processes, and procedures that align with organizational objectives.
- Creating oversight mechanisms to review and adjust the risk management strategy based on the performance of the organization's cybersecurity initiatives.

The introduction of the Govern function in NIST CSF 2.0 elevates cybersecurity to a more strategic level within the organizational hierarchy. Integrating cybersecurity into the corporate governance framework creates a unified vision that connects the boardroom with every team member. This function blends cybersecurity with corporate ethics, risk management strategies, and business continuity plans, advocating for a comprehensive, enterprise-wide adoption of a cybersecurity culture.

This proactive approach encouraged by the Govern function ensures that every layer of the organization, not just the IT department, is aware of its role in the cyber ecosystem. It dictates the creation of a common language for cybersecurity risks that is understood by all, fostering an environment where cyber risk decisions are made with clarity and confidence. The function's controls facilitate a top-down approach where leadership sets the tone, taking ownership and accountability for establishing cybersecurity as a priority that is as critical as any other business objective.

However, having documented cybersecurity policies, standards, and procedures is just the beginning. Some organizations mistakenly believe that once these documents are in place, the work is done. In reality, the governance framework must ensure that these policies, standards, and procedures are continuously updated and that compliance with them is rigorously enforced. This is where the Govern function plays a critical role, establishing that certain policies are nonnegotiable. These are the minimum standards that must be upheld across the organization. Over time, these nonnegotiable policies should translate into the organizational culture, where adherence to them becomes second nature and an integral part of how the organization operates.

In addition to internal governance, the Govern function emphasizes the need to look beyond the organization's immediate boundaries. A key focus is on supply chain risk management, marking a significant step forward in addressing the interconnected nature of business operations. The Govern function encourages organizations to scrutinize and secure their entire supply chain, understanding that their security is only as strong as the weakest link. This approach expands the cybersecurity perspective to cover not just internal operations but also external partners, suppliers, and third-party services. Integrating supply chain risk management into the governance framework contributes to make your organization's cybersecurity posture comprehensive and resilient, extending protection across all facets of the business ecosystem.

In practice, the Govern function fosters a cycle of continuous improvement. Organizations are encouraged to regularly review, update, and adapt their cybersecurity strategies in response to emerging threats, new technologies, and evolving business models. This dynamic approach ensures resilience, as cybersecurity practices must evolve alongside both the threat landscape and the organization's growth trajectory. Above all, the Govern function advocates for cybersecurity to be an essential part of organizational DNA. It aims to establish a mindset where cybersecurity is not viewed as an overhead but as an essential component of organizational success and longevity. The objective is to foster a cybersecurity-aware culture where every stakeholder is informed, vigilant, and proactive, ensuring cybersecurity is a key driver for operational excellence and strategic success.

Essentially, the Govern function ensures that cybersecurity becomes deeply integrated into the way we operate as an organization. If your approach to cybersecurity has been compliance-focused, it's time to evolve. Compliance doesn't equal security and never will because regulations can't move as fast as reality. Of course, compliance is something we need to factor into our risk assessments, but unfortunately, if we only do for security what compliance demands, we won't go at the speed our risks require. So, cybersecurity isn't about just ticking boxes; it's about recognizing risks and addressing them in ways that make sense for your organization and stakeholders. Stop seeing security as something required by a specific standard and start viewing it as essential to protecting your organization and enabling it to meet its business objectives. This shift in mindset is subtle but crucial to how you approach your cybersecurity program. The Govern function taps into company culture, using it to bring everyone on board with cybersecurity. In this way, staying secure becomes a natural part of our everyday work, not an extra task. Understanding our organizational culture helps foster empathy and creates a shared language around cybersecurity, making it an inherent part of our decisions and actions.

To effectively integrate cybersecurity into our organization, it's crucial to understand what culture truly is. Culture in an organization acts as a silent force, guiding the way things are done without the need for explicit instructions. It's the underlying current that shapes behaviors, decisions, and interactions among everyone in the organization. This invisible influence determines how people approach their work, interact with each other, and deal with challenges. A strong culture ensures that everyone, from top executives to the newest hires, understands the importance of the organization's values and priorities in every action taken, aligning everyone to move in the same direction. Culture is about creating an environment where the right choices are made naturally, reflecting what matters most to our organization. In a strong culture, important topics like cybersecurity go beyond mere policies to become a fundamental part of the organizational DNA, influencing every facet of daily operations.

Cybersecurity culture is about the collective mindset and behaviors of an organization's people toward cybersecurity. It's the atmosphere that permeates every level of the organization, from the boardroom to the break room, establishing a sense of responsibility and awareness in every individual about their role in maintaining security. Then, cybersecurity culture is the force that integrates security into the very essence of every activity and decision. It's about fostering an environment where security isn't seen as an afterthought or a barrier to productivity but as a vital component of success and innovation. A strong cybersecurity culture encourages proactive behavior, from recognizing and reporting potential threats or vulnerabilities to adhering to best practices for data protection. In such a culture, cybersecurity becomes a shared responsibility, empowering individuals to act as the organization's first line of defense. This shared commitment transforms cybersecurity from a series of technical challenges into a collective mission, embedding it deeply into the organization's way of life and making security second nature to its operations.

Together, governance and cybersecurity culture form the foundation upon which successful cyber risk management programs are built. They are what makes the difference between simply pushing everyone to work with security and fostering an environment where everyone naturally works securely, with a collective focus on achieving business objectives. This shift from a reactive stance, where organizations scramble to patch vulnerabilities as they arise, to a proactive posture, where potential risks are anticipated, understood, and managed before they can cause harm, is crucial. This transformation is not instantaneous but evolves through commitment, education, and continuous improvement. It requires a clear vision from leadership, one that communicates the importance of cybersecurity not as a departmental function but as a strategic imperative across the organization.

At its core, the establishment of robust governance and a vibrant cybersecurity culture marks the beginning of a journey toward an effective cybersecurity program and resilience. This is not an easy task, and it requires ongoing effort and commitment. You may find yourself returning to these chapters, as the concepts will resonate more and more as you progress in building the right foundations for your cyber risk management program. Remember, this is about creating an environment where the principles of cyber risk management are not just understood but are passionately advocated and embraced by everyone in the organization.

ALIGNING CORPORATE GOVERNANCE AND SECURITY CULTURE

Aligning corporate governance with security culture requires a conscious and strategic effort; and I'll be clear, it's an effort that will drain your energy and passion if it's not well planned. This alignment ensures that cybersecurity is not seen as an isolated technical task with the CISO as the exclusive owner, but as a vital part of the organization's overall strategic framework. Achieving this alignment transforms an organization's security posture, making cybersecurity a central element of corporate governance and embedding it into the organizational culture.

Integrating cybersecurity into the core of an organization's culture requires the involvement of every department, with human resources (HR) playing a particularly crucial role. As the backbone of any organization in matters related to its people, HR is an invaluable ally in fostering a strong cybersecurity culture. However, we must also recognize the critical importance of managers, team leaders, and everyone with a team under their responsibility. These individuals are on the front lines, ensuring that day-to-day practices align with the organization's cybersecurity goals. As Frank E. Adcock wisely noted, "Battles are sometimes won by generals; wars are nearly always won by sergeants and privates." Similarly, in cybersecurity, it's the leaders and managers who embed these practices into daily operations and drive the organization toward a resilient security posture. With this foundation in mind, let's explore how HR can be active in this mission.

Recruitment and onboarding: From the start, HR sets the tone for cybersecurity. Emphasizing cybersecurity in job descriptions and during onboarding introduces new hires to the organization's expectations immediately. HR ensures new employees understand their role in maintaining security from day one, embedding this awareness as a core part of their job. However, managers and team leaders are responsible for reinforcing these expectations in daily work, ensuring cybersecurity remains a priority beyond onboarding.

Cybersecurity awareness and training: HR departments often oversee training and professional development programs. Incorporating cybersecurity training as a mandatory part of these programs ensures all employees, regardless of role, receive ongoing education on best practices, emerging threats, and their role in defending against them. Leaders within the organization reinforce this training, encouraging a culture where cybersecurity is continuously practiced and discussed. Embedding cybersecurity awareness and training into the company culture ensures it becomes a fundamental part of the organization's DNA, supported by both HR and leadership.

Communicating policies: HR plays a key role in effectively communicating policies across the organization. Collaborating closely with the cybersecurity team, HR helps develop clear, understandable policies and procedures that outline expected behaviors and responses to potential threats. Managers and team leaders ensure these policies are consistently applied in day-to-day operations, making sure every team member understands and adheres to them. This collaboration turns policies into active guides for behavior in the workplace.

Handling security incidents: In the event of a security incident, HR plays a critical role in managing the situation from a people perspective. Whether it's dealing with the implications of a data breach on employee data, managing communications, or addressing the fallout of an insider threat, HR's involvement is essential to managing the human element of any security incident. At the same time, leaders must guide their teams through these situations, ensuring that the response is coordinated and that employees are supported throughout the process.

Performance management: HR can integrate cybersecurity practices into performance management processes. Including adherence to cybersecurity policies and procedures in performance reviews sends a clear message that cybersecurity is a fundamental part of every employee's role, not just an IT concern. Leaders reinforce this message by holding their teams accountable for their cybersecurity responsibilities, making it clear that security is a key component of job performance.

To achieve embedding cybersecurity into the organization's culture, a comprehensive strategy is required, one that considers every member of the organization, from the C-suite to frontline employees, as an ally in the fight against cyber threats. Working closely with leaders and HR helps create an environment where cybersecurity is understood, respected, and practiced by all, integrating cybersecurity into our organizational culture and transforming every employee into a vigilant guardian.

A key component of this strategy is the establishment of a network of cybersecurity champions across the organization. These are individuals from different departments who are passionate about cybersecurity and can serve as role models, promoting best practices among their peers. Peer influence is a powerful tool in changing behaviors and attitudes toward cybersecurity, making these champions invaluable in the cultural shift.

Identifying and empowering natural leaders within the organization to act as cybersecurity champions is essential in fostering the adoption of a cybersecurity culture. These champions often hold the respect and attention of their colleagues, making their endorsement of cybersecurity practices particularly impactful. Through demonstrating secure behaviors and advocating for cybersecurity awareness in their daily interactions, they help set a standard that others are inclined to follow.

In *Amazing Decisions*,[2] Chapter 8, Dan Ariely explores the compelling dynamics of social norms through a hotel towel reuse initiative aimed at environmental conservation. This case study sheds light on the profound influence that collective actions and shared goals have on individual decision-making. Ariely's investigation into how tailored messages affected guests' choices to reuse towels unveils the significant role of social cues in shaping behavior. This scenario not only emphasizes the sway of societal norms but also offers parallels to encouraging the adoption of a cybersecurity culture within organizations by crafting impactful communications.

The 2008 experiment had two guest groups at a hotel: one received a standard appeal emphasizing the environmental benefits of reusing towels, while the other was additionally informed that many guests were already participating in this eco-friendly practice. The outcome revealed a marked increase in towel reuse among the latter group, with a participation rate climbing from 37.5% to 44%. This outcome illustrates our intrinsic tendency to align with the actions of our peers, reinforcing the concept that social influences profoundly affect our decisions.

Building on this foundation, a subsequent 2012 experiment introduced an element of social commitment by inviting guests to publicly commit to the initiative. Participants were given a pin as a symbol of their pledge and asked to sign a commitment card. This approach skyrocketed participation to 73%, underscoring the potent combination of social motivation and personal commitment in driving collective action toward a shared objective. These findings highlight the potential of leveraging social dynamics and commitment mechanisms to foster behavioral changes, offering valuable insights for promoting cybersecurity awareness and practices within organizations.

The concept of social conformity plays a crucial role here. It refers to the human tendency to align attitudes, beliefs, and behaviors with those of the group. In an environment where respected peers actively practice and promote cybersecurity, individuals are more likely to adopt and mirror these behaviors. This becomes a powerful driver of cultural change, integrating cybersecurity into daily work life without the need for strict enforcement. Leveraging social conformity allows organizations to create a culture where secure behaviors become the norm, and deviations from that norm stand out. As more people follow cybersecurity best practices, collective behavior reinforces the culture, making it increasingly natural for others to follow suit. This creates a self-sustaining cycle of positive reinforcement, where secure actions become part of the organization's collective identity.

This concept of social conformity can be further understood through the lens of complexity theory and chaos theory. These theories, which have applications in fields like mathematics, physics, economics, and biology, suggest that within the apparent randomness of chaotic complex systems, there are underlying patterns, interconnectedness, constant feedback loops, self-organization, and a capacity for adaptation that eventually lead to order and harmony. Chaos theory, a subset of complexity theory, specifically addresses systems that are highly sensitive to initial conditions, often referred to as the butterfly effect, where small changes can lead to vastly different outcomes. This is similar to the impact we aim to achieve with cybersecurity champions. Complexity theory extends these ideas by exploring how interactions within a system can lead to emergent properties, new behaviors, and structures that cannot be predicted from the properties of individual parts. Together, these theories help us understand how systems, like an organization's cybersecurity culture, can evolve and adapt over time, exhibiting ordered patterns and structures out of seemingly disordered environments.

To enhance this effect, we need to create consistency and continuity by implementing regular training sessions, workshops, and awareness campaigns led by cybersecurity champions. This approach generates a multiplier effect because it is no longer just the CISO or HR carrying the cybersecurity message, but all those natural leaders who are embedded in operations and recognized by their peers. Cybersecurity should be integrated into the day-to-day operations of every department. Incorporating security into regular workflows, from project planning to daily tasks, keeps employees constantly aware of their role in maintaining security. This ongoing reinforcement helps keep cybersecurity top of mind. These initiatives not only spread knowledge but also reinforce the social norms around cybersecurity. Recognizing and celebrating the efforts and achievements of these champions further amplifies their impact, encouraging more individuals to take an active role in cybersecurity. We need to remember that actions speak louder than words, and when leaders and cybersecurity champions consistently demonstrate secure behaviors, they set a powerful precedent for the entire organization. This practical demonstration of commitment to cybersecurity resonates more deeply than any policy document or training manual could.

Leaders who actively participate in cybersecurity practices, such as consistently notifying suspicious emails, engaging in training sessions, and openly discussing the importance of cybersecurity, send a clear message about its value. This behavior signals to the rest of the organization that cybersecurity is not just a checklist item but a critical aspect of their role and the organization's success. It creates a standard that others are naturally inclined to follow, reinforcing the desired culture through observable actions.

Leading by example is a powerful way to build a strong cybersecurity culture within an organization. The goal is to create an environment where cybersecurity isn't seen as an external imposition but as an intrinsic part of the culture. Leveraging the human tendency toward social conformity and empowering internal leaders as cybersecurity champions can significantly enhance the organization's cybersecurity culture. When these leaders set a precedent through their actions, cybersecurity becomes a topic that everyone in the organization openly discusses.

Cybersecurity should be recognized as a critical concern not only in our professional roles but also in our personal lives. Sharing stories of real cybersecurity incidents helps employees understand the practical implications of breaches and highlights the importance of vigilance. This approach connects abstract security concepts with real-world impacts, making the need for robust cybersecurity more relatable and urgent. When individuals realize their actions can significantly influence the company's security posture, they are more likely to take their responsibilities seriously and act proactively to mitigate risks.

It is then that by fostering a culture that embraces change and encourages continuous learning, organizations can ensure that their cybersecurity practices remain effective over time. This adaptability is crucial in a world where cyber threats are constantly evolving and becoming more sophisticated. When all employees are allies in cybersecurity, and it becomes a core part of the organizational culture, companies can create a more resilient and proactive security posture. This collective approach not only enhances the organization's ability to prevent and respond to cyber threats but also fosters a sense of shared responsibility and commitment.

Throughout my career as a cybersecurity professional, I have worked with many organizations attempting to implement a risk management program. However, more often than I'd prefer, I've observed a common misconception: that risk management is a finite project, something to start, finish, and then return to business as usual. This couldn't be further from the truth.

I recall a particular instance when I was brought in to lead the implementation of a cyber risk program for an organization that prided itself on being 'risk-aware.' During the initial meetings, enthusiasm was high; everyone seemed keen on managing risks more effectively. However, as we went deeper, a simple reality emerged. Although there was much talk about risks, there was no foundational process in place for building a cyber risk program because "it was too much work." Inventories of assets, systems, and data were either nonexistent or severely outdated. Incidents that occurred within the organization were often undocumented, leaving us without historical data to learn from or patterns to analyze.

The concept of risk appetite was another area lacking clarity. Discussions around it were abstract, sometimes even contradicting the actions that were taken, with no concrete criteria or thresholds defined. It was as if the organization was navigating through fog without a compass. Also, the question of who owned the risk was met with uncertainty and, at times, outright avoidance. Departments operated in silos, each wary of assuming responsibility for risks that crossed multiple departments. The simplest answer was, "It's technology, IT owns the risk," without considering that IT did what was necessary to enable and support the company's operations, even when it wasn't done with cybersecurity in mind. This sometimes led to serious issues of obsolescence due to "not having had the time for migrations" since they had to implement the business requirements.

The resistance to change became increasingly apparent. Everyone was overwhelmed with work, and there was an underlying fear of the unknown, a comfort in the status quo, and a misconception that acknowledging and documenting risks would somehow make them more real or daunting. It was a challenge, to say the least, but also a turning point for me. I realized that my role was not just to implement a program but to facilitate a cultural shift. It was about transforming how the organization perceived risk, from a blurry concept discussed in passing to a tangible element that could be identified, assessed, and managed.

Navigating the maze of resistance and fostering a shift in the organizational culture required a better planned strategy. This approach is further explained in the book *Switch*[3] by Chip and Dan Heath. The book explores into the psychology of change, emphasizing the need to direct the rational mind, motivate the emotional mind, and shape the path for change. This triad became my blueprint for navigating the organizational inertia I encountered. Initially, the huge volume of work and the palpable fear of the unknown among team members seemed insurmountable. The organization clung to the comfort of the status quo, fearing that acknowledging risks would only exacerbate them. However, drawing inspiration from *Switch*, I realized the power of breaking down the monumental task of implementing a cyber risk management program into manageable, bite-sized pieces. This strategy not only made the goal seem more attainable but also minimized the resistance stemming from the fear of added workload.

I began by presenting a clear vision of the end goal without overwhelming the team with the enormity of the tasks ahead. Instead, I focused on outlining the immediate next steps, providing clear timelines and expected outcomes for each. This approach helped create short-term wins, each acting as a milestone that motivated the team and built momentum toward the larger objective. As we progressed, each completed task became a stepping stone to the next, gradually revealing the path to achieving our overarching goal of a robust cyber risk management program. This method of layering tasks, like building blocks, ensured that the team remained focused and not overwhelmed by the journey ahead. It also implanted a sense of achievement with each milestone reached, fostering growing confidence and a shift in how risk management was perceived within the organization.

This phased approach, inspired by the insights from *Switch*, transformed what initially seemed like an overwhelming effort into a series of achievable objectives. It proved to be an effective way to dismantle the resistance to change, paving the way for a fundamental shift in the organizational culture toward embracing risk management as a crucial aspect of our operations. This experience reinforced in me the importance of patience, perseverance, and the power of persuasion. It emphasized the need for a shift in mindset before any meaningful change in practice could occur. Implementing a cyber risk program was not merely about introducing new tools or processes; it was about leading an organization through a journey of transformation, one that would ultimately fortify its resilience against the many cyber threats the organization was facing.

How does cybersecurity culture connect with cybersecurity governance, and how does it help drive this change? To bridge the gap and achieve alignment, it's essential to recognize the strong relationship between the two. Establishing a clear line of sight from the boardroom to the front lines ensures that cybersecurity efforts flow both top-down and bottom-up. This integrated approach reinforces the significance of cybersecurity at all levels. The journey from establishing a resilient security culture to aligning it with governance principles is one of mutual reinforcement, where each element strengthens and supports the other, resulting in an effective cyber risk management framework.

Aligning corporate governance with security culture means ensuring that the principles guiding decision-making at the highest levels are reflected in the daily actions and attitudes of every employee. It involves clear communication from leadership about the importance of cybersecurity, backed by policies and practices that support a proactive security stance. It's also about creating a feedback loop where insights from the ground inform strategic decisions, and strategic objectives shape the security culture.

This alignment can be achieved through the combination of several practical steps:

- **Leadership involvement:** Executives and board members should lead by example, demonstrating a commitment to cybersecurity in their actions and decisions. This top-down approach encourages a company-wide embrace of security culture.

- **Education and training**: Regular, engaging cybersecurity training sessions for employees at all levels help to raise awareness and embed security-conscious behaviors.
- **Clear policies and procedures**: Developing and communicating clear cybersecurity policies and procedures ensures that everyone knows what is expected of them and how to contribute to the organization's security posture.
- **Open communication channels**: Encouraging open dialogue about cybersecurity challenges and successes fosters an environment of transparency and continuous improvement.
- **Recognition and rewards**: Acknowledging and rewarding security-conscious behaviors reinforces the value placed on cybersecurity within the organization.

Aligning corporate governance with security culture is not a one-time project but a continuous journey that requires commitment, investment, and a willingness to evolve. This alignment often begins with the establishment of an Information Security Forum, where strategic decisions around cybersecurity risks are made. The forum acts as a centralized body, bringing together key stakeholders from various departments such as IT, legal, HR, and operations to collaborate on cybersecurity matters. Its main purpose is to facilitate open dialogue, share best practices, and ensure a unified approach to managing cyber risks across the organization.

To formalize the role of the Information Security Forum, the creation of an Information Security Program Charter is a critical step. This charter serves as the foundational document that outlines the forum's mission, objectives, and responsibilities. It defines the governance structure, sets expectations for how cybersecurity will be managed across the organization, and establishes clear roles and responsibilities. The charter also grants the forum the authority needed to drive cybersecurity initiatives and ensure they align with the organization's strategic goals.

With the Information Security Program Charter in place, the forum can effectively carry out its crucial functions. It advises executive leadership, providing insights and recommendations on cybersecurity policies, strategies, and investment priorities. This ensures that decision-making at the highest level is guided by comprehensive, multidisciplinary insights that reflect the complexity and scope of the cyber risks the organization faces. The forum also fosters a culture of cybersecurity awareness throughout the organization. Involving representatives from different sectors of the business helps spread critical security information, raise awareness about potential risks, and emphasize the importance of cybersecurity best practices among all employees.

The Information Security Forum is also responsible for monitoring the effectiveness of the organization's cybersecurity measures. It stays informed on security incidents, analyzes trends in cyber threats, and evaluates the performance of implemented security controls. This ongoing evaluation process is vital for managing cyber risks and making decisions on how to address them. Here is where identified risks and their treatment plans are presented, providing a clear picture of gaps in the organization's cybersecurity defenses and recommending improvements.

The goal is to create a dedicated space for discussing cybersecurity risks and making well-informed decisions on how to mitigate them. This doesn't always require setting up a new forum, committee, or series of recurring meetings from scratch. Instead, leveraging existing structures or platforms that have proven effective for addressing other significant business matters can be a practical and efficient approach. Cyber risk management success depends not only on the implementation of robust technologies and processes but also on the engagement and cooperation of diverse teams and key stakeholders. Whether gathering critical information or making strategic decisions to mitigate identified risks, the involvement of various departments is indispensable.

While it's often said that the human element is a potential vulnerability in cybersecurity, sometimes referred to as the weakest link, this perspective overlooks the positive impact people can have when properly engaged and educated. Through cultivating a strong cybersecurity culture and a comprehensive awareness program, we can transform this so-called weakest link into our greatest asset. This shift is essential to strengthening our organization's defenses from within. A vibrant and adaptive culture is key to driving progress across all facets of our operations. Embedding cybersecurity into the core of our activities and digital initiatives not only accelerates our market pace but also creates a competitive edge. Our approach to cybersecurity awareness and culture ignites a collective commitment to stronger security practices. Empowering every team member to contribute to our security posture, along with establishing governance structures to guide us, paves the way for a more efficient and successful cyber risk management program.

CONNECTING THE DOTS IN CYBER RISK MANAGEMENT

Looking back on my experiences with organizations of all sizes and across different geographies, I've seen that the real journey of launching a cyber risk management program often begins with a moment of clarity. This isn't just any moment; it's when something clicks, and you realize that cybersecurity is much more than just a box to tick. For many, this realization comes after a close call with a security incident, new regulatory pressures, or simply recognizing the growing risks in the digital landscape. It's that moment when the importance of cybersecurity truly sinks in, and you understand that it needs to be integrated into every aspect of how the organization operates.

This moment of clarity often sparks the drive to start taking cybersecurity seriously, not as an isolated task, but as a core part of the organization's culture. It's not something you can fully prepare for just by reading textbooks or attending seminars. This shift in thinking requires more than just knowledge; it takes intuition, experience, and the ability to inspire change, helping others see the value in what you're doing. This is why I'm sharing all these pages with you about governance, people, culture, teams, and more. Over the years, I've learned that driving this kind of change means understanding the people you're working with, where they are in their own journey, and how to guide them along the path. It's an ongoing effort that requires a cultural shift.

Throughout my career, I've consistently observed the need for that initial spark, something that will ignite the creation or adaptation of essential elements within your cybersecurity program. When you create or modify something, you're inevitably talking about change. Driving change is an art in itself, requiring leadership, emotional intelligence, authenticity, and, above all, empathy. As I often say, to drive change effectively, you need to understand where everyone is positioned on the curve of change. You can't expect others to understand what you're saying if they haven't been prepared to receive the message.

Imagine trying to convince the American public and scientific community in the early 1960s that it was possible to land a man on the Moon. When President John F. Kennedy boldly announced this goal in 1961, many thought it was an impossible dream. The technology didn't exist, the challenges were immense, and the risks were unprecedented. If Kennedy had simply declared, "We can land on the Moon," without a clear plan, most people would have dismissed the idea as fantasy.

However, Kennedy didn't stop at the declaration. NASA approached the challenge with a phased strategy, working with experts to break down the monumental task into manageable steps. First, NASA focused on getting a human into space and back safely. Then, they tackled the challenges of space navigation and docking through the Gemini Program. With each success, what initially seemed impossible started to feel within reach. As the Apollo missions advanced, the vision of landing on the Moon gained credibility. Engineers, scientists, and the public began to see that it wasn't just a wild dream but a goal that could actually be achieved. By the time Apollo 11 launched, the once-skeptical masses were watching in anticipation, believing that the impossible was now possible. And when Neil Armstrong took that historic step onto the lunar surface, it wasn't just a victory for science, but a testament to the power of clear communication, systematic planning, and building belief through tangible progress.

This story shows that with the right approach, even the most ambitious goals can be achieved. It's about starting with a clear vision, breaking it

Figure 3.2 Weak foundations.

down into achievable steps, and guiding people along the way until they too can see what you saw from the beginning.

This is important because a significant part of our work involves encouraging teams to not only recognize cybersecurity as a necessity but also to embrace it as second nature, even in the face of their busy workloads. We must remember that the organization won't stop, and it can't stop. We need to change the wheel while the car is running. This means that our organization continues to build on the foundations we currently have, foundations likely established before cybersecurity was a big concern, which, by the way, wasn't too long ago. Often, as Figure 3.2 invites us to think, we inherit systems developed in an era that predates the cyber threats we face today, which poses a unique challenge. These legacy systems, often poorly documented and outdated, are what many of us are tasked with safeguarding against modern, sophisticated threats.

This is the backdrop against which we begin our cyber risk management programs, with a foundation that is less solid than we would like. As we tackle the complexities of risk management, we don't just look at weaknesses; we have to examine and understand the historical narratives of our environment where security was often an afterthought. It's a narrative that I, along with countless cybersecurity professionals like yourself, am working to rewrite.

Here are some of the hurdles that you might encounter when starting your program:

- **Lack of awareness**: Often, there's a fundamental gap in understanding the importance of cybersecurity across the organization, from the executive level to the operational teams.

- **Resource allocation**: Determining and securing the right amount and type of resources, be it financial, human, or technological, can be daunting, especially in organizations where cybersecurity has not been a priority.
- **Defining the scope**: It can be difficult to define the boundaries of what needs protection. This includes not just digital assets but also data, processes, and systems, which may span beyond the immediate IT environment.
- **Identifying assets and risks**: Creating an inventory of assets and associated risks can be overwhelming, especially when there are no previous records to build upon.
- **Establishing a baseline**: Without an existing cybersecurity baseline, it can be challenging to measure progress or understand what 'good' looks like.
- **Developing policies and procedures**: Drafting the necessary policies and procedures that align with best practices and regulatory requirements is a substantial task that requires specialized knowledge.
- **Implementing a culture of security**: Changing the mindset of an organization to prioritize security in everyday business processes is a significant cultural shift.
- **Dealing with evolving threats**: The threat landscape is constantly changing, with new vulnerabilities and attack methods developing all the time. Staying ahead of these can be a relentless task.
- **Training and education**: Providing adequate training for all employees, particularly those who are not in IT, can be a logistical and educational challenge.
- **Communication and buy-in**: Communicating the importance of cybersecurity and gaining buy-in from stakeholders across the organization, each with their unique perspectives and priorities, can be complex.
- **Measuring effectiveness**: Establishing metrics that accurately reflect the effectiveness of the cybersecurity program is critical but can be intricate to formulate.
- **Regulatory compliance**: Understanding and complying with a huge amount of industry and legal standards can be confusing, especially for those new to the field.

We might find ourselves thinking that navigating the world of cybersecurity often feels like chasing a mythical perfect world, a place where every piece of data is meticulously cataloged, resources are abundant, and every process runs seamlessly. Yet, reality is far from this utopian vision. This is reminiscent of Kennedy's audacious goal to land a man on the Moon, a mission that seemed nearly impossible given the challenges and limitations at the time. That's exactly why I felt motivated to write this book. The texts I've encountered throughout my professional journey often follow an idealistic 'happy path,' assuming an environment where everything needed for cybersecurity is readily at hand, and all organizations operate at the same maturity level. But, just as with the Moon landing, such perfect scenarios are rare, and real progress requires navigating complexities and uncertainties. Based on my experience, I'm certain that strong governance and a robust cybersecurity culture are essential in overcoming these challenges and achieving success.

This strong foundation of governance and culture not only sets the stage but also directly influences how we approach the broader challenges of cyber risk management. It's here that we begin to connect the dots between our governance principles, the culture we cultivate, and the methodologies we employ to manage risks effectively.

NOTES

1 National Institute of Standards and Technology. (2024, February 26). *Cybersecurity Framework 2.0*. National Institute of Standards and Technology. www.nist.gov/cyberframework

2 Ariely, D. (2019). *Amazing Decisions: The Illustrated Guide to Improving Business Deals and Family Meals* (p. 170). Hill and Wang.

3 Heath, C., & Heath, D. (2010). *Switch: How to Change Things When Change Is Hard*. Crown Business.

Chapter 4

Cyber risk management methodology and risk register

CYBER RISK MANAGEMENT METHODOLOGY

"And so goes the leader, so goes the culture. So goes the culture, so goes the company." As Simon Sinek suggests, leadership shapes the culture, and culture, in turn, drives the success of the organization. This applies directly to managing cyber risks. In the day-to-day battle of managing cyber risks, we struggle with incomplete datasets, resource constraints, and unexpected hurdles. The question arises: should we wait to solve all these problems before kicking off our cybersecurity program? Absolutely not! The organization is expecting results, and resolving these issues, should they exist, won't happen overnight. This is precisely where the importance of establishing clear guidelines becomes evident. Crafting a comprehensive cyber risk management methodology is crucial in setting the stage for how we'll navigate these challenges. Our risk methodology is about laying down the rules of the game, ensuring we have a structured approach to begin making strides in our cybersecurity efforts, even in the middle of uncertainty.

A well-defined cyber risk management methodology is based on several key pillars that uphold our work and will include defining clear roles and responsibilities for cyber risk management, setting forth a detailed process for all involved, and specifying how we'll characterize and prioritize risks.

The core of this methodology lies in its precision, outlining what constitutes a risk according to our risk matrix and its various levels or thresholds, such as extreme, high, medium, or low, tailored specifically to our organization's context in terms of impact and likelihood. It is a meticulously designed framework that guides us in assessing risks with a defined set of criteria, ensuring consistency and clarity in our approach. Beyond identification and assessment, our methodology details the decision-making process: where it happens, how it unfolds, and who holds the authority to make calls on risk acceptance. It specifies the formulas we'll use to calculate risk, embedding mathematical rigor into our evaluation process that transcends subjective judgment. Additionally, this document addresses the registration and ongoing monitoring of risks, establishing a systematic

DOI: 10.1201/9781003546207-6

approach for tracking and updating our risk landscape. It's about creating a transparent and accountable environment where decisions on risk management are made on solid ground, supported by a well-documented and accessible risk register.

Before we get into the depths of risk management and its assessments, it's crucial that our cyber risk management methodology is not only defined but also approved by the organization's governance structure, specifically through the Information Security Forum. This step is important because it ensures our methodology doesn't stand alone but is closely aligned with the broader information security policy of the organization. Getting management's approval through the Information Security Forum is a very important moment in our risk management journey. It reflects a shared understanding at the highest levels of how we'll approach and manage risks. This alignment is essential for ensuring that our methodology is embraced across the organization. While there's always room for improvement, having this framework in place provides us with the rules of the game as we move forward. When senior management and the Information Security Forum approve the methodology, they aren't just endorsing a document, but they're committing to these guidelines as a core part of how we operate. Once approved, the methodology becomes the official guide for managing risks within the organization, setting clear expectations for how we will navigate the complex landscape of cyber risks. Without a defined and approved cyber risk management methodology, we'll struggle with several challenges that can significantly hinder our ability to manage and mitigate cyber risks effectively. Here's some examples of what could go wrong:

- **Inconsistent risk assessment**: Without a unified methodology, different teams or individuals might assess risks based on their own understanding and criteria. This inconsistency can lead to gaps in risk identification, underestimation or overestimation of risks, and an overall fragmented view of the organization's risk posture.
- **Misaligned priorities**: Without clear guidance on how to evaluate and prioritize risks, efforts may be misdirected toward less critical issues, leaving the organization vulnerable to more significant threats. This misalignment can waste resources and delay the addressing of urgent vulnerabilities.
- **Lack of accountability**: A well-defined methodology assigns roles and responsibilities, ensuring accountability across the organization. Without this structure, it can be unclear who is responsible for managing specific risks, leading to overlooked vulnerabilities and uncoordinated response efforts.
- **Ineffective risk treatment**: An approved methodology outlines standardized processes for mitigating, transferring, accepting, or avoiding risks. Without these guidelines, risk treatment efforts may

be inconsistent, ineffective, or not aligned with the organization's risk appetite and business objectives.

- **Regulatory and compliance issues**: Many industries have strict regulations governing how organizations must manage cyber risks. Without a methodology that aligns with these requirements, organizations risk noncompliance, which can result in hefty fines, legal issues, and damage to reputation.
- **Difficulty communicating risk**: A common methodology provides a language for discussing risks within the organization and with external stakeholders. Without it, effectively communicating the nature, severity, and implications of risks can be challenging, hindering informed decision-making and strategic planning.
- **Barriers to building a risk-aware culture**: A defined methodology is crucial for embedding risk management into the organizational culture. Without it, fostering a shared understanding and proactive stance toward cybersecurity across the organization is significantly more difficult.

Therefore, our methodology has to be a living document, adaptable, and responsive to the ever-changing cyber threat landscape. As new threats emerge and our business evolves, so too does our approach to managing risk. It encourages a culture of continuous improvement, where lessons learned from past incidents inform future strategies, ensuring that our defenses grow stronger and more sophisticated over time.

Implementing this methodology will require collaboration across the entire organization, and we'll be required to connect all we've reviewed so far: cyber risk management concepts, governance, and culture. It's not just the responsibility of the IT department or security team; it involves everyone from the boardroom to the break room. Embedding cybersecurity considerations into every facet of our operations allows us to foster a shared sense of responsibility and a collective approach to safeguarding our digital assets.

Definition of the cyber risk methodology

Now that we're all aligned on the importance of defining our cyber risk management methodology within our governance structures, it's time to lay out a clear and structured approach. This methodology will guide us in the whole process of managing the cyber risks that could impact our organizations. The following sections are the ones we need to develop and will provide the foundation for our efforts, ensuring that our approach is comprehensive, consistent, and aligned with our overall cybersecurity strategy.

Purpose and scope: The methodology should begin with a clear statement of its purpose, guiding the organization in effectively managing cyber risks. The scope outlines the boundaries of the methodology, specifying which parts of the organization it covers and under what conditions it will be applied. This must be aligned with the scope of our cybersecurity program. If it is the entire organization, it is important to define what that means, do not make any assumptions because remember that this is about clarifying what we will do and how we will do it.

Applicable regulations and standards: This section identifies relevant laws, regulations, and industry standards that the organization must comply with. It ensures the methodology aligns with legal obligations and best practices in cyber risk management. Aligning with applicable regulations and standards is not just about compliance; it's about leveraging these guidelines to strengthen your organization's cybersecurity posture. For example, the ISO/IEC 27005 standard offers a structured framework for information security risk management that, as we reviewed in the "Cyber Risk Management Frameworks" (Chapter 2), provides a comprehensive yet pragmatic approach to identifying, assessing, and treating risks.

Beyond ISO/IEC 27005, other key regulations and standards may include the General Data Protection Regulation (GDPR) for organizations operating in or dealing with the European Union (EU), which emphasizes the protection of personal data and privacy. In the United States, the Health Insurance Portability and Accountability Act (HIPAA) sets the standard for protecting sensitive patient data for health-care entities. The Payment Card Industry Data Security Standard (PCI DSS) applies globally to all organizations that handle credit card information, outlining steps that must be taken to secure cardholder data.

For organizations in the energy sector, the North American Electric Reliability Corporation (NERC) standards ensure the reliability of the bulk power system in North America, including cybersecurity practices through its Critical Infrastructure Protection (CIP) standards.

The NIS2 Directive, an evolution of the original Network and Information Security (NIS) Directive within the EU, places a stronger emphasis on risk management practices for essential and important entities across various sectors. NIS2 mandates a more rigorous approach to identifying, assessing, and managing cyber risks, requiring organizations to adopt proactive and comprehensive risk management measures.

Specifically, NIS2 extends the scope of entities covered, emphasizing the need for enhanced security requirements, incident reporting, and risk management strategies to safeguard essential services and digital infrastructure. It introduces stricter supervisory measures and stringent enforcement requirements, including significant fines for noncompliance, and encourages information sharing and collaboration among member states to bolster overall cybersecurity resilience.

For organizations subject to NIS2, incorporating its risk management requirements into their cyber risk management methodology means not only complying with regulatory obligations but also significantly strengthening their defenses against cyber threats. This integration ensures a strategic, unified approach to managing cyber risks, aligning with NIS2's goal of a high common level of cybersecurity across the EU.

General guidelines and considerations: Here, broad principles and approaches for risk management are laid out. It includes the organization's stance on risk tolerance, methodologies for risk assessment, and criteria for prioritizing risks. This section is foundational, setting the tone and direction for the organization's entire approach to managing cyber risks. This section outlines the overarching principles and methods that govern how risks are identified, assessed, analyzed, and prioritized within the organization, serving as a compass for all cybersecurity efforts.

The organization's risk appetite, tolerance, and capacity are a critical aspect of these guidelines. As we defined before, they state the level of risk the organization is willing to accept in pursuit of its objectives, reflecting its overall appetite for risk. These levels are essential for making informed decisions about which risks require immediate attention and which can be accepted or monitored over time.

The methodology for risk assessment detailed in this section provides a standardized approach to identifying and evaluating risks. It might incorporate a range of techniques from qualitative assessments, which could involve expert judgment and risk matrices, to quantitative methods, such as statistical analyses and mathematical modeling. The choice of methodology depends on the organization's specific needs, resources, and the nature of its digital assets.

Also, the criteria for prioritizing risks are elaborated here. These criteria help determine which risks pose the greatest threat to the organization's objectives and should, therefore, be addressed first. Factors in this prioritization might include the potential impact of each risk, its likelihood of occurrence, the vulnerability of critical assets, and the organization's overall risk appetite.

Often defining this section uncovers foundational questions that many organizations find challenging to answer. Questions like "What's our risk appetite?" and "How much risk can we stand?" are deceptively simple on the surface but unpack layers of complexity involving the organization's values, objectives, and capabilities.

Defining risk appetite is a critical step in shaping our cybersecurity strategy. Yet, it requires a delicate balance. Set the appetite too low, and you might suppress innovation and growth; set it too high, and you expose the organization to unnecessary and potentially catastrophic threats. This decision demands input from across the organization, reflecting a comprehensive understanding of its mission, capacity for loss, and strategic priorities.

Besides, quantifying "how much risk we can stand" demands a nuanced understanding of the organization's resilience, financial stability, and operational flexibility. It involves assessing not just direct financial impact but also the potential for reputational damage, legal repercussions, and operational disruptions. Making these determinations requires a deep dive into the organization's risk profile, including its vulnerabilities, threat landscape, and the efficacy of existing controls.

These discussions can be challenging, as they force us to confront the inherent uncertainties of the digital age. However, they are essential for developing a clear, actionable cyber risk management strategy. Without a well-defined risk appetite and understanding of risk tolerance, organizations can either become paralyzed by fear of potential risks or overly cavalier, exposing themselves to unnecessary dangers. Establishing these definitions is the first step toward a mature, balanced approach to cybersecurity, where decisions are made based on a clear understanding of the organization's capacity to manage and mitigate risk.

Our journey on guiding your organizations in defining its risk appetite doesn't require a perfect starting point. Instead, it's about leveraging what we already know and have at our disposal. A practical first step could be utilizing an existing matrix to categorize risks as Extreme, High, Moderate, and Low, attaching monetary impacts to each category to illustrate what they represent in terms of impact and likelihood for our organization.

From there, management could decide, for example, to accept risks classified as Moderate and Low. While this initial stance on risk appetite might seem simplistic or insufficient, it serves as a starting point. The real value comes as you begin to apply this framework to your first risk assessments. These initial exercises into assessing risks with our initial methodology will likely reveal gaps and areas for refinement. It's a learning process, where each assessment brings new insights, allowing you to fine-tune our approach.

The success of risk management lies not in achieving absolute accuracy but in incrementally improving your understanding of risks and how they impact your organization. It's about progressively getting 'less wrong' with each assessment. This approach acknowledges the dynamic nature of cyber risks and the fact that our understanding of these risks evolves as we gain more information and context. Starting with what you know and are capable of now enables you to lay down a flexible foundation that can adapt and mature over time, aligning more closely with your organization's strategic objectives and tolerance for risk.

Together, these guidelines form a structured framework that guides the organization's cyber risk management efforts. They ensure that all actions taken are aligned with the organization's strategic goals, legal and regulatory obligations, and best practices in cybersecurity. This coherent, strategic approach is vital for building a resilient, proactive cyber defense posture.

As part of this section, it's essential to clearly articulate who within the organization has the authority to accept risks and the formal procedure for documenting such acceptances. Establishing this clarity ensures that risk acceptance is both responsible and aligned with the organization's strategic goals.

It's indispensable to understand that accepting a risk doesn't make it go away. Rather, it signifies a conscious decision to tolerate the risk under the current circumstances. Therefore, each accepted risk must be carefully documented, outlining the rationale behind the acceptance, the expected outcomes, and any conditions attached to this decision.

Importantly, every risk acceptance should be tagged with an expiration date. This built-in requirement for reassessment ensures that we'll reevaluate the risk considering any changes in the business environment, emerging threats, or shifts in the organization's risk tolerance. This approach to risk acceptance is about maintaining vigilance and adaptability, recognizing that the cyber threat landscape and the organization's own context are ever evolving.

This section of the methodology should specify that only certain levels of organizational leadership, such as senior management or specific governance bodies, have the authority to accept risks. The process for documenting risk acceptance must be straightforward and standardized, ensuring that all relevant information is captured and accessible for review.

Roles and responsibilities: Clearly defining who is responsible for what is crucial. This section details the roles and responsibilities of individuals and teams within the organization, ensuring accountability and efficient risk management processes. Providing this clarity ensures that each member of our organization understands their part in this process. Let's go deeper into some key roles that should be described in your methodology:

- **Information Security Forum:** This group brings together representatives from various parts of the organization to discuss and make decisions on cybersecurity matters. It acts as an advisory body to the Chief Information Security Officer (CISO) and plays a key role in setting cybersecurity policies, strategies, and priorities. The forum facilitates cross-departmental communication and ensures that cybersecurity considerations are integrated into all business decisions. This is the group that will be making final decisions based on the risks we identify.
- **Chief Information Security Officer (CISO):** The CISO oversees the organization's overall security posture, ensuring the alignment of

cybersecurity strategies with business objectives. They are responsible for the development, implementation, and management of the cybersecurity program.

- **Cyber risk management team**: Tasked with defining our methodology, identifying, analyzing, and characterizing risks, this team plays the core role in the risk assessment process. They collaborate with other departments to gather necessary information and ensure comprehensive risk coverage.
- **IT and cybersecurity teams**: These teams handle the technical aspects of cybersecurity, including the implementation of security measures, monitoring of security systems, and responding to security incidents. Their responsibilities also encompass conducting regular vulnerability assessments and ensuring the security of the organization's information technology infrastructure.
- **Risk owner**: Individuals designated as risk owners are directly responsible for managing specific risks. They are tasked with ensuring that risks are assessed accurately, that appropriate risk treatment plans are developed, and that measures are implemented effectively. Risk owners have the authority to make decisions about how to manage the risks for which they are responsible, within the guidelines set by the organization's risk management strategy.
- **Treatment plan owners**: These individuals are assigned to oversee the execution of specific risk treatment plans. They ensure that the actions outlined in the plan are carried out within the agreed timelines and budgets. Treatment plan owners coordinate with various teams and stakeholders to implement the risk mitigation measures and report on the progress and effectiveness of these measures to the risk owners and the broader cybersecurity governance structure.
- **Compliance Officer**: The Compliance Officer ensures that cybersecurity policies and practices meet regulatory and legal requirements. They keep abreast of new regulations and advise on compliance strategies.
- **Human resources (HR)**: HR is responsible for incorporating cybersecurity into organizational culture and practices. This includes managing cybersecurity training programs, ensuring that employees are aware of cybersecurity policies, and ensuring that they understand their roles in maintaining security.
- **Business area leaders**: Leaders within various business areas need to understand the cybersecurity risks relevant to their specific areas. They are responsible for implementing risk treatment plans within their departments and ensuring their teams comply with cybersecurity policies.
- **Cybersecurity champions**: Selected from different departments, these individuals advocate for good cybersecurity practices among their

peers. They act as a bridge between the cybersecurity team and the rest of the organization, promoting awareness and encouraging adherence to security policies.

Including a RACI matrix as the one we can see in Figure 4.1 as part of your cyber risk management methodology can be really valuable in ensuring clarity and alignment among all stakeholders. The matrix lays out the roles and responsibilities across different phases of the process, making it clear who is responsible, accountable, consulted, and informed at each step. This visual tool helps prevent overlap, confusion, and gaps in responsibility, facilitating smoother collaboration and more effective implementation of your risk management strategy.

Process map and description: This section is the core of the methodology because it outlines a step-by-step process for managing cyber risks. I found that if we want to make it pragmatic, we can take the best of the frameworks we reviewed before and establish the following sections: organizational context, risk assessment (identification, analysis, characterization), risk treatment strategies, communication and implementation, and risk monitoring and metrics. To effectively manage cyber risks, our methodology must articulate a clear and actionable process. Please keep in mind that in Section II we'll get in detail into each of these steps. However, for you to create your methodology, let's review a high-level overview of each phase:

- **Establishing the organizational context:** This initial phase sets the stage for effective risk management by understanding the organization's objectives, the environment in which it operates, its stakeholders, and the scope of the risk management process. This context shapes how risks are identified, assessed, and managed, ensuring that the risk management efforts are aligned with the organization's goals and capabilities.
- **Risk assessment:**
  - **Risk identification:** This involves identifying potential risks that could affect the organization. This step is about cataloging threats, vulnerabilities, and potential impact areas to create a comprehensive inventory of risks.
  - **Risk analysis:** Once risks are identified, this step evaluates the likelihood and impact of each risk, helping to prioritize them based on their severity. This analysis can be quantitative, qualitative, or a combination of both, depending on the organization's needs and the nature of the risks.
  - **Risk characterization:** This consolidates the findings from the risk analysis, providing a detailed picture of each risk, its potential consequences, and its priority level. This characterization

Task/Activity	*Information Security Forum*	*CISO*	*Cyber Risk Management Team*	*IT and Cybersecurity Teams*	*Risk Owner*	*Treatment Plan Owner*	*Compliance Officer*	*HR*	*Business Area Leaders*	*Cybersecurity Champions*
Define Cyber Risk Management Methodology	C	A	R	I	I	I	C	I	I	I
Establish Organizational Context	I	R	R	I	A	I	C	I	C	I
Risk Identification	C	A	R	R	I	I	I	I	C	I
Risk Analysis	I	A	R	R	I	I	I	I	C	I
Risk Characterization	I	A	R	R	I	I	I	I	C	I
Develop Risk Treatment Plans	I	A	R	I	R	R	I	I	C	I
Implement Risk Treatment Plans	I	I	I	R	I	R	I	I	C	I
Monitor and Review Risk Landscape	C	A	R	R	I	I	C	I	C	I
Risk Acceptance	R	R	C	I	A	I	I	I	C	I
Communicate Cybersecurity Policies	I	A	I	I	I	I	C	R	C	I
Conduct Cybersecurity Training	I	I	I	I	I	I	I	R	C	I

Legend:

R = Responsible (Those who do the work to achieve the task)
A = Accountable (The one ultimately answerable for the correct and thorough completion of the task)
C = Consulted (Those whose opinions are sought, two-way communication)
I = Informed (Those who are kept up to date on progress, one-way communication)

Figure 4.1 Cyber Risk Management RACI matrix.

helps in understanding the nature of risks in the context of the organization's operations and objectives.

- **Risk treatment planning**: Here, strategies for dealing with identified risks are developed. Options include avoiding, transferring, mitigating, or accepting risks. This phase involves selecting appropriate control measures and developing action plans to address the risks in line with the organization's risk appetite.
- **Implementation of treatment plans**: Once treatment plans are approved, they are put into action. This involves deploying the selected controls, carrying out mitigation strategies, and, where applicable, transferring risks. It's critical to ensure that the implementation is in accordance with the plans and that it effectively reduces the risks to acceptable levels.
- **Ongoing risk monitoring**: The final phase is about keeping a constant watch on the risk environment and the effectiveness of the treatment measures. This includes monitoring for changes in the organizational context, the emergence of new threats, and the performance of risk controls. Ongoing monitoring helps in identifying when adjustments to the risk management approach are needed, ensuring that the organization remains resilient against cyber threats.

In Figure 4.2 we can see a different approach to represent the cyber risk management process which in the next section we'll explore in detail these five phases and the strategies on how to implement each phase depending on our expertise and maturity level of our organizations.

Performance indicators: Key performance indicators (KPIs) and key risk indicators (KRIs) are defined to measure the effectiveness of the cyber risk management program. These metrics help the organization monitor progress and make informed decisions.

- **Key performance indicators (KPIs)**: These are metrics used to evaluate the effectiveness and efficiency of the cyber risk management program. KPIs might include measures such as the time taken to detect and respond to incidents, the percentage of employees who have completed cybersecurity training, or the number of identified risks that have been mitigated within a certain timeframe. KPIs provide tangible evidence of how well the cybersecurity program is performing against its set objectives, allowing for adjustments and improvements.
- **Key risk indicators (KRIs)**: These indicators signal potential increases in risk exposure before they materialize into actual incidents or losses. KRIs are forward-looking metrics, such as the number of failed login attempts, which could indicate a potential security breach, or the increase in unpatched systems within the network, signaling a

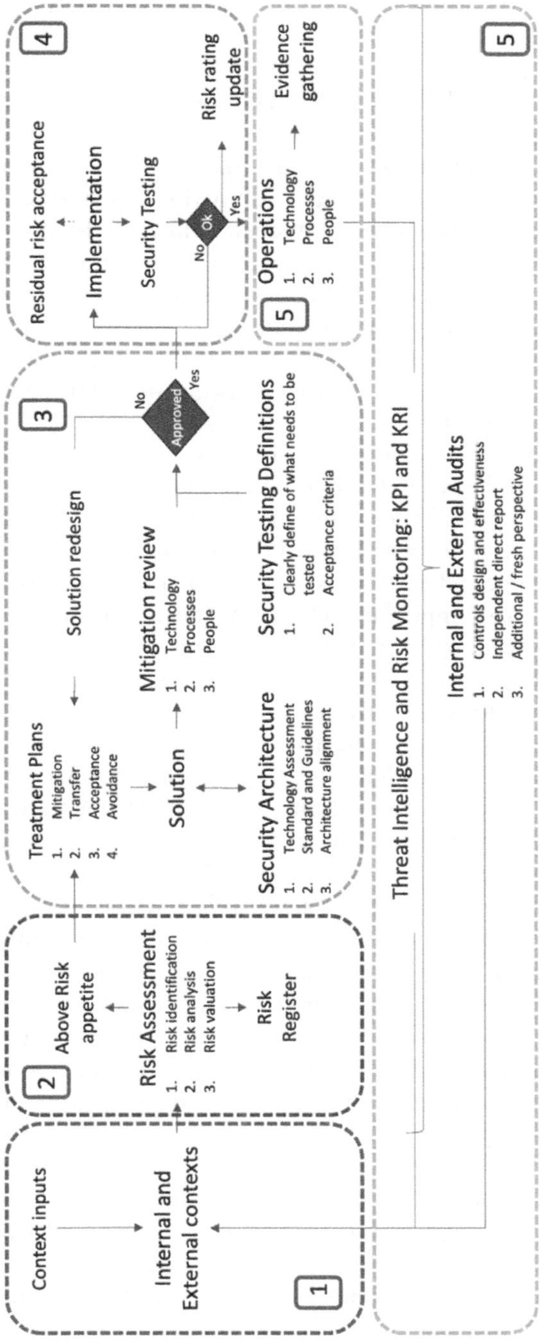

Figure 4.2 Simplified Cyber Risk Management process.

growing vulnerability. Monitoring KRIs enables organizations to proactively identify and address risks before they escalate into serious threats.

Together, KPIs and KRIs will offer a comprehensive overview of the cyber risk management program's performance and risk landscape. They should empower our organizations to make data-driven decisions, prioritizing resources effectively, and continually improving our strategies. Establishing these indicators requires a good understanding of the organization's risk appetite, strategic objectives, and operational context to ensure they are relevant, measurable, and aligned with the overarching goals of the cybersecurity program. Having metrics that are actionable and easy to constantly obtain with the same quality and level of confidence is equally important; don't forget about it, or you'll find yourself working all day trying to put together dashboards and reports.

To visualize these indicators effectively, as we can see in Figure 4.3, tools like Power BI can be really helpful. Power BI allows you to create dynamic dashboards that provide real-time insights into your KPIs and KRIs. For instance, you can set up a dashboard that tracks the number of failed login attempts over time, offering a visual cue when there's a sudden spike that might indicate an attempted breach. Another example might be a dashboard showing the percentage of unpatched systems, with color-coded alerts for when the numbers exceed your organization's acceptable thresholds.

These visualizations not only make it easier to monitor and interpret your data but also facilitate more effective communication with stakeholders. By presenting your KPIs and KRIs in a clear, visual format, you help ensure that everyone in the organization, from the IT team to the executive board, understands the current risk landscape and the effectiveness of your cybersecurity measures.

To ensure that these metrics are actionable and easy to consistently obtain with the same quality and level of confidence, it's important to look at the guidance provided by relevant standards and frameworks. For example, ISO 31000 and ISO 31010 emphasize the importance of developing metrics that reflect the organization's risk appetite and monitoring changes in risk exposure. These standards offer a foundational approach to identifying and developing KRIs, helping you monitor critical risk factors and adjust your strategy proactively.

Similarly, NIST SP 800-30 provides valuable insights into the continuous monitoring and assessment of risks, which aligns with the development of effective KRIs. Although it does not explicitly define KRIs, the principles outlined in NIST SP 800-30 can guide you in identifying metrics that signal changes in risk exposure, helping to ensure that your organization remains resilient against emerging threats.

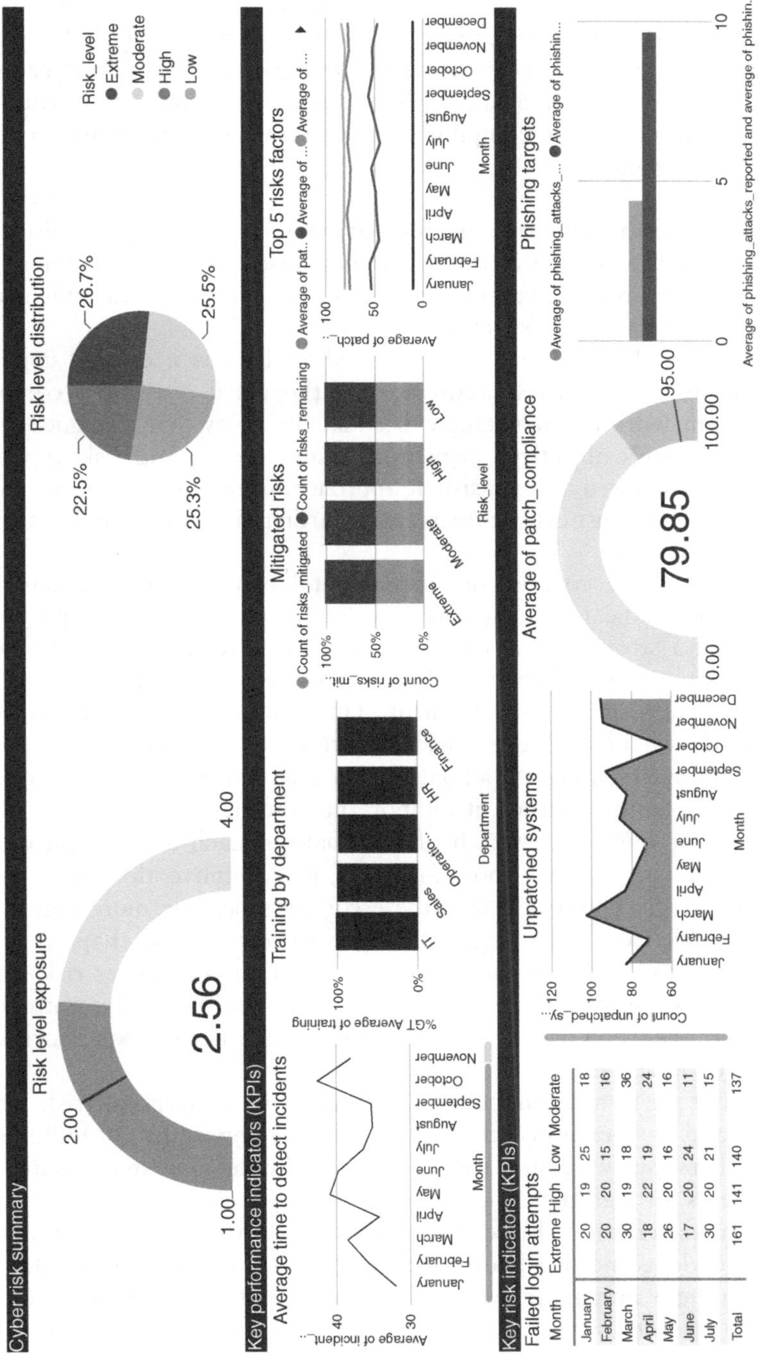

Figure 4.3 Example of a power BI Cyber Risk Management dashboard.

Incorporating these standards and frameworks into your cyber risk management methodology ensures that your KPIs and KRIs are not only compliant with best practices but also serve as effective tools for managing risks in real time. Having metrics that are actionable and easy to consistently obtain is crucial; without them, you might find yourself spending too much time compiling reports rather than focusing on strategic decision-making.

Glossary: A glossary of terms ensures that everyone in the organization has a common understanding of the terminology used in the methodology. It sounds obvious, but sometimes we assume that everyone will understand what we understand; that's a classic mistake.

Defining a cyber risk management methodology is a critical step for organizations to proactively address cyber threats. It provides a comprehensive framework for managing cyber risks in a way that is aligned with the organization's objectives, regulatory requirements, and risk appetite. Through a structured and consistent approach, organizations can enhance their resilience against cyber threats, safeguarding their assets and ensuring business continuity.

Now that we've covered the fundamental concepts of risk management, explored the role of governance, and understood the importance of fostering a strong cybersecurity culture, we're ready to take the next step. In the upcoming chapter, we'll dive into the key concepts and aspects of the five steps of risk management. This exploration will provide the final foundational knowledge needed before we can confidently move forward with implementing a pragmatic cyber risk management program. As you progress on this journey, it's important to recognize that the chapters in this section contain a wealth of information. Each topic could easily be expanded into its own book. However, as you move along your own curve of change, you'll find that these concepts become more digestible and applicable over time. I encourage you to revisit these chapters periodically. As you and your organization mature in your cyber risk management program, you'll discover that the messages here evolve with you. What might seem complex now will become clearer as your experience and understanding deepen.

Now that we're all equipped with the essential concepts of risk management and have explored governance and the importance of building a strong cybersecurity culture, we're ready to take the next step. Chapter 5 will guide us through the critical aspects and key concepts of the five steps of risk management. This exploration will provide the final foundational knowledge needed before we can confidently move forward with implementing a pragmatic cyber risk management program to drive our cybersecurity success, setting the stage for the practical application of everything we've discussed.

CYBER RISK REGISTER

The risk register is an essential tool, and it is vital to our cyber risk management program. It is the centralized repository for all information related to the cyber risks our organization is facing, serving not just as a record but as a dynamic management tool to track and analyze risks over time. Let's explore what a risk register is, why it's crucial, and how it functions within the broader scope of managing cyber risks.

At its core, the risk register is a detailed catalog that lists, describes, and analyzes every known risk to our organization. For each risk, it includes important details such as descriptions, the likelihood of occurrence, potential impacts, the controls and safeguards we have in place, the status of risk treatment plans, and the ownership assigned for managing those risks.

With the cybersecurity landscape always evolving, having a structured and organized method to keep track of risks is indispensable. The risk register gives us a snapshot of our organization's risk profile at any moment, offering clear insights into where our vulnerabilities lie and how we're addressing them. It's a key tool for communication, decision-making, and prioritization, helping stakeholders understand the cyber risk landscape and make informed decisions about where to allocate resources.

The risk register also allows us to take a holistic view of risk management. Without a centralized system, risks might be identified, analyzed, and managed in isolation, which can lead to a fragmented understanding of how they interconnect and what their collective impact might be. This can obscure the true nature of our cyber risks, much like how small, sporadic credit card purchases can quickly add up without a clear statement to summarize the total spending. Each small acceptance of residual risk might seem manageable on its own, but without a central overview, it's easy to overlook how these risks accumulate. It's like using a credit card for minor purchases that can quickly push you over your budget if you're not keeping track. Without a central record, like a credit card statement, it's challenging to get a clear picture of your overall spending, or in our case, the aggregated risk exposure.

The risk register is essential for effective risk management. It ensures that we maintain a clear, ongoing account of all risks, much like a financial ledger for purchases. This allows us to make strategic decisions and take action before risks accumulate beyond our ability to manage them effectively. It's not just about recording what's been done; it's about providing the insights we need to proactively manage our risk exposure and ensure we stay within our predefined risk appetite and capacity.

To fully understand the role of the risk register in our cyber risk management program, we need to realize that it is composed of three main sections: risk description and inherent risk, controls and actual risk, and treatment plans and residual risk. Each of these sections serves a specific moment in our risk management process. Understanding these sections helps us see how the risk register supports informed decision-making, effective communication, and proactive risk management. This breakdown will also show how the register helps us prioritize resources, manage residual risks, and maintain alignment with our strategic goals. Let's explore how the risk register functions through these sections, beginning with how we document and understand the inherent risks, then examining how we manage these risks through controls, and finally looking at how we plan and execute treatment strategies to address any remaining risks.

The first section of the risk register focuses on documenting the identified risks. Here, we carefully document each identified risk, capturing its description, attributes, and the inherent risk characterization it poses before any controls are applied. At this stage, we closely examine the nature of each risk, including its likelihood of occurring and the potential impact on our organization. At this stage, we examine the likelihood and potential impact of each risk, establishing a foundation for effective management.

As we move forward in our risk assessment, the focus shifts to managing risks through the application of controls. This involves assessing the controls we have in place and evaluating their effectiveness. We need to determine if these controls are reducing the risk and if they justify the investment. This means considering the return on investment (ROI) for each control, balancing the cost with the risk reduction it offers. Understanding the effectiveness of our controls allows us to document the actual risk our organization faces after applying these measures. This insight supports more strategic decisions about resource allocation and clarifies the difference between inherent and actual risk levels.

The final section of the risk register is about taking action. After identifying the risks and evaluating our controls, we must document treatment plans that will be implemented to address any remaining risks above our risk appetite. These plans outline the specific actions we need to take, along with commitment dates and the evidence required to demonstrate that these actions have been completed. The goal is to manage the residual risk that remains after all controls have been applied. This section ensures that we are not just identifying and analyzing risks but actively working to mitigate them, with clear timelines and accountability in place.

With the treatment plans in place, we move from understanding our risks to actively managing them. This ensures that risks are not just identified and evaluated but also addressed with concrete actions designed to reduce our exposure. The risk register, therefore, becomes much more than a static record; it transforms into a dynamic tool that guides our ongoing efforts to protect the organization. I hope that as we review how the risk register functions, it becomes clear that its value lies in its ability to evolve alongside our understanding and management of risks. The risk register is a living document, starting with identifying and documenting every risk uncovered during the assessment process. Including all potential risks ensures they are properly analyzed and addressed.

After documenting the risks, the next step is to analyze and prioritize them. The risk register records each risk's likelihood and impact, helping determine its severity and the urgency with which it should be addressed. This prioritization ensures we focus on the most significant risks first, allowing for effective resource allocation and timely action to address critical vulnerabilities before they escalate. The new risks are added as they emerge, and existing entries are revised to reflect changes in status. This includes updating the effectiveness of treatment measures and noting any shifts in severity or likelihood. Keeping the register current ensures it remains a reliable tool for guiding our risk management efforts.

In addition to tracking and updating risks, the risk register serves as a communication tool within the organization, offering a clear way for stakeholders to understand the current state of cyber risks. It fosters accountability and helps align our risk management efforts with broader business objectives. This clarity ensures that everyone, from technical teams to senior management, stays aligned and can contribute effectively to the overall strategy. The risk register also supports strategic decision-making by providing a comprehensive overview of the organization's risk profile. It helps determine which risks to accept, mitigate, or address through new security measures. Offering a complete view of the risk landscape empowers leaders to make decisions that align with strategic goals and the organization's risk appetite.

To keep the risk register effective, it's important to incorporate catalogs of risks and controls. These catalogs are detailed library, listing potential risks across business, security, and IT, along with corresponding controls. Aligning catalogs used in the risk register with recognized frameworks like CIS Controls V8.1 or NIST 800-53 rev 5 ensures that our approach is systematic and aligned with industry standards. These frameworks provide a common language and set of standards that facilitate discussions about risk at all levels, from technical staff to the boardroom.

These catalogs transform how we discuss and manage risk at all levels. By connecting the technical aspects of cyber risks with the strategic concerns of business risks, they foster meaningful dialogue on risk management. Breaking down business risks into security risks, and further into IT risks, allows us to trace high-level business risks, such as potential revenue loss due to a cyber incident, back to specific vulnerabilities and IT gaps. Presenting risks this way ensures that both technical teams and management understand how their roles contribute to the organization's broader objectives.

For technical teams, this approach provides insights into how their day-to-day activities and the risks they manage are directly connected to the organization's success. This understanding fosters a sense of ownership and responsibility toward mitigating those risks, reinforcing the importance of their contributions to the overall risk management strategy. For management and nontechnical stakeholders, this breakdown demystifies the complexities of cyber risks by presenting them in a context that highlights their impact on business goals and objectives. This clarity enables leaders to make informed decisions, ensuring that cybersecurity efforts are aligned with the strategic direction of the organization.

The strength of aligning with these frameworks lies in their ability to provide us with standardized language and clear guidelines for identifying, assessing, and managing cyber risks. For instance, the CIS Controls offer a set of prioritized actions that help protect against the most pervasive cyber threats, while NIST 800-53 provides a more granular set of security and privacy controls tailored to meet the needs of diverse organizations, including those with stringent regulatory requirements. Choose the one that better fits with your overall cybersecurity strategy because in this way you'll get a clear roadmap for mitigating risks, making it easier to prioritize actions based on the impact and likelihood of each risk. Additionally, it facilitates the tracking of our mitigation efforts, enabling us to monitor progress and adjust our strategies as needed.

Another significant advantage of structuring our risk register catalogs around these frameworks is the ability to generate actionable metrics because mapping risks to specific controls helps us to quantify our cybersecurity posture, track improvements over time, and identify areas that require additional focus. These metrics are really important for communicating risk management efforts to stakeholders, demonstrating compliance with regulatory requirements, and justifying investments in cybersecurity.

Another crucial aspect we must not overlook is the confidentiality of the risk register. Given its comprehensive detail on the organization's vulnerabilities, exposures, and mitigation strategies, this document contains sensitive information that could be exploited if it fell into the wrong hands. Protecting the risk register from unauthorized access is critical to maintaining the integrity and security of the organization's risk management efforts. Think of the risk register as a detailed blueprint of our organization's risks and the defense mechanisms we have in place, as well as those we plan to implement. It outlines not only where the organization is vulnerable but also how we intend to respond to these vulnerabilities, making it a potential goldmine for anyone looking to exploit these weaknesses. Just as a strategic plan in the hands of a competitor could be catastrophic, so too could the detailed information within a risk register if accessed by cybercriminals. In addition to guarding against external threats, it's vital to consider internal risks. Employees should be educated on the importance of the document's confidentiality and the critical role they play in safeguarding it. Regular audits and monitoring of access logs can help detect any unauthorized attempts to access the risk register, allowing for immediate action to prevent data compromise.

Access to the risk register should be tightly controlled, with permissions limited strictly to those who need the information to perform their roles effectively. This selective access minimizes the risk of internal leaks or external breaches. Additionally, the risk register should be encrypted and securely stored, with robust authentication mechanisms in place to verify the identity of those granted access, just as we would protect our most sensitive and critical information. One way of having a better management over our risk register is by integrating our centralized risk register into Governance, Risk, and Compliance (GRC) tools that elevate the efficacy of an organization's risk management strategy. GRC tools offer a dynamic platform where the risk register is not just a static document but a living, breathing part of the organization's risk management ecosystem. These tools facilitate the aggregation, analysis, and reporting of risks, ensuring that risk data is up to date, accessible, and actionable.

One of the standout benefits of housing the risk register within GRC tools is the automation of risk tracking and updating processes. As new risks are identified, or existing risks evolve, GRC tools can automatically update the risk register, ensuring that it always reflects the current risk landscape. This real-time update capability is crucial for maintaining an accurate and comprehensive overview of organizational risks. GRC tools enhance the visibility of risk management activities across the organization. They enable stakeholders from different departments to access relevant risk information, fostering a culture of transparency and shared responsibility for risk management. This cross-departmental visibility ensures that risk management is a collaborative effort that benefits from diverse perspectives and expertise.

Another significant advantage is the ability of GRC tools to facilitate risk analysis and prioritization. By leveraging built-in analytics capabilities, these tools can help organizations identify high-priority risks that require immediate attention, based on factors like likelihood, impact, and the effectiveness of existing controls. This prioritization supports more strategic allocation of resources toward mitigating the most critical risks. GRC tools also offer robust reporting features, making it easier to communicate risk information to stakeholders, including the board and senior management. Customizable dashboards and reports provide clear, concise, and relevant insights into the organization's risk profile, enhancing decision-making processes and enabling more effective risk management strategies.

Even when a formal GRC tool isn't within reach, either due to budget constraints or other limitations, organizations can still effectively manage their risks using more accessible resources like an Excel workbook. Starting with an Excel-based risk register is not ideal, but it certainly works as a practical interim solution. This approach enables organizations to maintain a centralized view of their risks, even when advanced tools are out of reach.

Using Excel for your risk register allows for the basic functionalities needed for effective risk management: listing risks, detailing their analysis (likelihood, impact, etc.), tracking mitigation strategies, and monitoring residual risks. Excel's formulae and functions can help in prioritizing risks based on defined criteria, and conditional formatting can highlight high-priority areas that require immediate attention. Excel's widespread availability and familiarity to most users lower the barrier to entry for maintaining a risk register. It requires no additional training or significant investment, making it an accessible option for organizations of all sizes. Collaboration can be facilitated through secure shared drives or cloud services, ensuring that relevant stakeholders can access and update the risk register as needed.

However, it's important to recognize the limitations of using Excel as a risk register. As the complexity of your organization's risk landscape grows, so does the need for more sophisticated tools that offer automation, real-time updates, and more comprehensive reporting capabilities. Excel lacks the ability to easily aggregate data for in-depth analysis or to automate the updating process as new information becomes available. Additionally, version control and ensuring the confidentiality and integrity of the data can become challenging as the number of stakeholders accessing the document increases.

In our journey for effective cyber risk management, the tools and technologies you employ are important, but the principles behind their use are the true key for success. Whether through a basic spreadsheet or advanced software, the goal remains the same: to have a clear, comprehensive understanding of your cyber risks and how they're being managed. This understanding enables organizations to navigate the complex cyber threat landscape with confidence, making informed decisions that protect and drive our businesses forward.

As we conclude this chapter, remember that the risk register is not just a requirement or a checkbox to tick off; it's a strategic asset that enhances our organization's ability to manage cyber risks. It's about continuous improvement and risk awareness that permeates every level of the organization, ensuring that cybersecurity is not just the responsibility of the CISO's department but a shared commitment across the enterprise.

Chapter 5

Laying the groundwork

Forever determined to turn effort into meaningful outcomes is one of our mantras. "Superhuman effort isn't worth a damn unless it achieves results." These wise words from Ernest Shackleton resonate with me, and I believe they capture the core of cyber risk management. As we prepare to start the journey of managing cyber risks within our organizations, it's crucial to remember that the ultimate goal is not just to perform assessments but to achieve tangible results that safeguard our digital and physical environments. The essence of a successful cyber risk management program lies in its ability to guide organizations toward making better, well-informed decisions that will minimize the materialization of cyber risks. Of course, we all now know that this is easier said than done, but that's the challenge we'll tackle with a pragmatic approach.

In the cybersecurity space, it's easy to get caught up in the complexities of identifying and analyzing risks. We often pride ourselves on the thoroughness of our risk assessments and delight in the granularity of our findings. However, without a clear focus on the end goal, implementing effective risk treatment strategies that truly protect our assets and operations, our efforts risk becoming pointless data collection exercises.

The purpose of cyber risk management is to provide clear guidance, enabling leaders to steer their organizations with foresight and confidence. It's about turning the insights from our detailed assessments into actionable strategies that reduce vulnerabilities, strengthen defenses, and build resilience against the constantly changing landscape of cyber threats. As we go further into the execution of risk management, we should always keep Shackleton's words in mind. Our efforts in identifying, assessing, and managing cyber risks must lead to outcomes that make our organizations stronger. Staying focused on results ensures that our cyber risk management program remains an effective tool, driving us toward a more secure and resilient future.

Before we get into the action, it's important to lay the groundwork for our cyber risk management program. The upcoming chapters will focus on

DOI: 10.1201/9781003546207-7

how to execute this in a way that's practical, scalable, and effective. But let's be clear: this journey requires strategic foresight, emotional intelligence, and patience. As you prepare to implement your cyber risk management program, it's crucial to go beyond traditional approaches that start with gap assessments and compliance checks. While many books and certifications emphasize the importance of identifying gaps and defining security initiatives to bridge them, I believe there's a more effective first step. Before diving into these assessments, take the time to fully understand the business model of the organization you're in or joining.

Understanding the organization's business model gives you a clearer view of its strategic goals, critical operations, and specific risks. This insight allows you to tailor your cyber risk management program to fit the organization's needs more precisely. Aligning security efforts with business objectives ensures that your program not only meets compliance requirements but also actively supports the organization's success. Focusing on the business model first guarantees that your cyber risk management strategies are relevant, effective, and seamlessly integrated into the broader organizational framework.

During my experience working in both government and complex industry sectors, enterprise risk management has traditionally been the domain of Enterprise Risk, Financial Risk, Business Risk, and typical non-cyber (i.e. COSO) Framework pillars. Over the past few decades, the emergence of another domain—cyber risk—has become woven into the fabric of all traditional risk pillars. This category of risk has often been feared by the business as it has been misunderstood and perhaps not well explained by the cyber risk management leadership. I have witnessed firsthand, through making errors myself along the way, that the ability of a cyber risk management professional to learn the business and understand the business drivers is key to success in achieving your mandate.

Unless you understand the context of the business and how it creates value (makes money, serves citizens efficiently, generates new products, develops advanced manufacturing products, provides commodity products, etc.) you cannot begin to build a right-sized cyber risk management program that will enable the business to succeed in its value-added mission while supporting the budget and resources you need to achieve the balanced mandate. Years ago, I worked for an outsourced electronics manufacturing company and initially attempted to develop a one-size-fits-all enterprise security risk management program for this organization. What I quickly realized was that I was alienating myself, my team, and my mandate from the business owners.

In this case, each plant general manager—worldwide—managed their own profit & loss (P&L) which included cyber risk management programs. As such, as the global lead for the programs, I needed to understand the nuances of each business. Some were providing commoditized manufacturing with lower profit margins and lower risks for intellectual property (IP) loss (commoditized products are not as protected as new product introduction (NPI) so the margins are thinner, and the level of risk accepted to achieve the right balance is higher in comparison). In stark contrast, we also had aerospace & defense (A&D) facilities that had higher profit margins per widget and had a significant security and compliance demand from federal regulators on IP protection. This basic example illustrates how I had to adjust my approach to cyber risk management across business units—within the same organization. The more time I spent learning the business of each general manager, the better I was able to shape the right-sized program and obtain budget approvals to deliver and support.

This holds true for many aspects of the cyber risk management mandate. Another example is digital resilience. Resilience is expensive to implement, support, and maintain. Some businesses require this from a compliance perspective, and as such, it is easier to force this aspect of cyber risk management. However, I have also experienced the success of developing a joint business case for a business general manager who was able to compete for and win higher margin business as we built a right-sized resilience and data protection capability. The cost of the implementation and support was measured and understood to allow the plant to win higher margin business and generate higher annual margins even with the investment in resilience and data protection measures. Working with the general manager of each business location allowed us to maximize cyber risk while balancing the unique risk appetite of the respective business operations.

Tyson Johnson
CIO of UNI Financial Cooperation

Once you have a clear understanding of the business model, the planning phase begins with an introspective look at your position within the organization, the state of your security department, and the organization's overall cybersecurity posture. A good starting point to better understand our current standing is to assess everyday aspects we might overlook, such as the existing cybersecurity policies and procedures. Are these policies regularly reviewed and updated, at least annually? Do we have mechanisms to enforce them? Do they emphasize the importance of a risk-based cybersecurity program?

The answers to these questions can help to reveal how deeply cybersecurity is embedded in our processes and its perceived importance within the organization. Also, as we discussed in previous chapters, understanding the organization's culture toward cybersecurity is just crucial. Is cybersecurity seen as essential to the organization's success, or is it treated as a checkbox exercise? This cultural insight is key because it influences how cybersecurity initiatives are embraced and supported across the board.

Your role and tenure within the organization also shape your perception of its cybersecurity landscape. Newcomers may bring a fresh perspective, spotting potential oversights that might be overlooked by those with more experience. However, we can't underestimate the learning curve for a newcomer, which can sometimes be steep. In these cases, it might make more sense to promote someone from within the organization and focus on developing their cybersecurity knowledge. It's about finding the right balance between technical or cyber-related experience and cultural fit. Those with a longer tenure can leverage their deep understanding of the organization's culture and processes to guide the cybersecurity strategy more effectively. Recognizing where we stand is the first step toward tailoring a cybersecurity approach that aligns with the organization's specific needs and challenges.

Whether you're new to the organization or have been with it for years, integrating a cyber risk management program comes with unique challenges and opportunities. Newcomers bring a fresh perspective, often questioning existing practices and proposing innovative solutions without the weight of "we've always done it this way." However, they may face resistance as they work to gain the trust of established teams and navigate internal politics.

In contrast, long-standing members possess valuable insider knowledge. They understand the key players, the unwritten rules, and the history of past challenges and successes. This deep understanding can be a significant advantage in anticipating obstacles and securing support for new initiatives. But with familiarity comes the risk of complacency or resistance to change. It's crucial for experienced members to remain open to new ideas and committed to continuous improvement.

Regardless of your tenure, resistance to change is a universal challenge. Newcomers may encounter skepticism about their understanding of the organization's culture, while seasoned members might face pushback when introducing changes that disrupt the status quo. In both cases, building trust, leveraging relationships, and demonstrating how changes align with the organization's goals are key to overcoming these barriers. Your role, whether as a fresh face or a seasoned veteran, is to advocate for meaningful change that benefits the entire organization.

Yet, even when we manage to navigate these internal challenges, the broader struggle remains: moving from understanding to action. In every organization, the journey toward transformation, especially in cybersecurity, is fraught with hurdles. It's one thing to recognize the necessity of protecting our organization to ensure the confidentiality, integrity, and availability of our cyber assets; it's another entirely to take decisive action. Often, I've encountered organizations that, while understanding the critical importance of cybersecurity, remain stationary, much like an ostrich with its head buried in the sand, pretending the threats in their environment are gone.

This absurd standpoint can come from various factors, each adding to the resistance that slows progress. Fear of the unknown, budgetary constraints, or even a deeply held belief that 'it won't happen to us' mindset can freeze an organization, preventing it from adapting to the challenges of the digital age. This kind of inertia is not just risky; it's a silent alarm signaling the urgent need for a shift in perspective.

In the spirit of overcoming the challenges that organizations face, especially the gap between recognizing the need for cybersecurity and actually implementing it, we can find important lessons in the book *The Knowing-Doing Gap*[1] by Pfeffer and Sutton. This book explores the perplexing issue of why knowledge often fails to translate into action, a theme that is very familiar in cybersecurity. Based on Pfeffer and Sutton's insights, it becomes clear that bridging this gap involves more than just sharing information; it's about fostering a culture where action is prioritized over talk, and where the practical implementation of cybersecurity measures takes precedence over theoretical knowledge. This aligns closely with our goal of not just recognizing the importance of cybersecurity, but actively engaging in practices that strengthen our defenses. One of the book's core tenets is that real change requires more than understanding; it demands a commitment to action, even when faced with uncertainty or resistance. In cybersecurity, this means moving beyond acknowledging the threats to our digital assets and committing to systematically implementing measures that protect them. It's about creating an environment where proactive management of cyber risk becomes the norm, rather than passive acknowledgment.

To bridge the knowing-doing gap in cybersecurity, we must confront the barriers head-on: fear of failure, bureaucratic inertia, and a lack of clear, actionable objectives can all slow progress. Setting specific, measurable goals aligned with our organization's capabilities and challenges allows us to create a path toward meaningful change. This means taking what we know about cyber threats and turning it into a solid framework of policies, procedures, and practices that are actively implemented and continuously improved.

The *Knowing-Doing Gap* also highlights the power of leading by example. Leaders and change agents within the organization must embody the principles they advocate for. In cybersecurity, this means fully embracing the practices we want to see adopted throughout the organization. When leadership is committed to cyber risk management, it sets a tone that encourages others to follow, turning knowledge into action.

Bridging the knowing-doing gap in cybersecurity requires persistence, leadership, and a focus on execution. By applying the insights of Pfeffer and Sutton, we can move our organizations from passive understanding to active engagement, strengthening our defenses against cyber threats. As leaders, it's our responsibility to challenge the status quo, inspire action, and articulate a clear vision that resonates across all levels of the organization, transforming apprehension into momentum.

So, if you find your organization playing the role of the ostrich, it's a call to action. It's time to lift heads from the sand and face the realities of our digital world. Through persistent effort, clear communication, and strong leadership, we can initiate change, no matter how resistant the organization might initially be. Whether you're a newcomer or a long-standing member of the organization, effective communication, patience, and strategic stakeholder engagement are key to building resilience. This means presenting clear, compelling reasons for change, supported by data or successful case studies, and listening to and addressing concerns. Cultivating a culture that values learning, adaptability, and innovation can gradually strengthen resilience, making the organization better prepared to tackle future challenges.

When talking to executives about cyber risks, it's very important to focus on how these risks directly impact the business. Start by translating technical jargon into business language, emphasizing what matters most to them: financial loss, operational downtime, and regulatory consequences. You don't need to dive into the specifics of the latest threat; instead, connect the risk to their world. For example, explain how a potential breach could affect revenue streams, disrupt supply chains, or harm the company's reputation. The key is to demonstrate that managing cyber risks is not just an IT responsibility but a business imperative that protects the bottom line and fosters long-term success. Executives are also looking for solutions, not just problems. So, when presenting risks, always follow up with actionable steps and potential outcomes. Show them the proactive measures being taken to mitigate those risks, whether it's enhancing security policies, training staff, or adopting new technologies. Be clear about what decisions need to be made, outlining the potential return on investment for each action. This way, you're not just presenting challenges but offering a clear path forward, helping them make informed decisions that align with the organization's overall strategy.

To achieve this, communication must be more than just a tool; it needs to be a fundamental part of your cyber risk management program. There are two critical points to keep in mind. First, remember that communication isn't just about delivering a message; it's about ensuring the message is understood. This means following up and seeking confirmation that the recipient has truly understood the essence of what you're trying to transmit.

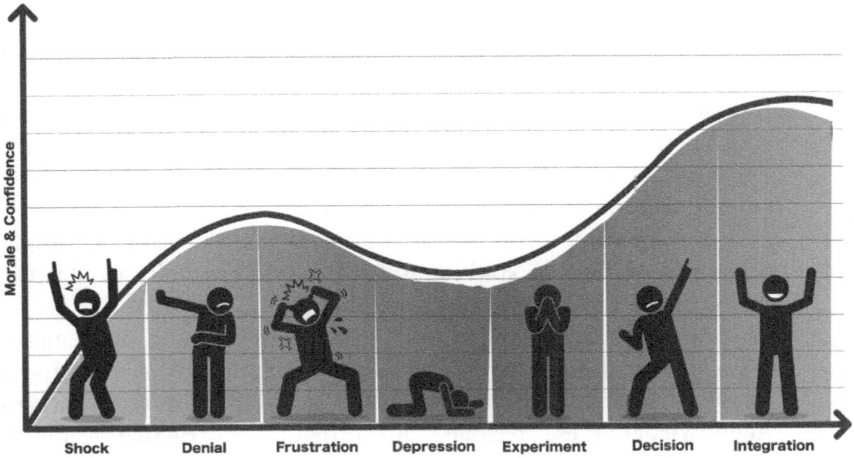

Figure 5.1 Curve of change.

This approach can prevent misunderstandings and save your valuable time. Second, it's important to tailor your communication style to your audience. This doesn't just mean avoiding jargon or technical terms with those who might not be familiar with them. It's about truly understanding where your audience is coming from, their level of knowledge, their perspective, what's important for them, and their concerns. When you align your message with their context, you're engaging in a two-way exchange that fosters better understanding and leads to more meaningful outcomes for your cyber risk management efforts.

As we work to overcome resistance and build resilience in our organizations through clear communication and strategic engagement, it's essential to remember that change involves more than just technical or procedural adjustments. It's also an emotional journey for everyone involved. As you can see, I believe that understanding and addressing the human side of change is crucial for the success of any cyber risk management initiative. In Figure 5.1 we can find a representation of the Kübler-Ross Change Curve which provides a powerful framework for understanding the emotional journey of change that each person within an organization navigates. Recognizing which stage each key player is in regarding our cyber risk management initiative can be transformative. Here's how you might address each stage:

- Shock: The initial reaction to change can range from disbelief to denial, similar to the surprise one might feel when learning about a significant, unforeseen cybersecurity threat. Leadership must step in with reassurance, offering clear, concise information about the change and the reasons behind it. Patience is key; allow individuals time to process the information and gradually come to terms with the new reality.

- Denial: Once the initial shock subsides, denial may take its place. This stage is marked by reluctance to accept the change, possibly due to a lack of understanding or fear of the unknown. Transparent communication becomes your most powerful tool here. Explain the need for enhanced cybersecurity measures and the risks of complacency. Use data, case studies, and real-world examples to illustrate the necessity and benefits of the change.
- Frustration: As the change begins to set in, frustration may emerge, often due to the perceived difficulty of adapting to new protocols or systems. It's important to listen actively to these concerns. Acknowledge these feelings and provide constructive feedback, showing how the change is not just a hurdle but an opportunity for personal and organizational growth.
- Depression: This stage may be characterized by a sense of loss or a decrease in motivation. The changes may seem overwhelming, leading to a drop in energy and engagement. Offer strong support during this phase. Highlight the benefits of the change, not just for the organization but for individuals' personal development and job satisfaction. Reinforce the idea that their contributions are vital to achieving a larger, communal goal.
- Experiment: With the acceptance of change comes the willingness to experiment. This is a crucial moment where individuals start to explore and engage with the new ways of working. Encourage this experimentation by providing the necessary resources, training, and support. Celebrate even small victories and milestones, as they are essential for building confidence and a positive outlook toward the change.
- Decision: As individuals experiment and begin to find their footing in the new environment, they reach a decision point. They start to see the benefits of their efforts and understand how the changes improve their work and the organization's security posture. Ensure that clear guidelines are in place and that the immediate benefits of the changes are visible and tangible. This clarity helps solidify the decision to embrace the new ways of working.
- Integration: The final stage is when the new practices become part of the norm. The changes are no longer seen as external impositions but as integral aspects of the daily workflow. At this point, it's important to recognize and celebrate the new behaviors. Reinforce them through positive feedback, rewards, and inclusion in the organization's culture. This reinforcement helps to solidify the changes, making them

a permanent part of the organization's approach to cybersecurity. Remember, the next phase will likely be 'Shock' again, as reaching the integration phase often means new changes are on the horizon to continuously improve our program.

Many years ago, I was deep in the trenches, pushing through the challenges of driving organizational change. The friction was evident, and no matter how much I tried, things just weren't moving in the direction I envisioned. I was frustrated. I couldn't see the whole picture, the individual motivations, the reasons behind the resistance, or even the subtle dynamics that were at play. I thought I had it all figured out, but I was missing something crucial. That's when Rick Doten, VP of Information Security at Centene, and a mentor and friend to me, stepped in.

Rick is one of those people who seems to have seen it all. His experience in cybersecurity is incredible, but it wasn't just his technical expertise that impressed me. It was his ability to listen, reflect, and then offer insights that were both practical and profound. He could see what was coming next, almost like he had a crystal ball, and he helped me understand the importance of stepping back to see the bigger picture. I'll never forget when he would listen patiently to me vent about the challenges I was facing and then, with a calm certainty, he'd say, "Okay, now you need to wait."

Patience was never my strong suit, but Rick was clear that sometimes, the best course of action is to let things unfold. And as hard as it was for me to wait, time and time again, he was right. What he said would happen, did happen. It was strange, but more than that, it was a lesson in listening, in observing the details that I'd previously been too focused to see. Rick taught me that when you're rushing to finish something, it's easy to shift from a growth mindset to a fixed one. This shift is normal, even necessary, because execution requires a certain level of focus and rigidity. But what I hadn't realized was how important it was to create feedback loops during that execution. You need those moments to check whether your strategy is working, and sometimes, it's the expertise of someone else, someone who can see what you can't, that makes all the difference.

Rick became that person for me. His mentorship wasn't just about giving advice; he opened doors, introduced me to the right people, and helped me build a deeper understanding of cybersecurity. He took me to industry events, where I met professionals who had been shaping the field for years. These were networking opportunities and moments of learning. Rick knew where I needed to be and who I needed to learn from. His hands-on, pragmatic approach resonated with me. I'm a practical person myself, and I found in Rick someone who understood that cybersecurity, at its core, is about getting the fundamentals right. He never overcomplicated things; he broke them down, showing me how to tackle challenges one step at a time.

A good example of this is when I decided to help Monterrey Tec design and create their cybersecurity master's program; I knew right away that this wasn't a task for one person. The goal was ambitious: to train the next generation of cybersecurity professionals with a strong alignment to the real needs of the industry. I put together a group of experts who shared the same vision, and we held several sessions to design the entire program that is now implemented. Rick was the first to confirm his participation, and, as always, he was actively involved from the start. We knew the importance of investing our time to shape a curriculum that would address the evolving landscape of cybersecurity, and together, we built a program that provides students with the knowledge and skills that matter most in today's field.

In many ways, Rick helped me become the cybersecurity professional I am today. He showed me how to navigate the complexities of driving change, how to listen to others, and, most importantly, how to be patient. His mentorship wasn't just about teaching me the technical aspects of cybersecurity, though there was plenty of that too. It was about showing me how to listen to others, how to bring people together, and how to stay grounded when things didn't go according to plan. Rick's influence helped me realize that leadership isn't just about pushing through obstacles, but it's about understanding the dynamics around you, creating space for feedback, and having the patience to let things unfold. If there's one lesson I've learned from this, it's the importance of finding a mentor who will guide you, challenge you, and help you grow. That person can offer perspectives you never considered, helping you develop into the professional, and leader, you're meant to be.

Just as the mission to send a man to the Moon required careful planning and communication, we can guide our colleagues through the cybersecurity change process. When we identify where everyone stands on this curve for the particular change we want to speed up, we can craft communications and strategies that will resonate with them, easing the transition and fostering acceptance. This understanding is a powerful tool in your arsenal to expedite the change process and minimize resistance within your organization. At the end of the day, the key to successfully implementing a cyber risk management program lies in striking a balance between leveraging your unique advantages and overcoming the inherent challenges. It involves building bridges, fostering dialogue, and creating a shared vision that aligns with the organization's goals and culture.

To support this vision, another critical aspect of preparation is defining your action plan with clear objectives and milestones. Your action plan serves as a compass, guiding each step of your cyber risk management implementation. Establishing this plan with concrete milestones allows you to track progress and quickly identify any deviations from the intended path. Think of it as a progress report that's transparent to all stakeholders, offering a clear snapshot of where you are versus where you need to be.

On the one side, you have the shared and formal plan. This version is visible to your team, business areas, management, and other stakeholders. It includes clear objectives, each with its own set of milestones, allowing everyone to track progress toward your cyber risk management goals. It's about creating accountability and fostering a shared sense of achievement as milestones are reached.

On the other side is your internal plan, the one you and your team use to drive effective change.[2] This internal roadmap integrates insights from our discussions about understanding organizational dynamics, effective communication, and resistance to change. It helps you navigate the softer side of the change management process, ensuring that you're not just checking off tasks but also cultivating the right environment for the change to take root and flourish.

A great tool you can use for this is to define your OKRs (objectives and key results), which is a collaborative methodology for goal setting used by teams and individuals to set challenging, ambitious goals with measurable results. It's an effective way of breaking down objectives into concrete, actionable steps, which aligns perfectly with the needs of cyber risk management programs.

When you're beginning to map out your cyber risk management journey, OKRs help in crystallizing what you aim to achieve (the objective) and how you'll gauge success (the key results). It's about establishing clear, measurable markers that not only guide your efforts but also keep the entire team focused and aligned. As you implement your cyber risk management plan, OKRs can serve as beacons, ensuring that each task contributes directly to your overarching cybersecurity objectives. They allow you to monitor progress, adapt to changes, and celebrate milestones along the way, keeping the whole team engaged and motivated toward achieving cybersecurity resilience.

To effectively use the OKRs methodology, it is essential to follow the guidelines outlined by John Doerr in his seminal book, *Measure What*

Matters.[3] I will describe the central steps of his work in the following sections, guiding us toward achieving our objectives:

1. **Set clear objectives**: Begin by defining clear, concise, and inspirational objectives. Objectives should be significant, action-oriented, and (ideally) inspirational. They articulate what the organization wants to achieve.
2. **Define Key Results**: For each objective, specify measurable outcomes called 'Key Results.' Key Results should be quantifiable, achievable, and lead to objective grading in a binary way. They act as milestones or benchmarks that measure progress toward the objective.
3. **Commit to objectives**: Ensure that objectives are publicly known within the organization to foster transparency and accountability. Everyone should understand what the organization is aiming for and how their work contributes to these goals.
4. **Make key results measurable and verifiable**: Each Key Result should have a clear metric with a starting value and a target value so that there is no ambiguity about whether it has been achieved.
5. **Update progress regularly**: Regular check-ins on progress toward Key Results are vital. This could be on a weekly or monthly basis, depending on the nature of the objectives and key results.
6. **Reflect and reset at the end of each cycle**: After a set period, usually a quarter, review the outcomes of your OKRs. Reflect on what was achieved, learn from failures and successes, and set new OKRs based on these insights.
7. **Focus and commit to priorities**: Prioritize the objectives that are most critical to your success and commit the necessary resources. It's important not to have too many OKRs at once to maintain focus.
8. **Align and connect for teamwork**: Align OKRs across different levels of the organization to ensure that everyone is moving in the same direction. Connecting OKRs between individual, team, and organizational levels fosters cohesion and teamwork.
9. **Stretch for amazing**: While some Key Results should be achievable, incorporating stretch goals can drive teams to exceed beyond what they thought possible, promoting innovation and growth.

We need to dream big while being clear about our goals. Picture yourself at the start of a huge journey, building the secure digital environment your organization needs. This is where we set our objectives, not just any goals, but ones that push us beyond the familiar. These objectives work as our guiding lights, helping us stretch further and aim higher. Now, let's talk about Key Results. These are measurable milestones that show us how far we've come. Each key result is a signpost, making sure we're on track and turning big goals into something real and achievable. These measurable outcomes help us see that success is not just a dream but something we can reach.

Next come the initiatives, the steps that bring us closer to our goals. These are the commitments to action. Each one is chosen to make sure we move with purpose. And this is about assigning responsibility but also empowering people to take ownership of their actions, ensuring that every move counts. As we move forward, it's indispensable to keep checking in on our progress. Regular reviews give us the chance to look at how far we've come and make adjustments where needed. These moments are perfect for celebrating wins but about learning from our challenges. It's all part of keeping the journey on course, making sure we stay aligned with our goals.

When we reach the end of a cycle of OKRs, it's time to reflect and prepare ourselves for what's next. We must examine what worked and what didn't, gaining insights that fuel the next round of objectives. This continuous cycle of learning and improvement pushes us forward, always reaching for more because with each cycle, our understanding expands and our methods improve. Using OKRs for our cyber risk management program gives us a clear method to align, act with purpose, and stay flexible. It turns high-level goals into concrete results, guiding us through the complexities of protecting our organizations.

Now that we have a better understanding of where we are and where our organization is, it is time to identify the scope of our first risk assessment because it's crucial to begin with a clear focus. Think about what's at the heart of your organization, what keeps the gears turning, and, perhaps more importantly, what's been causing headaches? Identifying a process or area that's both critical and currently problematic is your golden ticket. This isn't just about finding a starting point; it's about making a strategic choice that will demonstrate the value of your efforts and earn you the attention and appreciation of decision-makers.

So, how do you choose where to start? Ask yourself, "What's the most critical operation that, if improved, could significantly impact our organization?" It could be anything from customer data management to product development processes. The key here is to pinpoint something that, when assessed and subsequently fortified, will not only lessen some of those existing pains but also showcase the tangible benefits of a robust cyber risk management program. Starting with will reflect a strategic approach that not only protects the organization but also boosts its overall efficiency. Addressing what's most important to your organization allows us to solve real problems while showing how cyber risk management contributes directly to business goals.

Remember, the goal here is dual: to secure your organization's digital assets and to ensure that the fruits of your work are recognized and valued. Choosing a project with visible impact helps you achieve both. It's about making a statement that cybersecurity isn't just a technical requirement but a strategic asset, one that contributes directly to the organization's success and resilience. So, take the time to carefully select and scope your first assessment. Make it count, because this is your chance to show just how much value cyber risk management, and by extension you, can bring to the table.

Building on the strategic selection of your initial assessment area, the next critical step is identifying and engaging your key participants. These individuals are more than just stakeholders; they're your allies, collaborators, and, at times, your greatest challenge. Their involvement and buy-in are essential for the success of our cyber risk management efforts.

Keep in mind that this journey is about collaboration, not confrontation. It's crucial to communicate that this process isn't about pointing fingers or auditing for compliance's sake but about uniting to protect what's most important to your organization. That unity is the only path forward if we aim for our cyber risk management program to stand the test of time. As the African proverb goes, "If you want to go fast, go alone; if you want to go far, go together." This has been demonstrated in every journey I begin with a client or within the organizations I have served.

Invest time in explaining the process to these key participants. Sit down with them, one-on-one if necessary, and discuss not just the 'what' and the 'how' but, more importantly, the 'why.'[4] Make it clear how crucial their input and cooperation are to the success of the program. This is about ensuring everyone understands that we're in this together, working toward a common goal: protecting our operations and achieving our business objectives.

Frame this engagement as an opportunity for each participant to contribute meaningfully to the organization's security posture. It's essential they understand that their insights, knowledge, and everyday experiences are invaluable to making our cyber risk management program realistic, effective, and, ultimately, successful.

In a large multinational company, which we'll call "GlobalCorp," the journey to split the responsibilities of IT and Information Security was anything but smooth. The company had experienced rapid growth, and with that came the increasing complexity of managing both IT operations and security functions under one roof the conflicts of interest were evident. At the time, the IT director held responsibility for both IT and cybersecurity. The problem? The CIO wasn't keen on letting go of cybersecurity. In fact, cybersecurity was used as a bargaining chip to 'sell' services to other business units, making it an important part of IT's influence across the company. The friction was evident. The IT team saw no need for change except the cybersecurity manager. "We've always done it this way, and it's worked fine," the CIO would argue. To executives outside of IT, it seemed like a technical issue. However, those working on the security side were growing increasingly frustrated. They knew that having the same person oversee both IT and security functions was leading to conflicts of interest. Security often took a backseat when IT priorities, like project integrations or cost-saving measures, came first.

The tension boiled over when an external cybersecurity assessment was carried out. The findings showed that critical vulnerabilities had gone unaddressed because security wasn't being managed independently from IT. The company's board decided it was time to split the functions, but the resistance from the CIO and IT leadership was strong. Then, the Senior Leadership brought a team of consultants who help navigate this tricky transition. They knew that the key to success wasn't just about making the split on paper, it was about changing the way executives and staff across the organization thought about cybersecurity governance. The consultants worked closely with executives from every business unit to break down the old paradigms that had kept IT and Information Security tied together for so long. The first step was ensuring that the business units understood why separating these functions would benefit the company in the long run.

At first, the CIO and IT leadership were resistant to any meetings or discussions. But the consultants kept the messaging consistent: "This isn't about reducing IT's influence; it's about strengthening the company's overall security posture." They carefully made reports that resonated with executives in a way that no other consultant has done before, making sure to eliminate any room for excuses or misunderstanding. The key was to frame the change as a necessary step to ensure the company's resilience in the face of growing cyber threats, rather than an attack on IT's authority. Over time, the consistent messaging and effort to align with business goals began to take effect. Executives in other business units started to see the value of having Information Security operate independently, with its own leadership and resources. Slowly but surely, the tide began to turn. The CIO, seeing the growing support from the board and other executives, started to soften his stance. What made the difference? The consultants had taken the time to plan every step of the communication process, anticipating pushback and addressing concerns before they could derail the conversation.

Finally, after several months of discussions and careful planning, the decision was made to formally separate IT and Information Security. A new Chief Information Security Officer (CISO) in the corporate and CISOs for each Business Unit were appointed, and the new structure allowed for cybersecurity to operate independently with its own budget, staff, and governance processes. What's remarkable about GlobalCorp's story isn't just that they were able to make the split, it's that they did it without burning bridges. The CIO, who had initially resisted the change, remained a key ally in ensuring that IT and Information Security worked together after the separation. The message had been clear from the beginning: this wasn't about undermining IT, but about giving cybersecurity the focus and resources it needed to protect the company.

The key takeaway here? Change doesn't happen overnight, especially when there are long-standing power dynamics at play. It takes time, consistent communication, and careful planning to break old habits and build a new governance structure that works. Eliminating excuses, anticipating resistance, and focusing on the broader benefits for the business positioned GlobalCorp to create a governance structure that better aligned with its goals and significantly improved its security posture.

Encourage open dialogue, listen to their concerns, and address any misconceptions about the process. Fostering a sense of ownership and shared responsibility means you're not just gathering information for your assessment; you're laying the groundwork for a culture that values and actively participates in cybersecurity. This helps to ensure that when decisions are made, and actions are taken, they are done with a unified vision, making our cyber risk management endeavors even more potent and sustainable.

As we continue laying the groundwork for our cyber risk management program, one crucial step remains: developing or revisiting our cyber risk management methodology. Recall that this methodology serves as our playbook, providing a detailed framework that spells out the 'rules of the game' in unmistakable, actionable terms. It's the foundation that guarantees every participant is fully aware of their responsibilities and understands exactly how we will assess and manage cyber risks. Also, it should give us the tools we need to characterize risks, our risk matrix, and catalog of risks and controls.

Let's remember this methodology is a living guide that aligns everyone's efforts toward a common goal, ensuring a cohesive and informed approach to tackling cyber risks. If you're starting from scratch, now's the time to build your methodology from the ground up, drawing on the foundational concepts we've laid out at the end of Section I. But if a methodology is already in place, consider this an opportune moment to take a step back and reassess. The digital landscape evolves at a breakneck pace, and what worked yesterday might not hold up tomorrow. Review your existing methodology to ensure it's still fit for purpose, making any necessary tweaks or overhauls to align with current best practices and the unique challenges your organization faces today.

Equally important in our toolkit is the risk register, a tool we discussed in Chapter 4. Whether it's housed in a simple Excel workbook or a more sophisticated GRC tool, the risk register is essential for capturing and visualizing the risks we uncover. It allows us to see the entire identified cyber risks at a glance, tracking our progress and ensuring no threat is left unaddressed.

One last key aspect is to consider how we plan to approach risk assessments. As discussed throughout these chapters, there are several options, each with its own strengths. Will the assessments be purely qualitative, relying on descriptive analysis to evaluate risk levels? Or is there potential for a quantitative or semiquantitative approach, assigning numerical values to risks for a more data-driven perspective? This choice will influence our journey, guiding how we measure uncertainty and make informed decisions. Setting a clear methodology, keeping the risk register ready, and choosing an approach that aligns with our objectives and capabilities establish a foundation for a cyber risk management program where everyone understands their role in the process.

Before moving into Chapter 6, let's reflect on the journey we're about to embark on. Notice how this process doesn't commence by scrutinizing others or pinpointing their challenges. Instead, it begins with understanding the business model and a deep dive into our own standing. For change to take root, especially the kind spurred by our cyber risk assessments aiming to enact treatment plans for identified risks, a profound self-awareness is essential. We must assess our capabilities, motivations, and objectives to effectively navigate our environment and engage our key participants and stakeholders.

Understanding ourselves is the first step in navigating the vast landscape ahead. Leveraging our strengths and recognizing our limits creates the foundation for meaningful change. With exhaustive preparation, from defining our methodology to engaging stakeholders with clear purpose, we have established the groundwork for a successful cyber risk management effort.

Here a checklist based on all we've discussed in this section for laying the Groundwork:

1. **Understand your organization's cybersecurity posture:**
    a. Understand your organization's business model.
    b. Review existing cybersecurity policies and procedures.
    c. Determine if policies underscore the importance of a risk-based program.
    d. Gauge the organization's culture toward cybersecurity.

2. **Assess your position within the organization:**
    a. Consider your role and how it influences your perspective on cybersecurity.
    b. For newcomers: Leverage your fresh perspective to identify overlooked issues.
    c. For seasoned members: Use your deep organizational knowledge to navigate complexities effectively.
3. **Address resistance to change:**
    a. Recognize that both newcomers and veterans may face resistance.
    b. Use effective communication strategies to navigate and mitigate resistance.
    c. Embrace a culture of continuous improvement and openness to new ideas.
4. **Prepare for effective communication:**
    a. Ensure the recipient has understood your message to prevent misunderstandings.
    b. Tailor your communication to the audience's level of understanding and perspective.
5. **Understand participants' positions on the change curve:**
    a. Identify where key participants are on the Kübler-Ross Change Curve.
    b. Tailor strategies and communications based on their stage to minimize resistance.
6. **Define an action plan with milestones and clear objectives:**
    a. Establish a shared and formal plan with milestones for tracking progress.
    b. Create an internal plan incorporating strategies for driving effective change.
7. **Select and scope your first assessment:**
    a. Identify critical operations or problematic areas worth assessing.
    b. Choose a focus that will demonstrate the value of your efforts to decision-makers.
8. **Identify and engage key participants:**
    a. Emphasize collaboration and the importance of their participation.
    b. Foster a sense of unity and shared responsibility toward cybersecurity.
9. **Develop or review your cyber risk management methodology:**
    a. Ensure it serves as a clear guide for assessing and managing cyber risks.
    b. Review and adjust the methodology as necessary to align with current best practices.

10. **Prepare your risk register:**
    a. Ensure it's ready to capture and visualize identified cyber risks.
    b. Decide on the approach for risk assessments: qualitative, quantitative, or semiquantitative.

By following this checklist, you're not just preparing for the execution of your cyber risk management program; you're setting the stage for a transformative journey that aligns with your organization's specific needs and challenges. Remember, this is about more than just assessments; it's about driving meaningful change, improving your organization's cybersecurity posture, and ensuring the resilience and success of your business.

Now that you've built a strong foundation in the fundamentals of cyber risk management, you've likely gained a clearer understanding of its different layers, from the details of risk assessment to the value of maintaining an active and updated risk register. At this point, these concepts may still feel somewhat theoretical, but I see them as the driving force behind our cyber risk management program. Like an engine, they help keep us moving at the right speed and direction. Think of it like the core of a vortex, where the central force is what drives everything else forward, pulling the surrounding elements into motion. In Figure 5.2, you'll see how the fundamental elements we've discussed form the core of our approach. This image represents the first five chapters of the book, and as we move through the sections, we'll add layers to it. The further we go, the more we build upon this core, expanding our understanding while keeping the entire program in motion.

I'm confident that with these preparatory steps in mind, we're ready and well-equipped to initiate our cyber risk management process. Remember, this journey is as much about improving our organization's cybersecurity posture as it is about personal growth and leadership. Let's move forward with the assurance that we've done the groundwork to navigate this complex yet rewarding path. As we turn the page to the next section of our journey, we're moving into territory where theory meets practice, where the foundational knowledge we've laid becomes the bedrock for real-world application. This next phase is all about rolling up our sleeves and diving into the hands-on work of implementing the concepts and strategies we've discussed so far. It's here that the principles of cyber risk management leap off the page and into the operational reality of your organization.

In Section II: Executing cyber risk management in five steps, all the Section I concepts will become concrete tools in your arsenal, ready to be deployed in the ongoing battle against cyber threats and to enhance your organization's cybersecurity posture. The journey ahead is both challenging and rewarding, filled with opportunities to apply what you've learned in tangible ways that make a difference. Whether you're about to undertake

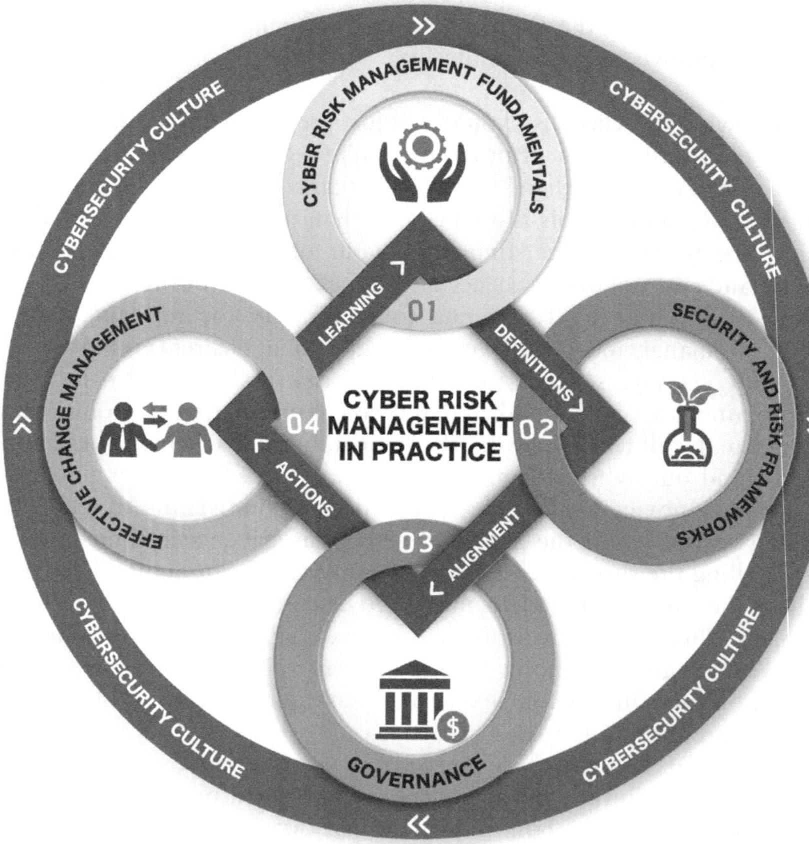

Figure 5.2 The core forces of Cyber Risk Management.

your first risk assessment, fine-tune your risk treatment plans, or enhance your risk monitoring practices, the path forward is clear.

Next section is designed to be your guide, offering practical advice, step-by-step instructions, and real-world examples that illuminate the path to effective cyber risk management. Let's move forward into this next phase with confidence and a shared commitment to achieving cybersecurity success. Implementing cyber risk management in the real world offers the opportunity to turn challenges into triumphs, using your newfound knowledge to create a secure, resilient, and thriving digital environment for your organization.

NOTES

1 Pfeffer, J., & Sutton, R. I. (2000). *The Knowing-Doing Gap: How Smart Companies Turn Knowledge into Action*. Harvard Business School Press.
2 Adizes, I. (1992). *Mastering Change: The Power of Mutual Trust and Respect in Personal Life, Family Life, Business, and Society*. Adizes Institute Publications.
3 Doerr, J. (2018). *Measure What Matters: How Google, Bono, and the Gates Foundation Rock the World with OKRs*. Portfolio/Penguin.
4 Sinek, S. (2009). *Start with Why: How Great Leaders Inspire Everyone to Take Action*. Portfolio.

Section II

Executing cyber risk management in five steps

Chapter 6

Starting the process

Contexts and information gathering

RISK CONTEXTS

My own experience has made me reflect on what is real and what's not. Reality refers to the state of things as they actually exist, rather than as they may appear or might be imagined. It incorporates everything that is happening around us, the facts, the physical universe, and the existence of everything within it, including ourselves, objects, events, and phenomena. Reality is distinguished from illusions, dreams, or fictional ideas, representing the objective truth or the actuality of existence as it is, independent of our perceptions, beliefs (or misbeliefs), or interpretations.

This concept intriguingly is not as fixed as it often appears. Our understanding and interpretation of reality evolve significantly as we gather more information and deepen our understanding. This phenomenon is rooted in the fundamental nature of human perception and knowledge acquisition. Initially, our understanding of reality is shaped by direct experiences and observations. We trust our senses to inform us about the world, assuming a direct correspondence between our perceptions and external reality.

However, as we gain more knowledge through personal experiences and shared discoveries, our understanding of reality changes significantly.[1] It's like slowly putting together a puzzle without knowing what the final picture looks like; each new piece of information adds to our understanding and changes how we see the whole picture. As we learn and understand more, we realize that what we once thought was the full picture of reality is actually just a small part of a much more complex, detailed, and interconnected world. The progress of science serves as a powerful illustration of this dynamic. For centuries, humanity's collective understanding of the universe, our planet, and even the nature of matter itself has been revolutionized by discoveries that challenged and expanded our prior conceptions of reality. The earth once stood at the center of the universe in the human perception of reality, only to be displaced by the heliocentric model. Similarly, the seemingly solid world around us revealed an invisible quantum world of particles and forces, reshaping our understanding of the very core of reality.

DOI: 10.1201/9781003546207-9

Also, it is necessary to mention that the notion of reality is deeply personal and varies from one individual to another, shaped by a cumulous of experiences, knowledge, and perceptions. Each person perceives the world through their unique lens, crafting a version of reality that is inherently subjective. This personal reality is a construct of our cumulative life experiences, the information we've been exposed to, and the meaning we derive from them. It's as if we each wear glasses tinted by our past, our beliefs, and our interpretations, coloring how we see and understand the world around us. Keeping this in mind is particularly important when we'll have qualitative risk assessments because this subjective nature of reality means that what is true or evident for one person might not hold the same truth for another. Our realities intersect, overlap, and sometimes diverge based on the diversity of our experiences and the breadth of our knowledge. It's a phenomenon that emphasizes the richness of human perception but also highlights the challenges in achieving shared understanding and consensus. In recognizing this, we come to appreciate the depth of individual perspectives and the value of diverse viewpoints in enriching our collective understanding.

Team members, stakeholders, and decision-makers each bring their interpretations of reality to the table, influenced by their backgrounds, expertise, and personal experiences. This diversity of perspectives is invaluable, as it broadens the scope of our understanding and uncovers risks that might otherwise remain hidden. However, it also requires effective communication and collaboration to align these varied realities toward a common goal.

Acknowledging the fluidity of reality and the diversity of individual perceptions enriches our approach to risk management. It encourages us to remain open and adaptable, to seek out and value different viewpoints, and to recognize that our understanding of risks and opportunities will continually evolve. In embracing this, we not only overcome the complexities of cyber risk with greater agility but also foster a culture of learning and innovation that strengthens our resilience in the face of uncertainty. This realization empowers us to approach cyber risk management with a mindset that is both inclusive and dynamic.

This better understanding of reality sheds light on why some organizations believe they are immune to cyberattacks, often perceiving such threats as issues reserved for the more prominent, headline-grabbing corporations. This misbelief can stem from a biased perception of reality, one where the narrative of cyber vulnerability does not align with their self-concept or past experiences. It's a reality shaped by the assumption that cybercriminals target only large entities, leaving smaller organizations to operate under the radar of such threats. This mindset, while comforting, overlooks the fundamental truth of the digital age: cyber threats are indiscriminate, and the lack of visibility or size does not provide immunity.

Recognizing this gap in perception is crucial because it highlights the need to expand the organization's understanding of cyber risks, challenge misconceptions, and align perceptions with the actual threat landscape. Education and awareness are key to closing the gap between misperception and the real-world risks of cyberattacks that affect organizations of all sizes. Shifting the collective perception to acknowledge these risks helps build a foundation for stronger cybersecurity measures, ensuring that preparedness and resilience become core elements of the organizational culture, no matter its size.

In his book *Misbelief: What Makes Rational People Believe Irrational Things*,[2] Dan Ariely explores the psychology behind why people are drawn to misinformation and how it can lead to the formation of deeply irrational beliefs. Ariely explains that to truly combat the appeal of misinformation, it's essential to understand the phenomenon of 'misbelief,' which involves the psychological and social processes that lead individuals to distrust established truths, consider alternative facts, and even adopt conspiracy theories. He identifies emotional, cognitive, personality, and social elements as key factors that drive individuals toward misbelief, emphasizing that anyone can fall victim to this process under certain circumstances. Being aware of these influences can help us avoid the pitfalls of accepting our perceptions as reality without scrutiny.

Building on Dan Ariely's insights into misbelief, we need to actively reduce biases and expand our understanding of both internal and external contexts within our organizations. This requires fostering a culture that values critical thinking, embraces diverse perspectives, and encourages continuous learning. Recognizing and addressing the psychological factors that contribute to misbelief helps create an environment that resists misinformation and is better prepared to handle the complexities of the cyber threat landscape. Reducing biases and broadening our perspective improves internal decision-making, enhances strategies, and leads to a more informed and balanced approach to cyber risk management.

Understanding our environment through the lens of internal and external contexts is crucial, particularly when assessing risks within any organization. This understanding forms the foundation of our overall context, the background against which we make decisions, plan strategies, and navigate challenges. The internal context encompasses everything within our organization, from our strengths, weaknesses, resources, and capabilities to our information and technology inventories, which are vital assets in today's digital age. Recognizing vulnerabilities, whether in our physical infrastructure, technological setups, or even within our personnel, is essential, as these vulnerabilities can become gateways for potential threats if left unaddressed.

A deep dive into our internal context also involves examining our business objectives, strategies, and operations. This includes our approach to managing human resources, financial capabilities, vendor relationships, and the structure of internal processes such as audits, network, and data flows. Each of these elements plays a significant role in shaping our risk landscape, helping us to identify areas of vulnerability and strength, and guiding us in deploying safeguards and controls effectively.

On the other side, the external context is everything outside our immediate control but still impacts our organization. This includes market trends, regulatory requirements, technological advancements, and the broader economic, geopolitical, and environmental conditions. External threats, whether from vulnerable third parties, cybercriminals, or other external forces, must be continuously monitored and assessed. The external context helps us understand the playing field. It highlights potential opportunities and threats, allowing us to adapt our strategies in response to external pressures and changes. For instance, a new regulation could mandate changes in how we handle data, or an emerging technology such as AI might offer a way to enhance efficiency but also introduce new vulnerabilities to our environment. Assessing risks based on our contexts allows us to make informed decisions. It helps us prioritize our actions based on where we are most vulnerable and what external factors we must prepare for. This understanding ensures that we are not just reactive but proactive in our approach to risk management. It enables us to align our resources and strategies with both our internal realities and the external environment, ensuring resilience and agility in the face of uncertainties.

Assessing risks requires a deep understanding of both our strengths and our blind spots, not just in cybersecurity but across all aspects of our organization. It's about navigating a complex landscape filled with hidden challenges, unexpected vulnerabilities, and the unknown. Understanding what we know and what we don't know is crucial for making informed decisions and safeguarding our organization. Here's how these four aspects apply:

We know we know: These are the areas where we have clarity and confidence. It includes the systems, processes, and knowledge that are well-documented and understood within the organization. For instance, we might know that certain critical systems are up to date and secure. However, even in these areas, there is always room for improvement. Regular reviews and updates ensure that our knowledge remains accurate and our controls effective.

We know we don't know: This refers to areas where we are aware of gaps in our understanding or documentation. For example, we might recognize that parts of our IT environment are not fully documented or that there are emerging threats we don't fully understand. The key here is acknowledging these gaps and actively working to close them through research, training, and continuous improvement. It's about turning these unknowns into knowns by seeking out the information we need.

We don't know we know: Sometimes, we have latent knowledge or skills within the organization that we're not fully aware of or aren't leveraging effectively. For example, certain team members might have experience with older systems or unique insights into particular processes that haven't been fully tapped into. Encouraging open communication and collaboration helps uncover these hidden strengths, ensuring they are recognized and applied where they are most needed.

We don't know we don't know: This is the territory of the truly unknown areas where we have no awareness of potential risks or gaps because they haven't yet come to light. This could include unknown vulnerabilities in our systems or future threats that haven't been anticipated. While we can't prepare for everything, fostering a culture of continuous learning and adaptability is crucial. Regular audits, scenario planning, and encouraging a proactive approach to emerging trends can help us mitigate the impact of these unforeseen challenges.

To explore the internal context in detail, we need to break down the elements that are central to any organization and are relevant for assessing cyber risks. First, it's important to define this context, which represents the DNA of the company. It shapes how we operate, why we do what we do, and the current state of the organization, including the challenges and opportunities we face.

Some concepts we can identify as part of the internal context include:

Information and technology inventories: These inventories encompass all the data we hold, from customer details to trade secrets, and catalog our digital and physical tech assets. Both are critical treasures that require vigilant protection and savvy management. Understanding what we have is the foundation for knowing what we need to protect.

Network diagrams: Network diagrams provide a visual map of our IT infrastructure, detailing how different components such as servers, routers, and endpoints are interconnected. These diagrams help us to understand the pathways data travels within our organization, identify potential bottlenecks, and pinpoint areas where security measures should be enhanced. They are essential tools for visualizing the architecture of our technology environment and ensuring that all components are adequately protected.

Data flow diagrams: Data flow diagrams illustrate how information moves through our systems, showing the flow of data between processes, storage points, and external entities. These diagrams help in identifying where sensitive data is processed, transmitted, or stored, and where it might be vulnerable to breaches. Understanding these flows allows for better control design, ensuring that data is protected at every stage of its life cycle, securing information assets from end to end.

Vulnerabilities: As clearly defined in the first section, vulnerabilities in our environment could stem from anywhere, such as outdated software, gaps in security protocols, or even a lack of awareness among our staff.

Internal culture and company's history: The culture within our company influences how we respond to challenges and embrace opportunities. Shaped by our company's history, including past successes, failures, and the lessons learned along the way, this cultural backdrop affects every decision and strategy, creating a unique approach to risk management.

Business objectives and strategies: Our business objectives outline what we aim to achieve, while our strategies define how we plan to get there. Understanding these elements helps us align our risk management efforts with our overall vision, ensuring that every action supports our end goals. This alignment ensures that our security efforts are not just reactive but strategically integrated into our broader business plans.

Safeguards and controls: Implementing safeguards and controls is how we protect our assets and ensure the continuity of our operations. These measures range from cybersecurity defenses to physical security protocols and internal policies that guide our team's behavior. They are the practical steps we take to translate our risk management strategy into action.

Human resources and vendors: Our people are our strength, and the vendors we choose are our allies. Managing these relationships wisely is crucial for operational success and security. Training and awareness programs for staff, along with due diligence and continuous assessment of vendor risks, form a critical part of our internal context. Strong relationships and well-informed teams are key to maintaining a robust security posture.

Financial resources: The availability and management of financial resources determine our capacity to invest in growth, innovation, and safeguards. Efficient financial planning and control are vital to sustaining operations and funding initiatives that drive us forward. The balance between risk management and financial investment is crucial for long-term success.

Audit reports: Audit reports provide a mirror to our operations, revealing efficiencies and exposing weaknesses. These reports help us identify areas where our controls may be lacking and where improvements are needed. These reports could include recent pentests, Privacy Impact Assessments (PIAs) performed on the environment and services in scope, etc.

Gathering information about these aspects of our internal context provides a better view of the organization's current state. This understanding evolves as new information emerges, and it's important to accept that knowing everything is impossible, which makes perfect risk management unachievable. However, focusing on the right information helps identify strengths and vulnerabilities. Proactively addressing these internal factors builds a strong foundation for managing risks, creating a secure, resilient environment that supports business objectives while adapting to challenges by leveraging strengths and mitigating vulnerabilities.

On the other side, we have the external context, which includes everything happening outside our organization that could impact us directly or indirectly. Understanding the external context is being aware of the environment in which we operate. It's about recognizing the factors beyond our immediate control that significantly influence our cybersecurity strategy and risk management efforts. Understanding our external context provides a broader perspective that helps us anticipate changes, adapt defenses, and ensure cybersecurity practices are proactive. This view is crucial not only for identifying threats but also for recognizing opportunities to strengthen our cybersecurity posture, supporting long-term success and resilience. Some factors to consider as part of our external context are as follows.

External threats include everything from sophisticated cyberattacks targeting our digital assets to physical threats that could indirectly compromise our cybersecurity. It's crucial to recognize that vigilance and adaptability are nonnegotiable in cyber risk management. Our approach to these external threats must be dynamic, continuously evolving to counter the various risks that could undermine the organization's security and integrity.

Competitors are not just rivals in the marketplace; their technological advancements or shortcomings can signal emerging threats or vulnerabilities in our systems. Analyzing competitor strategies gives us a dual advantage: identifying potential cybersecurity threats and highlighting opportunities to innovate securely and maintain a competitive edge.

Laws and regulations surrounding data protection and cybersecurity shape a significant part of our operational framework. Adhering to these legal standards is paramount, not just for compliance but as a basis of trust with our clients and partners. The regulatory landscape is always changing, demanding our constant attention to ensure that our cybersecurity measures are not just compliant but ahead of the curve, providing robust protection against potential legal and cyber threats.

Technological advancements and industry requirements set the pace for change in the cyber landscape. Staying current with these developments isn't just beneficial; it's essential for safeguarding against emerging cyber threats. This requires a proactive attitude on assessing new technologies anticipate and mitigate future risks.

Talent in the cybersecurity domain is a critical external factor influencing our ability to innovate and secure our operations. The global talent pool directly affects our capacity to manage cyber risks effectively. Therefore, strategies to attract, develop, and retain top cybersecurity talent are integral to reinforcement our defense mechanisms and fostering a culture of cybersecurity awareness across the organization.

Economic factors have a significant role in shaping our cybersecurity strategies. The broader economic climate impacts our financial planning and investment in cyber risk management initiatives. Understanding these economic dynamics allows us to tailor our cybersecurity efforts in a way that is both effective and economically viable, ensuring our organization remains resilient even in the face of financial uncertainties.

Geopolitical matters add another layer of complexity to cyber risk management. The stability of international relations and political landscapes can significantly impact our operations, especially for organizations with a global footprint. Navigating these geopolitical challenges requires a deep understanding of the potential cyber risks associated with international tensions and the strategies necessary to mitigate these risks effectively.

Environmental factors, including natural disasters and climate change, are increasingly relevant to cyber risk management. These factors can indirectly amplify cybersecurity vulnerabilities, emphasizing the need for comprehensive disaster recovery and business continuity planning that incorporates cybersecurity considerations.

Law enforcement is another factor to consider, especially when confronting cybercrime. Collaborating with law enforcement agencies not only aids in navigating the legal aftermath of cyber incidents but also strengthens our proactive defenses against cyber threats. Not all law enforcement organizations are equally prepared or trained to assist with cybersecurity attacks, so understanding their capabilities and processes is crucial for effective collaboration.

Cyber insurance has emerged as an external factor influencing our cybersecurity strategies. The requirements from insurers not only require high standards of cybersecurity but also serve as guidelines for industry best practices. Meeting these criteria ensures that our organization benefits from financial protection against cyber incidents while aligning with top-tier cybersecurity practices.

Third parties like vendors or service providers can be both a help and a potential risk to your business. They are deeply connected to your systems, yet you don't have direct control over their security practices. If they have a security problem, it could easily become your problem too. It's important to closely monitor these relationships, ensuring they meet strict security standards from the start. We'll discuss this in more detail later in the book, focusing on how to maintain your company's security while working with external partners. It's all about finding the right balance to ensure these partnerships enhance rather than compromise your cybersecurity efforts.

Making our context actionable and operational means turning it into something that's not just on paper but actively part of our decision-making process. It's like having all the pieces of a puzzle but needing a clear picture to see how they fit together. For example, having an inventory of information is crucial, but categorizing this information based on sensitivity or importance to the organization is as well important. This classification helps us understand what needs the most protection.

These pieces of information exist in various forms, within systems, on physical documents, or even with people. That's where technology inventories come into play, directly linking to our information inventories. Every piece of hardware and software listed in our technology inventory has its own state, showing us how vulnerable, exposed, or interconnected it is.

To better understand these vulnerabilities, we might scan our technology assets for weaknesses, using tools that provide a Common Vulnerability Scoring System (CVSS) score. The CVSS score helps us rate the severity of vulnerabilities on a scale, guiding us in prioritizing our risk management efforts. However, this score alone isn't enough. We need to see the bigger picture by considering how exposed our assets are, how they connect within our network, how critical they are based on the information they hold, their role in our operations, and whether those vulnerabilities are actively being exploited by threat actors. For example, a CVSS score of 5 might not seem like a top priority at first glance, but if we know that this vulnerability is being exploited in the wild by a threat actor targeting our industry, and it exists on a critical system within our organization, the context changes entirely. It's all about aggregating context, understanding more and more about our specific situation to make informed decisions.

Building a system that can take in all this varied context information and make sense of it is crucial for scaling our risk management program. It's not just about collecting data; it's about making that data work for us, helping us understand our risks better and make informed decisions on how to manage them. This approach ensures that we're not just reacting to risks as they arise but actively preparing for and mitigating them based on the understanding of our environment.

As we're seeing, in cybersecurity and risk management, understanding our environment in its entirety requires a meticulous combination of internal operations, external influences, and the dynamic interconnections between them. It's not just about recognizing the threats or acknowledging the assets we have; it's about understanding how every element, from technology vulnerabilities to geopolitical shifts, and even the stability of our third-party relationships, contributes to our overall risk profile. This holistic view enables us to design a more strategic, effective, and mature risk management program. Operationalizing context information turns raw data into actionable intelligence, helping us not only prepare for risks but also leverage strengths and opportunities in alignment with strategic goals. The objective is to build a better understanding of our operational landscape, where even the smallest details can offer valuable insights that shape our cybersecurity strategies and decisions.

LIMITING THE SCOPE

Defining our focus is essential. As Michael Porter said, "The essence of strategy is choosing what not to do." The act of limiting our scope is a strategic decision that not only prevents us from being overwhelmed by the huge volume of potential risks but also ensures we do not become distracted by less critical concerns that may arise along the way. The question at the heart of our assessments is: What is the key business process within the bounds of our initial risk assessment? It's common, particularly in organizations with risk management practices in development, to find a scarcity of formally documented business processes. If this sounds familiar, don't panic. We'll explore ways to concentrate on the areas where our efforts will make the biggest difference.

Having a process flow diagram for the business process in scope is a key asset. If it's not available, we should document it, as it helps outline the boundaries of our assessment and identify connections to other components within our environment, ensuring we have a thorough understanding before moving forward. Consider the complex relationships that sustain the process. Start by identifying who relies on this process, including clients, whether internal or external, who depend on its smooth operation. It is equally important to recognize who or what provides the necessary inputs to keep the process running.

Now, expand your view to include the three pillars that uphold every business process: People, Technology, and Processes. These are not isolated entities but a network that interconnects our operations. The true value of developing a process flow diagram lies in uncovering the links and dependencies that extend beyond our immediate scope. It's about seeing how our process integrates with the wider ecosystem, recognizing that our cybersecurity measures must account for these connections to be genuinely effective.

When working with the business process, it's essential to identify what information is used, stored, and transmitted. We need to understand how information flows and assess the sensitivity of each asset, as well as determine the technology that supports the process. This step is relevant for understanding the full scope of the process and making sure our cyber risk management efforts are aimed at protecting the most critical and sensitive assets. It also provides a clearer view of how the process functions. Knowing what information is involved, how it flows, and how it is managed allows for informed decisions that secure the data effectively and address potential vulnerabilities.

This methodical approach to defining our scope allows us to create a clear narrative, where every recommendation and treatment plan will be grounded in a deep understanding of the business and its critical dependencies. Building our cyber risk assessments from this perspective ensures that our efforts are technically sound and strategically aligned with the organization's broader objectives, providing a clear map of what will be assessed and what won't. So, as we sketch out our process flow diagram, let's do so with an eye toward narrative and strategy, ensuring that every line we draw and every connection we make adds to the story we're building. This is how we transform the often intangible concept of cyber risks into a tangible asset for our organization, making it an integral part of our journey toward operational excellence and resilience.

Focusing on delineating the business process for our assessment requires that we take a conscious approach to accurately defining and understanding the scope. Here is a simplified guide that focuses on the most relevant steps:

- **Identify the process**: Begin by pinpointing the specific business process or area that requires assessment. This could be determined by its criticality to your organization, known vulnerabilities, or both. Clarify the purpose of the process, its primary outcomes, and why it's been chosen for this risk assessment.
- **Develop a process flow diagram**: Utilize information gathered to map out a process flow diagram. This diagram should detail each step, action, and decision in the process, clearly showing how inputs are transformed into outputs. Ensure it highlights critical points where data is handled, decisions are made, or external interactions occur.
- **Identify critical assets and dependencies**: Within the flow diagram, identify and mark all critical assets involved, such as specific databases, applications, and hardware. Equally important is to note dependencies on other processes, services, or third-party providers. These elements are key for later understanding the full scope and potential points of vulnerability.
- **Define the process scope clearly**: With the diagram and critical components identified, concisely define the assessment scope. This includes outlining which parts of the process are included, any specific technologies or data considered critical, and acknowledging any external dependencies that could affect risk levels.
- **Validate with stakeholders**: Share the process flow diagram and your defined scope with the business process owner and key stakeholders for validation. This step ensures that your understanding aligns with those who work with the process daily and can provide insight into any areas that might have been overlooked or misunderstood.

Having our business process well defined, we should now start working on the internal and external context for our assessment. First, let's break down the process or subprocesses that fall within our chosen scope. This could mean diving deep into specific business operations, IT processes, or customer service protocols, anything that is critical to the functioning and success of the area we've decided to focus on. Start with what you know and build from there. So, let's take this challenge with a pragmatic mindset. It's okay not to have all the answers from the start or in the first assessment we perform. What's important is the commitment to keep looking, keep assessing, and keep improving. With each iteration, our cyber risk management efforts become more targeted and effective. Remember, it's not the pursuit of perfection that will secure our organizations, but the relentless drive to understand and protect them better with each step we take aiming for reducing cyber risk materialization.

Turning our focus to the architecture of our network, we must ask: How is it structured? Does it present as a flat landscape, where few to no barriers exist between segments, or is it a well-delineated environment with clear divisions and controls across different zones? This architectural blueprint holds significant influence over our risk assessment and subsequent treatment strategies. It's a common pitfall during the scope definition of a risk assessment to inadvertently 'isolate' the project or area under review, allowing the broader network environment to fade into the background. For example, when evaluating the cybersecurity implications of specific projects, there's a tendency to concentrate solely on the immediate changes introduced by these projects, without fully considering their impact on or interaction with the existing network environment. This approach can overlook vital aspects of our cyber ecosystem, emphasizing the importance of an assessment that includes the entirety of our network architecture.

That's why, we assess the cyber risks associated with specific processes or projects, it's important to try to maintain a holistic perspective. Understanding not just the piece of the network directly involved but also how it fits within the greater network architecture ensures a better risk evaluation. This holistic approach allows us to identify and address dependencies that may not be immediately apparent when focusing solely on the project at hand.

Dependencies play an important role in defining our scope and require our careful attention. This includes middleware that links different systems, directory services like Active Directory that manage user permissions and identities, and external services our scope relies on. These key systems are the connections that support the organization's operations, and any oversight could expose us to unexpected risks. Dependencies can introduce vulnerabilities that may not be immediately obvious. For example, outdated or poorly configured middleware can be a weak point, allowing cyber threats to spread across systems.

Dependencies also add complexity to our risk management assessments. They create additional layers in our cybersecurity landscape, making it essential to identify and understand them fully. We need to ask the right questions: What are these dependencies? How do they interact with the systems within our scope? What risks do they introduce, and how might these risks affect our overall security posture?

This exploration of dependencies is about mapping the unseen, redrawing trying to get a complete picture of what will be our well-defined scope. So, the task of identifying all these components within our scope requires a meticulous approach to effectively limit our scope, a keen eye for detail, and an understanding of the broader implications of these connections. As we examine these layers, we must maintain an open dialogue with stakeholders in the relevant areas. Their input can shed light on aspects we might overlook and help us understand the real-world applications and limitations of the systems we are examining. Working in this way ensures that when we move forward to understanding the business environment and gathering essential information, we do so with a clear view of what's at stake and what needs to be protected. This preparation paves the way for effective risk assessment and management.

UNDERSTANDING THE BUSINESS ENVIRONMENT

Having defined our scope, we've started to get a clearer picture of how things work, but we need to dig deeper to truly understand the process. The business environment, with its unique challenges and opportunities, shapes our cyber risk landscape. Building on the foundational knowledge from Section I, we need to closely examine both the internal dynamics and external factors that impact our organization. This deeper understanding will refine our focus and enhance our ability to identify and prioritize the risks that matter most.

Gaining a better understanding of the internal and external contexts of our organization is vital for examining each layer to learn about the essence of our operations, alongside recognizing external influences that might impact us. This process involves the examination of our procedures, personnel, and technology, aiming to identify the strengths that we can capitalize on and the vulnerabilities that require mitigation. To conduct this exploration effectively, it's essential to engage various departments across the organization, each contributing unique insights critical to painting a full picture of our cybersecurity landscape. This collaborative effort involves many departments in our organization, some of the most common departments involved are:

- Information management, playing an essential role in the identification, classification, and labeling of information. This department ensures that our data is accurately categorized and protected according to its sensitivity and value, serving as a critical input for our risk assessments. This allows us to prioritize our focus effectively, directing our resources and efforts toward safeguarding the most critical information assets.

- Human resources (HR), which sheds light on matters related to our workforce, including the cultivation of our organizational culture, the enforcement of disciplinary processes, and adherence to policies.
- Supply management, which offers a perspective on vendor relationships, detailing the specifics of contracts and the cybersecurity implications tied to our external partners.
- Legal department, providing guidance on compliance with regulatory requirements and the specifics of contractual obligations that might influence our cyber risk posture.
- Information technology (IT) department, offering invaluable information on ongoing and planned transformational projects, the current technological capabilities, available licenses, and the proficiency and training of the teams responsible for maintaining our cybersecurity controls.
- Sales department, contributing insights on customer demands and potential limitations, which could shape our approach to managing cyber risks.
- Privacy officer, identifying the presence of personally identifiable information (PII) within our scope, underscoring the criticality of safeguarding this data.
- Finance and senior management, providing a macro view on our organization's risk capacity, tolerance, and appetite, alongside outlining the business objectives that influence our process in scope.
- Governance structures, clarifying the decision-making processes, ensuring that our cyber risk management efforts align with the broader organizational goals.

Each department brings a unique lens through which we can view our organization, contributing to a holistic understanding of our internal environment. All this is about capturing a snapshot of where we stand today. Asking questions: What are our core capabilities? In what areas do we excel, and where are opportunities for improvement? By conducting a detailed analysis of our internal environment, we establish a baseline that serves as the yardstick against which all identified risks are evaluated. However, we can't limit our exploration within the confines of our organizational boundaries. We also extend analysis considering external factors like market trends, competitor activities, regulatory changes, and technological advancements.

As part of this exercise to better understand our environment, we scrutinize the effectiveness of our implemented controls. Are they performing as intended, or are there gaps that leave us vulnerable? This inquiry is supported by historical data, which provides empirical evidence of the controls' performance over time, highlighting any instances of failure or inefficiency. The competence and training of the teams responsible for maintaining these controls come under review. Understanding the depth of their expertise and the adequacy of their training is crucial.

This evaluation of our internal capabilities and external influences enables us to identify where we stand strong and where fortification is needed, all while keeping an eye on the dynamic external environment that continuously shapes our cyber risk profile.

Prepared with a clear understanding of both our internal and external contexts, we employ the SWOT analysis tool to distill this information into actionable insights. This analysis helps us identify our Strengths (what we do best), Weaknesses (where we could improve), Opportunities (external factors we can capitalize on), and Threats (external challenges we need to navigate). It's a tool that transforms our understanding into a strategic asset, enabling us to align our cyber risk management program with our broader organizational objectives.

The SWOT analysis is a strategic planning tool that originated in the 1960s, developed by Albert Humphrey, who led a research project at Stanford University. This project aimed to understand why corporate planning failed. Through rigorous analysis and study, Humphrey and his team developed the SWOT framework. The primary objective of SWOT analysis was to assess the strategic position of a business within its environment, allowing organizations to identify internal strengths and weaknesses alongside external opportunities and threats.

This approach was revolutionary and stays after all these years as valuable tool providing a clear, simple way to evaluate a company's competitive stance and facilitating strategic planning. Over the years, SWOT analysis has transcended its business origins to become a fundamental tool across various fields, including cybersecurity risk management, where it can help us to better understand our organizations.

Preparing a SWOT analysis based on the information you've gathered will help you to clear your mind and digest the huge amount of information you received, processing it and strategizing the approach by dissecting your cyber risk landscape into manageable parts, identifying Strengths, Weaknesses, Opportunities, and Threats. Here's how you can effectively prepare a SWOT analysis for your cyber risk management efforts:

- **Consolidate your information**: Start by organizing all the data and insights you've collected from your information-gathering techniques. Whether from surveys, enterprise systems, workshops, or site visits, ensure you have a better understanding of your organization's internal and external environments.
- **Identify your strengths**: Strengths are your organization's assets and capabilities that can be leveraged as competitive advantages in cybersecurity. Look for areas where you excel, such as robust security protocols, advanced technology, skilled cybersecurity personnel, or

strong leadership in cyber risk management. These are your defensive and offensive tools against cyber threats.

- **Pinpoint your weaknesses**: Weaknesses are internal factors that might make your organization more susceptible to cyber risks. This could include outdated technology, lack of employee cybersecurity awareness, insufficient security policies, or gaps in your incident response plan. Recognizing these weaknesses is the first step toward mitigating them.
- **Spot opportunities**: Opportunities are external factors that you can exploit to strengthen your cybersecurity posture. This might include emerging technologies, cybersecurity grants, partnerships with security firms, or shifts in regulatory landscapes that favor more robust security measures. Identifying these can help you pivot or adapt your strategy to stay ahead.
- **Acknowledge threats**: Threats are external challenges or risks that could harm your organization. These could be new forms of cyberattacks, regulatory changes posing compliance risks, or even the activities of your competitors. Understanding these threats is crucial for preparing defensive strategies.
- **Organize your findings into a SWOT matrix**: Figure 6.1 is a visual representation that helps to see how these elements interact and where your priorities should lie. Then with your SWOT matrix complete, analyze the relationships between the different elements. How can you use your strengths to seize opportunities or counter threats? Can your opportunities help mitigate your weaknesses? This analysis will form the basis of your cyber risk management strategy.

When conducting a SWOT analysis, we don't just catalog facts; we are synthesizing knowledge to illuminate the path forward. It is a fundamental step to ensure that our risk management efforts are based in reality and aligned with the aspirations of where we want to go. Remember that understanding the business environment is an ongoing practice, not a task to be completed just once. Yet, it's essential to set a deadline for moving to the next phase with the information we've collected. Without this, we risk remaining indefinitely in this stage of the process.

GATHERING ESSENTIAL INFORMATION

With a solid understanding of our scope and a clear understanding of our business environment, we're now ready to gather the information needed for our risk assessment. This phase involves collecting detailed data on the topics and categories we've identified. But before jumping in, there's one important step that can make a big difference, setting a deadline. Decide

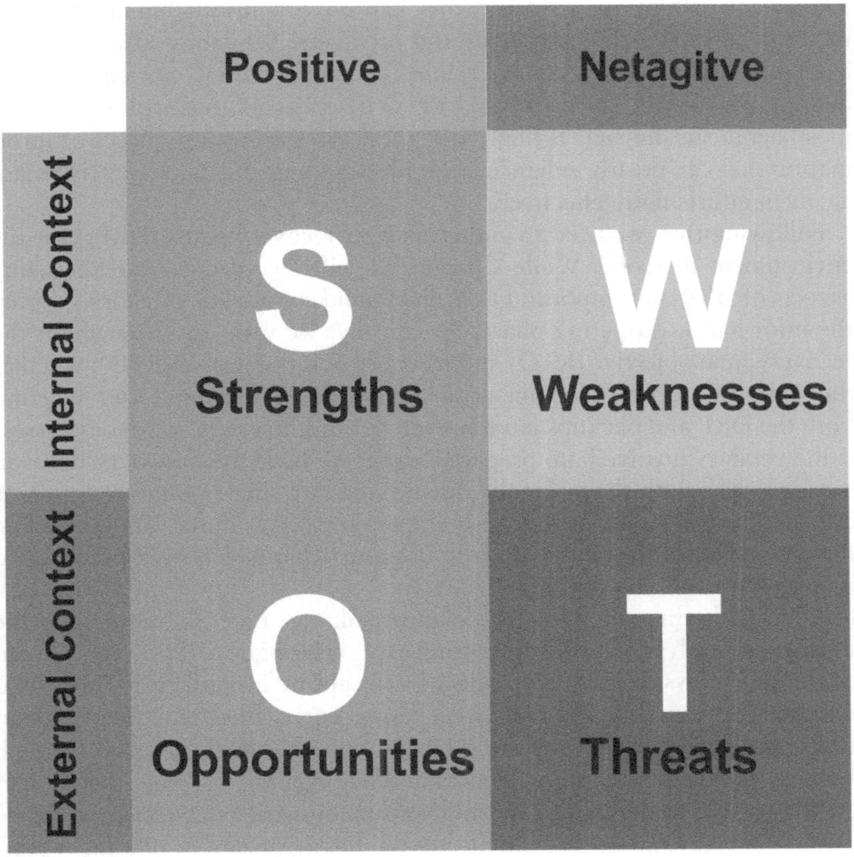

Figure 6.1 SWOT analysis.

upfront how long you'll spend gathering information. Once that deadline hits, you'll work with whatever data you've collected by then. Without a set time frame, it's easy to get stuck in this phase, constantly uncovering new details that lead to even more research. Since we'll never know everything, this can quickly turn into an endless process. So, give yourself a limit, gather what you can, and be confident moving forward with the information you have. So, now, let's dive into gathering this crucial information using various techniques, ensuring we have a good foundation for a full and informed risk assessment process.

Our initial step in gathering information should focus on reviewing our existing documentation, such as standard operating procedures (SOPs), guidelines, processes, and policies. This review not only clarifies how processes and systems within our scope operate but also highlights what is currently defined and where gaps may exist. Additionally, if business impact assessments (BIAs) are available, they can provide invaluable insights into the criticality of different systems and processes. While not always readily available, BIAs offer a detailed look at the potential consequences of disruptions, helping to prioritize our focus on areas that would have the most significant impact. If they exist, these assessments are pieces of information that can greatly enhance our understanding and guide our risk management efforts more effectively.

Following this, we need to gather disaster recovery plans (DRPs) for the environment in scope. While Chapter 12 will dive deeper into the many aspects of DRPs, it's important to keep in mind certain key categories during the information-gathering phase. Specifically, we want to know about the recovery time objective (RTO) and recovery point objective (RPO), whether the plan is properly documented, the status of backups, and whether both the DRP and backups have been tested. Additionally, we should assess if the vendors involved are prepared and if we have the necessary terms in our contracts with them. Finally, identifying any single points of failure is critical, as these could significantly impact recovery efforts. Understanding these seven categories now will help us ensure that we are well-prepared to manage potential disruptions effectively.

After gathering all what is documented, it's time to jump into the unknowns and gather the undocumented information. For this we can count on surveys, because they allow us to capture insights from those who interact with our systems daily uncovering unrecorded practices that can shape our cybersecurity posture. Engaging directly with the team through surveys provides a baseline understanding, helping us map the human element of our digital landscape and guiding our risk assessment.

Surveys create an open dialogue across the organization, offering a platform for everyone, from IT specialists to front-desk operators, to contribute their insights. This method ensures that we hear from a wide range of voices, reflecting diverse experiences and perspectives across the organization. Each survey response adds to our understanding of the cyber risk landscape. Well-crafted questions help gather detailed and relevant information, revealing patterns and outliers that might otherwise go unnoticed. When data is scarce, surveys provide rich, qualitative insights that complement quantitative information. Beyond data collection, surveys promote a culture of cybersecurity awareness. Recognizing and valuing each contribution reinforces the importance of everyone's role in maintaining the organization's cyber health.

The design of the survey, including the questions asked and the distribution strategy, directly impacts the quality of responses. Ensuring that the survey is clear, accessible, and relevant maximizes the chances of receiving actionable feedback. Creating and utilizing surveys effectively to gather information for your cyber risk assessment involves a careful blend of clarity, conciseness, and engagement. Here's a step-by-step guide to help you craft surveys that yield useful insights:

- **Define your goals**: Before drafting your survey, clearly define what information you need to gather. This could range from details about asset usage, understanding specific cybersecurity practices, to identifying areas of concern from the employees' perspective. Your goals will shape your questions, so it's crucial to be specific.
- **Craft concise and clear questions**: Each question should be easy to understand and answer. Avoid technical jargon that might confuse respondents not familiar with cybersecurity terminology. Use simple language and be as specific as possible to avoid ambiguous answers. Open-ended questions can provide valuable insights, but balance these with closed-ended questions for easier analysis.
- **Organize your survey logically**: Structure your survey so it flows naturally from one topic to the next. Group related questions together to keep respondents engaged and make the survey easier to follow. Starting with less sensitive or easier questions can warm up respondents before moving to more detailed or sensitive topics.
- **Test your survey**: Before deploying your survey widely, conduct a pilot test with a small, diverse group of colleagues. This can help you identify any confusing questions, technical issues with the survey platform, or any other obstacles that could hinder the survey's effectiveness. Use the feedback to refine your survey for clarity and engagement.
- **Choose the right tool**: Select a survey tool that is user-friendly and accessible to all participants. Ensure it offers the features you need, such as anonymity for respondents, various question types, and easy data analysis. Familiarity for your audience is key, so choose a platform they're likely comfortable using. I found Microsoft forms particularly useful when a GRC tool wasn't available.
- **Communicate the purpose and anonymity**: When inviting participants to take the survey, clearly explain its purpose and how their responses will be used. If responses are anonymous, make sure to state this explicitly to encourage honesty. Assuring respondents of the confidentiality of their answers can significantly increase the quality and honesty of the feedback received.
- **Set a deadline and send reminders**: Define a clear deadline for completing the survey and communicate this with your invitation. Send reminders as the deadline approaches, particularly to those who have not yet responded. However, be mindful of not overcommunicating and causing survey fatigue.
- **Normalize and analyze the responses**: Once the survey period has closed, collect the responses and begin normalization to ensure

consistency in the data, especially for open-ended questions. Look for patterns, trends, and outliers that can inform your risk assessment process.
- **Act on the findings**: The ultimate goal of the survey is to gather actionable insights. Review the data collected to identify areas of strength, potential vulnerabilities, and gaps in knowledge or practice within your organization. Use these insights as a basis for making informed decisions in your cyber risk management strategy.
- **Share results and next steps**: Depending on the nature of the survey and the confidentiality of the responses, consider sharing general findings and next steps with the participants. This can help demonstrate the value of their input and encourage participation in future initiatives.

I'm sure that as you examine the responses from these surveys, you'll see that what emerges is a narrative map of our operations and our cybersecurity posture, shaped by the same people who inhabit and navigate its business process every day. This map not only guides our next steps in the risk assessment process but also highlights areas where knowledge sharing and training can further strengthen our defenses.

As surveys won't be our only source and technique to gather information, it is time for exploring the structured world of enterprise architecture (EA) and configuration management database (CMDB) systems which is similar to accessing a detailed map of our technological infrastructure. These systems offer a bird's-eye view of our organization's technological framework, presenting a complete record of our assets, configurations, and connections. Utilizing EA and CMDB systems allows us to quickly identify critical technological components and understand their interrelations, streamlining our assessment process by leveraging existing documentation and insights.

While EA systems grant us a panoramic understanding of our technological infrastructure's assembly, it's paramount to recognize their potential limitations, particularly from a cybersecurity vantage point. Originating in an era before cybersecurity concerns reached their current zenith, EA systems sketch a vast, interconnected view of technological assets and their links. Yet, they may not always drill down to the granular level of detail critical for an exhaustive cyber risk assessment. The clear understanding of data flows, protocols, and the multilayered integration across databases, applications, operating systems, servers, and network infrastructure might remain elusive.

This observation doesn't detract from the value of EA systems but rather illuminates the necessity of weaving them together with complementary data sources, notably CMDBs. CMDBs are often the key to unlocking the details left uncharted by EA systems, shedding light on device maintenance protocols, access controls, and the minutiae of network pathways and protocols. This synergetic approach empowers us to marry the strategic, high-level insights offered by EA systems with the operational depth provided by CMDBs.

Imagine EA systems as the structural framework outlining our organizational technology's vast expanse. They delineate the major landmarks and the pathways connecting them. Yet, securing our digital and physical domains, especially against cybersecurity threats, mandates a journey through the less explored paths. It requires delving into the specifics of data handling, user access, and system upkeep elements essential to our risk profile but potentially glossed over by EA systems.

Our strategy for cyber risk assessment must be all-encompassing, ensuring we leave no stone unturned. While EA systems lay down an essential groundwork for our understanding, the treasure of cybersecurity insights often resides in the details these systems might overlook. Integrating the overarching views from EA systems with the granular insights from CMDBs and other informational reservoirs enables us to forge a more precise and actionable understanding of our cybersecurity risks. As we gather information using EA and CMDB systems, we need to stay alert for details that might not be immediately visible and be ready to uncover additional data. This broad view is crucial for spotting vulnerabilities, understanding their potential impacts, and developing strategies that fit the specific needs of our organization's technology environment.

But what if we don't have all what we need from the EA or CMDB systems? We can work with another technique: workshops. They serve as a dynamic forum, bridging gaps where structured data is not available. These interactive sessions stand out for their capacity to consolidate fragmented knowledge, align perspectives, and unearth critical information that might not be documented. Imagine workshops as collaborative endeavors where the collective wisdom and experiences of participants coalesce, offering a rich tapestry of insights into our technological and operational landscape.

The real magic of workshops lies in their ability to foster consensus among varied stakeholders, simultaneously serving as a crucible for information gathering and classification. In instances where our databases offer a skeletal framework or are conspicuously absent, workshops can flesh out the details, painting a better picture of our cyber risk environment. This process not only aids in capturing elusive data but also in ensuring that the information reflects a shared understanding, aligning with the organization's reality.

However, navigating the complexities of workshops, especially in an era dominated by virtual meetings, presents its own set of challenges. Virtual workshops, conducted via platforms like Zoom or Microsoft Teams, require creative approaches to engage participants effectively. The lack of face-to-face interaction can sometimes lessen the depth of communication, making it crucial to use strategies that promote active participation and openness.

On the other hand, on-site workshops, while offering the advantage of direct interaction, require detailed planning to ensure that discussions are structured and yield the intended outcomes. If you'll be the facilitator, you must skillfully guide conversations, ensuring that every voice is heard, and no critical insight is overshadowed. This balancing act is crucial in creating a space where participants feel comfortable sharing, even when the information might reveal vulnerabilities or gaps in the organization's cybersecurity posture.

Building trust among participants is essential to the success of our workshops. Creating an environment where participants clearly understand that the collective goal is to strengthen the organization's cyber resilience is key. This starts with clearly communicating the workshop's objectives, emphasizing that the focus is on collaboration, not blame, in identifying and addressing cybersecurity challenges. A culture of transparency and support ensures that workshops go beyond information gathering, becoming drivers of meaningful change and improvement.

Additionally, workshops can be an indispensable resource, particularly if you're relatively new to an organization. They offer a unique platform to deep dive into the processes and systems that are part of your scope. Think of them as your orientation session into the organization's operations, a chance to get up close and personal with the very mechanisms you'll be assessing. When you're stepping into a new role or organization, the challenge isn't just about understanding what needs to be protected; it's about appreciating the intricacies of how things operate, the interconnectedness of systems, and the cultural approach to cybersecurity. Workshops provide this complete overview in an interactive format, allowing you to ask questions, challenge assumptions, and get a feel for the cybersecurity pulse of the organization.

This is particularly valuable because it offers a holistic view of the cybersecurity environment from multiple perspectives. You're not just getting a run-down from IT; you're hearing from various departments about how they use systems, perceive risks, and implement security in their day-to-day operations. This multifaceted insight is gold for someone new to the organization, as it helps build a rounded understanding of what's at stake and what needs to be prioritized in your risk assessment efforts. In fact, workshops can accelerate your integration into the organization's cybersecurity culture. They're an opportunity to introduce yourself, outline your objectives, and explain how your work will contribute to the organization's overall security posture. This helps in establishing your role and the value of the cyber risk management program, fostering collaboration and support from various quarters of the organization right from the start.

Preparing for an effective workshop to gather information for your cyber risk assessment involves a thoughtful approach to ensure it is both engaging and fruitful. Here's how you can structure this preparation:

- **Define clear objectives**: Start by pinpointing exactly what you aim to achieve with the workshop. Is it to understand specific processes, identify assets, or clarify how information flows within the scope? Having clear objectives will not only guide your planning but also help participants understand the importance of their contributions.
- **Identify the right participants**: The success of a workshop heavily depends on having the right mix of people in the room. Identify stakeholders from various departments who interact with or have knowledge about the systems and processes within your scope. This may include IT staff, department heads, and end-users who can provide diverse perspectives.
- **Develop a structured agenda**: Create a detailed agenda that aligns with your objectives. This should include topics for discussion, activities planned, and allocated times. A structured agenda helps keep the workshop focused and ensures all critical areas are covered.
- **Prepare engaging materials**: Depending on the objectives, prepare materials that can facilitate discussion and engagement. This could be diagrams of the systems being assessed, lists of assets for verification, or scenarios that might require risk evaluation. Visual aids and interactive elements can help make complex information more accessible.
- **Foster an open environment**: Workshops are most effective when participants feel comfortable sharing their thoughts and experiences. Set the tone early by emphasizing the collaborative nature of the session, reassuring everyone that the goal is to improve security, not to assign blame. Encouraging an atmosphere of openness and respect is key.
- **Facilitate productively**: As the facilitator, your role is to guide the conversation, ensure all voices are heard, and keep the session on track. This might involve asking probing questions, summarizing discussions to ensure clarity, and steering the conversation back to the agenda when necessary.
- **Capture everything**: Designate someone to take detailed notes or record the session (with participants' consent) to ensure that no insights are lost. Capturing the details allows you to revisit the discussions later and ensures that the information gathered can be accurately incorporated into your risk assessment.
- **Plan for follow-up**: A workshop is often just the starting point. Plan for how you will follow up on the information gathered, including verifying details, addressing unanswered questions, and integrating

insights into your risk assessment. Communicate these next steps to participants, so they understand how their input will be used and what to expect next.

- **Express gratitude**: Recognize and thank participants for their time and contributions. Acknowledging the value of their input not only fosters goodwill but also encourages continued cooperation throughout the cyber risk management process. Really this has to be genuine and if you think about it, gratitude is something we all must keep in mind. All participants of our workshop are giving us their time although they, I'm sure, are super busy but recognize the importance of what they can provide to better assess and manage cyber risks. Remember, just as any other process or activity in the organization, cybersecurity isn't about technology, always it's all about people.

Workshops are great tools in our information-gathering process, providing a way to collect, classify, and validate information that might otherwise go unnoticed. The key is recognizing their potential, addressing the challenges, and implementing strategies to maximize their effectiveness.

When it comes to deepening our understanding of the cyber risks within our organization, there's no substitute for getting your boots on the ground and seeing things for yourself. That's where conducting site visits comes into play. Conducting site visits offers us the opportunity to observe our cybersecurity practices in their natural habitat. This hands-on approach provides a ground-level view of how policies and protocols are implemented, how physical assets are secured, and how information flows within our network. Site visits enable us to spot vulnerabilities that might be overlooked in document-based assessments, offering tangible insights into the physical and operational aspects of our cyber risk landscape.

When walking through the hallways of your organization, stepping into server rooms, and visiting workspaces, you're not having just a casual walk; you're on a mission to uncover the real situation beyond what's written in policies and system diagrams. It's about seeing firsthand how well our cybersecurity measures hold up in the day-to-day running of the business. During these site visits, I encourage you to engage in conversations with the people you meet. These folks operate, manage, and safeguard our information and assets every day. They're the unsung heroes who often have insights that you won't find in any report. Ask them about their challenges, the workarounds they've devised, and what they think could improve. You'll be surprised at how much you can learn from these interactions.

Pay attention to the physical setup too. How secure do the physical assets appear? Are the server rooms well-guarded? Is access to sensitive areas controlled effectively? It's the little things, like an unmonitored entry point or an outdated access system, that can open up avenues for risk that we hadn't considered. Observing the flow of information within the organization is equally enlightening. Look at how data moves, where it's stored, and who has access to it. Sometimes, the way information is handled in practice can be quite different from what's outlined in the protocols. Identifying these discrepancies can provide valuable insights into potential vulnerabilities.

When gearing up for an on-site visit as part of our cyber risk assessment, it is as if we're embarking on a detailed exploration mission. Our goal? To dive deep into the physical and operational realities of our cyber environment. To make this visit as impactful as possible, let's sketch out a roadmap for preparation:

- Set clear goals: I know this may sound repetitive but it's key for us to always remind what are the goals we want to achieve by doing these activities. I'm sure you have seen or you'll about to see how easy is to get lost in an ocean of information pointing to so many directions at the same time. So, to set clear goals you need to think on what do you hope to uncover or verify during this visit? Pin down your objectives to ensure your on-site time is targeted and efficient. This clarity will guide your interactions and observations, focusing your attention on areas critical to your cyber risk assessment.
- Engage and inform: Reach out to the teams and individuals you'll be interacting with. Explain the purpose of your visit and how it plays into the broader goal of strengthening our cybersecurity posture. This step is vital for fostering an atmosphere of cooperation and openness, ensuring that staff are prepared and receptive to your inquiries.
- Craft a detailed checklist: Based on your objectives, put together a checklist of specific areas, systems, or practices you need to examine. This could range from physical security controls to the setup of workstations or the implementation of access management protocols. A checklist keeps you on track and guarantees the coverage of all critical points.
- Schedule key conversations: Identify and arrange meetings with personnel who have hands-on experience with the systems and processes within your scope. These conversations can unveil operational insights that documentation alone cannot capture, offering a richer, more detailed understanding of your cyber environment.
- Prep your knowledge base: Immerse yourself in existing documentation and diagrams that detail the operational and technological landscape of your scope. This prep work will sharpen your ability to spot inconsistencies, outdated practices, or unaddressed vulnerabilities during the visit.
- Equip yourself with the right tools: Depending on your objectives, ensure you have the necessary equipment to document your findings

effectively. This might include a camera (if permitted) for capturing physical security setups, a notebook for jotting down observations, or any specialized tools for testing access controls or other security measures.

- Adopt an observer's mindset: Approach the visit with curiosity and an open mind. While you're there to assess and identify risks, also be receptive to learning about the operational challenges and constraints the staff face. This understanding can enrich your risk assessment, making your recommendations more practical and actionable.
- Follow-up thoroughly: After your visit, take the time to debrief with the teams you interacted with. Share preliminary observations and express also gratitude for their cooperation. This debrief is also an opportunity to clarify any points of confusion and ensure that your understanding is accurate.

Preparing for our on-site visit sets the stage for a successful assessment and demonstrates our commitment to collaborating with the wider organization. This approach deepens our understanding of the cyber risk landscape and strengthens relationships with those on the front lines of cybersecurity. These visits are about gathering the missing pieces scattered across the organization, building a complete picture of the processes and systems in scope, and assessing our cybersecurity posture in the context of daily operations. Stepping away from our desks and into the field allows us to gather valuable insights that will shape our cyber risk management strategies, ensuring they are as robust and responsive as the environments they are designed to protect.

The next technique for gathering information we're going to explore requires us to dive into the world of automated scanning tools, which feels like unlocking a new level of capability in our cyber risk assessment journey. These tools are like having a dedicated, indefatigable team that works around the clock, exploring every nook and cranny of our digital landscape. Their role? To uncover the hidden and highlight the overlooked, ensuring that our assessment is as thorough as possible.

When we use automated scanning tools in our network, they work around the clock, exploring our environment, listing assets, identifying vulnerabilities, and providing insights that might take a human team months to uncover. This detailed and wide-ranging coverage is especially valuable in complex environments, where the sheer amount of data and interconnected systems can easily overwhelm traditional manual assessments.

These tools don't just reveal what's present; they expose the cracks in our defenses, highlighting vulnerabilities that could be exploited by cyber threats. Their value extends beyond identification, as they also provide insight into the effectiveness of existing controls. This dual perspective, showing where we are vulnerable and where our defenses are strong, helps prioritize our risk management efforts, focusing attention where it's most needed. The historical data these tools provide adds further depth. Analyzing trends over time allows us to spot recurring issues, measure the impact of previous actions, and anticipate future vulnerabilities.

It's crucial, however, to use automated tools strategically. While they offer valuable insights, the data must be contextualized within the broader scope of our cyber risk management program. This involves integrating these findings with other techniques to create a cohesive view of our cyber risk landscape. Aligning insights from automated scans with information gathered through other methods ensures a detailed understanding of our cybersecurity posture. Leveraging these tools strengthens our information-gathering process, broadening our reach and sharpening our insights.

Another key technique involves using threat intelligence sources. Incorporating threat intelligence services and feeds uncovers unknown risks. These sources act as advanced early-warning systems, offering real-time insights into the evolving threat landscape. Tapping into these intelligence streams enables us to anticipate risks and refine our defenses, ensuring that our strategies are robust and responsive to the latest cyber threats, vulnerabilities, and attack patterns.

Think of threat intelligence services as having an informant that aggregates information from a variety of sources, including incident reports, hacker forums, and malware samples, analyzing this data to identify emerging threats and trends. This overview enables us to adjust our defenses in real time, staying one step ahead of potential attackers, and actually, this is what helps us to bridge the risk monitoring phase with the context analysis that will determine when a new cyber risk assessment is required because something has changed and whatever we assessed before is no longer valid. But all this we'll review it later in Chapter 10.

Utilizing threat intelligence effectively requires filtering, prioritizing, and contextualizing information relevant to our organization's specific context and vulnerabilities. The goal is to transform raw data into actionable knowledge, aligning security measures with the most pressing threats and ensuring resources are directed where they are needed most. Threat intelligence feeds act as a bridge between our organization and the wider cybersecurity community, allowing the exchange of information and learning from others' experiences. This collective defense mentality is essential in today's interconnected world, where a breach in one system can ripple across the digital ecosystem. This collaborative approach highlights the power of shared knowledge in strengthening defenses against adaptive adversaries. Incorporating threat intelligence into cyber risk management enhances resilience, helping tailor strategies to future threats and ensuring that defenses remain proactive rather than reactive. This strategic advantage enables us to protect assets with precision and foresight.

As we wrap up this chapter on gathering the key information for cyber risk management, it's a good time to reflect on where we've come. We started with what we already knew, our organization's existing knowledge, and then stretched that further using tools and techniques that helped uncover hidden details about our digital environment. Now, we're better prepared with the data needed to work our risk assessments. But there's something else that's just as important: realizing that this part of the process will only get smoother as you and your organization mature. Early on, you might feel like the information is scattered, and gathering everything takes longer than expected. Trust me, that's normal. But as your organization grows, and as you work to improve the documentation along the way, you'll notice a shift. The next time you dive into a risk assessment, you'll have better-organized, more reliable information right at your fingertips. This makes future assessments faster, less stressful, and, ultimately, more effective.

This is where you have a great opportunity. While working on gathering the information you don't have right now, you can sell the idea of keeping documentation up to date. It's not just about doing the work now, but it's about setting yourself up for an easier, more streamlined process next time. The more current and well-organized your data, the less time you'll spend collecting basics and the more time you can invest in really expanding your understanding of the organization's current risk contexts.

This journey from the known to the unknown has required patience and a commitment to getting better with each step. Gathering information exhaustively as possible gives us the knowledge we need to address risks in a meaningful way. It's all about seeing the bigger picture, how the various parts of your digital ecosystem interact, and where potential failure points lie and adjusting your strategies accordingly. As we conclude this first phase of our journey into cyber risk management, where defining the scope and meticulously gathering information set the stage for effective risk assessment, I hope you feel ready to move forward with confidence. Here is a checklist designed to guide you through this critical phase:

1. **Define the scope:**
   a. Identify the key business process for the initial risk assessment.
   b. Develop a process flow diagram to clarify the scope in terms of information, technology, and identify connections and dependences.
   c. Consider criticality, known vulnerabilities, or regulatory requirements.
2. **Set a deadline:**
   a. Define a clear deadline for moving to the next phase with the information gathered.

   b. Ensure the process remains focused and time-bound to prevent stagnation.
3. **Engage with departments**:
   d. Collaborate with Information Management, HR, IT, Legal, Supply Management, Sales, and other relevant departments.
   e. Gather insights on organizational culture, compliance requirements, technological capabilities, and risk tolerance.
4. **Gather all relevant information using different techniques**:
   1. **Documentation review**:
      a. Review existing standard operating procedures (SOPs), guidelines, policies, and processes.
      b. Identify gaps and update documents as necessary.
   2. **Use surveys**:
      a. Design and distribute surveys to gather insights from across the organization.
      b. Ensure questions are clear and concise to collect meaningful data.
   3. **Leverage EA and CMDB systems**:
      a. Utilize EA and CMDB systems for a high-level overview of technological assets and configurations.
      b. Identify gaps in cybersecurity perspectives and supplement with additional data sources.
   4. **Conduct workshops**:
      a. Organize workshops with key stakeholders to gather, classify, and validate information.
      b. Address challenges of virtual and on-site workshops by fostering an open environment and building trust.
   5. **Perform site visits**:
      a. Conduct on-site observations to understand the implementation of cybersecurity controls and practices.
      b. Engage with personnel to gain operational insights and assess physical security.
   6. **Automated scanning tools**:
      a. Deploy automated scanning tools to identify assets, vulnerabilities, and assess control effectiveness.
      b. Analyze trends and historical data to inform risk management strategies.
   7. **Threat intelligence services**:
      a. Integrate threat intelligence feeds to stay informed on the latest cyber threats and vulnerabilities.
      b. Tailor intelligence to the organization's context and vulnerabilities for actionable insights.

5. **SWOT analysis:**
   a. Prepare a SWOT analysis based on gathered information to identify strengths, weaknesses, opportunities, and threats.
   b. Use the analysis to inform and refine your cyber risk assessment making sure it is aligned to business objectives and will add real value to your organization.

Let this chapter serve as a reminder of the power of knowledge and the critical role it plays in our cyber risk management program. At this point, you should have gathered the essential information needed for your assessment. While it's important to acknowledge that you may not have everything you want to know, also remember that there are many aspects you and your organization might not even realize you need to know. This is part of the process. Keep in mind that cyber risk management is a continuous improvement journey. As you progress, you'll have the opportunity to expand your understanding of the environment in scope, gradually enhancing your assessments and making them even more effective. As we move forward to the risk assessment phase, let us carry with us the knowledge gained, the lessons learned, and the understanding deepened through this process. It is through this meticulous preparation and informed perspective that we can navigate the complexities of cyber risk assessments, leading our organization toward a more secure future. Remember, the cyber risk management journey is continuous, a perpetual cycle of learning, action, and improvement. And it starts with understanding our environment: knowing more, knowing better, and using that knowledge to protect what matters most.

We're on the edge of an exciting phase where all the theory we've absorbed and the extensive knowledge we've gathered start paying off. The groundwork we've laid is about to bear fruit, simplifying the complex process of assessing risks and formulating treatment plans. This is where our diligent preparation meets practical application, and the real fun begins. So, buckle up, because the adventure is just getting started, and the rewards of our efforts are within reach. Remember, results are what matter not the superhuman effort.

NOTES

1 Hawkins, J. (2021). *A Thousand Brains: A New Theory of Intelligence*. Basic Books.
2 Ariely, D. (2023). *Misbelief: What Makes Rational People Believe Irrational Things*. Harper Collins Publishers.

Chapter 7

Risk assessment

From identification to characterization

RISK ASSESSMENT

Inspiration often helps us look beyond the surface to uncover and identify the critical risks that may otherwise go unnoticed. "There is nothing more deceptive than an obvious fact." This insightful observation by Arthur Conan Doyle, through the voice of his legendary detective Sherlock Holmes, serves as a fitting preamble to our exploration of risk assessment. At first glance, the risks facing an organization might seem straightforward, easily identifiable by their outward manifestations. Yet, as Holmes appropriately highlights, the truth often lies beneath the surface, obscured by the apparent simplicity of observable facts. This chapter examines into the process of risk assessment, a journey from the initial identification of risks to their characterization.

Risk assessment is a critical phase in the journey of risk management, where the goal is to understand and evaluate the risks that your organization faces. This phase can be seen as the bridge between knowing there are potential dangers (acknowledged during the risk context phase) and deciding what to do about them (the following risk treatment phase). Let's break it down into its three main components: risk identification, risk analysis, and risk characterization.

Risk assessment is often seen as the heart of the entire risk management process because it is where risks are identified and translated into terms that the organization can understand and act on. Its importance lies in its ability to identify, analyze, and characterize the risks an organization may face. This serves as the key mechanism that turns abstract concerns about potential dangers into actionable information, allowing the organization to make informed decisions about how to manage these risks. Also, it plays a central role in determining the overall effectiveness of the risk management process. A clear understanding of the risks allows the organization to allocate resources efficiently, prioritize efforts to address the most

DOI: 10.1201/9781003546207-10

significant threats, and develop strategies that align with its objectives and risk tolerance.

Risk assessment is often mistaken as the entirety of the risk management process. This misconception proves the importance of the assessment phase, which involves the detailed work of identifying and mapping potential risks in a structured manner. However, it's important to remember that risk assessment is just one part of a larger process that includes setting the context, treating the risks, and ongoing monitoring and review. Each component is vital for a risk management program. The risk assessment phase also ensures that the organization's approach to risk is both proactive and based in reality. This alignment between understanding risk and taking action is what makes risk assessment not just a step in the process but the very core of effective risk management.

We'll begin with risk identification, where, based on the information gathered, we uncover the cyber risks our organization faces, describing them in a way that decision-makers can better understand. This stage requires vigilance and foresight, recognizing that what may seem minor could unravel into significant vulnerabilities. It's about bringing together diverse perspectives from across the organization, whether it's the IT department highlighting technological flaws or the finance team pointing out market-related risks, to ensure a comprehensive understanding of the risk landscape.

As we move forward to the next step: risk analysis, we'll dive deeper into each identified risk to understand its nature, including its likelihood and potential impact. This step often involves both quantitative and qualitative methods to gauge risks, providing a clearer picture of which ones are more pressing. By the end of this process, we'll have a prioritized list of risks, laying the foundation for effective risk characterization.

Finally, we'll bring everything together in the risk characterization phase, where we'll paint a detailed picture of each risk, understanding it in a way that is meaningful to your organization. This understanding is crucial as we move into the risk treatment phase, ensuring that the strategies we develop are not only technically sound but also strategically aligned with the organization's broader goals.

In this chapter, you'll find practical guidance on gathering essential information, engaging with stakeholders, and applying both quantitative and qualitative techniques to create a solid risk assessment framework. The aim is to provide you with the guidance, tools, and knowledge necessary to perform complete and insightful risk assessments, enabling your organization to navigate the complex and ever-evolving cyber threat landscape with confidence and strategic foresight. As we progress through this phase, remember Holmes' wisdom: the most significant discoveries often come from looking beyond the obvious, challenging our assumptions, and fully engaging with the complexities at hand. Let's start!

THE ART OF RISK IDENTIFICATION

At this stage, I'm sure you've been thinking on potential risks while gathering information to better understand your organization's internal and external context, and I know it's tempting to start assessing these risks immediately. However, it's crucial first to focus on understanding our environment without jumping to conclusions prematurely. Quick judgments could lead to oversights or inaccuracies which in the best scenario we'll have to rework part of our assessment but in the worse scenario we'll increase our biases and provide information to decision-makers that is not accurate. Having said that, once we've collected all the information, we can, within the time allocated for this phase of risk assessment, shift our focus. Now, we base our efforts on identifying risks with the information at our disposal.

This initial step in the risk assessment phase is both a science and an art, demanding a blend of technical knowledge and intuitive insight to uncover the risks that can compromise our cybersecurity posture and, ultimately, the business objectives. Adopting a pragmatic standpoint on risk identification involves leveraging a variety of tools, techniques, and frameworks to guide our quest. Yet, the true artistry in risk identification lies in our ability to synthesize this information, drawing connections between seemingly disparate pieces of data to reveal the bigger picture.

Before we fully dive into the risk identification, it's time to organize it in a way that allows us to tell a coherent story about the cyber risks within our scope. Think of this as setting the stage for identifying inherent cyber risks, those risks that exist regardless of the controls in place. To begin, we should dive into the nature of the process, service, or specific scope we're examining. Start by reviewing the collected data, including network diagrams, data flow charts, and technology inventories. The goal here is to map out where critical information resides, how it's processed, and the channels through which it's transmitted. This step is really important for pinpointing what needs protection and where potential vulnerabilities might lie.

For example, during one of my previous engagements, I worked with an organization that was implementing a new digital payment platform. The scope of the assessment was clearly defined, with a statement that described what the company aimed to achieve. This statement was our starting point for identifying the "Crown Jewels," the critical assets that are vital to the operation. These could be anything from customer payment information and personal identifiable information (PII) to transaction data and platform security protocols. Once we've identified these key assets, we need to trace their paths within the system where they are stored, how they are transmitted, and where they are processed. This process involves organizing the gathered information into a structured format, which might include tables that detail the storage locations, transmission paths, and processing points for each critical asset.

This structured organization will help us clearly visualize where our most important data lives, moves, and is used. It's the foundation for the next steps, where we will identify vulnerabilities, threats, and, then, the inherent risks associated with these critical assets.

With our information now organized, we have a clearer view of where our most critical data lives, moves, and is used. Now, we begin the process of listing all potential risks that could impact your organization. This step is crucial as it allows us to identify and document risks from every possible angle, ensuring nothing is overlooked. As you start this task, use the organized information you've gathered to guide your thinking. Consider the various sources from which risks might arise, technical flaws in your systems, human errors, external threats like cyberattacks, third parties, or even natural disasters that could disrupt your operations.

Start by methodically reviewing each critical asset you've identified in the previous step. For each asset, ask yourself:

- What could go wrong? Consider potential failures, especially the single point of failure where if affected, we'll find ourselves in a very bad day, breakdowns, or breaches in the technology or processes surrounding this asset.
- What human errors could occur? Reflect on the potential for mistakes, whether intentional or accidental, by individuals who interact with this asset.
- What external threats exist? Think about third parties in scope, how good is their security posture? Cyber threats, such as hackers or malware, as well as physical threats like natural disasters that could impact this asset.
- What are the environmental factors? Consider how environmental changes or disasters might impact the physical or operational aspects of your assets.

As you compile this list, remember to be comprehensive but also realistic. Your goal is to create a detailed inventory of risks that covers all aspects of your organization's operations, without getting bogged down in unlikely scenarios. This inventory will serve as the basis for the risk analysis and prioritization that follows, helping you to focus your resources and efforts on the most significant threats. Keep in mind we must identify and include in our risk description the three components of risk: Vulnerability, Threat, and Impact.

Here's a practical approach to listing potential risks:

- **Start with the "Crown Jewels"**: Begin by focusing on your most critical assets. For each asset, consider the different ways it could be compromised. Think broadly, include everything from a failure in encryption to a flood that could damage your data center.

- **Expand to interconnected systems:** Once you've identified risks to your primary assets, think about how these risks might extend to interconnected systems or processes. A vulnerability in one area could potentially lead to risks in another.
- **Consider external factors:** Don't forget to include risks from outside your organization. External threats such as cyberattacks, supply chain disruptions, or changes in regulations can have significant impacts on your assets.
- **Document everything:** As you identify risks, document them in detail. Include a brief description of the risk, the asset it relates to, and any initial thoughts on its potential impact or likelihood.

For example, if your critical asset is "customer payment information," potential risks and its descriptions might include:

Risk of data breach: There's a risk that customer payment information could be accessed without authorization. This could happen because of weak points in our system, such as insufficient data encryption or flaws in access control mechanisms. If these vulnerabilities are exploited by cybercriminals or even insiders with malicious intent, it could lead to the exposure of sensitive payment data. The impact of such a breach would not only harm customer trust but could also result in significant financial loss and legal consequences for the organization.

Risk of compliance failure: Our organization faces the risk of failing to meet the stringent requirements set by PCI standards or GDPR if we think on compliance with Privacy Regulations. This risk is tied to vulnerabilities in our systems that may not fully comply with these regulations. The threat here comes from audits or breaches that reveal these shortcomings, leading to possible regulatory fines, enforced changes, and increased scrutiny from governing bodies and authorities. The impact of this could be major, affecting our ability to operate smoothly and damaging our reputation in the industry.

Risk of internal threats: There is a potential risk from within our organization, where employees might mishandle payment data, either through carelessness or with harmful intent. This risk is rooted in vulnerabilities like lack of proper training, poor access controls, or insufficient monitoring systems. If these weaknesses are exploited, it could result in unauthorized access or accidental leakage of sensitive information. The impact could range from minor operational disruptions to significant data breaches that damage customer trust and incur legal penalties.

Risk of system failure: Our payment processing system is not immune to breakdowns, which could lead to the loss or corruption of payment data. This risk is associated with vulnerabilities in our technology infrastructure, such as outdated software or inadequate backup systems. The threat could come from system errors, hardware failures, or cyber criminals targeting these weak points. If such a failure occurs, the impact could disrupt business operations, result in financial losses, and cause a decline in customer confidence.

By systematically listing these risks, you'll build a complete picture of the potential risks your organization faces. This process not only highlights where you are most vulnerable but also sets the stage for analyzing these risks in detail, prioritizing them, and developing strategies to mitigate their impact.

The success of the risk identification process relies heavily on involving a diverse group of individuals from across the organization. It's challenging to identify risks in areas you may not be fully familiar with, which is why bringing together different perspectives is essential. This collaborative approach allows various departments to contribute their unique insights and expertise. For example, your IT department might highlight technological vulnerabilities, while the finance team could identify risks related to market fluctuations or financial fraud. Similarly, the HR department can provide insights into potential internal threats, such as data breaches resulting from employee actions, whether accidental or intentional. Incorporating these varied perspectives helps you to ensure a more complete understanding of the risk landscape, allowing the organization to uncover hidden risks that might not be apparent to a single department or individual.

Another crucial aspect of involving people from different parts of the organization is that it fosters a sense of ownership and responsibility toward the risk management process. When individuals contribute their knowledge and insights, they are more likely to be invested in the outcomes of the risk management efforts. This collective involvement also aids in breaking down silos within the organization, encouraging cross-departmental communication and collaboration. As a result, the risk management process becomes a unifying force, bringing together various parts of the organization to work toward a common goal of resilience and security.

With your initial list of risks identified, you now have a starting point for a rich conversation with other teams in your organization. Risk identification requires effective techniques to uncover all potential vulnerabilities, threats, and impacts an organization might face. One popular method is brainstorming sessions, where team members from different departments gather to discuss and identify possible risks based on their experiences and expertise. This approach encourages open communication and leverages the diverse knowledge within the organization, fostering a collaborative environment where even the smallest risk can be brought to light.

Another technique is the use of checklists, which can be developed from industry standards, past incidents, or regulatory requirements. These lists ensure that common and recurring risks are not overlooked and serve as a guide for the team. Checklists can be particularly helpful for new team members or organizations just starting their risk management journey, providing a structured way to think about potential threats.

Interviews and surveys are also valuable tools, especially for gaining insights from staff members who might not feel comfortable speaking up in group settings. These methods can uncover risks that are unique to specific roles or departments, offering a more detailed and nuanced understanding of the organization's risk profile.

To effectively involve your entire team in the risk identification process, especially those who may not be familiar with the intricacies of cyberattacks, it's essential to use tools that can bridge the gap between technical and non-technical understanding. These tools help to demystify how attacks unfold, making the concepts accessible to everyone involved in the risk management process. A good technique is scenario analysis, which involves imagining possible adverse events and their potential impacts on the organization. This method requires a creative and analytical approach, encouraging teams to think beyond the obvious and consider complex interdependencies and the cascading effects of various risk events.

Threat modeling is another valuable technique that serves as a structured approach to identify and assess the risks stemming from various vulnerabilities and the threats that could exploit them. For example, when focusing on customer payment information, threat modeling can help organize potential attacks using the framework of the cyber kill chain.[1] This model reveals a sequence in which threat actors might employ tactics, from initial reconnaissance to eventual data exfiltration or system disruption, allowing the team to map vulnerabilities and threats to each stage:

- **Reconnaissance**: Attackers may employ various techniques to gather preliminary information about the organization, such as scanning for exposed devices, conducting external network scans, or mining data from social media and the dark web for sensitive information.
- **Weaponization**: Tailoring malware to exploit specific vulnerabilities, such as software flaws or weak security configurations.
- **Delivery**: Using phishing or spear-phishing emails to gain initial access, exploiting weaknesses like unencrypted transmission channels or weak authentication protocols.
- **Exploitation**: Targeting vulnerabilities during processing and storage, such as software flaws or spreadsheet manipulation.

- **Installation**: Establishing persistence, like installing ransomware by exploiting weak backup protocols.
- **Command and control (C2)**: Using insider threats to leverage access control weaknesses for further exploitation.
- **Actions on objectives**: Executing the final goal, such as data breach/exfiltration or privilege escalation, directly exploiting identified vulnerabilities.

Understanding this sequence not only helps your team anticipate how vulnerabilities might be exploited but also highlights the importance of a layered security strategy that addresses all technological, procedural, and human factors. Also, this is particularly helpful when communicating with nontechnical stakeholders because it translates the complex process of a cyberattack into a series of logical steps. Each step can be visualized and discussed in terms of what specific risks it poses and what measures can be taken to mitigate those risks.

Other similar techniques to consider include:

- **Attack trees**: These are hierarchical diagrams that map out all possible attack vectors aimed at compromising critical assets. They can be particularly effective in showing how different vulnerabilities could be exploited in combination, helping teams visualize the full scope of potential threats.
- **Vulnerability assessments and penetration testing**: These are systematic evaluations of your systems to identify exploitable vulnerabilities. Performing these tests by professional ethical hackers where they are attempting to exploit these vulnerabilities in a controlled environment helps your team gain a deeper understanding of the most critical risks and how to mitigate them effectively.
- **Internal audits**: Regular internal audits are another tool in risk identification. These audits review the effectiveness of your current security controls, compliance with policies, and overall risk management practices providing great insights you may sometimes overlook.

As you work through scenario analysis and threat modeling, it's helpful to consider specific risks that might impact your organization. This list serves as a practical guide, illustrating various risks associated with vulnerabilities and threats that could arise in different areas. These examples will help you and your team think more broadly about the potential impacts on your critical assets and refine your approach to identifying and assessing risks.

For instance, when considering the risk of regulatory noncompliance, you might explore the following potential issues:

1. Inadequate data classification and protection measures.
2. Lack of encryption for sensitive data both at rest and in transit.
3. Insufficient access controls and authentication mechanisms.
4. Poor data retention and deletion practices.
5. Inadequate training on regulatory requirements for IT staff.

When assessing the risk of unauthorized access, consider these vulnerabilities:

1. Weak password policies and absence of multifactor authentication.
2. Insufficient network segmentation and firewall configurations.
3. Insecure remote access solutions.
4. Lack of role-based access control and least privilege enforcement.
5. Outdated or unpatched operating systems and applications.

Similarly, for data theft, loss, or leakage:

1. Unencrypted data storage and transmission.
2. Vulnerable storage solutions and misconfigured databases.
3. Lack of data loss prevention (DLP) strategies and tools.
4. Insecure application programming interfaces (APIs) and web services.
5. Inadequate backup and disaster recovery solutions.

These examples are not exhaustive but provide a starting point to guide discussions and analysis. They help identify gaps in your current security posture and prioritize areas needing immediate attention. Considering these scenarios prepares your organization to anticipate, prevent, and respond to potential threats, strengthening your overall risk management strategy. Using these tools not only enhances your ability to identify and assess risks but also helps you to better communicate these risks effectively across your organization.

This is particularly important when collaborating with individuals who might not be fully aware of how an attack develops or how vulnerabilities can be exploited. Once your team has a clear understanding of how risks might manifest through tools like threat modeling and attack trees, the next step is to leverage historical data and incident reports. This data-driven approach allows you to identify trends and recurring issues, highlighting areas of vulnerability that have been problematic in the past. By combining qualitative insights from tools like threat modeling with quantitative data, you can prioritize risks based on actual past events, providing a factual basis for the next step in the risk management process.

Incorporating a mix of techniques allows for a broad and detailed exploration of potential risks. Using various methods helps you create a more accurate and complete risk list, setting the stage for effective analysis and treatment in the next phases of risk management. This inclusive approach brings diverse insights and enables a more informed risk analysis and characterization. Drawing on the collective expertise of the organization helps the risk management team better assess the likelihood and impact of each risk. With this solid understanding, you are ready to move on to the next step: risk analysis, where the identified risks will be carefully evaluated to determine their likelihood and potential impact. This collaborative foundation ensures that decisions on risk treatment are well-informed and tailored to the organization's specific context, strengthening the overall effectiveness of the risk management program.

ASSESSING THE IMPACT AND LIKELIHOOD OF RISKS

Now, it's time for us to take the next step: assessing the impact and likelihood of the risks we've identified. Assessing impact is about understanding what could happen if these risks turn into reality. It's like asking ourselves, "What's at stake?" and "How much damage could this cause?" Whether it's a small disruption or something more severe, we need to understand what we're up against. Then, we'll look at likelihood. This is where we first evaluate the inherent risks by considering how likely and impactful the identified risks are, without considering the controls we have in place. Understanding both impact and likelihood helps us clearly describe the inherent risks, providing an initial prioritization and preparing us for the next step: assessing the actual risk levels.

So, to assess the inherent risk levels we need to understand its nature. This step often involves quantitative and/or qualitative methods to measure risks, providing a clearer picture of which ones are more pressing. By the end of this process, you should have a prioritized list of risks based on their potential to impacts your organization.

When assessing the likelihood of risks, particularly in the context of cybersecurity, it's important to consider a range of factors that contribute to the overall risk equation. These factors help us understand not just if a risk could happen, but how likely it is given the current landscape. Here's what we need to keep in mind:

- **Velocity**: How quickly can a threat materialize? This looks at the speed with which a vulnerability can be exploited and the damage can begin to spread.
- **Vulnerability**: This is a repeat, but for clarity, it's crucial to assess the weaknesses within our systems that could be exploited by threats. A higher number of vulnerabilities increases the likelihood of an attack.
- **Interdependence**: Systems are often interconnected, meaning a breach in one area could quickly affect others. Understanding these connections helps us gauge how a threat could propagate.

- **Motivation**: What's driving the threat actors? Whether it's financial gain, political motives, or just the challenge, understanding the motivation behind potential attacks can help us assess how likely they are to target us.
- **Skills of the threat**: The capabilities of potential attackers play a significant role in determining risk likelihood. Skilled hackers might exploit vulnerabilities that others can't, increasing the risk.
- **Exposure**: How much of our system is exposed to potential attackers? Systems that are more accessible to the outside world, such as public-facing web applications, might have a higher likelihood of being attacked.
- **Historical data**: Looking at past incidents can provide valuable insights into the likelihood of future risks. Trends in attacks against similar organizations or technologies can inform our assessment.
- **Threat landscape**: The current state of the cybersecurity world, including prevalent types of attacks, common targets, and emerging threats, all factor into assessing likelihood.
- **Control effectiveness**: While we assess inherent risk without considering safeguards, understanding the current state of our defenses can provide context for how exposed we really are.
- **Resource availability to threat actors**: Consider the resources that potential attackers have at their disposal. Well-funded groups might pose a higher risk due to their ability to employ sophisticated tools and techniques.

Quantitative and qualitative methods offer two distinct approaches for evaluating risks, each providing valuable insights into the nature and severity of potential threats facing an organization. Understanding these methods is crucial for a balanced risk analysis.

Quantitative methods involve the use of numerical values to estimate the likelihood and impact of risks. This approach typically relies on historical data, statistical analysis, and mathematical models to assign probabilities to potential incidents and quantify their potential consequences in financial terms. Quantitative analysis is particularly useful when precise data is available, allowing organizations to make calculations such as the annual loss expectancy (ALE), which estimates the yearly cost of risks. This method provides clear, objective data that can be used to prioritize risks based on their potential financial impact, facilitating decision-making processes about where to allocate resources for mitigation efforts.

Without going into too much detail because we will explore risk quantification in the last section of this book and using the definitions we have from Chapter 1, the ALE represents an estimate of the financial loss an organization might expect from a risk event over a year. ALE is calculated by multiplying the annual rate of occurrence (ARO) of a risk event by its single loss expectancy (SLE), which is the estimated monetary loss from a single occurrence of that risk. This calculation provides a dollar figure that can be compared against the cost of implementing controls, helping organizations to make informed decisions about whether the cost of mitigation measures is justified by the potential reduction in annual losses.

Value at risk (VaR) is another important concept used alongside ALE, particularly in financial sectors, to estimate the maximum potential loss over a specific period and with a certain confidence level. VaR offers a way to assess and compare the potential impact of different risks, providing a quantifiable measure of the extreme losses that could occur. When used together, ALE and VaR can provide a better view of the financial implications of risks, guiding strategic decisions on where to allocate resources for risk mitigation efforts.

These quantitative methods are great tools for supporting decision-making processes, enabling organizations to prioritize risks based on their potential financial impact. Quantifying risks in monetary terms allows them to be ranked and compared, offering a more objective assessment of which risks require investment in controls. This approach also supports cost–benefit analyses of various risk treatment options, ensuring that resources are allocated efficiently to reduce risk exposure to an acceptable level.

However, quantifying risks with ALE and VaR comes with its challenges. Accurately estimating the ARO and SLE for various risks can be difficult, especially for cyber risks where data on past incidents may be limited or not directly applicable due to the rapidly evolving threat landscape. Similarly, calculating VaR requires complex statistical models and assumptions that may not always capture the full range of uncertainties associated with cyber risks. These challenges highlight the importance of complementing quantitative assessments with qualitative insights to ensure a holistic understanding of risks.

So, thinking on the other side of this coin, qualitative methods assess risks based on subjective judgments about their severity and likelihood. This approach often uses rating scales (such as high, medium, and low) and relies on the expertise and experience of key personnel in the organization that know the ins and outs of the business process or systems that are part of the scope of our assessment. These *magic people*, as some friends call them, are guided and complemented by us as cybersecurity professionals to evaluate risks without necessarily converting them into numerical values. Qualitative analysis is invaluable when precise data is scarce or when assessing intangible factors, such as the potential reputational damage from a data breach. This is because everyone in the organization is the result of years of experience, knowledge acquired through practice or studies that are contained in the individual. This person sees the world from his own perspective and knowledge. Therefore, as we can see in Figure 7.1, when evaluating risks qualitatively, we must have different perspectives that are relevant to the

Figure 7.1 Different Perspectives assessing the same risk.

risk we are evaluating. That is, we must make use of the wisdom of the crowds.[2] Having this focus on qualitative evaluations will help us eliminate biases and add the knowledge that all these magic people have.

Also, by facilitating discussions among stakeholders, qualitative methods can help analyze risks building a consensus on risk priorities and foster a deeper understanding of the organization's risk landscape, reducing resistance to change. Both quantitative and qualitative methods have their advantages and limitations. Quantitative analysis offers the clarity of numerical data but may be constrained by the availability and reliability of historical information. Qualitative analysis, while more flexible and adaptable to different scenarios, may be subject to biases and variability in judgment.

In practice, the most effective risk assessment strategies often combine quantitative and qualitative methods. Leveraging the strengths of both approaches provides organizations with a more realistic understanding of their risk landscape. This hybrid approach enables objective prioritization based on numerical data while incorporating the insights and context offered by qualitative assessments. This balance is crucial for developing risk management strategies that are both data-driven and adaptable to the complex realities of cybersecurity and the organization.

Risk analysis is then where the intricate details of each risk are examined, drawing attention to various crucial aspects that determine the risk's overall threat to the organization. One key factor is risk exposure, which assesses how exposed the organization is to potential threats. This involves evaluating how frequently the organization encounters situations where vulnerabilities could be exploited and the extent to which these vulnerabilities are accessible to potential threats.

The analysis requires a detailed evaluation of the number and criticality of vulnerabilities within the organization's systems and processes. Not all vulnerabilities pose the same level of threat; some may allow for minor disruptions, while others could lead to significant breaches or data loss. Understanding the criticality of each vulnerability, in relation to the organization's assets and objectives, helps prioritize risks and focus efforts where they are needed most.

Threats that could exploit these vulnerabilities are also a crucial component of the risk analysis. It's important to consider not just the existence of threats but also their capability, motivation, and the resources they might have at their disposal. Assessing how easy it would be for these threats to exploit vulnerabilities gives insight into the likelihood of a risk eventuating, which is vital for prioritizing risks effectively.

It is equally crucial considering the potential impact of each risk on the organization. This goes beyond the immediate consequences to include longer-term effects on reputation, financial stability, and compliance with regulations. The potential impact should be analyzed in both qualitative and quantitative terms, providing a complete view of how each risk could affect the organization's operations, objectives, and stakeholders. Impact can be understood in five dimensions: financial, operational, legal and regulatory, reputational, and environmental or safety. All of them can be quantified in monetary terms.

Financial impacts are often the most apparent, including direct losses from theft of assets or information, costs of incident response, and any necessary remediation efforts. However, financial ramifications can also arise indirectly, such as through lost revenue due to system downtime or increased insurance premiums following a breach.

Operational impacts reflect the effect on an organization's ability to function effectively. A cybersecurity incident can disrupt business processes, degrade service quality, or completely halt operations, leading to lost productivity and the cost of overtime work or outsourcing to address the issue.

Legal and regulatory impacts arise from noncompliance with data protection laws, breach notification requirements, and other regulations. Penalties can include fines, sanctions, and the costs associated with legal actions taken by affected parties. Additionally, organizations may face costs related to regulatory compliance improvements post-incident.

Reputational impacts can be particularly challenging to quantify but are no less significant. Damage to an organization's reputation can lead to lost business, difficulty in attracting talent, and strained relationships with partners and customers. Quantifying this impact often involves assessing the potential loss in market value or a decrease in customer trust and loyalty.

Environmental or safety impacts concern the potential harm to people or the environment resulting from a cybersecurity incident. This could involve physical harm due to compromised safety systems, environmental damage from industrial control system breaches, or risks to public health. While these impacts may be less common, they can have profound consequences and carry significant cleanup, legal, and reputational costs.

Quantifying these impacts in monetary terms involves estimating the potential costs for each dimension, considering direct and indirect expenses, potential fines, and long-term effects on the organization's market position and operational capacity. Aggregating impacts across these dimensions provides a clearer picture of the total potential cost of cybersecurity risks, helping guide more informed risk management and investment decisions. Remember to set the values not just the levels that information will help you to later perform a quantitative analysis of the risks you assessed.

Now that we've discussed how to assess the impact and likelihood of risks, let's walk through a practical example using the customer payment information scenario we previously identified. Throughout this example we'll be working with Figure 7.2 as it will help you understand how to apply the concepts of impact and likelihood to determine the inherent risks associated with this asset. We begin by revisiting the identified risks related to the customer payment information asset, such as data breaches, compliance failures, internal threats, and system failures. These risks were identified based on the vulnerabilities within the system and the threats that could exploit them. Now, it's time to analyze these risks by assessing their inherent impact and likelihood.

To start, we need to evaluate the impact of each identified risk without considering any existing controls. The goal here is to understand the worst-case scenario if the risk were to materialize. For instance, in the case of a data breach, the impact could be major. The exposure of customer payment information might lead to financial fraud, identity theft, and significant reputational damage. The financial cost could include fines, legal fees, and compensation for affected customers. Additionally, the organization might suffer long-term reputational damage, leading to a loss of customer trust and market share. Similarly, consider the impact of a compliance failure. Failing to comply with PCI standards or GDPR could result in hefty fines

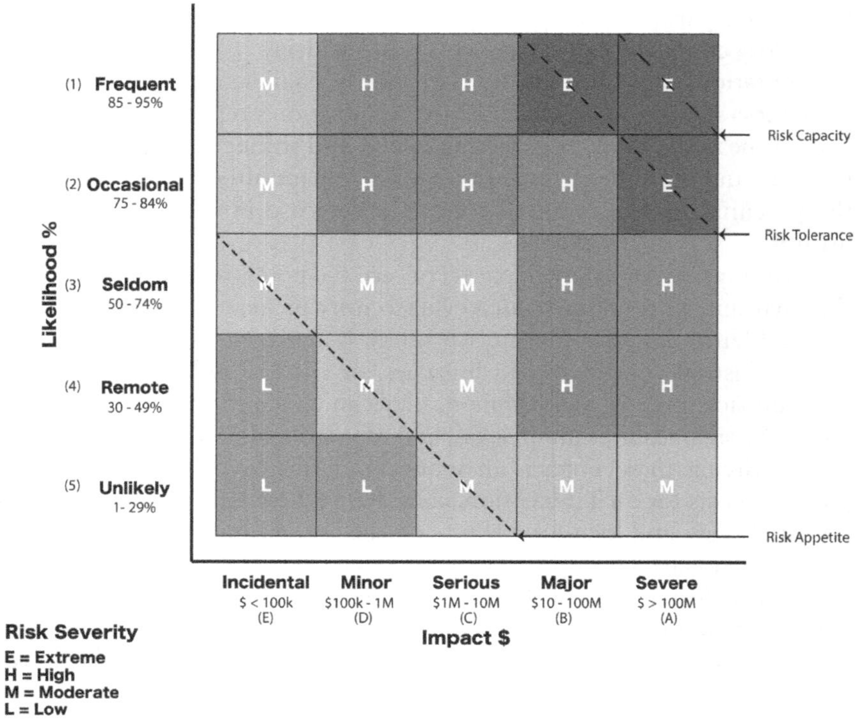

Figure 7.2 Typical risk heatmap chart.

and increased regulatory scrutiny. Beyond the immediate financial penalties, the organization might also face operational disruptions as it implements corrective measures. The reputational impact could be substantial, as non-compliance often signals to customers and partners that the organization is not taking its data protection responsibilities seriously.

Now, let's think about the impact of internal threats. An internal threat, such as an employee mishandling payment data, could lead to unauthorized access or accidental data leaks. The impact might range from minor operational disruptions to significant data breaches, depending on the nature of the mishandling. If the incident becomes public, it could also harm the organization's reputation and lead to legal consequences. Finally, consider the potential impact of a system failure. A failure in the payment processing system could lead to data loss, corruption of payment information, and interruptions in business operations. The financial impact might include lost revenue from downtime, the cost of system repairs, and the potential loss of customers who cannot complete transactions. The operational impact could also extend to delays in other business processes that rely on accurate and timely payment data.

To quantify the impact of a data breach, let's assign realistic estimates to the potential costs associated with the incident. First, you should ask what could go wrong and cost us money? For example, let's consider regulatory fines for noncompliance with PCI standards or GDPR. Depending on the scale of the breach, these fines could range from $500,000 to $5 million. Next, legal fees and compensation for affected customers could add another $2 million to $4 million, considering the costs of litigation, settlements, and customer reimbursements. Operational disruptions during the recovery period might lead to a loss of revenue, especially if the breach occurs during a critical business period. Let's estimate that downtime could result in a loss of $1 million in sales. Additionally, the cost of hiring external cybersecurity experts, implementing new security measures, and replacing compromised systems could add up to another $1.5 million. Opportunity costs, such as delayed projects or missed business opportunities due to diverted resources, might amount to $500,000. Reputational damage is harder to quantify but could lead to a loss in market share, translating to an estimated $3 million in lost revenue over the next year.

When we aggregate these values, the total estimated impact of the data breach could range from $6.25 million to $17.25 million. This figure represents the cumulative financial consequences of the breach, providing a better understanding of the potential severity of the risk. This quantified impact helps in prioritizing the risk and determining the level of investment needed in mitigation strategies to prevent or minimize such a loss. These estimated impact ranges can then be translated into the categories defined in our risk methodology, such as major, moderate, or low, depending on the thresholds set in our risk matrix. For instance, if our risk matrix defines a major impact as anything exceeding $10 million, then a data breach with a potential cost of $6.25 million to $17.25 million would clearly fall into the major category. This classification helps in aligning the quantified impacts with our organization's risk appetite and tolerance, ensuring that the assessment is consistent with the overall cyber risk management methodology. I understand these impacts are not exhaustive, and there may be many more potential consequences a data breach could have on an organization. However, we must remember that these numbers might not be even exact, but coming from the right people, they are a great starting point for our analysis. I hope this has helped you see the importance of assessing inherent impact.

A compliance failure can have wide-reaching effects across multiple areas. Let's start with regulatory fines. When an organization falls short of industry standards like GDPR, HIPAA, or PCI DSS, the penalties can vary significantly based on the severity and nature of the violation. In this scenario, fines could range from $1 million to $4 million, representing the potential financial consequences of not meeting regulatory expectations, particularly in industries where compliance is strictly enforced. Legal costs often accompany regulatory fines, especially if the compliance failure affects customers or partners. This could lead to lawsuits, with legal fees, settlements, and other associated expenses potentially adding another $1 million to $2.5 million. These costs cover attorney fees, court proceedings, and compensation to affected parties. Legal processes can be lengthy, meaning these expenses may continue to accumulate over time, further straining the organization's resources. Operational disruptions are also likely. Addressing a compliance issue usually involves halting certain business activities to correct the gaps, which may require reconfiguring systems, revising processes, or delivering urgent training to staff. These disruptions can lead to revenue losses, estimated between $500,000 and $1 million, as the organization reallocates resources and adjusts operations to meet compliance requirements. The extent of these disruptions depends on how efficiently the organization can manage the corrective actions and resume normal activities. Reputation is another area at risk. A compliance failure can erode customer trust and damage relationships with partners, potentially resulting in a loss of market share or future business opportunities. To mitigate the damage, organizations may need to invest in public relations efforts or customer retention strategies, with costs in this scenario estimated between $500,000 and $1.5 million. The longer-term effects on reputation can be challenging to quantify but should not be overlooked, as rebuilding trust often requires substantial time and effort. Finally, the financial impact extends beyond direct losses to include opportunity costs. As the organization diverts resources to address the compliance issue, projects may be delayed, and growth initiatives could stall. This diversion can result in missed business opportunities and lost sales, with potential costs ranging from $1 million to $2 million.

Combining these estimates, the total impact of a compliance failure could range from $4 million to $11 million. This range captures the diverse ways in which noncompliance can affect an organization, from immediate financial penalties to longer-term consequences like operational disruptions and reputational harm. Evaluating these factors helps in prioritizing compliance efforts and aligns risk management strategies with the organization's broader goals. However, keep in mind that during the workshops or surveys you're using to gather this information, participants of your assessment may be saying "moderate impact" or "frequent likelihood" where they may or may not be specific in the range they have in mind. If that's the case what you can do is take the values of the range you have, after few risk assessments people will get more confidence and refine the estimates. Also, this is a starting point, you'll refine as you further assess your risks.

Let's continue with the next risk in our example. For the insider threat risk, operationally, addressing this risk can strain resources, as the organization may need to conduct a thorough investigation, implement new security protocols, or even stop certain activities temporarily to contain the damage. The impact on operations: Let's imagine it could cost between $500,000 and $1 million, depending on how extensive the mitigation efforts are and how quickly the organization can return to normal operations. From a legal and compliance perspective, internal threats can lead to regulatory scrutiny or contractual penalties, especially if the incident exposes sensitive data covered by regulations like GDPR or industry-specific requirements. Legal fees, settlements, and compliance-related remediation could amount to between $1.75 million and $3 million, covering costs related to audits, fines, or legal actions that may follow the incident. Reputation is also at risk when an internal threat is involved, rebuilding that trust might involve public relations efforts and customer outreach, which could add up to another $500,000 to $1 million in costs, reflecting the need to repair relationships and restore confidence. Finally, financial impact of an internal threat such as employee misconduct or data theft can lead to opportunity costs. If sensitive information is leaked or stolen, the organization might lose competitive advantage or suffer delays in projects as resources are diverted to investigate and address the issue. The financial impact in terms of lost business opportunities and disrupted operations could range from $500,000 to $1.5 million. This estimate reflects the potential revenue losses or additional expenses incurred due to the internal disruption.

Combining these estimates, the overall potential impact of an internal threat could range from $3 million to $6 million. This range captures the diverse consequences that such incidents can have, from immediate financial losses and operational disruptions to longer-term effects on reputation and legal exposure. Understanding these potential costs helps prioritize preventive measures and shape a more resilient approach to managing internal risks.

Finally, for the last risks of our imaginary case, for system failure, operationally, a system failure can cause significant disruptions, especially if it affects critical business functions or essential services. When a key system goes down, it often halts business activities, resulting in downtime, reduced productivity, and delayed projects. The costs associated with restoring operations, repairing systems, and compensating for lost work hours could range from $1 million to $1.5 million. This estimate captures the expenses related to bringing systems back online and catching up on delayed tasks. From a legal and compliance perspective, system failures can also expose the organization to regulatory scrutiny or contractual penalties. For example, if the failure leads to a breach of service-level agreements (SLAs) with clients or causes data loss that triggers compliance requirements, the organization may face fines, legal fees, or the need to undergo additional audits. The costs related to legal and compliance challenges could range from $300,000 to $800,000, covering potential fines, settlements, and expenses for addressing regulatory requirements. Reputation can take a hit when a system failure disrupts services or prevents the organization from delivering on its commitments. Customers and partners may question the reliability of the company, leading to a loss of trust or even future business. Restoring confidence might involve public relations efforts, customer outreach, or offering compensatory services, with estimated costs between $200,000 and $500,000 to manage the reputational fallout and reassure stakeholders. Financially, the opportunity costs resulting from a system failure can add up quickly. Revenue losses may occur if sales are interrupted, transactions are delayed, or projects are postponed due to the outage. Additionally, resources allocated to fix the issue could have been used for other growth-focused initiatives. The financial impact from these missed business opportunities and diverted resources could be estimated at $500,000 to $1.2 million.

When we add these estimates together, the total potential impact of a system failure ranges from $2 million to $4 million. This range provides a comprehensive view of the various costs associated with system failures, highlighting the need for robust preventive measures and swift recovery strategies to minimize disruption and protect the organization's overall resilience.

The second part of the risk equation is likelihood. With a clear understanding of the potential impact, it's important to evaluate the likelihood of each risk occurring, again without considering the existing controls. For instance, the likelihood of a data breach could be high, given the attractiveness of payment information to cybercriminals and the commonality of attacks targeting financial data, especially if the system has known vulnerabilities and is exposed to the internet. For compliance failures, the likelihood depends on how well the organization's practices align with regulatory requirements. If there are significant gaps in data encryption or access controls, the likelihood of noncompliance is higher, particularly during an audit or if a breach occurs. The likelihood of internal threats materializing might vary depending on factors such as employee training, the strength of access controls, and the presence of monitoring systems. If these areas are weak, the likelihood of an insider incident might be moderate to high. As for system failures, the likelihood might depend on the age and complexity of the payment processing system, as well as the organization's maintenance and upgrade practices. If the system is outdated or poorly maintained, the likelihood of failure might be significant.

When assessing the likelihood of these risks materializing, we need to consider several contributing factors. For instance, with internal threats, the likelihood might be influenced by factors such as the frequency of employee errors, the level of access controls, and the presence of monitoring systems. If we know that similar incidents have occurred in the past within our organization, we might estimate a higher likelihood. For example, if the company has experienced two incidents of mishandling payment data in the past year, we might estimate the likelihood of another incident occurring within the next year as seldom to occasional. We could quantify this by assigning a likelihood value, such as a 50%–60% chance. For system failures, the likelihood could be influenced by the age and reliability of the technology in use, the regularity of maintenance, and the presence of redundancies. If our payment processing system is outdated and has failed twice in the past 12 months, we might assess the likelihood of another failure as high, perhaps in the range of 60%–80%. For cyberattacks that could cause a data breach, the likelihood might be assessed based on the current threat landscape, the industry's risk profile, and recent attack trends. If our organization operates in a sector frequently targeted by cybercriminals and has identified vulnerabilities in its defenses, we might assess the likelihood of a cyberattack as frequent, perhaps 80%–90%. Finally, for compliance failure, we can consider factors such as regulations applicable to our organization, jurisdictions where we operate, penalties for noncompliance, and so on. For this case we may imagine that for our scenario we'll assign a 70%–80% chance. So, we can summarize this information in Table 7.1 as follows.

Once we've assessed both impact and likelihood, we can determine the inherent risk level for each risk. For example, a data breach with major impact and frequent likelihood would result in an extreme inherent risk level. Similarly, compliance failures might be categorized as moderate inherent risk, internal threats as moderate inherent risk, and system failures as moderate inherent risk. As we can see in Table 7.2, this initial prioritization of inherent risks provides a clear understanding of which risks pose the most significant threats to the organization. Identifying these inherent risk levels gives us a foundation to move forward into the next phase, where we assess the effectiveness of the controls in place and evaluate the residual risk after considering those controls.

The inherent risk level is great because by assessing it, we can estimate the effectiveness of our controls. So, continuing with the risk analysis, another critical aspect is the safeguards or controls currently in place to mitigate these risks. Understanding the actual effectiveness and design of these safeguards is vital for a correct analysis; even the most comprehensive

Table 7.1 Inherent and Actual Risks in Ranges

Ranges	*Risk*	*Inherent Impact*	*Inherent Likelihood*	*Actual Impact*	*Actual Likelihood*
	Data Breach	$6.25–17.25 million	80%–90%	$4–8 million	30%–50%
	Compliance Failure	$4–11 million	70%–80%	$2–5 million	30%–40%
	Internal Threats	$3–6 million	50%–60%	$1.5–3 million	20%–30%
	System Failure	$2–4 million	60%–80%	$1–2 million	20%–30%

Table 7.2 Inherent Risks Summary

Average	*Risk*	*Inherent Impact*	*Inherent Impact*	*Inherent Likelihood*	*Inherent Likelihood*	*Inherent Risk*	*Risk Severity*
	Data Breach	$ 11,750,000	Major	85%	Frequent	$9,987,500	Extreme
	Compliance Failure	$7,500,000	Serious	75%	Seldom	$5,625,000	Moderate
	Internal Threats	$4,500,000	Serious	55%	Seldom	$2,475,000	Moderate
	System Failure	$3,000,000	Serious	70%	Seldom	$2,100,000	Moderate

security measures can fail if they are not correctly implemented or if they do not align with the specific risks they are meant to mitigate. Therefore, a complete assessment of existing safeguards' effectiveness is essential to understand how they reduce risk likelihood and impact.

Considering attack scenarios plays a crucial role in assessing how susceptible our organization is to potential cyber threats. Envisioning various attack scenarios, from initial penetration through lateral movements within the network and ultimately data exfiltration, organizations can evaluate the effectiveness of their cybersecurity measures across different stages of an attack. This approach helps to identify potential weaknesses in the security posture that could be exploited by attackers.

For example, imagine a scenario where an attacker gains access to your network through a phishing email. If your organization has strong email filters, multifactor authentication, and effective user training, the likelihood of the attack succeeding might be significantly reduced. However, if these controls are not fully implemented or if there are gaps, such as unpatched vulnerabilities in your systems, the risk of a successful breach increases. Assessing the controls in this scenario allows us to determine whether the inherent risk we identified earlier, such as the high likelihood and major impact of a data breach, has been effectively mitigated or if further action is required.

This evaluation of controls also involves assessing their resilience against evolving threats. Cyberattackers are constantly developing new methods to bypass existing defenses, so it's crucial to ensure that your controls are not only effective today but also adaptable to future threats. This continuous assessment process enables organizations to maintain a proactive security posture, where risks are regularly reevaluated in light of new intelligence feeds and emerging attack techniques, but we'll get deeper into that in Chapter 10.

For now, let's consider the assessment of controls implemented to prevent, detect, and respond to cyber incidents. This assessment is crucial for understanding how well your organization is prepared to handle potential threats. While the NIST Cybersecurity Framework (CSF) 2.0 provides high-level guidance by organizing cybersecurity activities into six core functions: Govern, Identify, Protect, Detect, Respond, and Recover, NIST 800-53r5 complements this by offering a detailed catalog of specific controls that can be implemented to achieve these objectives. This was further reviewed in Chapter 2, and if there are doubts, I strongly recommend you read that section again.

Starting with the Protect function, the NIST CSF guides organizations to focus on preventive controls, which form the first line of defense. These controls, such as firewalls, antivirus software, and secure coding practices, are designed to prevent attackers from gaining access to systems. NIST 800-53r5 provides a great set of controls under various families, such as access control (AC), system and communications protection (SC), and configuration management (CM), which support this preventive focus. The effectiveness of these controls directly impacts the likelihood of an attacker successfully initiating an attack. However, preventive measures alone are not enough.

Detection controls are equally essential because they enable the organization to identify ongoing attacks before they cause significant damage. NIST 800-53r5 offers controls related to security monitoring, continuous diagnostics, and vulnerability management under control families like system and information integrity (SI) and audit and accountability (AU). These controls include intrusion detection systems, security monitoring, and anomaly detection algorithms. The quicker an attack is detected, the less time the attacker has to move laterally within the network and access sensitive data.

Finally, in the Respond function, the NIST CSF emphasizes the need for effective incident response strategies. NIST 800-53r5 provides detailed controls within the incident response (IR) family, which includes guidelines for developing, implementing, and testing incident response plans. Response controls are the organization's ability to react to detected threats effectively. This includes disaster recovery procedures and the ability to isolate affected systems to prevent further spread of the attack. Assessing these controls involves understanding how quickly and effectively the organization can contain and mitigate an attack, minimizing its impact.

Leveraging the high-level structure of the NIST CSF in synchrony with the detailed controls offered by NIST 800-53r5, organizations can create a robust cybersecurity posture that not only addresses but also anticipates potential threats. This combined approach ensures that preventive, detective, and responsive measures are all in place and functioning effectively, ultimately reducing the overall risk to the organization.

Analyzing the organization's defenses across the entire kill chain of an attack, from penetration to exfiltration, risk analysis gains a more detailed understanding of potential attack scenarios. This approach not only identifies the most significant vulnerabilities and threats but also assesses the robustness of the organization's cyber defenses at each stage of a potential attack. This detailed evaluation guides strategic decisions on where to enhance cybersecurity measures from a very pragmatic standpoint, ensuring that resources are allocated to areas where they will have the most significant impact on reducing cyber risk.

Building on the attack scenarios and kill chain framework shown in Figure 7.3, that were developed during the information-gathering phase, we can now analyze where our controls are in place and how effective they are in mitigating the inherent risks we've identified. This involves mapping the existing controls to each phase of the attack chain and evaluating their efficiency based on historical data, industry statistics, and insights shared

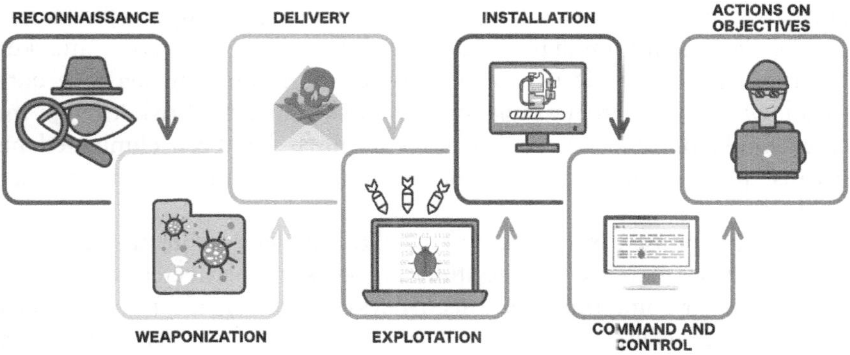

Figure 7.3 Lockheed Martin Kill Chain Framework.

by peers. By doing it, we can identify gaps in our defenses and areas where our controls may need strengthening or updating. This analysis is crucial because it allows us to understand not just where we are protected, but how well these protections align with the specific threats and vulnerabilities we face. Likewise, by incorporating real-world data and industry trends, we can ensure that our risk assessments are based in reality, reflecting the latest developments in the cybersecurity landscape.

Now that we've mapped out our controls and evaluated their efficiency against the identified inherent risks, it's time to assess the actual risk level. This step involves understanding how much the existing controls reduce the impact and likelihood of these risks. Essentially, we're moving from a theoretical understanding of potential threats to a more practical evaluation of how these threats are mitigated in the real world by our current security measures.

To begin, let's consider the effectiveness of the controls in place. For instance, if our preventive controls, such as firewalls and intrusion prevention systems, are robust and consistently updated, they may significantly reduce the likelihood of an attack successfully breaching the perimeter. This reduction in likelihood means that while the inherent risk might have been high, the actual risk, after accounting for these controls, is much lower. The effectiveness of these controls can often be quantified by examining past incidents and determining how frequently they've stopped or slowed down similar attacks. If we know that our firewalls have successfully blocked 90% of attempted breaches in the past year, we can confidently adjust the likelihood of that risk materializing.

Next, let's consider how our detection controls, such as intrusion detection systems and security monitoring, influence the actual risk level. These controls don't prevent attacks from occurring but instead focus on quickly identifying and responding to them. If our detection systems are efficient and can identify suspicious activity within minutes, the impact of an attack can be significantly mitigated. This rapid detection can prevent attackers from gaining deeper access to the network or exfiltrating sensitive data, thus lowering the potential impact of the risk. The actual risk level, in this case, would be reduced not because the threat has been eliminated but because its potential impact has been minimized by the controls we have in place.

Finally, response controls play a crucial role in determining the actual risk level. Even if an attacker successfully breaches the perimeter and remains undetected for some time, the effectiveness of the organization's response controls, such as incident response plans and disaster recovery procedures, can greatly reduce the overall impact. If these controls are well-practiced and can be deployed swiftly, the damage from an attack can be contained, reducing the long-term effects on the organization. For example, a well-executed incident response might reduce downtime from days to hours, thus limiting the operational and financial impact. The actual risk level, therefore, becomes a function of not just the inherent risk but also the efficiency and speed of the organization's response.

Now that we've evaluated the inherent risks, it's time to reassess those risks in light of the controls we have in place. The goal here is to determine the actual risk levels by considering how effectively our existing controls mitigate both the impact and likelihood of these risks. Starting with the data breach scenario, we previously identified a potential impact range of $6.25 million to $17.25 million, assuming no controls were in place. However, our organization has implemented several key controls, such as robust encryption protocols, regular security audits, and a well-maintained firewall system. These measures are designed to prevent unauthorized access and minimize the damage if a breach does occur. With these controls in place, the actual impact of a data breach might be significantly reduced. For instance, while fines and legal fees might still be a concern, the extent of reputational damage and financial loss could be less severe, perhaps lowering the impact to a range of $4 million to $8 million. Similarly, the likelihood of a breach occurring could be reduced from the inherent range of 80%–90% to something more moderate, such as 30%–50%, due to these preventive measures.

Next, let's consider the compliance failure scenario. Initially, the inherent impact of noncompliance with PCI standards or GDPR could result in severe financial penalties and operational disruptions, with an estimated impact of $4 million to $11 million. However, let's imagine our organization has implemented strong access controls, conducts regular compliance audits, and ensures continuous monitoring of data protection practices. These controls could significantly reduce the likelihood of noncompliance or at least demonstrate we're not negligent taking the risk level from an inherent range of 70%–80% down to an actual range of 30%–40%. As a result, the actual impact might also decrease, potentially ranging from $2 million to $5 million, as the chances of a significant breach or audit failure are mitigated by these controls.

For the internal threat example, where an employee mishandling payment data could lead to unauthorized access or accidental data leaks, we initially estimated an inherent impact of $3 million to $6 million with a likelihood of 50%–60%. With the implementation of employee training programs, strict access controls, and effective monitoring systems, the actual risk level is lowered. The impact might now be reduced to $1.5 million to $3 million, and the likelihood of such an incident occurring might drop to 20%–30%, reflecting the effectiveness of the controls in preventing or detecting misuse.

Finally, consider the system failure scenario. The inherent risk of a failure in the payment processing system, which could lead to data loss and operational disruptions, was estimated with an impact of $2 million to $4 million and a likelihood of 60%–80%. By implementing redundant systems, conducting regular updates, and maintaining proactive maintenance schedules, the actual likelihood of a critical failure could be reduced to 20%–30%. The impact, too, could be mitigated, perhaps lowering it to a range of $1 million to $2 million, due to the ability to quickly recover from a failure or prevent data loss altogether.

Our updated assessments of both impact and likelihood provide a clearer picture of the actual risks our organization faces, after considering the effectiveness of our controls. For example, in the data breach scenario, we previously estimated an inherent impact ranging from $6.25 million to $17.25 million with a likelihood of 80%–90%. However, after considering the implemented controls such as encryption protocols and security audits, the actual impact is reduced to a range of $4 million to $8 million, with the likelihood dropping to 30%–50%. Also, for compliance failure, where noncompliance with regulations like PCI standards or GDPR could result in severe penalties and operational disruptions, the inherent impact was estimated between $4 million to $11 million, with a likelihood of 70%–80%. With strong access controls, regular compliance audits, and continuous monitoring in place, the actual impact might now range between $2 million and $5 million, and the likelihood could decrease to 30%–40%. Similarly, for internal threats, where mishandling of payment data by employees could lead to unauthorized access, the inherent impact was estimated between $3 million and $6 million, with a likelihood of 50%–60%. With effective training and monitoring controls in place, the actual impact might now be between $1.5 million and $3 million, and the likelihood could decrease to 20%–30%. Lastly, for a system failure, where the inherent risk included lost revenue and repair costs, initially estimated between $2 million and $4 million with a likelihood of 60%–80%, the actual risk is now mitigated by redundancies and maintenance practices, reducing the impact to

$1 million to $2 million and the likelihood to 20%–30%. This reassessment of actual risks provides a more accurate understanding of where our organization stands, highlighting the effectiveness of our current controls while also indicating areas where further improvements may be necessary, which is with we'll work on.

With the actual risks now clearly assessed and summarized in Table 7.3, we can take this analysis a step further by evaluating the monetary value of our controls and their efficiency. Knowing the cost of implementing and maintaining these controls, along with how much they reduce the risk in financial terms, allows us to calculate the return on investment (ROI) for each control. This process helps us determine whether our controls are truly effective or if they are simply adding unnecessary expense.

For example, if a control costs $1 million annually but only reduces a potential risk by $500,000, its ROI might show that it's not as effective as expected. On the other hand, a control costing $200,000 but reducing a risk by $1 million demonstrates a strong ROI, highlighting its value in the risk management strategy. This evaluation ensures that controls are not more expensive than the risks they mitigate, aligning security investments with the organization's financial health and strategic goals. Let's imagine that for our examples, the data breach risk involves an annual cost of $1.5 million, covering controls like robust encryption protocols, regular security audits, and a well-maintained firewall system. For compliance failure, the annual cost is $750,000, which includes strong access controls, regular compliance audits, and continuous monitoring of data protection practices. Internal threats, such as employee mishandling of sensitive data, the controls, employee training programs, strict access controls, and effective monitoring systems, come with an annual cost of $220,000. Lastly, for system failure, the cost of $500,000 is associated with maintaining redundant systems, conducting regular updates, and ensuring proactive maintenance schedules. For your convenience, all control costs and its effectiveness are summarized in Table 7.4. Continuously assessing this balance allows for informed decisions on resource allocation, whether to enhance existing controls or explore more cost-effective solutions. While this might not be part of your first risk assessment, keeping it in mind for future iterations can help ensure that control effectiveness is clearly understood, especially when the organization has the necessary data in place.

All the information we've now assessed for our inherent risks, controls, and actual risks should be documented in our risk register. While this may initially serve as a draft, because these risks have to be characterized, reviewed, and calibrated with other stakeholders to ensure that our assessments are accurate, and we have consensus on them. This collaborative review process allows for adjustments and refinements based on different perspectives within the organization, helping to build a more robust and aligned understanding of our risk landscape. Here our risk register becomes a living

Table 7.3 Actual Risks Summary

Average	*Risk*	*Actual Impact*	*Actual Impact*	*Actual Likelihood*	*Actual Likelihood*	*Actual Risk*	*Risk Severity*
	Data Breach	$6,000,000	Serious	40%	Remote	$2,400,000	Moderate
	Compliance Failure	$3,500,000	Serious	35%	Remote	$1,225,000	Moderate
	Internal Threats	$2,250,000	Serious	25%	Unlikely	$562,500	Moderate
	System Failure	$1,500,000	Serious	25%	Unlikely	$375,000	Moderate

Table 7.4 Control Costs and Its Effectiveness

Controls	*Risk*	*Cost*	*Risk Reduction*	*Effectiveness*
	Data Breach	$1,500,000.00	$7,587,500.00	61%
	Compliance Failure	$750,000.00	$4,400,000.00	65%
	Internal Threats	$220,000.00	$1,912,500.00	68%
	System Failure	$500,000.00	$1,725,000.00	58%

document, evolving as we gather more information and insights throughout the risk management process.

Before moving into the next step, I have to remind you there's one final aspect of risk analysis that we will address later in the process: the evaluation of residual risks. Residual risks are the risks that remain after we have implemented our treatment plans, those strategies and controls designed to reduce or mitigate the risks we've identified. Once we have our treatment plans in place, we can return to our analysis to assess the effectiveness of these plans and understand the level of risk that will remain after their implementation. For now, let's move on to risk characterization.

RISK CHARACTERIZATION: AGGREGATION OF RISKS ABOVE THE RISK APPETITE

The final step in the risk assessment phase is risk characterization, where the information from identification and analysis comes together to form a detailed understanding of each risk. This step involves understanding the origin, potential triggers, and possible consequences of each risk in a way that resonates with your organization. This understanding will shape the decisions made in the risk treatment phase. Our cyber risk management methodology serves as the key guide for this process. Standardizing how risks are characterized ensures a consistent approach across the organization. This consistency is crucial for effective communication, allowing everyone from the IT team to the boardroom to speak the same language when discussing cyber risks. This unified approach supports clear discussions and helps align risk priorities with the organization's strategic objectives.

Risk characterization is crucial for aligning risk priorities with the organization's goals. Clearly defining the potential impact of each risk in terms that all stakeholders understand, we can prioritize those that pose the most significant threats to critical assets and objectives. This prioritization ensures that resources are allocated efficiently, focusing on risks that could derail the organization's strategic plans. A clear and consistent characterization of risks also fosters informed decision-making. Leadership can use this detailed understanding to make strategic decisions about risk treatment, whether to mitigate, transfer, accept, or avoid risks, based on a

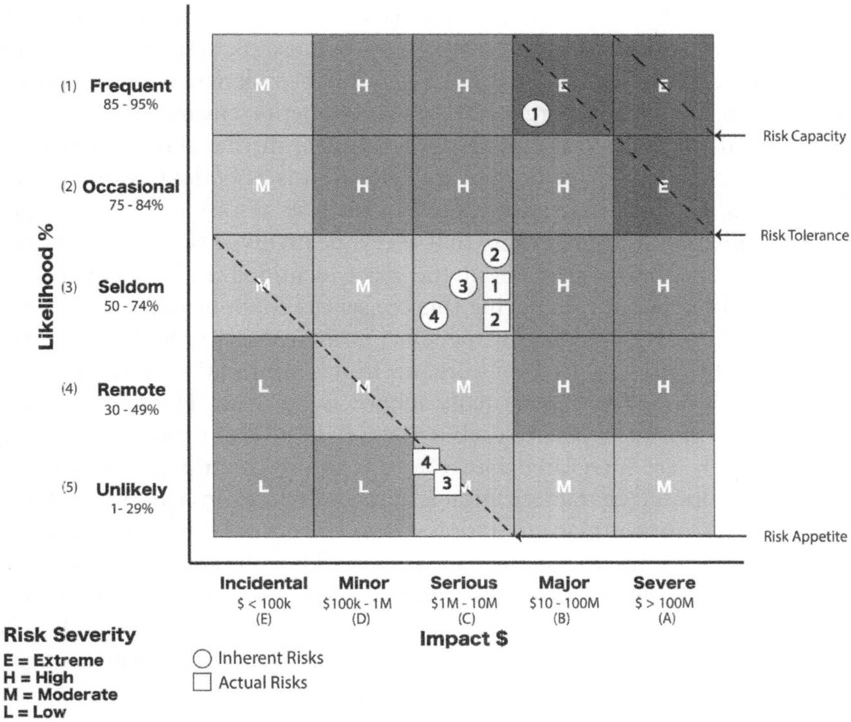

Figure 7.4 Risk Matrix with risk appetite, tolerance, and capacity levels.

good understanding of the potential consequences and the organization's capacity to manage those risks.

Once risks are characterized, as we can see in Figure 7.4, they are evaluated against the organization's risk appetite, the level of risk the organization is willing to accept in pursuit of its objectives. Risks that fall within the organization's risk appetite might be accepted and monitored, with the understanding that further mitigation could be unnecessary or unjustified in terms of cost. However, these risks must still be actively managed to align with the organization's willingness to take on certain levels of risk as part of its strategic pursuits. On the other hand, risks that exceed the organization's risk appetite require our attention. These risks signal where the potential impact is greater than what the organization believes is acceptable, requiring additional resources for mitigation, risk transfer strategies, or changes in business practices to avoid the risk altogether. Decisions in this phase are made with a clear understanding of the organization's risk tolerance, ensuring that actions are aligned with strategic objectives.

This stage in risk characterization emphasizes the importance of flexibility and adaptability. As the organization's objectives, external environment, and risk landscape evolve, so too must its assessment of what constitutes acceptable risk. Regular reviews of the risk management process, including reassessing the organization's risk appetite, ensure that the organization remains agile and responsive to changing threats and opportunities. After the actual risks have been characterized, it is essential to present these findings to the team that participated in the risk assessment process. This step is really important to ensure that everyone involved is on the same page and to generate consensus about the risks identified and their respective impact and likelihood. Achieving this consensus is about building a shared understanding of the risk landscape. Once consensus is reached, the assessed risks should be presented to your organization's information security forum, where decision-makers can formally acknowledge them. This step is crucial as it ensures that the risks are visible at the right levels in your organization and that they are integrated into the organization's strategic discussions. Once the proposed characterization is agreed upon, teams can proceed with developing treatment plans to address these risks, marking the beginning of the next phase in the risk management cycle. This phase of risk assessment is cyclical and iterative, requiring multiple rounds of review and adjustment until all identified risks have well-defined treatment plans. The cycle continues until there is a clear strategy in place for managing every significant risk, ensuring an actionable approach to risk management.

Risk characterization culminates in documenting these risks in a cyber risks report. Create a report with your risk assessment; it's always helpful to document your work, helping others understand it and leaving evidence of our understanding so we can go back and review from where we were coming from. Also keep in mind we're not in this world forever; this will help future CISOs and risk managers in your organization. Additionally, make sure you register all this information in the risk register, including their descriptions, sources, impacts, likelihoods, and chosen management strategies. As we discussed in Section I of the book, the risk register is a critical tool for maintaining structure and visibility in the risk management process, enabling continuous monitoring and updating as conditions change. Incorporating a characterized risk into the risk register involves detailing its nature, analysis findings, and treatment plans. This step ensures that all relevant information is captured in a standardized format, making it accessible to stakeholders across the organization. Assigning a risk owner, responsible for managing the risk, ensures accountability and active management. The risk register is a dynamic document, reflecting the ever-changing nature of the organization's risk landscape. As new risks are identified, they are added, and as existing risks evolve or are mitigated, their entries are updated. This continuous process ensures that the risk register remains an accurate and up-to-date tool for decision-makers, providing a clear snapshot of the organization's risk profile at any given time.

The risk register also facilitates prioritization and resource allocation, providing a clear view of all risks and enabling organizations to focus their efforts where they are needed most. This strategic approach to risk management ensures that resources are used efficiently to mitigate risks with the greatest potential impact on the organization's objectives. In essence, risk characterization lays the foundation for a proactive and strategic approach to cyber risk management. It transforms raw data about vulnerabilities and threats into actionable intelligence, enabling the organization to navigate the complex cyber threat landscape with confidence and strategic foresight. This not only enhances the organization's cybersecurity posture but also supports its overall mission and strategic objectives, making cyber risk management an integral part of organizational success and allowing leadership to make informed decisions on how these risks should be treated.

Now that we've assessed both the inherent risks and the effectiveness of our existing controls; it's time to characterize the actual risks our organization faces. As we can see in Figure 7.5, this step involves synthesizing all the information we've gathered to create a profile for each risk, which includes the residual impact and likelihood after considering our current controls, as well as their alignment with our organization's strategic objectives and risk appetite.

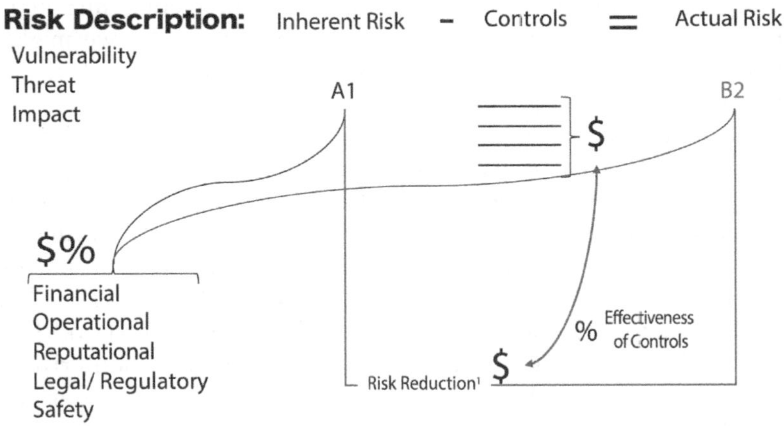

Risk Reduction1 = (Inherent likelihood x Inherent Impact) - (Actual likelihood x Actual Impact)
Effectiveness of Controls = (((Risk Reduction1) - (Control Cost)) / (Inherent likelihood x Inherent Impact)) x 100

Figure 7.5 Actual risk assessment.

Take, for instance, the data breach scenario. Initially, we identified the inherent impact of such a breach as potentially major, with costs ranging from $6.25 million to $17.25 million. After evaluating our controls, such as encryption, access management, and monitoring systems, we might determine that these controls effectively reduce the financial impact. However, while encryption might significantly lower the risk of unauthorized access, it does not entirely eliminate it. The likelihood of a breach might be reduced from an inherent 80%–90% to an actual likelihood of 30%–50%, and the impact might now range between $4 million and $8 million. Given this characterization, we must evaluate how this actual risk aligns with our organization's risk appetite. If our risk appetite is such that any impact above $6 million is considered unacceptable, this risk, with its upper potential impact of $8 million, would require further mitigation or risk transfer strategies. On the other hand, if this risk falls within our tolerance levels, we may decide to monitor it closely rather than take immediate additional action.

Now, consider the compliance failure scenario, where noncompliance with PCI standards or GDPR could result in severe financial penalties and operational disruptions. Initially, we assessed this risk with a significant financial impact between $4 million and $11 million, and a likelihood range of 70%–80%. After reviewing the controls, such as strong access controls, regular compliance audits, and continuous monitoring, we might find that these measures effectively reduce both the likelihood and impact of this risk. The likelihood might drop to 30%–40%, and the impact could be lowered to $2 million to $5 million. When we compare this with our organization's risk appetite, if an average financial impact up to $3.5 million is within our acceptable threshold, we might decide that this risk can be accepted and monitored, as the controls in place sufficiently align with our risk appetite.

Next, consider the internal threat of an employee mishandling payment data. Initially, we assessed this risk with a serious financial impact between $3 million and $6 million, and a likelihood range of 50%–60%. After reviewing the controls, such as strict access controls, regular training programs, and data handling protocols, we might find that these measures effectively reduce both the likelihood and impact of this risk. The likelihood might drop to 20%–30%, and the impact could be lowered to $1.5 million to $3 million. When we compare this with our organization's risk appetite, if an average financial impact up to $2.25 million is within our acceptable threshold, we might decide that this risk can be accepted and monitored, as the controls in place sufficiently align with our risk appetite.

Finally, think about the system failure scenario. Initially, we considered the impact of such a failure, including lost revenue, repair costs, and customer churn, with an inherent likelihood range of 60%–80%. After analyzing controls like redundancy systems, regular maintenance schedules, and failover procedures, the actual risk might be characterized by a reduced likelihood of 20%–30%, with the potential impact minimized to S1 million to $2 million. If our organization's risk appetite allows for disruptions up to $2 million with an unlikely (<29% annual chance), we might choose to accept it and continue monitoring.

Each of these actual risks is now characterized by a detailed profile that includes the adjusted impact and likelihood, providing a better view of the organization's current risk landscape. This characterization also involves assessing how each risk aligns with the organization's business objectives and risk appetite. We'll review further this into Chapter 8 but let's remember: Risks that fall within the acceptable range can be accepted and monitored, while those that exceed the organization's risk tolerance may require mitigation, transfer, or even avoidance strategies. This alignment ensures that our risk management efforts are closely tied to the organization's strategic goals and capacity for risk, enabling informed decision-making about where to focus resources and how to proceed with each identified risk.

As we reach the end of our journey through the steps of risk assessment, I want to take a moment to reflect on the ground we've covered together. We've walked through the process of identifying risks, analyzing their potential impact and likelihood, evaluating our existing controls, and, finally, characterizing those risks in a way that truly matters to our organization. It's been a deep dive into the realities of managing cyber risk, and if there's one thing, I hope you take away, it's that this process is not just about ticking boxes or following a formula. It's about understanding the differences of your unique environment and making informed, strategic decisions that align with your organization's goals and risk appetite.

Risk management is, at its core, a dynamic and continuous process. It's about staying ahead of the curve, anticipating what's around the corner, and being ready to adapt as new threats emerge and the business landscape evolves. The steps we've covered are not static; they are part of an ongoing cycle that requires vigilance, collaboration, and a willingness to revisit and revise your approach as needed. As you apply these concepts in your own organization, remember that risk management is as much an art as it is a science. It involves not only the technical skills we've discussed but also the human elements of judgment, communication, and collaboration.

Throughout this chapter, we've looked at risk assessment from every angle, but the real value lies in how you bring these ideas to life within your own organization. Whether you're refining your existing risk management practices or building a new framework from scratch, know that the effort you invest now will pay dividends in resilience, security, and peace of mind for your organization in the future. So, as you move forward, keep these lessons close. Use them as a guide, but also trust your instincts and gained experience. Here a checklist you can follow to remember key steps of the risk assessment phase:

1. **Organize gathered information:**
   a. Review and structure the data collected during the information-gathering phase, including network diagrams, data flow charts, and technology inventories.
   b. Map out where critical information resides, how it's processed, and the transmission paths to ensure a clear understanding of what needs protection.
   c. Organize information in a structured format, such as tables or flowcharts, to visualize the system and identify potential vulnerabilities.
2. **Identify critical assets:**
   a. Identify the "Crown Jewels" of your organization critical assets essential to operations and business continuity.
   b. Trace the paths of these assets within the system, documenting storage locations, transmission paths, and processing points.
   c. Evaluate how these assets interact with other systems and dependencies to uncover potential risk areas.
3. **List potential risks:**
   a. Create a complete inventory of potential risks, considering technical flaws, human errors, external threats, and environmental factors.
   b. Document each risk with a detailed description, including the associated asset, potential impact, likelihood, and vulnerability.
   c. Prioritize risks based on their potential to affect the organization's critical assets and business objectives.
4. **Engage stakeholders:**
   a. Involve a diverse group from across the organization, including IT, HR, Legal, Finance, and other relevant departments, to gather different perspectives on potential risks.
   b. Conduct brainstorming sessions, interviews, and surveys to uncover risks from all relevant angles, ensuring full coverage of the scope.
   c. Facilitate workshops or focus groups to validate and refine the list of identified risks, fostering collaboration and shared understanding.
5. **Assess inherent impact:**
   a. Evaluate the potential impact of each identified risk without considering existing controls, focusing on the worst-case scenarios.
   b. Quantify impacts in monetary terms across five dimensions: financial, operational, legal and regulatory, reputational, and environmental or safety.
   c. Use historical data, industry benchmarks, and expert judgment to estimate the potential financial consequences of each risk.

6. **Assess inherent likelihood:**
    a. Analyze the likelihood of each risk occurring by considering the threat landscape, historical data, exposure levels, and the capabilities of potential attackers.
    b. Assign likelihood values to each risk, helping prioritize them based on their potential to materialize and cause harm.
    c. Consider factors such as system vulnerabilities, external threat actors, and environmental conditions that could influence the likelihood of risk occurrence.
7. **Determine inherent risk levels:**
    a. Combine the assessments of both impact and likelihood to determine the inherent risk levels for each identified risk.
    b. Rank risks based on their inherent risk levels, focusing on those that pose the greatest threat to the organization.
    c. Document the inherent risk levels in a clear and consistent manner, using a risk matrix or similar tool for visualization.
8. **Evaluate control effectiveness:**
    a. Assess the effectiveness of existing controls, including preventive, detective, and responsive measures, in reducing the impact and likelihood of identified risks.
    b. Evaluate the design and implementation of these controls to ensure they align with the specific risks they are meant to mitigate.
    c. Identify gaps or weaknesses in controls that may require enhancement or additional measures to address evolving threats.
9. **Determine actual risk levels:**
    a. Reassess the risks by considering the effectiveness of the controls in place, determining the actual impact and likelihood after mitigation.
    b. Calculate the actual risk levels, which reflect the organization's true risk exposure after accounting for existing controls.
    c. Compare the actual risk levels to the organization's risk appetite to determine if further action is needed or if the risks are acceptable.
10. **Characterize risks:**
    a. Synthesize the information from identification, analysis, and control evaluation to create a detailed profile for each risk, including residual impact and likelihood.
    b. Align the characterized risks with the organization's strategic objectives and risk appetite, determining which risks can be accepted and which require further treatment.
    c. Present the characterized risks to stakeholders and decision-makers, ensuring consensus and alignment with the organization's risk management strategy.
11. **Document risk assessment and update the risk register:**

a. Create a report with your risk assessment.
b. Record all assessed risks in the risk register, including detailed descriptions, sources, impacts, likelihoods, and chosen management strategies.
c. Regularly update the risk register to reflect changes in the risk landscape, control effectiveness, and organizational priorities.
d. Ensure the risk register is accessible to relevant stakeholders, providing a clear and up-to-date view of the organization's risk profile.

12. **Review and calibrate with stakeholders:**
    a. Present the actual risks and their characterization to the team involved in the risk assessment process to ensure consensus and accuracy.
    b. Review and calibrate assessments with relevant decision-makers, such as the Information Security Forum, before proceeding to develop risk treatment plans.
    c. Engage in iterative reviews to refine the risk assessment, ensuring alignment with the organization's evolving risk appetite and strategic goals.
13. **Plan for residual risk analysis:**
    a. Prepare to revisit the risk analysis after developing and implementing treatment plans to assess residual risks and ensure they align with the organization's risk tolerance.
    b. Monitor the effectiveness of treatment plans over time, adjusting strategies as necessary to manage residual risks effectively.
    c. Document residual risks in the risk register and ensure they are actively managed as part of the ongoing risk management process.

Let's continue to Chapter 8 and develop treatment plans strategies for our assessed risks.

NOTES

1 Martin, L. (2024). Cyber kill chain [THE-CYBER-KILL-CHAIN-body.png.pc-adaptive.1280.medium]. Lockheed Martin. www.lockheedmartin.com/en-us/capabilities/cyber/cyber-kill-chain.html
2 Recommended book: *The Wisdom of Crowds* by James Surowiekie.

Chapter 8

Risk treatment strategies

RISK TREATMENT PLANNING

Strength lies in our ability to anticipate and act, turning potential risks into opportunities for growth and resilience. "The best way to predict the future is to create it." These words from Peter Drucker encapsulate the proactive nature of risk treatment planning. Now that we know our risks and their actual risk levels, it's time to act. This phase is inherently proactive because if we're dealing with risks that have already materialized, we're talking about incidents, which require immediate response which means we're reacting. But with the risks we've just discovered and assessed, we have the opportunity to take a proactive approach that, ideally, will prevent these risks from ever materializing. This is the moment where we take control of our organization's destiny, moving beyond merely identifying risks to actively shaping how we will address them. In the space of cybersecurity, it's not enough to simply understand the threats that loom over us. The real power lies in the strategic decisions we make to manage these risks effectively.

As we enter this phase of risk management, our focus starts to shift from analysis to action. This is where we determine how to handle the risks that exceed our organization's risk appetite, ensuring that our responses align with our overall business objectives. Whether it's avoiding, mitigating, transferring, or accepting these risks, the decisions we make here will have an important impact on our organization's security posture. In this chapter, we'll explore how to identify, design, and implement risk treatment strategies. We'll transform the knowledge we've gained into concrete actions that protect our assets, operations, and, ultimately, our future.

When planning how to treat risks, we're talking about what response we'll recommend to the risks we've assessed. Each treatment option comes with its own set of potential new risks, so it's important to choose a strategy that introduces fewer or more manageable risks than the ones you're addressing. You have different options at your disposal, each leading to a different way of handling risks. Here are the key options in the order I always recommend you follow.

DOI: 10.1201/9781003546207-11

Avoid the risk: This option involves eliminating the source of the risk entirely. Sometimes, the best choice is to sidestep the risk altogether, which might mean changing plans to prevent the risk from impacting your organization. For instance, if a particular business initiative carries too much uncertainty, you might choose not to pursue it. Or, if you have an obsolete system that's introducing significant risks, replacing it with a newer system could eliminate those old risks, though it will bring new ones associated with the replacement. However, avoiding a risk isn't always possible or even desirable, especially if the potential benefits outweigh the risks.

Mitigate the risk: While avoiding a risk entirely is often impossible, you can reduce its impact or likelihood through mitigation strategies. This is typically the option we focus on because it allows us to manage risks without halting business operations. Mitigation involves implementing safeguards or adjusting existing controls to lessen potential harm. For instance, you might strengthen access controls, enhance monitoring systems, or improve incident response protocols.

In practice, this means working closely with Security Architects who design security solutions tailored to your organization's specific needs. These solutions must be carefully integrated into the existing environment and aligned with the overall Enterprise Architecture to ensure they function effectively within your unique context. The goal is to create a layered defense that reduces the chances of a risk materializing and minimizes its impact if it does. Please keep in mind that simply implementing security tools doesn't necessarily mitigate the risk. A correct implementation that considers people, processes, and how the technology will be supported, configured, and architected for your environment is key. It's about balancing security with usability, ensuring that protective measures enhance rather than disrupt business operations while effectively addressing the identified risks.

Transfer the risk: In some cases, when a mitigation strategy isn't enough to bring the risk level within your organization's risk appetite, you can transfer the remaining risk to someone else. This typically involves using insurance or outsourcing, with the right security clauses in place within the contracts. While this approach doesn't eliminate the risk, it does shift the responsibility for managing it and responding to potential impacts. For example, you might purchase insurance to cover potential financial losses or outsource a high-risk operation to a third party that's better equipped to handle it. The key here is to ensure that the terms of the transfer are clear and that the third party is fully capable of managing the risk in a way that aligns with your organization's standards and expectations.

Accept the risk: When there's still risk above your organization's risk appetite that couldn't be addressed through avoidance, mitigation, or transfer, it might be necessary to formally accept it. Sometimes, the cost of avoiding, mitigating, or transferring a risk is higher than simply accepting it. In these cases, you may decide to acknowledge the risk and prepare to deal with it if it materializes. This is a calculated decision, where you understand the potential impact but determine that it's manageable or worth the potential reward.

It's important to keep in mind that, according to your risk methodology, the authority to accept risks typically resides with specific roles or organizational levels. Not everyone should have the power to accept risks. Additionally, risk acceptances should be reassessed periodically, at least annually, to determine if circumstances have changed and whether new actions can be taken to address the risk. Accepted risks must be actively monitored because the threat landscape can shift at any time, potentially altering the nature of the risk. What was once an acceptable risk might no longer be the same, and it's crucial to stay vigilant and responsive to these changes.

In practice, a combination of these strategies is often used to manage risks effectively. The choice of how to treat each risk depends on its specific nature, the potential impact on the organization, and the resources available for managing it. The focus of this analysis was on how effectively the proposed avoidance, mitigation, and transference strategies align the identified actual risks with the organization's risk appetite. We need to recognize that every change in our environment introduces its own set of risks; the goal is to ensure that these new risks are lower than the ones we're currently addressing. This analysis also involved an examination of the remaining threats and vulnerabilities, alongside the potential impacts, to determine the level of risk the organization is willing to accept or needs to further mitigate. This approach reflects my view of risk management as a spiral rather than a cycle, as the intention is to move toward improvement. When we revisit the process, we should find ourselves in a stronger position than during the previous assessment.

It is then that the assessment of residual risk serves several key purposes. First, it provides a clear picture of the expected risk posture after implementing mitigation plans, allowing decision-makers to evaluate the balance between cost, effort, and risk reduction. Second, it helps determine whether additional risk treatment options are needed to reduce the risk to an acceptable level. Assessing residual risk enables cyber risk management professionals to evaluate the effectiveness and cost-efficiency of risk treatment plans, ensuring the right balance between reducing risk and allocating resources. This process prioritizes risk treatment actions based on their impact on the organization's risk profile, guiding strategic decisions on risk acceptance, further mitigation, or risk transfer strategies.

If, after evaluating the mitigation strategies, the risk level remains above your organization's risk appetite, we must explore risk transfer options. This could involve negotiating contracts with vendors that include liability clauses for security breaches or purchasing cyber insurance to cover potential losses from a data breach. It's crucial to understand that what you're transferring is the residual risk; as we said, it is the risk that remains after we've implemented our mitigation efforts. However, not all risks can be fully transferred. There may be scenarios where the cost of insurance is prohibitively high or where contracts can't fully indemnify your organization against all potential consequences of a risk. In such cases, if the residual risk cannot be entirely offloaded, a formal risk acceptance process is needed. This means your organization decides to consciously and formally accept the remaining risk, acknowledging the potential consequences but determining that the benefits of continuing the operation outweigh the risks. Let's explore an example to see how the risk treatment process develops in practice, from the initial assessment all the way through to acceptance if necessary.

EXPLORING RISK TREATMENT OPTIONS

We all know that the cyber threat landscape evolves all the time, challenging us constantly, and maintaining consistency and constancy is difficult. That's why mastering the security basics is so important. These foundational controls are the no-brainers of your security program, providing the essential support needed to manage the risks your organization faces effectively. Without a strong foundation, risks can quickly escalate. However, when these basics are firmly in place, they do more than just protect your assets; they enable your organization to pursue its business objectives with greater confidence and agility.

At the core of any robust cybersecurity strategy are a set of core controls that are the basics of your security framework. These include: Technology and information inventories, identity and access control, vulnerability and patch management, network security, monitoring and detection, incident response and recovery, physical security, endpoint protection, application protection, and awareness and training. What holds everything together? Risk management, ensuring that we understand our issues, prioritize them correctly, and take action to improve.

Understanding these basics as a cohesive group is key to building a security program that truly acts as a business enabler. Technology and information inventories ensure you know what assets you have and where they're located, which is fundamental for protecting them. Identity and access control, guided by the authentication, authorization and audit (AAA) framework, ensures that only authorized individuals have access to your systems and data. Vulnerability and patch management keeps your systems up to date and protected against known threats. Network security goes beyond segregation, also encompassing encryption and other measures to protect data flow, limiting the spread of potential breaches. Monitoring and detection provide the real-time insights needed to stay vigilant against emerging threats. Incident response and recovery ensure that when incidents do occur, your organization can recover quickly, and physical security keeps your locations, data centers, premises, and people safe. Endpoint protection safeguards individual devices from threats, while application protection secures the software your organization relies on, reducing the risk of vulnerabilities being exploited. Finally, awareness and training program equips your team with the knowledge and skills necessary to do their jobs correctly, use tools to their full potential, and recognize and respond to security challenges, fostering a culture of security across the organization.

With strong basic controls, your organization is better positioned to adapt to new opportunities and challenges without compromising security. This proactive approach to cybersecurity allows you to move at the speed of business, turning security from a potential obstacle into a competitive advantage. With this solid foundation in place, we can now dive deeper into each of these core fundamental controls.

Let's begin with **technology and information inventories**. Building a strong cybersecurity foundation starts with knowing exactly what you have. That's where technology and information inventories are our starting point. These inventories are truly critical for understanding and managing your organization's assets, providing a clear picture of the hardware, software, and information that make up your environment. Without this knowledge, it's impossible to protect your assets effectively, and gaps in your security could go unnoticed.

First, let's talk about Technology Inventories. This involves cataloging all the hardware and software within your organization. It's not just about listing what devices and applications you have; it's about knowing their locations, purposes, and how they fit into the bigger picture. Whether it's servers, workstations, mobile devices, or the specific software versions running on them, having a detailed inventory allows you to manage your technology life cycle effectively. This includes identifying and addressing potential obsolescence, outdated hardware and software can become significant security risks if they're no longer supported by vendors with updates and patches. Sometimes, dealing with obsolescence causes major headaches. The fear of touching these aging systems can be so great that we freeze, worried that we might break something critical to the organization, right? And with so much on our plates, these old projects are frequently pushed off, again and again, until that inevitable bad day arrives, and everyone asks, "Why didn't we handle this before?"

A well-maintained technology inventory also includes complete documentation of your environment. This means keeping up-to-date network diagrams, data flow diagrams, and detailed records of how your systems are configured. Network diagrams show how devices and systems are interconnected, highlighting potential points of vulnerability. Data flow diagrams illustrate how information moves through your organization, helping you understand where sensitive data is stored, processed, and transmitted. This documentation is not static; it needs to be regularly updated to reflect any changes in your environment, ensuring that your security measures are always aligned with the current state of your network and data flows.

Software versions have a key role in your technology inventory. Knowing exactly which versions of software are in use across your organization allows you to manage updates and patches more effectively. Remember the SolarWinds security hack back in 2020? The affected versions were 2019.4 through 2020.2.1 HF1. Why is it important to know the versions we have? Because without this knowledge, we might invest significant effort investigating potential threats that don't even affect our environment, or even worse, we might overlook a critical vulnerability simply because no alert was triggered, not realizing that we're actually running an impacted version. Outdated software can be a significant vulnerability, as older versions may have known security flaws that attackers can exploit. Regularly reviewing and updating your software inventory helps you stay ahead of potential threats and ensures that all systems are running the most secure versions available that our environment supports. If your environment doesn't support more secure versions, then you're falling behind. The concept of obsolescence ties directly into this. As technology ages, it eventually reaches a point where it can no longer be supported or updated. This can happen with both hardware and software, creating security gaps that need to be addressed.

In addition to traditional on-premises assets, data centers and cloud computing must also be part of your technology inventory. Data centers house your organization's critical infrastructure, and understanding what's stored where, and how it's protected, is vital. With the increasing reliance on cloud services, it's equally important to include cloud-based assets in your inventory. This includes understanding the cloud providers you use, the services they offer, and the data that's being stored or processed in the cloud. Just because your data is in the cloud doesn't mean it's out of sight or out of mind; it is still your responsibility to ensure it is secure.

Information inventories are equally important. This involves cataloging the types of data your organization collects, where it's stored, and how it's used. Sensitive information, such as personal data, financial records, or intellectual property, needs to be identified and protected. Understanding what information is held and where it's located ensures that the right security measures are in place. This inventory also helps with compliance to data protection regulations and reduces the risk of data breaches.

The second security basic is **identity and access control**. Understanding who has access to your systems and what they can do is fundamental to any cybersecurity strategy. This is where identity and access control comes in, providing the mechanisms that determine who can enter your environment and what actions they can perform once inside. Without strong identity and access control measures, your organization is vulnerable to unauthorized access, potentially leading to data breaches, insider threats, and other security incidents.

The AAA framework has been a fundamental part of network security for decades, originally developed to manage access control in telecommunications and networked systems. Its origins trace back to the early days of computer networks, when the need to secure access grew as systems became more interconnected. As networks evolved, the framework was adopted and expanded by various industries, becoming a standard approach for managing user access and maintaining secure environments. The AAA framework's enduring relevance is due to its flexibility and effectiveness in addressing the core needs of security: verifying identities, controlling access, and keeping detailed records of user activities. Today, it remains a key component of cybersecurity strategies, helping organizations balance security needs with operational efficiency.

Authentication is the first one of the AAA framework; it is about ensuring that users are who they claim to be before granting access to your resources. This step is basic for establishing trust in each individual's identity. Traditionally, the electronic authentication model has been used, which relies on three types of verification factors: something the user knows (like a password), something the user has (like a security token), or something the user is (like a biometric trait). These factors form the basis of how users prove their identity when accessing systems.

As technology has evolved, so have authentication approaches. One of the most effective methods today is multi-factor authentication (MFA), which requires users to provide two or more types of the previous verification factors. For example, a user might need to enter a password (something they know) and then confirm their identity using a code sent to their mobile device (something they have). This layered approach significantly increases security by making it much more difficult for unauthorized users to gain access, and these days is a must to have it implemented everywhere.

As technology has evolved, so have authentication approaches. While MFA remains one of the most effective methods today, requiring users to provide two or more types of verification factors, the next evolution in authentication seeks to simplify the user experience while maintaining security. Emerging technologies have introduced passwordless authentication, which eliminates the need for traditional passwords by using alternatives such as biometrics (like fingerprints or facial recognition), hardware tokens, or one-time codes. While this approach enhances security by reducing reliance on passwords and simplifies the user experience, it's important to understand that a password, in some form, still exists. For example, when you enroll in a biometric authentication system, your fingerprint is scanned, creating an image that is measured and converted into a sequence of ones and zeros using an encoding standard. This digital representation becomes the template of your fingerprint, according to the standard used for its creation. Later, when you use your fingerprint to authenticate, the system compares the new scan to the stored template. Each time your fingerprint is scanned, it is translated into a unique sequence of ones and zeros because each time the image captured is a little bit different but effectively serves as your password. Now, what if the template matches 100% with the fingerprint you're currently scanning? At first glance, this might seem like a perfect match is the best possible answer, proving your identity. However, this could actually indicate a security breach, suggesting that someone has stolen your fingerprint template and is using it to authenticate as you. This example shows the fact that even in passwordless systems, there is always something functioning as a password. It's important to understand that true passwordless authentication doesn't mean there's no password, but it just means the password takes a different form.

While technologies like passwordless authentication offer new ways to secure access, they highlight the ongoing need for vigilant monitoring and management of user behavior within systems. As authentication methods evolve, so must our strategies for detecting and responding to potential threats. This is where user access behavior management becomes relevant. Even with these advanced authentication methods, ensuring the security of access requires more than just the right credentials. How users behave once inside the system is just as critical. User access behavior management focuses on monitoring and analyzing how users interact with systems to identify patterns that could indicate potential security risks. This involves tracking user activities, such as logins, file access, and system usage, to detect anomalies that deviate from normal behavior. For instance, if a user suddenly starts accessing sensitive data they've never interacted with before, or if there are unusual login attempts from different locations within a short time frame, these could be red flags signaling a potential breach or misuse of privileges. When you implement user access behavior management, you enhance your security posture by more effectively identifying and responding to insider threats or compromised accounts. This proactive approach prevents unauthorized access and reduces the likelihood of data breaches by flagging suspicious activities in real time, allowing your security teams to take immediate action.

In addition to monitoring user behavior, implementing structural safeguards within your organization is essential to prevent misuse of access. This is where the principle of separation of duties (SoD) becomes key. SoD is a fundamental principle in identity and access control that ensures no single individual has control over all critical aspects of a process. This principle is designed to reduce the risk of fraud, errors, and unauthorized actions by distributing responsibilities among multiple users. For instance, in a financial system, the person approving a transaction should not also be the one processing it. Separating these duties minimizes conflicts of interest and lowers the risk of misuse of power. To effectively implement SoD, organizations must carefully define roles and responsibilities, ensuring that conflicting duties are assigned to different individuals. This requires a complete analysis of business processes to identify potential conflicts and adjust access controls accordingly. Regular audits and reviews are also essential to ensure that SoD is maintained over time and that any changes in roles or responsibilities are properly managed to avoid introducing new risks.

Another important aspect of maintaining secure access is transparency with your users about their roles and the monitoring in place. This can be achieved through clear notifications of system use. Notification of system use is a practice that involves informing users about their access rights, responsibilities, and any monitoring that may be in place. This typically includes providing users with a notification or acknowledgment when they log into a system, reminding them that their activities may be monitored and that unauthorized use is prohibited.

This practice serves multiple purposes: it reinforces the organization's security policies, deters unauthorized behavior by reminding users of the consequences, and provides a legal basis for monitoring activities. Notifications of system use are especially important in regulated industries, where compliance with data protection and privacy laws is critical. When it comes to controlling access within an organization, several models can be employed, each with its own strengths and suitable use cases. Here's an overview of the four primary types.

In a discretionary access control (DAC) model, the owner of an asset, such as a file or database, has the authority to decide who can access it and what permissions they have. Permissions are typically granted by the asset owner based on their discretion, which is why it's called 'discretionary.' While DAC offers flexibility and ease of use, it can also introduce security risks. Users may inadvertently grant access to unauthorized individuals or fail to manage permissions effectively over time, leading to potential security gaps.

Mandatory access control (MAC), on the other hand, is a more rigid model where access to resources is determined by a central authority based on predefined security policies. In a MAC system, users are assigned security clearances, and assets are classified with security labels. Access is granted or denied based on these classifications, leaving no discretion to individual users. This model is often used in environments where security is critical, such as military or government organizations, because it provides strict control over access and ensures that users cannot override established security policies.

Role-based access control (RBAC) is another widely used model, where access decisions are based on the roles that users have within an organization. Instead of assigning permissions to individual users, permissions are assigned to specific roles. Users are then granted access based on the roles they hold. This approach simplifies management by grouping permissions under roles, ensuring that users receive appropriate access based on their job functions. RBAC is particularly effective in organizations with well-defined roles and responsibilities, as it aligns access with business processes and reduces the risk of unauthorized access.

Attribute-based access control (ABAC) takes things a step further by making access decisions based on a combination of attributes. These attributes can include user characteristics, such as job title or department, as well as environmental factors, like time of day or location. ABAC provides a highly dynamic and flexible approach to access control, allowing organizations to create fine-grained policies that adapt to different situations. For example, a user might be allowed to access certain data during business hours but not after-hours or from an unauthorized location. ABAC is powerful for environments where access needs to be closely aligned with a variety of contextual factors.

While these access control models help structure who gets in and what they can do, managing how authentication is carried out across these models is equally important. Authentication management is the process of issuing and revoking, overseeing and maintaining these various authentication methods to ensure they are functioning correctly and securely. This is particularly important for privileged accounts, which have elevated access rights and are often targeted by attackers. Proper management of these accounts includes enforcing strict controls such as requiring MFA, regularly updating credentials, and closely monitoring account activity to prevent misuse or unauthorized access. A privileged access management (PAM) solution can help to ease the workload that comes with it.

Lastly, to ensure that all these layers work together seamlessly, a strong Identity management system is critical. Identity management ties all these elements together by ensuring that each user's identity is accurately verified and that they have the appropriate level of access based on their role within the organization. Identity management systems automate and enforce policies, ensuring that access rights are aligned with job functions and that security risks are minimized.

Authorization comes next, determining what authenticated users can do within your environment. It's about setting boundaries, defining who has access to what data, which systems they can interact with, and what actions they can perform. Authorization ensures that users have the minimum level of access necessary to perform their roles, reducing the risk of accidental or intentional misuse of resources.

A key concept in authorization is the need-to-know principle. This principle asserts that access to information should be granted only if it is necessary for the user to perform their specific job tasks. Even within the same department, employees might have access to different sets of data based on their particular responsibilities. For example, within a financial department, one employee may need access to payroll information, while another may only need access to budget reports. The need-to-know principle ensures that sensitive information is protected by restricting access to only those individuals who truly need it. This not only strengthens security but also helps to maintain the confidentiality and integrity of sensitive data.

Closely related to the need-to-know principle is the least privilege principle. This principle dictates that users should be granted the minimum level of access necessary to perform their job functions. For example, an employee who needs to view certain data should not have permission to edit or delete it unless their role specifically requires it. Limiting access in this way reduces the potential damage that could occur if a user's credentials are compromised. It also lowers the risk of accidental changes or access to information outside the user's scope of responsibility.

Together, the least privilege and need-to-know principles form the foundation of an effective authorization strategy. Applying these principles ensures that users have only the access needed to do their jobs, no more, no less. This careful control of access rights protects the organization from internal threats and human error, while also supporting compliance with regulatory requirements that mandate strict access controls. Implementing these principles in your authorization processes is a critical step in creating a secure, well-managed environment where risks are minimized, and resources are safeguarded.

Auditing is the final component of the AAA framework, and as authorization and authentication, it has a key role in maintaining the integrity and security of your systems. Auditing involves systematically reviewing and recording user activities to ensure that all actions within your environment are authorized and comply with established security policies. This process helps in detecting potential security breaches and also provides a trail of evidence for compliance audits and forensic investigations. Here is where we close the loop and validate everything works as expected.

There are several types of auditing that can be implemented, each serving a specific purpose in maintaining security. User activity auditing tracks the actions of individual users, recording details such as files accessed, modifications made, and resources used. System auditing focuses on the overall health and security of the system, monitoring for unusual behavior or configuration changes that could indicate a security issue. Access auditing specifically examines who accessed what, when, and from where, ensuring that access controls are functioning as intended and that unauthorized access attempts are flagged.

In addition to these types of auditing, implementing User access control restrictions can further enhance security. For example, unsuccessful sign-ins should be monitored closely, as repeated failed attempts can indicate a brute-force attack or unauthorized access attempts. Last sign-in notifications can alert users to any suspicious account activity, such as logins from unknown devices or locations, giving them the opportunity to report potential security incidents. Time-based access is another effective control, where user access is restricted to specific time frames, reducing the risk of unauthorized access during off-hours. Similarly, location-based access restricts access to certain systems or data based on the user's physical location. For instance, access could be limited to users within a specific office or geographic region, preventing logins from potentially risky or unverified locations.

Integrating these auditing practices and access control restrictions, your organization can maintain a high level of security, ensuring that only authorized users perform actions within your environment. Regularly reviewing audit logs and access controls helps to identify and respond to potential security threats promptly, while also providing the documentation needed to demonstrate compliance with regulatory requirements. Auditing is about monitoring and ensuring that your systems remain secure and that any deviations from expected behavior are quickly identified and addressed. This final 'A' in the AAA framework is critical for maintaining the ongoing security and integrity of your organization's digital assets.

The AAA framework has remained current over the years helping organizations to develop their identity and access control strategy. With it you will create a layered approach that protects your systems but also empowers your organization to operate securely and efficiently. These controls are not just technical implementations; they're strategic tools that help align security with your business objectives.

The third cybersecurity basic is **vulnerability and patch management**. Staying ahead of threats in cybersecurity requires a proactive approach to both identifying vulnerabilities and applying patches. While these two areas might seem to overlap, they actually complement each other. Vulnerability management is focused on identifying and assessing security weaknesses, while patch management addresses how to fix those weaknesses. Typically, security teams handle vulnerability management, identifying potential risks, while IT teams take charge of patch management, ensuring those risks are mitigated through updates and fixes. Both processes are essential and must work seamlessly together to effectively protect your organization.

Vulnerability management begins with the identification of vulnerabilities. This step is closely tied to your technology inventories, as having a clear picture of your hardware and software assets allows you to understand where potential weaknesses might exist. Vulnerabilities can be discovered through various means, such as automated scanning tools, threat intelligence feeds, or manual assessments.

Once vulnerabilities are identified, they must be cataloged and assessed to determine their priority for remediation. Not all vulnerabilities are created equal, so it's crucial to focus on those that pose the greatest risk. Prioritization involves several factors, including the severity of the vulnerability (often rated using standardized metrics like CVSS), the potential impact on your critical systems, and the likelihood of exploitation. Context also matters; factors like existing mitigating controls, the value of the assets at risk, and the current threat landscape play significant roles in deciding which vulnerabilities to address first. In many cases, you might find that vulnerabilities rated as medium on the CVSS scale are actively exploited by threat actors targeting your industry. This could mean that, for you, the risk level of that vulnerability is actually higher than its CVSS rating suggests.

Once vulnerabilities are identified and prioritized, effective communication is essential. This involves informing the relevant stakeholders within your organization about the risks and the necessary steps to mitigate them. Clear communication ensures that everyone understands the urgency and importance of addressing these vulnerabilities, from IT teams responsible for deploying patches to leadership who may need to allocate resources or adjust priorities. Finally, monitoring vulnerabilities is an ongoing process. It's not enough to identify and communicate vulnerabilities once; you need to continually track their status until they are resolved. This involves keeping an eye on newly discovered vulnerabilities, monitoring the effectiveness of any mitigations or patches that have been applied, and adjusting your approach as new information becomes available.

On the IT side, patch management plays the execution role by addressing the vulnerabilities identified. This process starts with change management, where any planned patch deployment is carefully reviewed and approved to ensure it doesn't negatively impact systems. Patching isn't just about applying updates; it involves doing so in a controlled, deliberate way that minimizes disruption. Testing patches before deployment is essential, as patches can sometimes introduce new issues or cause compatibility problems with existing systems. Testing in a controlled environment allows potential problems to be identified and resolved before reaching production systems. Having technology inventories and detailed diagrams is valuable here, as they provide a better understanding of what could be affected.

In addition to manual patching, automated patching can streamline the process, particularly for less critical systems or when managing a large number of devices. However, automation needs to be balanced with proper oversight to ensure patches are applied correctly and don't unintentionally cause issues. Just like the automated updates we receive for security tools, things can occasionally go wrong, and it's important to maintain oversight in case problems arise.

When it comes to deploying patches, having a rollback plan is essential. Despite the best planning and testing, things can go wrong during patch deployment, and being able to quickly revert to a previous state can save your organization from significant downtime or data loss. Finally, flexibility in your patch schedule is another important aspect of effective patch management. While regular patch cycles are important, sometimes critical vulnerabilities arise that require immediate attention. Being able to adjust your patching schedule to address these urgent issues is key to maintaining a strong security posture.

The fourth cybersecurity basic is **network security**. At its core, network security is about designing and maintaining a network architecture that protects an organization's assets from unauthorized access, misuse, or attacks. One of the most effective ways to achieve this is through security by design, which involves embedding security controls into every phase of network development and design. When adopting this approach, you are able to build networks that are secure by design, rather than trying to retrofit security measures after the fact. To fully understand how to integrate security into network design, it's important to consider the seven layers of the OSI Model (Figure 8.1). The OSI Model, or Open Systems Interconnection Model, is a conceptual framework that standardizes the functions of a telecommunication or computing system into seven distinct layers. Each layer has its own security requirements and vulnerabilities, and understanding these can for sure help in architecting a secure network.

- **Physical layer**: This is the lowest layer of the OSI Model and includes all the physical components of the network, such as cables, switches, and routers. Security at this layer involves protecting the physical

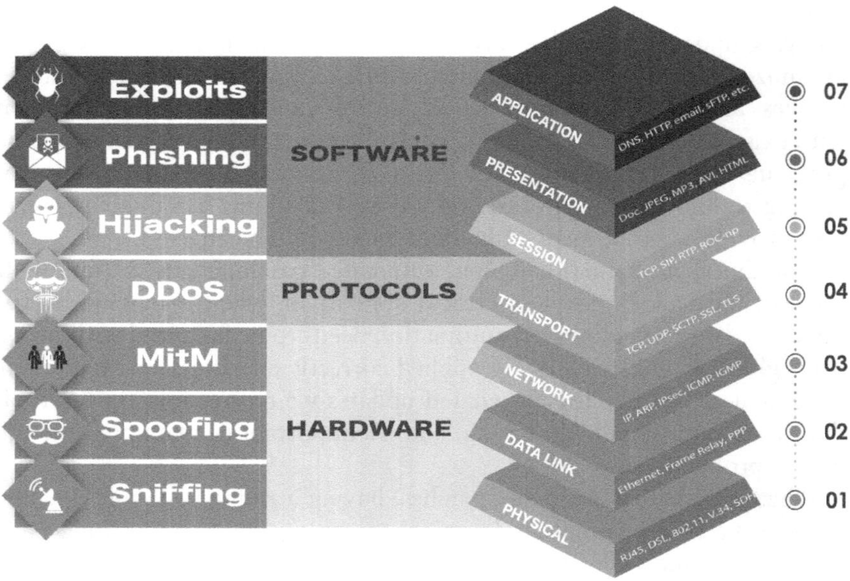

Figure 8.1 OSI model.

devices and connections from tampering or damage. This can be achieved by controlling physical access to network equipment, using secure cable management, and implementing environmental controls to prevent damage from external factors like power surges or water leaks.

- **Data link layer**: The data link layer is responsible for node-to-node data transfer and error detection and correction in the physical layer. At this level, security measures include protecting against MAC address spoofing and implementing VLANs (virtual local area networks) to segregate network traffic, preventing unauthorized access between different network segments.
- **Network layer**: This layer manages the routing of data packets between devices across different networks. Security controls at the network layer include implementing IPsec for secure communication, using firewalls to filter traffic, and configuring routers to block or restrict unwanted traffic, thus preventing potential threats from entering the network.
- **Transport layer**: The transport layer is responsible for end-to-end communication and error handling. Security at this layer often involves using protocols like TLS (transport layer security) to encrypt data in transit, ensuring that sensitive information remains confidential and protected from interception or tampering during transmission. However, TLS is, in a strict sense, providing security services to the application layer (layer 7), by protecting information transmitted at transport layer (layer 4).
- **Session layer**: This layer establishes, manages, and terminates connections between applications. Security considerations here include implementing session management protocols that ensure only authenticated users can initiate or maintain a session. This might involve using secure tokens or certificates that validate user identities before allowing access to network services.
- **Presentation layer**: The presentation layer translates data between the application layer and the network. At this level, security measures often focus on data encryption and decryption, ensuring that sensitive information is protected during transmission. Data compression and conversion formats should also be scrutinized for vulnerabilities that could be exploited by attackers.
- **Application layer**: This is the top layer of the OSI Model and provides network services directly to end-users and applications. Security at the application layer involves ensuring that applications are designed with security in mind, including input validation, authentication, authorization, and regular security testing to identify and fix potential vulnerabilities.

Considering the security needs of each layer in the OSI Model helps to create a multilayered defense strategy that addresses potential threats from multiple angles. This approach to network security ensures that if one layer is compromised, the other layers can still provide protection, reducing the overall risk to the organization. However, implementing a comprehensive security strategy that covers all these layers is not without its challenges.

As networks become more complex and interconnected, designing a secure network architecture becomes increasingly difficult. One of the primary challenges is managing the growing number of devices and endpoints. Over time, networks evolved, incorporating various technologies, devices, and protocols many of which, like FTP or HTTP, were not originally designed with security in mind and, unfortunately, are still commonly found in organizations today. This evolution results in a patchwork of different systems with varying capabilities to implement security controls, making it challenging to maintain a unified security strategy. With the rise of IoT (Internet of Things) devices, mobile workforces, and remote access solutions, networks now extend far beyond traditional office environments. This expansion increases the attack surface, making it harder to monitor and secure all entry points effectively.

Another significant challenge is ensuring consistent security across diverse environments. Modern networks often span multiple locations, including on-premises data centers, cloud environments, and hybrid setups. Each of these environments has its own security requirements and vulnerabilities, and the diversity can lead to inconsistencies in security capabilities. Older network devices and software may not support modern security standards or updates, leading to potential security gaps that can be exploited by attackers.

Additionally, keeping up with evolving threats is also a constant challenge. Cyber threats are continually evolving, with attackers developing new tactics and tools to exploit vulnerabilities. This dynamic environment means that network security measures must be regularly updated and adapted to stay ahead of potential threats. Finally, I can say that balancing security with performance is an ongoing concern. Security measures, such as encryption, firewalls, and intrusion prevention systems (IPSs), can introduce latency and impact network performance if not properly configured. Ensuring that security measures are robust without degrading the user experience or business operations is a delicate balance that requires ongoing optimization and tuning.

These challenges highlight the importance of a structured approach to network security, which is where network security standards, like ISO 27033, become essential. These standards provide guidelines and best practices for designing, implementing, and managing network security, helping you address these challenges effectively and align your security practices with recognized industry standards. At a high level I'll describe ISO 27033 but

I strongly recommend you go deeper in its review when working on network security because it will help you create a structured and robust approach to network security. ISO 27033 is part of the broader ISO/IEC 27000 series, which, as discussed in Chapter 2, focuses on information security management systems. Specifically, ISO 27033 offers a framework that encompasses all network components, from physical devices to virtual environments and cloud services. The standard is divided into several parts, each addressing different aspects of network security:

- **Part 1: Overview and concepts**: This part provides a general introduction to network security and outlines the basic concepts and principles that underpin the standard. It emphasizes the importance of understanding the network security context, including the assets to be protected, the threats and vulnerabilities that could affect those assets, and the overall risk management strategy.
- **Part 2: Guidelines for design and Implementation of network security**: This part provides detailed guidance on designing and implementing network security. It covers various network architectures and topologies, providing best practices for securing each type. This section also addresses the importance of integrating security into the network design process from the outset, ensuring that security controls are not just added as an afterthought but are built into the network's foundation. Topics include selecting appropriate security controls, designing secure network segments, and ensuring secure communication between different parts of the network.
- **Part 3: Reference networking scenarios, threats, design techniques, and control issues**: This part provides practical examples and scenarios that illustrate common network security challenges and how to address them. It discusses typical threats faced by networks, such as denial-of-service attacks, unauthorized access, and data breaches, and offers strategies for mitigating these risks. The scenarios help organizations understand the application of the standard in real-world contexts, providing insights into how to design and implement effective security measures tailored to specific situations.
- **Parts 4–6: Specific technical controls and technologies**: These parts focus on the technical controls and technologies that can be used to secure networks. They provide detailed guidance on implementing specific security measures, such as firewalls, intrusion detection and prevention systems, virtual private networks (VPNs), and secure web gateways. Each control is discussed in terms of its role in the network security strategy, offering practical advice on deployment, configuration, and management.
- **Part 7: Guidelines for network virtualization security**: The final part of the standard published in 2023 addresses the security considerations

to virtualized network environments. With the increasing adoption of virtualization technologies in data centers and cloud environments, securing virtual networks has become super relevant. Part 7 provides guidelines on securing virtualized network infrastructures, including virtual switches, routers, and firewalls. It also covers best practices for managing virtual machines, ensuring that security controls are consistently applied across both physical and virtual environments.

Following ISO 27033 allows you to create a network security framework that aligns with international best practices. This approach not only protects your networks from a wide range of threats but also demonstrates a strong commitment to security, which can enhance trust with your customers, partners, and regulators. As you establish a solid foundation with ISO 27033, it's important to understand the main security controls that can be implemented to strengthen your network security.

Let's start by the beginning. Firewalls are one of the most essential security controls, acting as gatekeepers by filtering incoming and outgoing network traffic based on predetermined security rules. Controlling the flow of data, firewalls help block unauthorized access and protect networks from external threats. Whether hardware-based or software-based, they form a critical first line of defense in any network security setup.

Edge routers work in tandem with firewalls, directing traffic between different networks and adding another layer of security. Managing the data entering and leaving the network, edge routers ensure that only authorized traffic passes through. When properly configured, edge routers can prevent certain types of attacks, such as distributed denial of service (DDoS) attacks, by filtering out malicious traffic at the network's edge.

Intrusion detection systems (IDSs) and IPSs are critical for monitoring network traffic and identifying potential security threats. IDSs monitor traffic for suspicious activity and alert security teams when anomalies are detected, while IPSs go a step further by actively blocking or mitigating these threats in real time. Together, these systems provide a robust layer of defense against both known and unknown threats, enhancing the overall security posture of your network.

VPNs are essential for securing remote connections to your network. VPNs create encrypted tunnels for data transmission, ensuring that sensitive information remains private even when transmitted over public networks. This is particularly important in today's world, where after COVID remote work is common and employees often need to access corporate resources from various locations.

Web proxies and secure web gateways (SWGs) are tools designed to control and monitor users' web access. Web proxies act as intermediaries between users and the internet, filtering requests based on security policies. SWGs take this a step further by providing advanced security features like

URL filtering, anti-malware scanning, and data loss prevention, ensuring that users can safely access the web without exposing the network to risks.

Network encryption and transport layer security (TLS) are key components for protecting data in transit. Network encryption involves converting data into a secure format that can only be read by authorized users, preventing unauthorized access during transmission. TLS (1.2 and 1.3), a widely used encryption protocol, ensures secure communication over the internet by encrypting data between web browsers and servers. Implementing these encryption methods is crucial for protecting sensitive information from interception and ensuring the integrity of data.

Network segregation is an essential control that involves dividing a network into smaller segments or subnets. This approach helps limit the spread of potential breaches, ensuring that if attackers gain access to one segment, they cannot easily move laterally to other parts of the network. Isolating sensitive areas and controlling access between segments reduces the impact of a security incident, making it easier to contain threats. I like to think of network segregation as being similar to the compartments designed to protect the Titanic from sinking. The ship's compartments were created to isolate sections, minimizing the risk of flooding and keeping the ship afloat even if some parts were breached. In theory, this compartmentalization was a smart design to prevent a single breach from becoming catastrophic. However, there was a flaw: the compartments weren't fully sealed at the top. In an effort to improve the user experience on board, the designers left the tops of the compartments open, which ultimately allowed water to flow between them once the ship was breached. This design flaw caused more compartments to flood than intended, leading to the ship's tragic sinking.

In the same way, network segregation works to limit the damage in the event of a breach, isolating different sections of your network to prevent an attack from spreading. But if the 'compartments' of your network aren't fully isolated or properly designed, a breach can escalate, spreading far beyond the intended boundaries. It's a reminder that good design isn't just about user experience or convenience, it's about ensuring security measures are robust enough to prevent the worst-case scenario. This is exactly what happens to our networks when they are flat; if we're hit by ransomware, it can spread across the entire network, potentially causing our company to 'sink.'

Monitoring and detection is our fifth cybersecurity basic because with cyber threats constantly evolving, having the ability to continuously monitor your network and detect potential threats in real time is very important. Just think on this; if we assess and manage risks then we're bringing the proactive approach to our security program; however, we can't know and manage all risks, right? Then we need to monitor and detect everything that could be happening in our environments so we keep learning and improving our risk management program. This proactive approach helps identify unusual activities, allowing you to respond quickly before they escalate into serious incidents. This involves tracking network traffic, user activities, system performance, and other indicators that could signal a potential threat. Effective monitoring goes beyond simply watching for threats; it also involves understanding the normal patterns of your network and systems. This is where behavioral analysis comes into play. Learning what typical behavior looks like, monitoring tools can better identify deviations that may indicate malicious activity. For example, if a user who normally logs in from one location suddenly attempts to access your network from another country; this could trigger an alert for further investigation. In addition to behavioral analysis, anomaly detection is another critical component of effective monitoring. Anomaly detection tools are designed to identify patterns that do not match the expected behavior within your network. These could be anything from a sudden spike in network traffic to an unusual login attempt outside of normal business hours.

Security information and event management (SIEM) systems are great tools in the monitoring and detection arsenal. SIEM systems collect and analyze log data from various sources across your network, providing a centralized view of security events. They help identify potential threats by correlating data from different systems, generating alerts for suspicious activities, and providing insights that are critical for effective incident response.

Finally, remember that monitoring and detection are not static activities. The threat landscape is constantly changing, and your monitoring tools and strategies must evolve accordingly. Regularly reviewing and updating your monitoring policies, tuning your detection systems, and staying informed about new threats are essential practices for maintaining a strong security posture.

Monitoring and detection are about being proactive, staying ahead of potential threats, and ensuring that your organization is prepared to respond quickly and effectively when incidents occur. But even with the best monitoring in place, incidents can still happen, which is where **incident response and recovery** come into play as the sixth cybersecurity basic.

Incident response and recovery is focused on minimizing the impact of security incidents and ensuring a swift return to normal operations. When a security breach or other incident occurs, having a structured response plan in place is critical. This plan should outline the steps your organization will take to identify, contain, and eliminate the threat, preventing further damage and protecting your assets. As I mentioned earlier, if your risk management program is not strong, your response and recovery capabilities must be even stronger. At the core of Incident response is the ability to act quickly and decisively when risks materialize because we weren't able to manage them effectively. The moment an incident is detected, your response team needs to jump into action, following a predefined process to assess the situation and determine the best course of action. This might involve isolating affected systems, removing malicious software, or shutting down certain parts of the network to prevent the incident from spreading. The goal is to contain the threat as swiftly as possible, reducing the risk of further compromise. Communication is another key element of effective incident response. It's important to keep all stakeholders informed throughout the process, providing regular updates on the status of the incident and the actions being taken to resolve it. This transparency helps maintain trust and ensures that everyone is on the same page, working together to manage the situation effectively.

Once the immediate threat is contained, the focus shifts to Recovery. This phase involves restoring affected systems and data to their normal state, ensuring that your organization can resume its operations with minimal disruption. It also includes a complete investigation to understand how the incident occurred, what vulnerabilities were exploited, and what can be done to prevent similar incidents in the future. Documenting the incident and the response actions taken is a crucial part of the recovery process. This documentation provides valuable insights that can be used to improve your security posture, refine your response plan, and strengthen your defenses against future threats. It's about learning from each incident and continuously enhancing your organization's resilience. Regular testing and updating of your incident response plan are also vital. Cyber threats are constantly evolving, and your response strategies need to keep pace. Conducting simulated attacks and drills can help your team practice their response and identify any gaps in the plan, ensuring that you are always ready to tackle the next challenge.

Incident response and disaster recovery are about being prepared, staying resilient, and ensuring that your organization can handle whatever comes its way. With a robust response plan in place, you can minimize the impact of security incidents and maintain confidence in your ability to protect your assets and continue your business operations. We'll explore these capabilities in greater detail in Chapter 12, where we'll dive deeper into effective strategies and best practices to enhance your organization's resilience.

The seventh cybersecurity basic to keep in mind is **physical security**. While cybersecurity often focuses on digital defenses, physical security is equally important in protecting your organization's assets. Physical security measures help prevent unauthorized access to buildings, data centers, systems, and data, ensuring the overall security of your environment.

Geographic location is a key factor in physical security. The location of your data centers, offices, and other facilities can influence your security strategy. Facilities in regions prone to natural disasters, such as earthquakes, floods, or hurricanes, require additional safeguards to protect against physical damage and ensure business continuity. Similarly, facilities located in high-crime areas may need enhanced security measures to prevent theft, vandalism, or unauthorized access.

Geopolitical factors are also important in physical security planning. Organizations with facilities in politically unstable regions may face risks, such as government intervention, civil unrest, or targeted attacks. Understanding the geopolitical landscape helps you develop appropriate security measures, such as stricter access controls, enhanced surveillance, or considering the relocation of critical assets to more stable regions.

Multi-tenancy is another consideration, especially for organizations that share facilities with other businesses. In multi-tenant environments, securing your specific areas is crucial. This involves implementing strict access controls to prevent unauthorized individuals from entering your spaces and using barriers, such as secure doors and partitions, to separate your areas from those of other tenants. In these settings, collaborating with building management and other tenants to establish and maintain security policies is essential.

Building materials can impact the effectiveness of your physical security measures. The construction and materials used in your facilities influence how easily an attacker might gain unauthorized access or how well your assets are protected from environmental hazards. Facilities built with reinforced concrete or steel offer greater resistance to physical breaches compared to those constructed with less durable materials. Additionally, buildings designed with security in mind, such as those with limited entry points or blast-resistant windows, provide added protection against physical threats.

Integrating physical security into your overall cybersecurity strategy creates a more effective defense against both digital and physical threats. Ensuring that your facilities are secure and well-protected helps safeguard your organization's assets, data, and operations from a wide range of potential risks. A strong cybersecurity program addresses the digital aspects of security and the physical elements that are essential for maintaining a secure environment.

The eighth cybersecurity basic to focus on is **endpoint protection**. As the number of devices connecting to your network increases, securing these endpoints becomes crucial. Endpoint devices, such as computers, laptops, mobile phones, tablets, handhelds, or even POS machines, are often the primary targets for cyber attackers. Protecting these devices from unauthorized access, malware infections, and other security threats that could compromise your organization's data and operations is the goal here.

Endpoint device hardening is a fundamental aspect of endpoint protection. Hardening involves configuring devices to reduce their vulnerability to attacks. This includes replacing default configurations and passwords by strong and secure ones, disabling unnecessary services and features, setting strong password policies, and applying the latest security patches and updates. One effective way to achieve this is by following the CIS (Center for Internet Security) Hardening Benchmarks. These benchmarks provide detailed guidelines on securely configuring operating systems, applications, and network devices, helping to minimize security risks and improve the overall security posture of your endpoints.

Device logging is a critical element of endpoint protection. Enabling and monitoring logs on endpoint devices allows you to track user activities, detect suspicious behavior, and identify potential security incidents. Logs provide valuable insights that help understand what occurred during an incident, how it happened, and what steps are necessary to prevent recurrence. Ensuring that logging is configured correctly and that logs are stored securely is essential to protect them from tampering or unauthorized access, safeguarding the integrity of the information for accurate analysis and response.

Device security goes beyond just hardening and logging. It involves implementing a range of security measures to protect endpoint devices from various threats. This can include using endpoint detection and response tools to detect and remove malicious code, deploying software firewalls to control incoming and outgoing traffic, and using encryption to protect sensitive data stored on devices.

Mobile device security controls are especially important in today's work environment, where employees often use personal devices to access corporate resources. These controls help protect mobile devices from threats like malware, phishing attacks, and unauthorized access. Key security measures include enforcing strong passwords or biometric authentication, enabling remote wipe capabilities to erase data if a device is lost or stolen, and restricting access to sensitive data based on the device's security posture. Mobile device management (MDM) solutions can be used to enforce security policies, manage device configurations, and monitor device compliance across your organization. A strong endpoint protection strategy helps secure individual devices as well as contributes to the overall security of your network, creating a more resilient environment for your business operations.

Building on the strength of a robust endpoint protection strategy, application protection is the next essential cybersecurity basic to consider. As applications serve as the interface between users and your organization's data, ensuring their security is paramount. Applications are often targeted by attackers seeking to exploit vulnerabilities and gain unauthorized access to sensitive information or systems. Protecting these applications helps maintain the integrity, confidentiality, and availability of your data and services.

Application hardening involves securing the application's code to make it more resistant to attacks. Techniques like code obfuscation make the code more difficult for attackers to understand, while anti-debugging measures prevent attackers from analyzing the application. Regular updates and patch management are also critical to fixing known vulnerabilities and keeping applications secure against emerging threats.

Implementing secure coding practices is another important aspect of application protection. Developers should be trained to write code with security in mind, following best practices to avoid common vulnerabilities such as SQL injection, cross-site scripting (XSS), and buffer overflows. Secure coding standards, along with regular code reviews and static analysis, can help identify and address security flaws before applications are deployed, minimizing the risk of exploitation.

Application security testing (AST) is a comprehensive approach to identifying vulnerabilities in applications throughout their life cycle. Several types of security testing can be utilized to ensure that applications are secure:

- **Static application security testing** (SAST) examines an application's source code, bytecode, or binary code without executing it. This method identifies security vulnerabilities such as syntax errors, coding flaws, and insecure coding practices early in the development process. Analyzing the code itself helps developers catch and fix vulnerabilities before the application goes into production, reducing the potential attack surface.
- **Dynamic application security testing** (DAST) evaluates applications in their running state to identify security vulnerabilities that can be exploited in a live environment. Unlike SAST, DAST does not require access to the source code; instead, it simulates attacks on the application to identify issues like runtime vulnerabilities, configuration errors, and other security weaknesses. This testing is particularly useful for detecting vulnerabilities that arise from the interaction of various components within the application, such as input validation flaws and session management issues.
- **Interactive application security testing** (IAST) combines elements of both SAST and DAST by analyzing applications in real time while they are running. IAST tools are typically integrated into the application environment and monitor the application's behavior during execution, providing detailed insights into how the code behaves in different scenarios. This approach helps identify vulnerabilities that may not be evident through static or dynamic testing alone, offering a more complete view of the application's security posture.
- **Penetration testing** (Pentesting) simulates real-world attacks on an application to evaluate its security in an operational environment. During a pentest, ethical hackers attempt to exploit vulnerabilities within the application to determine how far they can penetrate into the system. This method provides an in-depth assessment of the application's defenses, highlighting not only technical weaknesses but also procedural and configuration flaws. Pentesting helps organizations understand the potential impact of an attack and improve their overall security posture by addressing identified vulnerabilities.

Web application firewalls (WAFs) play a significant role in application protection. A WAF monitors and filters HTTP traffic between a web application and the internet, blocking malicious requests that may exploit vulnerabilities. WAFs help protect web applications from common attacks such as SQL injection, cross-site scripting, and other threats listed in the OWASP Top Ten, reducing the risk of application-level attacks.

The final cybersecurity basic to focus on is **awareness and training**. Security awareness is about ensuring that the entire organizational culture embraces security as a fundamental part of its operations. This isn't a one-time effort but an ongoing process that evolves continuously. There's always something new to improve or a creative approach to explore. I always recommend keeping a positive approach to security awareness, encouraging learning and growth rather than taking a punitive stance. When people understand the importance of security and feel supported in their efforts to improve, they are more likely to adopt secure behaviors and integrate them into their daily routines.

On the other hand, training focuses on making sure that everyone responsible for managing security controls, whether they are employees, vendors, or contractors, is properly trained. This training ensures they know how to configure, execute, and maintain these controls correctly. Human error can be just as impactful as a cyberattack; the difference is in the intention behind the action. We must not forget that a well-intentioned mistake can still lead to significant security breaches. That's why it's crucial to provide ongoing training to ensure everyone understands their role in maintaining security and is equipped to do so effectively.

Fostering a culture of security awareness and providing training, you can minimize the risk of human error and enhance your organization's overall security posture. A positive, proactive approach to awareness and training helps create an environment where everyone feels responsible for security and is empowered to contribute to protecting the organization's assets and data. Together, these cybersecurity basics will help you design better treatment plans, keeping in mind the fundamental aspects that will truly improve your security posture. Remember, security technology is effective only when it's fully integrated into your environment and properly configured, operated, and maintained. Don't become a tool jockey, that's just a waste of money and creates a false sense of security for your organization.

SELECTING THE OPTIMAL PATH FORWARD

Now that we've explored the cybersecurity basics that form the foundation of a solid security solution, it's time to discuss how to decide the best way to address the risks your organization faces. This is where we move into selecting the optimal path forward. Choosing whether to avoid, mitigate, transfer, or accept a risk depends on various factors, including the nature of the risk, your organization's risk appetite, available resources, and overall business objectives.

When considering Avoidance, this strategy is most suitable for risks with an impact that is well above your organization's risk capacity and has a medium to high likelihood of occurring. These are risks that, if materialized, could cause severe damage to your organization, potentially threatening its survival. In such cases, avoiding the risk altogether by altering plans or changing business strategies might be the best course of action. This could mean canceling a project, discontinuing a risky activity, or changing business models to eliminate exposure to the risk. The key is to recognize that some risks are too significant to manage through mitigation or transfer alone and that the only viable option is to remove the threat entirely.

Mitigation is often the best choice when dealing with risks that have a high impact but are still within your organization's risk capacity. If these risks occur, they could cause substantial harm, but they are not necessarily catastrophic. Mitigating these risks involves implementing controls and safeguards to reduce their likelihood or impact to an acceptable level. When considering mitigation, it's important to prioritize risks that pose the greatest threat to your operations and to allocate resources effectively to minimize these risks as much as possible.

Transferring risks is a strategic option for risks that have a high impact but a medium to low probability of occurring. These are risks that, while potentially severe, are not likely to materialize frequently. Transferring these risks to another party, through contracts, outsourcing, or insurance, can be an effective way to protect your organization from significant financial losses or operational disruptions. For example, cyber insurance can cover costs related to a data breach, while outsourcing a high-risk function can shift the responsibility to a third party with better expertise or capabilities. It's crucial, however, to ensure that the terms of risk transfer are clear and that the other party is fully prepared to handle the risk appropriately.

Finally, accepting risks is appropriate when the risk is below your organization's risk appetite. These are risks that, even if they occur, are not expected to cause significant harm or disruption to your operations. Accepting these risks means acknowledging them but deciding that no further action is needed. This approach requires a careful assessment to ensure that the potential impact is truly within acceptable limits and that the organization is prepared to manage the risk if it materializes. It's also important to regularly reassess accepted risks, as changing circumstances or emerging threats could alter their status and necessitate a different approach.

In choosing the optimal path forward, it's essential to make sure risk owners and treatment plan owners are assigned and aware of their role. Also, we must weigh the cost-benefit of each option against the specific characteristics of the risk and the overall context of your organization. Remember, risk treatment is not about eliminating all risks but managing them in a way that aligns with your business objectives and risk appetite. As you assess each risk, consider how each strategy fits into your broader risk management plan and how it will help you achieve a stronger security posture. Ultimately, selecting the right risk treatment strategy involves a detailed understanding of your organization's risk capacity, the nature of the risks, and the resources at your disposal. Think thoughtfully when applying these principles as you can create a balanced approach that protects your organization while allowing it to achieve its business objectives.

TREATMENT PLANS IN PRACTICE

Now, taking the same examples we've been using in our risk assessment; we'll now analyze treatment plan options and create risk treatment strategies for each actual risk we assessed. If you remember, these include the risks of a data breach, compliance failures, internal threats such as employee mishandling of payment data, and system failures in the payment processing system.

Let's start with Avoidance. For the data breach risk, to truly avoid this risk involving customer payment information, our organization would need to essentially modify its business model so that it no longer collects, stores, or processes any customer payment information. This could mean reverting to cash-only transactions, where no digital or electronic payment data is required, thus completely eliminating the risk of a data breach involving payment information. However, this approach is likely impractical in today's digital economy and may not even be legally viable due to regulations designed to prevent money laundering, which often require some form of traceable data for transactions above certain amounts. Therefore, while true avoidance of this risk is theoretically possible, it would require significant changes to the business model that might not align with modern operational requirements or legal obligations. As a result, this strategy would be rarely considered the best option for most organizations. So just for making things easier let's keep this in mind: Risk Impact = \$4 million to \$8 million, Likelihood = 30% to 50%.

Similarly, avoiding the risk of compliance failure might involve deciding not to engage in activities that require adherence to specific regulations. For instance, if the organization chooses not to process or store payment data, it could bypass the need to comply with PCI-DSS standards. While this strategy avoids the risk of regulatory noncompliance, it might not be feasible if payment processing is integral to the business. The cost of avoidance here could be the need to alter business models or revenue streams significantly. So just for making things easier let's keep this in mind: Risk Impact = \$2 million to \$5 million, Likelihood = 30% to 40%.

For internal threats, avoiding the risk would involve ensuring that customer payment information is never stored or processed within the organization's environment. Removing this sensitive data from internal systems eliminates the risk of employee mishandling or internal breaches since the data simply doesn't exist within the organization to be compromised. However, this approach would likely require relying on an external payment processing provider, which means losing control over certain aspects of the payment process. Additionally, while the internal threat is removed, new risks related to the third-party provider would be introduced. To simplify things, let's consider the following: Risk Impact = $1.5 million to $3 million, Likelihood = 20% to 30%.

For system failures, avoiding the risk might involve decommissioning an outdated payment processing system known for reliability issues. Replacing it with a more modern, stable system avoids the risks associated with the old system's failures but introduces new risks with the modern system. This decision would require investment in new technology and could cause disruptions during the transition. Let's imagine we take this route. The cost of replacing the system is estimated at $250,000. After implementing the new system, the likelihood of failure is expected to drop to between 10% and 20%, and the potential impact, if a failure occurs, would decrease to a range of $500,000 to $750,000. To quantify this effectiveness, let's compare the new risk levels with the original ones. Previously, the risk impact averaged $1.5 million, with a likelihood of 20% to 30%. After the upgrade, the new risk impact averages $625,000, with a likelihood of 10% to 20%. This change represents a significant decrease in both the financial risk and the likelihood of occurrence.

The value of the control's effectiveness can be measured by comparing these new risk levels to the original ones. Originally, the potential risk impact was $1.5 million with a 25% likelihood. With the new system in place, the risk impact is reduced to $625,000, and the likelihood drops by 41.65%. The effectiveness of the control in reducing risk, therefore, saves the organization an estimated $875,000 ($1.5 million–$625,000) over the lifespan of the system. This, combined with the reduction in likelihood, further justifies the investment in the new system. To keep things simple, refer to Table 8.1 for our figures. Keep in mind that the current risk impact is $1.5 million with a 25% likelihood. After investing $250,000, the risk impact decreases to $625,000 with a 15% likelihood.

Now, you may be asking yourself, how did we arrive at those levels of residual risks? Remember we mentioned earlier that there would be a final risk analysis to perform with treatment plans? Well, this is it. When we assess treatment plans, we need to analyze them just as we did for actual risks, but this time, we're thinking about the future controls that will be implemented.

In this case, if we're avoiding the direct risks of having an obsolete system, we also need to assess the risks that the new system will bring. This means conducting a risk assessment specifically for the new system, where we

Table 8.1 Summary Table of Residual Risks after Avoidance

Avoidance	*Risk*	*Actual Impact*	*Actual Likelihood*	*Post-Avoidance Impact*	*Post-Avoidance Likelihood*	*Investment Cost*
	Data Breach	$6,000,000	40%	No change	No change	N/A
	Compliance Failure	$3,500,000	35%	No change	No change	N/A
	Internal Threats	$2,250,000	25%	No change	No change	N/A
	System Failure	$1,500,000	25%	$625,000	15%	$250,000

Note: Let's remember that the residual risk after the avoidance of replacing the system is not the same risk but the new one introduced by the new system.

calculate the expected risks after its implementation. The outcome of this assessment, after considering the new controls and potential vulnerabilities, gives us what we refer to as residual risks. It is then that the residual risks are those that remain after we have applied our treatment plans, in this case, the new modern system that replaces the old one. These risks are lower, but they still exist and must be managed. Understanding this process is key to effective risk management, as it allows us to make informed decisions about which controls to implement and how to best protect the organization moving forward.

When it comes to mitigation, the focus shifts from avoiding risks entirely to reducing their impact or likelihood. In our examples, we didn't have strong options to avoid the first three risks, so mitigation becomes our next step. For the data breach risk, mitigation could involve implementing strong encryption protocols, regularly updating security systems, and conducting frequent security audits. These measures protect customer payment information by making it significantly more difficult for unauthorized individuals to access or exploit the data. However, while these steps reduce the likelihood and potential impact of a data breach, they do not eliminate the risk entirely. Vulnerabilities can still exist, and new threats can emerge, leaving us with a residual risk where the impact could still range between $1 million and $3 million, with a likelihood of 10% to 30%.

Since the mitigation strategy we're proposing for addressing the data breach risk requires a multilayered approach, let's break down these controls to understand their costs and effectiveness.

First, implementing strong encryption protocols is critical in safeguarding customer payment information. The cost of deploying advanced point-to-point encryption across all relevant systems could be estimated at $150,000, including software licensing, integration, and ongoing maintenance. Encryption is highly effective in protecting data, but it's not foolproof, especially if attackers find vulnerabilities elsewhere in the system. We can estimate the effectiveness of encryption alone in reducing the risk to be around 60%. Next, regular updates to security systems are essential to protect against the latest threats. This involves patching vulnerabilities, upgrading firewalls, and ensuring that all systems are configured correctly. The ongoing cost of these updates could be approximately $50,000 per year, which covers software updates, IT staff time, and potential downtime during updates. The effectiveness of regular updates in reducing the likelihood of a breach is significant, but again, not absolute. Let's estimate this at an additional 20% reduction in risk. Finally, frequent security audits help identify and address potential weaknesses before they can be exploited. Conducting these audits might cost around $30,000 annually, factoring in both internal resources and external auditors. The effectiveness of these audits can vary, but for the purposes of this analysis, let's assume they contribute an additional 10% reduction in risk.

Now, let's quantify the residual risk after implementing these controls. Initially, the data breach risk was estimated to have an impact of $1 million to $3 million, with a likelihood of 10% to 30%. The combined effectiveness of the proposed controls, encryption (60%), system updates (20%), and security audits (10%) comes to an approximately total likelihood reduction of 90%. However, considering the complex and evolving nature of cybersecurity threats, the actual reduction in likelihood may not be as dramatic as the sum of individual control effectiveness might suggest. Instead, we might expect the likelihood of a data breach to reduce to approximately 10% to 30%, with an average of 20%. While these controls greatly reduce the likelihood of a breach, it's important to note that the potential impact, if a breach were to occur, remains largely unchanged. The organization could still face significant consequences, with an impact still ranging between $1 million and $3 million. Therefore, the total investment in these mitigation controls is estimated at $230,000 ($150,000 for encryption, $50,000 annually for updates, and $30,000 annually for audits). After these investments, the residual risk shows a reduced likelihood now averaging around 15%, while the potential impact remains between $1 million and $3 million. This analysis demonstrates the value of these mitigation efforts in substantially reducing the likelihood of a data breach, while acknowledging that the impact, if it were to occur, would still be considerable. So just for having the numbers handy: Actual Average Risk Impact = $1.5 million, Likelihood = 25%. New Average Risk Impact = $1.5 million, Likelihood = 20% with an investment of $230,000.

Mitigating the risk of compliance failure could involve adopting strict access controls, continuous monitoring, and regular compliance audits to ensure that the organization meets all necessary regulatory requirements. For instance, enforcing strong data encryption standards and ensuring that all systems handling payment data are PCI-DSS compliant can reduce the likelihood of noncompliance. Additionally, training employees on data protection practices helps prevent unintentional violations of regulations. While these actions mitigate the risk, they require ongoing effort and resources, and there's always a possibility of compliance gaps emerging over time. Even with these measures in place, the residual risk might still result in an impact ranging from $500,000 to $1 million, with a likelihood of 5% to 10%.

As we're seeing, mitigating the risk of compliance failure requires an approach that involves adopting more than one control. In this case those controls are: strict access controls, continuous monitoring, and regular compliance audits. These measures are designed to ensure that the organization meets all necessary regulatory requirements and reduces the likelihood of noncompliance.

First, adopting strict access controls is essential to limit who has access to sensitive payment data. Implementing RBAC and ensuring that only authorized personnel can access certain information can significantly reduce the risk of unauthorized access. The cost of deploying and maintaining these controls, including software, training, and ongoing management, could be estimated at $120,000. The effectiveness of these controls in reducing the risk of noncompliance could be estimated at around 50%, given that access control is a key factor in protecting sensitive data. Next, continuous monitoring is vital to detect and respond to any potential compliance issues in real time. This involves implementing monitoring tools that can track access to sensitive data, identify unusual activities, and generate alerts for potential violations. The cost for continuous monitoring, including tools and staff to analyze the data, might be around $90,000 per year. The effectiveness of continuous monitoring in reducing the likelihood of compliance failures could be estimated at an additional 30%. Finally, regular compliance audits help ensure that all systems and processes are in line with regulatory requirements. These audits could involve internal reviews and external audits to validate that the organization is adhering to standards like PCI-DSS. The cost of these audits, including external auditors and internal preparation, could be approximately $60,000 annually. The effectiveness of these audits in reducing the risk of noncompliance might contribute an additional 10% reduction in risk.

Now, let's quantify the residual risk after implementing these controls. Initially, the compliance failure risk was estimated to have an impact of $2 million to $5 million, with a likelihood of 30% to 40%. The combined effectiveness of the proposed additional or improved controls, strict access controls (50%), continuous monitoring (30%), and regular compliance audits (10%) suggests a total likelihood reduction of approximately 90%. Given this reduction, the likelihood of noncompliance would drop significantly, from the initial 30% to 40% range to approximately 5% to 10%. However, while these controls greatly reduce the likelihood of a compliance failure, the potential impact if such a failure were to occur would still be significant, ranging between $500,000 and $1 million. Therefore, the total investment in these mitigation controls is estimated at $270,000 ($120,000 for access controls, $90,000 annually for continuous monitoring, and $60,000 annually for audits). The residual risk, after these investments, shows as expected a decrease in likelihood, now ranging between 5% and 10%, while the impact remains between $500,000 and $1 million. This analysis demonstrates the value of these mitigation efforts in substantially reducing the likelihood of compliance failures while acknowledging that the impact, if it were to occur, would still be considerable. So just for having the numbers handy: Actual Average Risk Impact = $3.5 million, Likelihood = 35%. New Average Risk Impact = $750,000, Likelihood = 7.5% with an investment of $270,000.

For internal threats, mitigation might involve implementing strict access controls, employee training programs, and real-time monitoring systems. These measures aim to reduce the likelihood of an employee mishandling or misusing payment information. For instance, limiting access to sensitive data to only those employees who absolutely need it, combined with regular monitoring of data access, can help detect and prevent insider threats before they lead to significant issues. However, the risk remains that internal threats could still occur if an employee with access acts maliciously or makes a critical mistake. Despite these efforts, the residual risk might still have an impact ranging from $1.1 million to $2.5 million, with a likelihood of 10% to 20%.

Just like the previous two risks, mitigating the risk of internal threats requires a strategy that involves implementing strict access controls, employee training programs, and real-time monitoring systems. These measures are designed to reduce the likelihood of an employee mishandling or misusing payment information.

First, implementing strict access controls is crucial to ensure that only authorized personnel can access sensitive payment data. Since we've already accounted for the cost of strict access controls in the compliance failure example, we'll maintain that consistent cost estimate of $120,000. The effectiveness of these controls in reducing the risk of internal threats could be estimated at around 40%, given that limiting access significantly reduces the chances of misuse.

Next, employee training programs are essential to ensure that employees understand the importance of data protection and are aware of the policies and procedures in place. These programs should cover topics like data security, recognizing potential threats, and the correct handling of sensitive information. The cost of developing and delivering these training programs could be around $100,000 annually, factoring in both the initial setup and ongoing training sessions. The effectiveness of these programs in reducing internal threat risks could be estimated at an additional 30%. Finally, real-time monitoring systems are necessary to detect and respond to potential internal threats as they occur. These systems should monitor access to sensitive data, flag unusual activities, and generate alerts for any suspicious behavior. The cost of implementing and maintaining real-time monitoring systems might be around $90,000 annually. The effectiveness of these systems in further reducing the likelihood of internal threats could be estimated at 20%.

Now, let's quantify the residual risk after implementing these controls. Initially, the internal threat actual risk was estimated to have an impact of $1.5 million to $3 million, with an average impact of $2.25 million and a likelihood of 20% to 30%. The combined effectiveness of the proposed controls, strict access controls (40%), employee training (30%), and real-time monitoring (20%) suggests a significant reduction in both likelihood and impact. After implementing these controls, the likelihood of an internal threat materializing is expected to drop to approximately 10% to 20%, with an average of 15%. Simultaneously, the impact of such a threat, if it were to occur, is expected to decrease from an average of $2.25 million to $1.8 million. Therefore, the total investment in these mitigation controls is estimated at $310,000 ($120,000 for access controls, $100,000 annually for employee training, and $90,000 annually for monitoring systems). The residual risk, after these investments, shows a good decrease in likelihood, now ranging between 10% and 20%, and a reduced impact averaging $1.8 million. This analysis demonstrates the value of these mitigation efforts in substantially reducing both the likelihood and impact of internal threats. So just for having the numbers handy: Actual Average Risk Impact = $2.25 million, Likelihood = 25%. New Average Risk Impact = $1.8 million, Likelihood = 15% with an investment of $310,000.

To mitigate the risk of system failures, the organization might explore investing in redundant systems, regular maintenance schedules, and robust backup procedures. For example, implementing a failover system that automatically takes over if the primary payment processing system fails can help ensure business continuity. Regular system updates and proactive maintenance can also reduce the likelihood of system failures. While these measures can significantly mitigate the risk, the possibility of failure still exists, especially in the face of unforeseen technical issues or during the deployment of new updates. For illustration purposes, let's imagine this will require an investment of $200,000. After these mitigating actions, the residual risk might still present an impact between $1 million and $1.5 million, with a likelihood of 20% to 25%. In this case, avoidance may be the better option, as it offers greater effectiveness in reducing the risk to a level that is within the organization's risk appetite.

As you can see from the analyses, certain controls, like strict access controls, can impact more than one risk. This overlap is not just a coincidence; it's a strategic advantage in risk management. Implementing controls that address multiple risks simultaneously, your treatment plan strategy maximizes the return on investment (ROI). For instance, the cost of implementing strict access controls at $120,000 is justified not only because it reduces the likelihood of compliance failures but also because it significantly mitigates the risks associated with internal threats. Similarly, continuous monitoring and employee training programs, while essential in their own right, provide compounded benefits by reducing risks across various scenarios.

This approach ensures that every dollar invested in your risk management strategy delivers the greatest possible impact. Selecting and implementing controls with broad applicability allows you to maximize your budget, reducing overall risk exposure without unnecessary or excessive spending. The treatment plan strategy goes beyond addressing individual risks in isolation, it's about building a cohesive, cost-effective defense that protects the organization from multiple angles and as you can see one treatment plan can address more than one risk.

Based on the numbers after mitigation (Table 8.2), we can now analyze the potential benefits of transferring the remaining risks that are still above the organization's risk appetite, which we've set at $1 million for this example.

For the data breach risk, even after mitigation, the residual impact is $1.5 million with a likelihood of 20%. Since this impact is still above the risk appetite of $1 million, transferring this risk through a cybersecurity insurance policy could be a viable option. The cost of such a policy, as previously estimated, might be $150,000 annually, with a deductible of $500,000. This would reduce the financial impact on the organization to $500,000 in the event of a breach, while the likelihood remains at 20%. After transferring the risk, the organization would have a residual impact that is now below the risk appetite, at $500,000, with the same likelihood.

For the compliance failure risk, after mitigation, the residual impact is $750,000 with a likelihood of 7.5%. Since this is already below the risk appetite, there's no need to transfer this risk. The organization might decide to retain this residual risk, considering it within acceptable limits without further investment.

For the internal threats risk, the residual impact after mitigation is $1.8 million with a likelihood of 15%. Since this impact is still above the $1 million risk appetite, it becomes a candidate for risk transfer. Instead of solely relying on internal measures, the organization could choose to outsource the processing of customer payment information to a third-party provider, ensuring that all necessary security and indemnification clauses are included in the contract. The agreement with the third-party provider should stipulate that the provider is financially responsible for any breaches or mishandling of payment information. This means that if a breach occurs due to their negligence or internal threats within their organization, they will cover all associated costs, including legal fees, compensation, and any fines incurred. The cost of outsourcing this service might be estimated at $150,000 annually, depending on the provider and the scope of the service.

Even with these measures in place, the reputational impact of a breach remains a concern. To address this, the organization can utilize the same cybersecurity insurance policy previously discussed, which would cover residual risks that the third-party provider cannot fully mitigate, particularly those related to reputational damage. The cost of this insurance policy would be approximately $150,000 annually, shared between the two risks it will cover, with a deductible of $500,000. After transferring this risk, the residual impact on the organization could be reduced to $1 million for the reputational impact that cannot be completely transferred, down from the $1.8 million initially estimated, with the likelihood remaining at 15%. In the event of a breach, the insurance would cover $500,000, leaving the organization with a residual impact of $500,000 and a likelihood of 15%. The total annual cost of this combined transfer strategy (outsourcing

Table 8.2 Summary Table of Residual Risks after Mitigation

Mitigation	*Risk*	*Actual Impact*	*Actual Likelihood*	*Post-Avoidance Impact*	*Post-Avoidance Likelihood*	*Investment Cost*
	Data Breach	$6,000,000	40%	$1,500,000	20%	$230,000
	Compliance Failure	$3,500,000	35%	$750,000	7.50%	$210,000
	Internal Threats	$2,250,000	25%	$1,800,000	15%	$250,000
	System Failure	$1,500,000	25%	$1,250,000	22.5%	$200,000

Table 8.3 Summary Table of Residual Risks after Transference

Transference	*Risk*	*Post-Mitigation Impact*	*Post-Mitigation Likelihood*	*Post-Transfer Impact*	*Post-Transfer Likelihood*	*Investment Cost*
	Data Breach	$1,500,000	20%	$500,000	20%	$75,000
	Compliance Failure	$750,000	7.50%	No change	No change	N/A
	Internal Threats	$1,800,000	15%	$500,000	15%	$225,000
	System Failure	$1,250,000	22.5%	No change	No change	N/A

and insurance) would then be around $225,000. For the system failure risk, after mitigation, the residual impact is $625,000 with a likelihood of 15%. This is below the risk appetite of $1 million, meaning that there is no need to transfer this risk. The organization could retain this residual risk as it falls within acceptable limits. For convenience you can see in Table 8.3 a summary of residual risks after transference.

Finally, when it comes to managing risk, we need to recognize that even after applying the best strategies, some level of risk will always remain unless we avoid. This residual risk must be documented carefully, ensuring that it aligns with our organization's risk appetite and strategic goals.

Here's how we should approach the acceptance of the remaining risks:

For the data breach risk, after implementing mitigation and transfer strategies, we've reduced the impact to $1.5 million with avoiding the outdated system and then to a residual risk of $500,000 with a 20% likelihood. The investment totaled $305,000, resulting in an effectiveness of 83%. Although the risk is not entirely eliminated because we had to replace a system by another one that will introduce new risks, the measures we've put in place significantly reduce the potential impact, making this level of residual risk acceptable within the organization's risk appetite. In the case of compliance failure, our mitigation efforts have brought the residual impact down to $750,000, with the likelihood decreasing to 7.5%. With a $210,000 investment and an effectiveness of 78%, this risk is well-managed and falls within acceptable limits. The reduction in likelihood indicates that the remaining risk is now at a level that aligns with our organization's risk appetite. For internal threats, after mitigation and transfer plans proposed, we see a residual impact of $500,000 with a 15% likelihood. However, the investment cost was higher, at $475,000, leading to an effectiveness of 2%, indicating that the measures did not produce the expected return on effectiveness in risk impact or likelihood, which means that that plan should be revisited, or we'll be putting more money than necessary, and we'll may end up not getting back good value from those plans. Finally, for the system failure risk, after employing avoidance measures, the residual impact is reduced to $625,000 with a 15% likelihood. The total investment amounted to $250,000, resulting in an effectiveness of 8%. This residual risk is within our risk appetite, making it manageable given the steps we've taken to replace systems and prevent future failures.

In all these scenarios, accepting the residual risks is not about ignoring them but about understanding that they are at a level where potential impacts align with our strategic objectives. The measures taken have reduced the risks to manageable levels, ensuring the organization is prepared to respond effectively if any of these risks were to materialize. Putting all the numbers together as I did in Table 8.4 is easier now.

After completing our analysis, we can see in Figure 8.2 how our risks have shifted across the heatmap. Even though risks 3 (insider threat) and 4

Table 8.4 Summary of Risk Treatment Plan Analysis

Avoidance	*Risk*	*Actual Impact*	*Actual Likelihood*	*Post-Avoidance Impact*	*Post-Avoidance Likelihood*	*Investment Cost*
	Data Breach	$6,000,000	40%	No change	No change	N/A
	Compliance Failure	$3,500,000	35%	No change	No change	N/A
	Internal Threats	$2,250,000	25%	No change	No change	N/A
	System Failure	$1,500,000	25%	$625,000	15%	$250,000
Mitigation	*Risk*	*Actual Impact*	*Actual Likelihood*	*Post-Mitigation Impact*	*Post-Mitigation Likelihood*	*Investment Cost*
	Data Breach	$6,000,000	40%	$1,500,000	20%	$230,000
	Compliance Failure	$3,500,000	35%	$750,000	7.50%	$210,000
	Internal Threats	$2,250,000	25%	$1,800,000	15%	$250,000
	System Failure	~~$1,500,000~~	~~25%~~	~~$1,250,000~~	~~22.5%~~	~~$200,000~~
Transference	*Risk*	*Post-Mitigation Impact*	*Post-Mitigation Likelihood*	*Post-Transfer Impact*	*Post-Transfer Likelihood*	*Investment Cost*
	Data Breach	$1,500,000	20%	$500,000	20%	$75,000
	Compliance Failure	$750,000	7.50%	No change	No change	N/A
	Internal Threats	$1,800,000	15%	$500,000	15%	$225,000
	System Failure	$1,250,000	15%	No change	No change	N/A
Acceptance	*Risk*	*Residual Impact*	*Residual Likelihood*	*Treatment Plan*	*Total Investment Cost*	*Effectiveness*
	Data Breach	$500,000	20%	Mitigate and Transfer	$305,000	83%
	Compliance Failure	$750,000	7.50%	Mitigation	$270,000	78%
	Internal Threats	$500,000	15%	Mitigate and Transfer	$535,000	2%
	System Failure	$625,000	15%	Avoidance	$250,000	8%

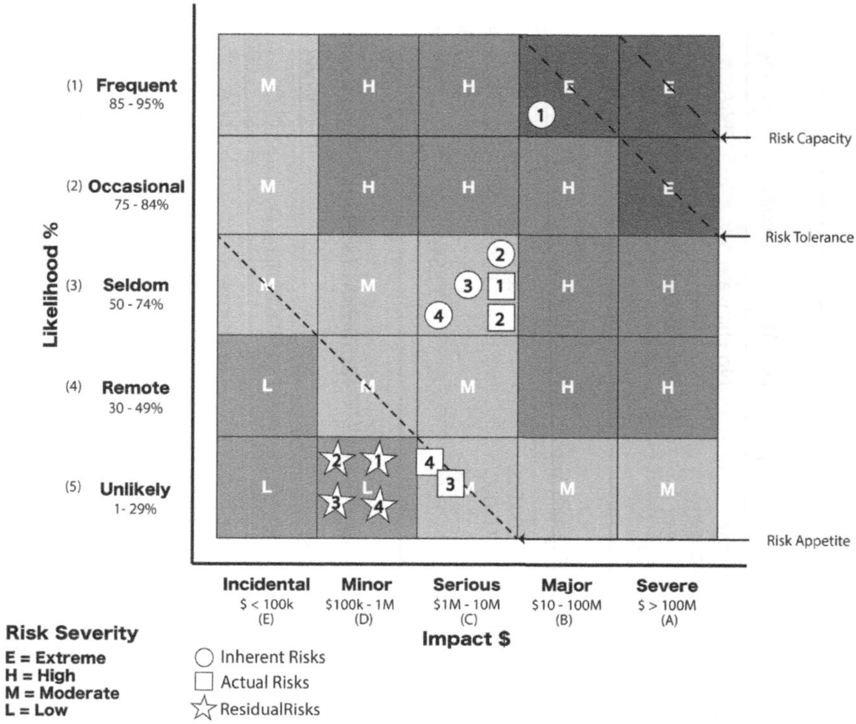

Figure 8.2 Heatmap with inherent, actual, and residual risks.

(system failure) were within the risk appetite, we decided to review treatment plans for all four risks. I wanted to highlight how low the effectiveness of additional controls can be once a risk is already at an acceptable level. It's important to remember this and aim for a balance between security and effectiveness, rather than striving for perfection. Achieving that balance allows organizations to maintain both agility and security, which is where cybersecurity truly becomes a business enabler.

Another way to represent this information is by using a loss exceedance curve through a quantitative approach. With the same data we compiled for our examples, we can run some thousands of Monte Carlo simulations to generate the chart. For instance, the aggregation of data breach, compliance failure, insider threat, and system failure risks would produce a result similar to what is shown in Figure 8.3. We'll dive deeper into this in Section III, but for now, I just wanted to give you a glimpse of what's possible. By organizing and gathering information correctly, the same data used for a qualitative approach can easily transition into a quantitative analysis as well.

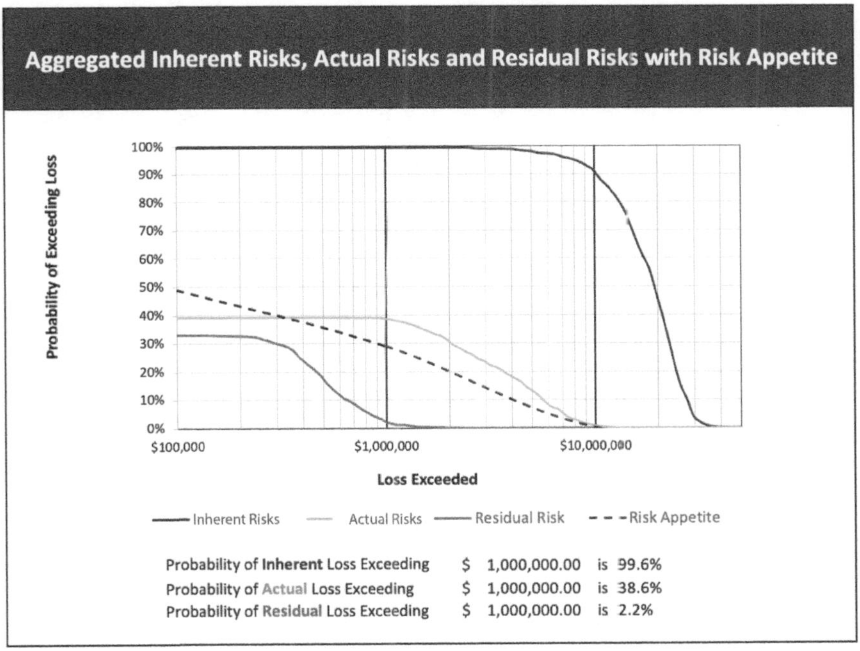

Figure 8.3 Aggregation of the four example risks.

After all this analysis you may have more questions, and that's great because it means you're truly understanding the cyber risk management process. How complex is this analysis in practice? Well, I would say that it depends on three factors: time constraints, the amount of information, and the tools you have available to perform the assessment. You can complete on your own the analysis represented in Figure 8.4 which is what we've just reviewed, using the information you already know, or you can enrich the process by bringing others into the discussion.

This collaboration can add valuable perspectives, statistical data, threat intelligence, and more. As I mentioned from the beginning, we assess risks based on what we know and understand. As you improve your information gathering and systematize that knowledge, you'll need better tools to manage the growing sets of information and the teams working with you. Then, there's the issue of time. There's never enough time to assess everything we'd like, so you'll need to find the balance between exhaustive risk assessment and moving forward to take action. The time you need will also depend on how mature your organization is and how well-established your security posture is. If your organization has significant gaps, it's crucial to focus on what matters most. Prioritize continuous improvement with smaller

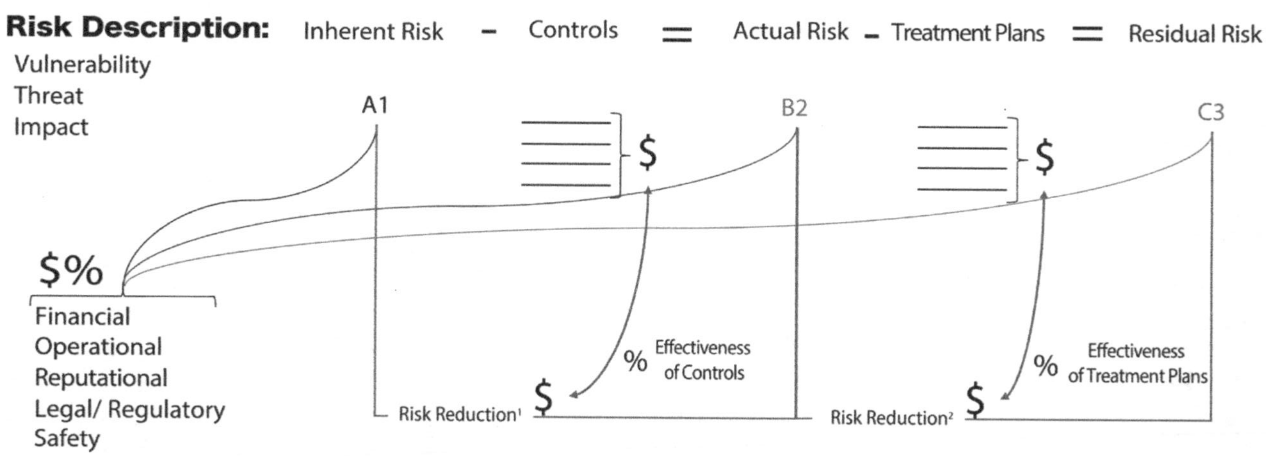

Risk Reduction1 = (Inherent likelihood x Inherent Impact) - (Actual likelihood x Actual Impact)
Effectiveness of Controls = (((Risk Reduction1) - (Control Cost)) / (Inherent likelihood x Inherent Impact)) x 100
Risk Reduction2 = (Actual likelihood x Actual Impact) - (Residual likelihood x Residual Impact)
Effectiveness of Treatment Plans = (((Risk Reduction2) - (Treatment Plan Cost)) / (Actual likelihood x Actual Impact)) x 100

Figure 8.4 Residual risk after treatment plans.

assessments but faster action plans to get things done. This is where getting the basics right becomes so important, remember those strong foundations we discussed in Section I? Start there.

Ok, continuing with the phase of risk treatment strategies, we need to remember that after formulating treatment plans, the next significant step is presenting these strategies to the management team. This presentation is not just a formality; it's an essential process that ensures decision-makers fully understand the scope, implications, and requirements of the proposed mitigation strategies. A key aspect of this discussion involves a detailed breakdown of costs associated with implementing each plan. This includes not only the initial outlay for technologies or services but also any potential hidden costs, such as training employees on new systems or the potential for increased operational expenses.

The effort and time required for implementation are also critical components of the conversation. Management needs to understand the timeline for deploying mitigation strategies, including any periods of increased risk or operational disruption. This helps in planning and ensures realistic expectations about when the organization can expect to see the benefits of these measures. Additionally, the resources needed for operation and maintenance must be clearly outlined. It's vital to present a complete view of the ongoing commitment required to sustain these safeguards effectively. This includes detailing the need for continuous monitoring, regular updates, and potential future investments to keep defenses robust against evolving threats.

By presenting a complete picture that includes costs, effort, time, and ongoing resource needs, you can facilitate informed decision-making and turn plans into action. This approach ensures that management not only supports the proposed treatment plans but also understands their long-term implications, setting the stage for a successful implementation and maintenance of cybersecurity measures. This process highlights the strategic decision-making involved in risk treatment planning. It requires a deep understanding of the risk, the effectiveness of existing controls, and a thoughtful assessment of the organization's capacity to manage or mitigate the risk. Throughout this process, formal documentation and clear communication are vital, ensuring that all stakeholders understand the rationale behind the treatment decisions and the steps taken to protect the organization's interests.

As we conclude this phase, an essential step involves updating the risk register with the treatment plans approved for implementation. This update is not merely about recordkeeping; it's about ensuring transparency and accountability within the organization regarding how risks will be managed. The updated risk register will detail the specific treatment strategies that have been chosen, whether they involve avoiding, mitigating, transferring, or accepting the risk. For each risk, the register will outline the actions to be taken, who is responsible for implementing these actions, and the timelines for completion. It's a roadmap that guides the organization from the decision-making process in the boardroom to the practical, on-the-ground actions that will safeguard the organization's digital assets.

Keeping our risk register up to date gives all stakeholders a clear and current view of the organization's risk landscape and how it's being managed. This practice fosters a culture of informed decision-making and continuous engagement with the risk management process. Documenting the approved treatment plans allows the organization to track progress toward its cybersecurity objectives, identify any gaps or delays in implementation, and make the necessary adjustments to stay aligned with its risk management goals. Ultimately, updating the risk register with approved treatment plans is a critical link between planning and action. It marks the transition from theoretical risk management strategies to tangible steps aimed at enhancing the organization's security posture.

Chapter 9

Making things happen

Communication and implementation

ORGANIZING PROJECTS FOR TREATMENT PLANS IMPLEMENTATIONS

"And the belief in a thing makes it happen." These words from Frank Lloyd Wright align with the structured approach needed for successful project management. Adopting a formal project management methodology, such as the Standard for Project Management ANSI/PMI 99-001-2021[1] and the *Project Management Body of Knowledge* (PMBOK), 6th edition, is crucial for executing security initiatives in a structured and consistent manner. The Project Management Institute (PMI) approach provides a comprehensive framework, organizing projects into five key process groups: initiating, planning, executing, monitoring and controlling, and closing. These groups are supported by ten knowledge areas: integration, scope, schedule, cost, quality, resources, communications, risk, procurement, and stakeholder.

Leveraging this structured approach helps align each security initiative with the risks it seeks to address and the organization's priorities. This methodology ensures that every project follows a clear process from start to finish, improving resource management, setting expectations, and maintaining detailed documentation. Additionally, it facilitates tracking changes and updates in the environment, providing a transparent record of how risks are managed and ensuring accountability throughout the project life cycle.

The first step in implementing a risk treatment measure is the initiation phase, as outlined in the PMBOK framework. This phase marks the beginning of the project, involving formal authorization, setting objectives, and defining scope. Here, you identify the specific risks the initiative will address and establish the desired outcomes. This is where all necessary information, such as risk assessments, stakeholder input, and technical requirements, is gathered to ensure the solution is well-designed and effective. In a cyber risk management context, this phase aligns with the ideation stage, where the initiative is conceptualized, and a foundational strategy is developed to

DOI: 10.1201/9781003546207-12

address identified risks. This dual focus ensures that both project management principles and cybersecurity needs are integrated from the outset.

An integral part of the Initiating phase is developing the project charter. This formal document authorizes the project and provides the project manager with the authority to allocate resources. It outlines the project's purpose, objectives, high-level requirements, and stakeholders, serving as a reference throughout the project's life cycle. The project charter also includes an overview of risks, assumptions, and constraints, establishing a baseline for planning and decision-making.

Once the project is initiated, the Planning phase begins. This involves developing a project management plan that outlines how the initiative will be executed, monitored, and controlled. It includes selecting the appropriate technologies and controls, defining necessary processes, and identifying the resources required. The Planning phase covers all aspects of the project, from scope, time, and cost management to quality, human resources, communication, risk, procurement, and stakeholder management.

During the Planning phase, it's important to dive into the specifics of each aspect to ensure nothing is overlooked. When defining the project scope, clarity is key. You need to be precise about what the project will cover and, just as importantly, what it won't. This helps in setting the boundaries for the work ahead, preventing scope creep, which can derail even the best-laid plans. The activity definition process is about breaking down the project into manageable tasks, making it easier to understand what needs to be done and in what order.

Resource planning is another part of this phase which it is about identifying what you'll need, be it personnel, technology, or materials, and ensuring that these resources are available when needed. Proper resource allocation helps to prevent bottlenecks and ensures that the project stays on schedule. Activity sequencing comes into play here, as it's all about understanding the dependencies between tasks and making sure everything flows smoothly from one step to the next. Estimating activity duration and costs goes hand in hand with sequencing; you need to have a realistic idea of how long each task will take and what it will cost to avoid surprises down the line.

Risk management planning involves identifying potential risks to the project, analyzing their impact, and developing strategies to mitigate them. This allows you to anticipate challenges and prepare solutions in advance, reducing the likelihood of being caught off guard. Schedule development and cost budgeting are intertwined with risk management, as they both rely on accurate estimates and a good understanding of the project's requirements.

Quality planning is about setting the standards that the project must meet and determining how these will be achieved. This ensures that the final output not only meets the project's requirements but also satisfies the stakeholders' expectations. Organizational planning and staff acquisition are about getting the right people in place. It's important to have a clear plan for how teams will be structured and how new members will be integrated into the project.

Communication planning is key to keeping everyone informed and aligned. It's about deciding what information needs to be shared, who needs to receive it, and how it will be delivered. Good communication helps to build trust and ensures that everyone is on the same page, reducing the risk of misunderstandings or conflicts. Risk identification, qualitative risk analysis, and quantitative risk analysis are ongoing processes throughout the planning phase. They involve continuously assessing potential risks and adjusting the plan as needed to ensure that the project remains on track.

With a solid plan in place, the Execution phase is where the actual work happens. Building on the foundation laid during the Initiation and Planning phases, this stage is all about translating plans into tangible results. During the initiation phase, we defined the project's scope and objectives, secured formal authorization, and gathered all necessary inputs to ensure a well-rounded approach. The Planning phase then took these inputs and developed a roadmap, detailing every aspect of how the initiative would be carried out, from identifying required resources and defining tasks to estimating costs and planning for potential risks. Now, in the Execution phase, we take that carefully crafted plan and begin to implement it in a structured and controlled manner, putting all the pieces together to move the project forward effectively.

Project plan execution is at the heart of this phase. It's where all the strategies, schedules, and resource allocations come into play as we start deploying the controls, technologies, and processes identified in the planning stage. This is a highly coordinated effort, where project managers are crucial in ensuring that every task is performed as planned. They are responsible for orchestrating activities, managing the team, and ensuring that every action taken aligns with the project's goals and objectives.

Quality assurance is another integral part of the Execution phase. As tasks are carried out, it's essential to maintain a high standard of work to ensure that the project deliverables meet the predefined requirements and quality benchmarks. This involves continuous monitoring and regular checks to verify that the work being done aligns with the project's objectives and that any deviations are quickly identified and corrected. Quality Assurance is an ongoing process throughout the Execution phase, ensuring that each step of the project contributes to achieving its overall goals without compromising quality. This helps to prevent issues from escalating, ensuring that any problems are addressed early on and that the project stays on track.

Team development also plays a significant role in the success of the Execution phase. As the project progresses, it's crucial to foster a strong, collaborative team environment where everyone is motivated and aligned with the project's objectives. This might involve additional training, coaching, and team-building activities to enhance skills and improve communication. A well-developed team is more likely to perform efficiently, overcome challenges, and deliver high-quality results.

Effective information distribution is key to keeping everyone aligned and informed throughout the Execution phase. Regular communication with stakeholders ensures that they are aware of the project's progress, any changes in scope or timelines, and any emerging risks or issues. This transparency helps build trust and ensures that all parties involved are on the same page, reducing the likelihood of misunderstandings and fostering a collaborative environment where everyone is working toward the same goals. Clear and consistent communication also allows for timely decision-making, enabling the project team to address any issues promptly and keep the project moving forward.

In addition to managing internal activities, the Execution phase often involves solicitation and source selection, where external vendors or partners are engaged to provide necessary services or products. This requires a careful selection process to ensure that these external resources align with the project's quality and budget requirements. Once selected, contract administration becomes a critical task and something you as part of managing cyber risks must review and make sure that all security contractual obligations are in place, and that vendors deliver as expected. Throughout the Execution phase, the focus is on maintaining momentum, managing resources efficiently, and ensuring that all activities are aligned with the project's objectives. It's about keeping the project on track, addressing any issues that arise promptly, and ensuring that the initiative is implemented effectively with minimal disruption to business operations. Combining planning with diligent execution is what ultimately ensures the success of any risk management initiative.

The monitoring and controlling phase runs concurrently with the Execution phase and focuses on tracking the project's progress to ensure it stays aligned with the plan. This phase involves measuring performance against the project management plan, identifying deviations, and implementing corrective actions as needed. It also includes managing risks, quality, and scope to ensure the project stays on track and meets its objectives. The goal is to maintain control over the project by documenting changes and managing risks effectively. Continuously measuring performance, addressing deviations, and applying corrective actions as required ensures the project remains on course and achieves its intended outcomes.

One of the key components of the Monitoring and Controlling phase is performance reporting. Regular performance reports provide a clear picture of the project's status, highlighting what has been accomplished, what still needs to be done, and any areas where the project is falling short. These reports are vital for keeping stakeholders informed and engaged, ensuring transparency, and enabling timely decision-making. Scope verification is another important activity during this phase. It involves reviewing and validating that the project deliverables meet the requirements defined during the planning phase. This step ensures that the project is producing the right outputs and that all deliverables are completed to the agreed-upon standards. It's a process of checking that what is being delivered matches what was promised, preventing scope creep, and ensuring that the project stays focused on its original objectives. Alongside scope verification, scope change control is necessary to manage any changes that might arise. Changes are inevitable in any project, but this control process ensures that all changes are evaluated for their impact on the project's objectives, timeline, and budget before they are approved or rejected. Schedule control is important in keeping the project on track and within its intended timeframe. When such discrepancies are detected, Schedule Control involves implementing corrective actions to bring the project back on track. This might mean reallocating resources, adjusting timelines, or revising project activities to ensure that deadlines are met without compromising the quality of the deliverables. Similarly, cost control ensures that the project remains within its budget.

Quality control is another significant element of the monitoring and controlling phase. This involves continuously assessing the project's outputs to ensure that they meet the required standards and quality benchmarks. Quality Control activities help to identify any defects or issues with the deliverables, allowing the project team to address these problems before they become more significant. Risk monitoring and control is also part of this phase, as it involves keeping a close watch on identified risks and identifying any new risks that might arise during the project's execution. This continuous monitoring allows project managers to respond quickly to any changes in the risk landscape, implementing mitigation strategies or adjusting the project plan as needed to minimize the impact of risks on the project's success.

Integrated change control involves coordinating all changes across the project, ensuring that any modifications to the project scope, schedule, or cost are systematically evaluated and managed. Throughout the Monitoring and Controlling phase, the emphasis is on maintaining control over the project and ensuring that it remains aligned with its original objectives. This phase is about being vigilant, responsive, and adaptive, ensuring that any changes or deviations are promptly addressed and that the project stays on track to achieve its goals.

The final phase, closing, is where the project is formally completed and all activities are finalized. This phase isn't just about ticking off remaining tasks but about ensuring a smooth transition from project work to everyday operations, cementing the project's outcomes, and capturing valuable insights for future use. During this stage, every aspect of the project is reviewed to confirm that all objectives have been met and that the deliverables align with the agreed-upon standards. This includes obtaining formal acceptance from stakeholders, which is essential for officially closing the project and handing over the results to the organization. The Closing phase is an opportunity to solidify the project's contributions to the organization's risk management practices by documenting outcomes and learning from the project experience.

A key component of this phase is contract closeout, which involves verifying that all contractual obligations have been fulfilled by both the organization and its partners, such as vendors and contractors. This means checking that all work has been completed satisfactorily, all deliverables have been received and meet the necessary quality standards, and there are no unresolved issues or disputes. Resolving any outstanding contractual matters is important to avoid future legal complications and to maintain positive relationships with external partners. Ensuring that all agreements are fully satisfied helps protect the organization and contributes to a clean project closure.

Administrative closure includes wrapping up all administrative tasks related to the project, such as finalizing documentation, archiving records, and releasing project resources. It's about making sure that all project information is accurately captured and stored in a way that can be easily accessed for future reference. This includes updating the risk register and other related documents to reflect the final state of the project. Proper administrative closure ensures that all aspects of the project are formally concluded and that there is a detailed record of the project's life cycle, which is invaluable for future project planning and risk management efforts.

During the closing phase, project managers need to conduct a project review. This involves gathering feedback from all stakeholders and team members to evaluate the project's successes and challenges. This step is about fostering an environment of continuous improvement. The insights gained here can lead to better project management practices and more effective risk management strategies in the future. Finally, as the project concludes, it's important to ensure that all documentation is up to date and that any loose ends are tied up. This includes updating project plans, technology inventories, network diagrams, finalizing financial records, and ensuring all project files are properly archived. It means that all project information is preserved, providing a clear and accurate record of what was achieved, which can be used as a reference for future initiatives.

RISK TREATMENT PLAN IMPLEMENTATION

Once management gives the green light, these treatment plans become security initiatives that need to be followed closely to ensure they're executed as intended. This follow-through is crucial to confirm that each initiative is not only implemented but also seamlessly integrated into the organization's operations. After approval, it's important to act quickly and kick off the project management process without delay. Any lag between approval and implementation can lead to shifts in priorities, and suddenly, your project might be pushed down the list or delayed indefinitely. When you have the chance to execute a plan, take it.

Starting the project process varies from organization to organization. Some have designated windows where projects are reviewed, prioritized, and assigned to project managers to initiate. Others maintain a continuous pipeline of projects, constantly feeding new initiatives into the system. However, regardless of the approach, the process generally begins with allocating resources and defining responsibilities. No one is just sitting around waiting for a new task, so it's essential to identify who will be involved, assess their current workloads, and allocate time accordingly. Ensuring resource availability at the start is key to avoiding delays and keeping the project on track. In our case, our project has already been approved, and the initial idea has been conceptualized. So, at this stage the architects have created a conceptual design, which has been assessed by you and your team to evaluate the residual risk after its implementation. With this initial work, we are ready to move directly into the design phase, where the security architects alongside with the project team will develop a detailed solution design. This phase is critical as it defines every aspect of the project needed for a successful execution. We need to consider all details, such as selecting vendors, determining the necessary technology, adjusting existing processes or developing new ones, and identifying the training or personnel required to operate the solution effectively.

It's also during this phase that we must define the security testing requirements. While IT teams are accustomed to testing new deployments before they go live, they don't always include security testing. This oversight can be risky. At the time of conceptual design, we operated under the assumption that the implementation wouldn't introduce new risks beyond those we had already identified. However, as we move into the detailed design phase, this assumption needs to be validated. For example, if we are developing a new web application as part of the solution, we couldn't initially assess risks related to the code because the code didn't exist yet. Now, as we finalize the solution design, it's a must to include requirements for security testing to identify any new risks that the web application might introduce. These risks need to be addressed before the application goes into production to ensure the solution is secure and aligns with the organization's risk management strategy. So, if you can see, at this stage, we conduct another risk assessment, this time based on the final and detailed solution design. This step allows us to confirm the assumptions made during the treatment plan strategy phase. We take a closer look at the specifics of the solution to ensure that it aligns with our initial expectations and doesn't introduce any new, unexpected risks.

During this assessment, we also communicate final cost estimates, outline the expected timeline for implementation, and identify any potential risks that the solution might introduce. It's essential that these newly identified risks are lower than the risks we're aiming to mitigate. The end goal is to ensure that, after implementing the solution, the overall risk level is brought within our organization's risk appetite. This phase of reassessment and confirmation ensures that our approach is not only effective but also aligned with the broader risk management strategy of reducing exposure to an acceptable level. Taking this information to the Risk Committee, whether it's called the Information Security Forum, Information Risk Forum, Risk Review Board, or any other name your organization uses, is a step in the right direction before moving into the execution phase. This step is particularly important if gaps in costs, time, or residual risks have been identified during the detailed solution design. Presenting these findings to the committee ensures that all stakeholders are aware of any deviations from the original plan and can discuss and approve adjustments as needed. This process provides transparency and also aligns everyone's expectations, ensuring that the project moves forward with a clear understanding of the potential challenges and the strategies to address them.

Timing is crucial once we have the green light to proceed with implementation. Rolling out each security initiative according to the planned schedule is vital. Delays can leave your organization vulnerable to risks longer than necessary, making adherence to timelines a top priority. Effective project management, clear communication, and sometimes flexibility are essential to adjust as situations evolve. Ensuring everyone involved, from IT staff to department heads, receives clear instructions on their roles within the initiatives is key. It's not just about knowing the 'what' and the 'when,' but also understanding the "why" behind each action. This clarity ensures that all participants are aligned and committed to the common goal of mitigating cyber risks.

It is then that effective risk communication strategies are key for bridging the gap between the approval of risk treatment plans and their actual implementation. Once management has approved these plans, the next critical step is ensuring that everyone involved understands their responsibilities and the importance of their role in executing the plan. This phase is not just about passing down orders; it's about creating a shared understanding of the risks, the tasks at hand, and the overall goals. Effective communication is key to ensuring a smooth transition from planning to action.

First, it's essential to clearly communicate the risks that have been identified and the reasoning behind the chosen treatment strategies. Stakeholders across the organization need to understand why certain actions are being taken and what the potential consequences might be if these actions are not effectively implemented. This requires providing context for each risk, including its impact, likelihood, and how it fits into the broader risk landscape of the organization. Presenting this information in an understandable way ensures that everyone is aligned on the urgency and importance of the tasks ahead. Next, clearly define and assign tasks. Each team member, department, or external partner involved in the implementation must know precisely what is expected of them. This involves breaking down the treatment plan into actionable steps and assigning these steps to the appropriate individuals. Defining tasks clearly helps avoid misunderstandings and ensures that everyone knows their role in advancing the plan. Setting realistic timelines for each task and communicating deadlines effectively is also crucial, so everyone understands the timeframe in which their work needs to be completed.

In addition to defining tasks, it's critical to emphasize the importance of each role within the context of the larger objective. When individuals understand how their specific actions contribute to the overall security posture of the organization, they are more likely to be engaged and motivated. Highlighting the importance of collaboration and how different teams' efforts intersect can foster a sense of shared responsibility and drive a collective effort toward successful implementation. Effective risk communication also requires regular updates and feedback loops. Keeping lines of communication open allows for real-time updates on progress and enables teams to address any challenges or obstacles as they arise. Regular check-ins and status meetings can help keep everyone aligned, track progress against timelines, and identify any issues that might need attention. This continuous dialogue helps maintain momentum and ensures that the project stays on track.

Now that we have the final approval to move into the execution of the project; the project team will implement exactly what was approved. Any deviations from the original plan need to be identified and reported so we can reassess risks based on those changes. For instance, let's imagine following the example of the risk avoidance treatment plan for the risk of system failure, we were implementing a new solution replacing the outdated one and this will require migrating from version A to version C. During the execution of the project, the team discovers that version C is failing and doesn't integrate with your environment as expected, causing issues and not functioning properly. As a result, they decide to switch to version B, which works without those issues. This change means that your risks were initially assessed according to version C, and switching to version B could introduce different risks. Version B might have vulnerabilities or lack some of the security features you had considered in your assessment. Alternatively, it could be more secure but more expensive. The point here is that the possibilities are endless, and every change can impact your risk landscape. With this example I want to highlight the importance of constant feedback during the implementation phase to avoid losing time and to fully understand the risks that may be introduced with the new solution. Regular communication and reassessment ensure that your security posture remains aligned with your risk appetite, even when unexpected changes occur.

Of course, if a situation like this arises, a change request should be documented. This involves taking that part of the solution back for review and confirmation with the architecture and risk management teams. Approvals for the change might also be required, depending on the nature of the adjustment. Once the change is reviewed and approved, the project can then return to the execution phase. This process ensures that any deviations are properly vetted and that the risks associated with the new approach are fully understood and managed before proceeding. The same applies to security testing. In fact, we can think on this feedback process as what is essentially updating our understanding of the current state, providing new insights into what we are assessing. As we learn more about the system or solution through testing, we may uncover new vulnerabilities or unexpected behavior that wasn't initially considered. This requires us to adjust our understanding of the risks and respond accordingly.

Similar to what we did at the end of the previous phase, as we can see in Figure 9.1, once risk treatment plans are put into action, it's necessary to revisit the risk register and update it to accurately reflect the progress made and the current state of cyber risks within the organization. This updating process is the step that ensures the risk register remains a living document, reflecting a true representation of the organization's risk landscape at any given time. Updating the risk register involves documenting the outcomes of the implemented treatment plans, including any mitigation efforts, risk transfers, or acceptances that have occurred. This might mean adjusting the likelihood or impact scores of certain risks, removing risks that have been fully mitigated, or adding new risks that have emerged as a result of the treatment actions. Our updated risk register should clearly indicate the residual risks that remain even after the treatment plans have been executed.

Sometimes we're good at identifying problems but not as good as we wish in getting those treatment plans implemented. This is not because we're really bad at getting things done but because this phase requires collaboration from many more areas. Sometimes, the work to implement these plans isn't even in our hands. We talked about these aspects in more detail in Section I, where we discussed how important it is to work with others and the realities of putting plans into action.

Finally, it's important to celebrate milestones and successes along the way. Acknowledging the completion of key tasks and recognizing the efforts of individuals and teams reinforces the importance of the work being done and keeps morale high. Celebrating these achievements not only boosts motivation but also reinforces the value of effective risk management in protecting the organization. Make sure you and everyone around you enjoys the job, try to consciously do that until it becomes a habit.

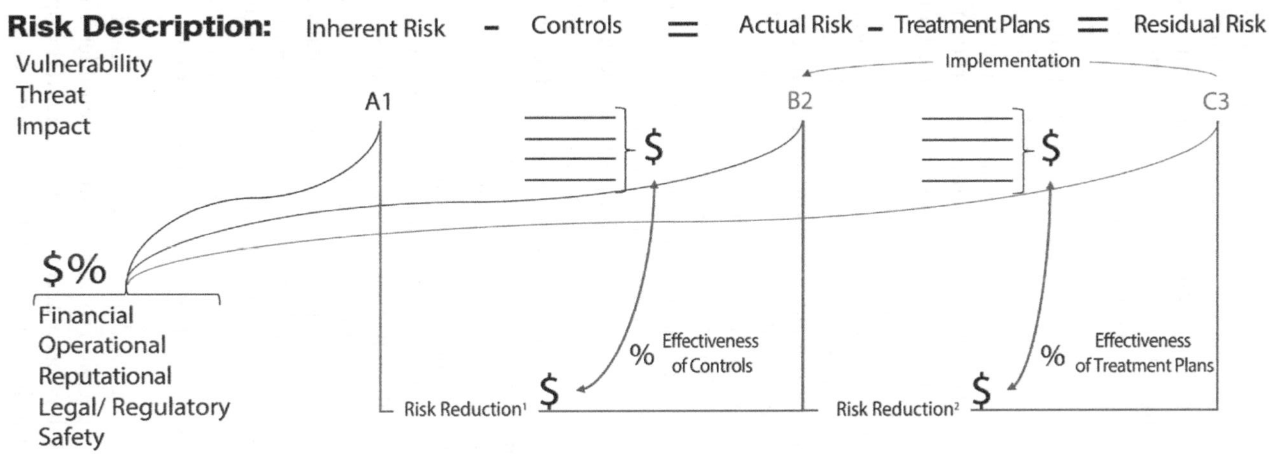

Risk Reduction1 = (Inherent likelihood x Inherent Impact) - (Actual likelihood x Actual Impact)

Effectiveness of Controls = (((Risk Reduction1) - (Control Cost)) / (Inherent likelihood x Inherent Impact)) x 100

Risk Reduction2 = (Actual likelihood x Actual Impact) - (Residual likelihood x Residual Impact)

Effectiveness of Treatment Plans = (((Risk Reduction2) - (Treatment Plan Cost)) / (Actual likelihood x Actual Impact)) x 100

Figure 9.1 Treatment plans implementation.

EXECUTING RISK ACCEPTANCE

When we talk about risk acceptance, we're referring to a deliberate and strategic decision made after the analysis. This decision acknowledges that the cost or impact of implementing additional controls to mitigate, avoid, or transfer a particular risk outweighs the benefits of reducing that risk further. It's important to note that accepting a risk doesn't mean ignoring it; rather, it's about recognizing that the risk level is within the organization's risk appetite and that the resources required to mitigate it could be better allocated elsewhere. However, this process needs to be formalized to ensure clarity and accountability. This is where risk acceptance letters come into play. These documents are formal records that outline the rationale behind the decision to accept the risk, ensuring that everyone involved understands the reasoning and the boundaries of this acceptance.

The first step in executing risk acceptance is to clearly document the decision-making process. This involves detailing the specific risk, its potential impact, and why it has been deemed acceptable within the context of the organization's risk management strategy. The risk acceptance letter must be signed off by the appropriate authority, which explicitly states that the risk is being accepted, along with the reasons for doing so and the date of the acceptance will expire as the risk acceptance should never be open-ended; setting a timeframe for reassessment ensures that the risk is regularly reviewed in light of any changes in the organization or external environment. This letter should also outline any conditions under which the risk was accepted, such as specific circumstances or mitigating factors that were considered. Formalizing this decision ensures transparency.

Risk acceptance is not a static decision. It requires ongoing monitoring to ensure that the risk level remains within acceptable limits over time. As the organization evolves and external conditions shift, the factors that made the risk acceptable initially may also change. For this reason, accepted risks must be formally recorded in the risk register, a living document that captures the current state of all identified risks and their treatment plans. The risk register should include details about the risk acceptance, such as the justification for acceptance, the expiration date, and any conditions that were set. Regular reviews of accepted risks are key to determine if they still fall within the organization's risk appetite or if new treatment measures need to be considered.

Once the decision to accept a risk has been documented and formalized, it's time to communicate this decision to all relevant stakeholders. They need to understand why the risk has been accepted, the potential implications, and any limitations or conditions attached to this acceptance. Effective communication ensures that there are no surprises down the road and that everyone is prepared to manage any potential consequences should the risk materialize. However, even when a risk is accepted, it's important to have contingency plans in place. These plans outline the steps the organization will take if the risk materializes, providing a clear roadmap for response and recovery. This will help you to maintain your organization resilient, even in the face of accepted risks, and supports continuous improvement in risk management practices. Formally documenting, communicating, and monitoring accepted risks ensures that the organization remains proactive in managing risks, safeguarding its assets, and aligning with its strategic goals.

At the end of the day, risk acceptance is a strategic decision that must involve careful consideration and formal documentation. Making informed choices that align with your organization's overall goals and risk management strategy, ensuring that risks are formally accepted, documented, monitored, and reviewed regularly.

So, as we bring this chapter to a close, it's important to emphasize the significance of translating strategy into action. The fourth phase of risk management, which is about communication and implementation, is where all the planning and assessment truly come to life. It is in this phase that we turn intentions into implemented actions, ensuring that risks are not just identified and analyzed but are actively managed and mitigated. The success of this phase relies heavily on a structured approach, using methodologies like project management professional (PMP) to ensure that each initiative is systematically planned, executed, and monitored. This structured process helps in aligning the risk treatment initiatives with the organization's priorities, making sure resources are allocated efficiently and that all changes are meticulously documented. This meticulous documentation is not just for recordkeeping; it is a critical component of accountability and continuous improvement, providing a clear trail of how decisions were made, actions were taken, and how risks were ultimately treated.

Implementing risk treatment plans requires immediate action once they have been approved. Delays can compromise the effectiveness of the entire risk management process, potentially leaving the organization vulnerable to risks that could have been mitigated earlier. It's not just about starting projects quickly but also about maintaining momentum and ensuring that each step is completed as planned. Effective project management is essential in this regard, as it helps keep the project on track, prevents scope creep, and ensures that all stakeholders are kept informed of progress and any changes that may arise. Communication is the backbone of this process. Clear, consistent communication ensures that everyone involved understands their role, the reasons behind the actions being taken, and the expected outcomes. This clarity helps prevent misunderstandings and ensures that all team members are aligned toward the common goal of reducing the organization's risk exposure.

Risk acceptance, as discussed, is a vital aspect of risk management that requires careful consideration and formalization. It's not a decision to be taken lightly, nor should it be made without complete analysis and documentation. When an organization decides to accept a risk, it must be because the cost of mitigation outweighs the benefits, and it is within the organization's risk appetite. This decision must be documented in a risk acceptance letter, clearly outlining the reasons for acceptance, any conditions or limitations, and an expiration date for reassessment. This formalized approach ensures that all stakeholders understand the decision and are prepared to manage any potential consequences should the risk materialize. Besides, accepted risks should be continuously monitored to ensure that they remain within acceptable limits and do not pose a greater threat as conditions change. Whether it's through careful project management, clear communication, or formalizing risk acceptance, the key is to maintain a proactive posture. This means being vigilant, staying informed, and ensuring that your risk management practices are flexible aligned with both current needs and future challenges. Remember, the goal of risk management is to safeguard your organization's assets contributing to the achievement of the strategic objectives. So, keep pushing forward, continuously improve your processes, and always remember that people expect results, not activity.

NOTE

1 Project Management Institute. (2021). *A Guide to the Project Management Body of Knowledge (PMBOK® guide)* (7th ed.). Project Management Institute.

Chapter 10

Risk monitoring and metrics

RISK MONITORING

Support from robust systems and vigilant processes is what ensures our efforts remain resilient, allowing us to adapt and succeed in the face of evolving challenges. Risk monitoring is the final, yet ongoing phase of the risk management cycle. It's like being the lookout on a ship, constantly scanning the horizon for changes in the weather, obstacles in the path, or signs of opportunities. This stage is about keeping a vigilant eye on the risks we've identified, treated, and accepted, making sure we understand how they evolve over time and how our defenses hold up against them. At its core, risk monitoring involves the regular review and tracking of the risk environment and the effectiveness of our risk management efforts. It's about asking, "Are our safeguards working as expected?", "Have any new threats emerged?", and "Are there changes in our operational environment that might affect our risk profile?". This continuous scrutiny helps us adapt and respond to new information or changes in the external and internal context that might impact our cybersecurity posture.

Risk monitoring is inherently tied to both internal and external contexts, functioning as a dynamic feedback loop that ensures our risk management strategies stay relevant and responsive while new risks are promptly identified and managed. Continuously revisiting and reassessing our operational environment allows us to recalibrate our focus based on the latest developments, threats, and opportunities. This ongoing evaluation requires examining changes within the organization, such as shifts in strategic priorities, new technologies, or workforce transitions, as well as external factors like evolving cyber threats, regulatory updates, and geopolitical changes. Recognizing that both our organization and the broader cyber landscape are fluid and ever-changing, we must adopt a proactive, adaptive approach to risk monitoring.

Through regular reviews of these shifts, we can identify emerging risks early and adjust our risk treatment plans accordingly. This might involve strengthening cyber defenses against new threats, adapting compliance

DOI: 10.1201/9781003546207-13

strategies in response to regulatory updates, or revisiting our risk appetite in light of changes in business objectives or market conditions. Maintaining this constant vigilance enhances our understanding of the effectiveness of existing controls and safeguards, enabling us to measure actual performance against expected outcomes and identify areas for improvement. This feeds into a continuous improvement cycle as shown in Figure 10.1, where insights gained from monitoring help detect opportunities for enhancing our risk management efforts.

A key part of risk monitoring is generating actionable metrics through key performance indicators (KPIs) and key risk indicators (KRIs). KPIs help us measure how well the cybersecurity program is performing against its goals, like how quickly we can detect and respond to incidents. KRIs, on the other hand, give us early warnings about potential increases in risk exposure, such as a spike in phishing attempts or unusual network traffic, signaling the need for closer inspection or immediate action. One concept that might be new to you is the role of KRIs; they act as our digital canaries in the coal mine, providing early warning signals that alert us to potential danger before it escalates. Just as miners used canaries to detect invisible, harmful gases, in cyber risk management, we use KRIs to sense shifts in our risk landscape. These indicators might track trends in threat intelligence reports, anomalies in user access patterns, or unexpected changes in system performance, among others. When a KRI crosses a predefined threshold, it's a cue for cybersecurity risk management teams to take a closer look, potentially averting a crisis through proactive intervention.

For KRIs to be effective, they need to follow the SMART criteria: Specific, Measurable, Attainable, Relevant, and Timely. This means each KRI should clearly define what it is tracking, be quantifiable for objective assessment, be realistic within the organization's capabilities, directly relate to the risks being monitored, and provide timely data that supports quick decision-making. A balanced approach to KRIs is also crucial. Including a mix of indicators that focus on past results, predict future risks, and track ongoing trends ensures that the organization is prepared for what might happen next, not just reacting to what has already occurred. Efficiency is another key aspect when measuring KRIs. This involves evaluating the impact of each indicator, the effort required to collect and analyze data, the reliability of the information, and the ability of the KRI to be consistently measured over time. KRIs should provide meaningful insights, helping to guide decisions rather than simply adding numbers to a report.

KPIs complement KRIs by serving as benchmarks to assess the effectiveness of cybersecurity programs and risk strategies. KPIs help evaluate the efficiency of incident response processes, the impact of training programs on reducing user errors, and the resilience of the organization's infrastructure against breaches. Systematically measuring these aspects gives a clear picture of where the cybersecurity program stands, highlighting strengths

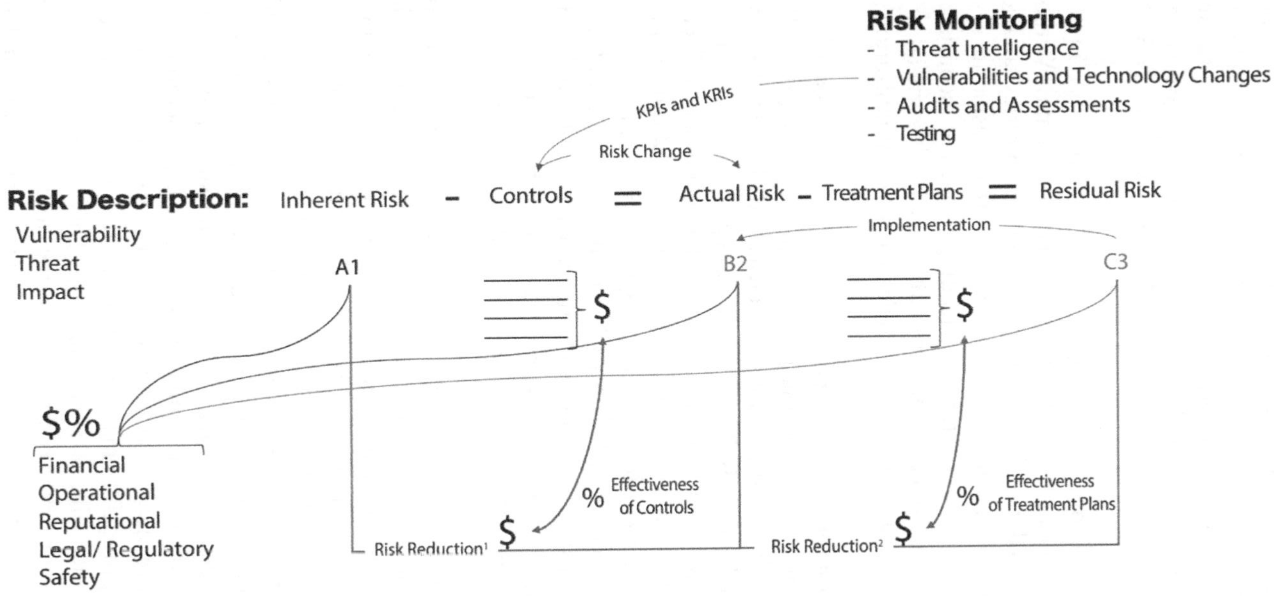

Risk Reduction1 = (Inherent likelihood x Inherent Impact) - (Actual likelihood x Actual Impact)

Effectiveness of Controls = (((Risk Reduction1) - (Control Cost)) / (Inherent likelihood x Inherent Impact)) x 100

Risk Reduction2 = (Actual likelihood x Actual Impact) - (Residual likelihood x Residual Impact)

Effectiveness of Treatment Plans = (((Risk Reduction2) - (Treatment Plan Cost)) / (Actual likelihood x Actual Impact)) x 100

Figure 10.1 Risk monitoring to be proactive.

and identifying areas for improvement. Together, KRIs and KPIs are essential tools for guiding risk management. Incorporating them into regular reporting promotes a culture of continuous improvement and accountability. Sharing these metrics with stakeholders fosters a shared understanding of cybersecurity priorities and challenges, encouraging engagement across the organization and reinforcing the idea that cybersecurity is a shared responsibility.

One significant challenge in developing effective cyber risk metrics is maintaining comprehensive and consistently recorded data. Without a structured approach to data collection and management, metrics can become unreliable and misleading. The problem often stems from disparate systems and processes that are not well integrated, leading to gaps or inconsistencies in data logging. To create reliable and actionable metrics, it's crucial to have data that is comprehensive, accurate, and reflective of the organization's risk landscape.

To address this, establishing data governance practices is essential. This involves standardizing data recording processes and ensuring that all relevant cybersecurity incidents and actions are consistently logged in a way that is accessible and analyzable. Building a reliable repository of cybersecurity data allows organizations to develop metrics that genuinely reflect their security posture and risk exposure. Educating employees about the importance of accurate data recording can also improve the quality of the data collected. If you've ever struggled to gather evidence for an audit, you'll understand how critical it is to improve how evidence is collected and logs are recorded. Doing so ensures the metrics you rely on for decision-making are grounded in reliable data, allowing for more informed and effective risk management.

Another important aspect to consider when working on risk monitoring and metrics generation is the assurance process. This process should be embedded in risk monitoring and ensures that we're not just looking at numbers but also understanding what they mean in the context of our overall cybersecurity health. It involves validating that the controls we've put in place are effective and functioning as intended. This could be achieved through regular audits, testing, and reviews, providing an additional layer of confidence that our cybersecurity measures are robust and capable of protecting the organization against current and emerging threats. One approach that I really like is the three lines of defense model because it offers a structured approach to managing risks and ensuring comprehensive oversight and assurance within an organization. This model is particularly useful in the context of cybersecurity, where the landscape is continually evolving, and the stakes are high. Let's break down how each line of defense contributes to the overall assurance process in cyber risk management.

The first line of defense consists of the operational management and teams directly responsible for managing and securing the organization's daily operations. This includes IT and cybersecurity teams who implement and oversee security measures, policies, and procedures. However, it also extends to all employees and third parties working within the environment, as cybersecurity is a shared responsibility. Everyone must follow and comply with the organization's information security policies, standards, and procedures. For those in the first line of defense, the focus is on ensuring that controls are applied effectively to mitigate identified risks. Regular self-assessments, continuous monitoring, and swift responses to security incidents are essential activities at this level. These teams, positioned on the front lines, play a crucial role in maintaining the organization's security posture and resilience against cyber threats.

The second line of defense is made up of the internal governance structures, such as cyber risk management and compliance functions, which provide oversight and support to the first line. This layer is responsible for ensuring that the cybersecurity strategies and controls are aligned with the organization's risk appetite and compliance requirements. It involves making sure that risk management methodologies, security policies and procedures are in place, as well as the monitoring of their compliance across the organization. This line also plays a critical role in conducting risk assessments and reviews to identify potential gaps or weaknesses in the organization's cyber defenses, providing a crucial check on the efficacy of the first line's efforts.

The third line of defense is the internal audit function, an independent and objective assurance body that evaluates the effectiveness of the organization's overall risk management, governance, and control processes. In the context of cybersecurity, internal audits assess the adequacy of both the first and second lines of defense in managing cyber risks. They provide senior management and the board with an impartial evaluation of the effectiveness of the controls and the risk management practices, highlighting areas of improvement and verifying that risk management processes are functioning as intended across the organization.

This structured approach ensures a broader coverage of risk management and assurance activities, with each line of defense playing a distinct but complementary role (see Figure 10.2). Implementing the three lines of defense model helps organizations build a strong framework for managing cybersecurity risks, ensuring that controls are effective, compliance is upheld, and the organization's cyber resilience is continuously strengthened.

We can't ignore the role of internal audit, which acts as the third line of defense in protecting an organization from cyber risks. As an independent and objective function, internal audit supports the organization by improving operations through its consulting and assurance activities. Regularly assessing the effectiveness of risk management, controls, and governance will help senior management, and the board ensure that the first two lines of defense are working as intended and that the organization's risk management strategies are aligned with its goals.

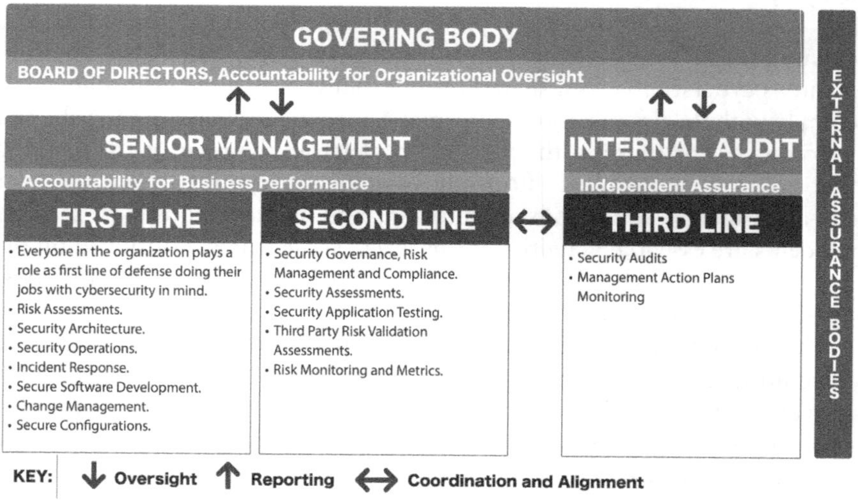

Figure 10.2 Three lines of defense model.

Internal auditors can identify gaps, inefficiencies, or instances where policies and procedures aren't being followed, things that might have slipped through the cracks in the second line of defense. Addressing these issues strengthens the organization's protection against cyber threats and improves overall resilience. Internal audit is essential in keeping cybersecurity practices up-to-date and flexible in response to the evolving threat landscape. Ultimately, risk monitoring keeps the risk management process adaptable and responsive.

ONGOING MONITORING PRACTICES

Ongoing monitoring is about maintaining a vigilant watch over the threat landscape that is always evolving, meaning our defenses can't remain strong and effective indefinitely. As a result, our risks also change, making cyber risk management an endless cycle. Ongoing monitoring involves regularly gathering and analyzing data, understanding the implications of new threats, and being prepared to adjust our risk management strategies as needed. It's an ongoing, iterative process that keeps our cybersecurity efforts aligned with both current situations and future possibilities, ensuring our organization remains resilient against emerging risks. To effectively monitor risks, we need an approach that integrates various tools and techniques, designed to provide unique insights into our cybersecurity posture. One of the fundamental components of ongoing monitoring is threat intelligence. Threat intelligence goes beyond simply gathering information, it involves transforming raw data into actionable insights by adding context and relevance. This evolution from simple information to intelligence is crucial because it provides a deeper understanding of potential cyber threats, making it meaningful and actionable.

Threat intelligence can come from public and private threat feeds, government bulletins, and information-sharing communities that provide insights into the latest cyberattack techniques, malware, and threat actors. Often, threat intelligence is outsourced as part of the services offered by Security Operations Centers (SOCs). The key to leveraging these services effectively is ensuring that your SOC understands your operations and integrates these intelligence feeds into the use cases configured in your Security Information and Event Management (SIEM) system. This integration ensures that the intelligence is not just passive information but becomes a dynamic part of your defense strategy. Additionally, if your organization has the capacity and expertise to handle threat intelligence internally, there are various tools and services available to support these efforts. Platforms like Recorded Future, Falcon Adversary Intelligence, SOCRadar, Digital Risk Protection Platform, Cyble Vision, and Microsoft Defender XDR offer full threat intelligence solutions. These tools provide real-time data and analytics, helping your team to stay ahead of potential threats and integrate these insights into your security operations effectively.

When a trend detected by these intelligence feeds crosses a predefined threshold set for our KRIs, it signals that something significant is occurring. This trigger prompts a risk assessment to better understand what's happening and to evaluate the risks we are facing. By having this integrated approach, we ensure that our threat intelligence is directly tied to actionable steps, allowing us to respond promptly and effectively to emerging threats.

Another vital tool is statistical reports. These reports provide valuable data on past incidents, helping us spot trends and patterns that may indicate emerging risks. Reviewing reports from sources like government entities, such as the FBI's Internet Crime Complaint Center (iC3), the Canadian Centre for Cyber Security, and the Cybersecurity & Infrastructure Security Agency (CISA), alongside reports from security vendors like IBM, CrowdStrike, and Verizon, as well as institutions like the Cyentia Institute, Ponemon Institute, and the World Economic Forum, helps us better understand which types of attacks are becoming more frequent or severe. This insight enables us to allocate resources more efficiently and adjust our risk management strategies accordingly. Also, statistical analysis allows us to benchmark our cybersecurity performance against industry standards, giving us a clearer picture of where we stand in comparison to our peers and revealing areas that may need improvement.

In addition to threat intelligence and statistical reports, industry events and reports are invaluable resources for ongoing risk monitoring. Attending conferences, participating in webinars, and reading industry publications keeps us up-to-date with the latest developments in cybersecurity. These events provide opportunities to learn from experts, hear about new technologies and best practices, and understand how other organizations are tackling similar challenges. Engaging with the broader cybersecurity community allows us to continually refine our strategies and stay ahead of new risks.

SIEM systems play a crucial role in real-time monitoring of our network and systems. SIEM tools collect, correlate, and analyze security events from across the organization, providing a centralized view of all activities. This allows us to detect anomalies and potential security incidents as they happen, enabling a quick response to mitigate threats before they can cause significant damage. SIEM systems also help in identifying patterns that might indicate a larger, coordinated attack, allowing us to take preventive action to protect our assets. Learning from these events can help to detect risks in a timely manner.

To complement SIEM systems, we also rely on IT problem management logs. These logs provide detailed records of incidents and issues that have occurred within our IT infrastructure. Regularly reviewing these logs, can identify recurring problems that may indicate vulnerabilities or misconfigurations that need to be addressed. This approach to problem management helps us stay ahead of potential threats. Vulnerability reports are another key component of ongoing monitoring. These reports highlight weaknesses in our systems and applications that could be exploited by attackers. Regular vulnerability scanning and assessments help us identify and prioritize these weaknesses, allowing us to patch or remediate them before they can be exploited.

A critical aspect of ongoing monitoring that we shouldn't forget is change management. In any IT dynamic environment, changes are inevitable, whether they involve system updates, new software deployments, or modifications to existing infrastructure. Each change introduces the potential for new risks or alters the risk landscape, making it crucial to integrate risk assessments into the change management process. Before any change is implemented, a thorough risk assessment should be conducted to evaluate how it might impact the organization's security posture. This ensures that all potential risks are identified and mitigated before they can be exploited by attackers. Effective change management is about maintaining a clear and accurate understanding of the entire environment. This helps us keep our understanding of the environment current and aligned with reality, enabling us to respond quickly and effectively to any new threats that arise. Without this continuous updating, each risk assessment will become a challenge and we'll find ourselves struggling to gather current information of our environments as they may have already changed since the last assessment. Without proper change management, there's a risk that our monitoring efforts could become outdated or misaligned with the actual state of our systems, leaving us vulnerable to unseen threats.

Each of these tools and techniques serves a specific purpose in the broader context of risk monitoring. Leveraging threat intelligence, statistical reports, industry events, SIEM systems, IT problem management logs, and vulnerability reports helps build a monitoring strategy that offers a well-rounded view of our cybersecurity posture. However, as Richards J. Heuer suggests in his book *Psychology of Intelligence Analysis*,[1] having an avalanche of available information does not necessarily lead to better results. In fact, Heuer presents results of some experiments that showed that after reaching a certain threshold where experts have enough information, additional data often doesn't significantly improve the quality of the analysis and, in some cases, can even lead to worse outcomes. This phenomenon highlights the importance of balancing the quality of our information with the quantity of data available for our analysis. With all this being said, we need to keep this in mind and ensure that our risk monitoring strategy is not just focused on collecting large amounts of data, but also on the quality and relevance of the information collected. Carefully selecting and filtering the data ensures that analyses remain actionable and meaningful. This balanced approach allows for better detection and response to threats, continuously improving defenses, and maintaining readiness in an ever-evolving cyber threat landscape.

CYBER RISK MANAGEMENT METRICS

Effective cyber risk management relies not only on continuous monitoring but also on clear, actionable metrics that help us measure the effectiveness of our risk strategies and adjust them as needed. While the earlier section on risk monitoring highlighted the importance of vigilance and adapting to a changing landscape, this section will focus on the specific metrics that form the foundation of a robust cyber risk management program. Defining and using these metrics effectively will help us to better understand our risk posture, make informed decisions, and communicate our cybersecurity status to stakeholders.

Starting with the basic idea that if we don't measure our program, we can't improve it. Metrics in cyber risk management are tools that provide quantifiable insights into our cybersecurity efforts. They help us understand where we stand today and how well we are prepared to handle future challenges. When defining these metrics, it's crucial to consider what information is most valuable for our organization and how it can be used to drive meaningful action.

Referring back to what we discussed earlier, we should focus on two primary types of metrics: KRIs and KPIs. It's important to first establish a baseline understanding of your current cybersecurity posture. This involves selecting a set of initial metrics that can give a snapshot of your current risk exposure and the effectiveness of existing controls. These metrics could include incident response times, the number of vulnerabilities identified and remediated within a set time frame, the number of identified risks without treatment plans, the number of security exceptions authorized, the total risk accepted, or the frequency and success rate of phishing simulations among employees. Establishing these baseline metrics will help you understand your starting point and serve as a reference for measuring progress over time. However, it's important to keep in mind Goodhart's law: "When a measure becomes a target, it ceases to be a good measure." This is critical because people will often focus on improving a specific metric, even if that means sacrificing the actual goal. For example, consider a compliance approach where the metric is to have zero compliance issues on your Payment Card Industry (PCI) program. You might find people checking boxes just to meet PCI requirements, even if that means sacrificing broader security measures. So, while metrics are vital, they should always align with the overall objective of enhancing security, not just meeting targets.

As you develop your metrics framework, applying the SMART criteria is helpful to ensure that your metrics are effective and actionable. Let's break down each of these criteria:

- **Specific**: Each metric should have a clear objective and focus. For example, instead of a vague metric like 'improve cybersecurity,' a specific metric could be 'reduce the average time to detect and respond to a phishing attack by 20% over the next six months.'
- **Measurable**: The metric should be quantifiable. It must allow for tracking and assessment over time to evaluate progress. Using numerical values or percentages helps in maintaining objectivity and clarity.
- **Attainable**: Metrics should be realistic and achievable within the constraints of your organization. Setting unattainable goals can lead to frustration and disengagement.
- **Relevant**: Your metrics should directly relate to your organization's risk management objectives and cybersecurity strategy. Avoid metrics that do not add value or inform decision-making.
- **Timely**: Each metric should have a time frame for assessment. This could be weekly, monthly, quarterly, or annually, depending on the specific goals and the nature of the metric.

Once you have established baseline metrics and ensured they are SMART, the next step is to evolve your metrics program by incorporating more advanced indicators. As your organization matures in its cybersecurity practices, your metrics should also become more sophisticated, allowing for deeper insights and more detailed understanding of your risk posture.

First, start with fundamental metrics that provide a straightforward view of your cybersecurity landscape. These could include the number of detected incidents, average time to resolve incidents, patching cadence, and the number of compliance violations. These metrics should focus on capturing the essential elements of your security posture, offering a baseline from which to measure progress. Key metrics in this category could include:

- **Technology environment visibility**: This metric evaluates the extent to which your security technology stack is deployed and operational across your organization's technology environment. It measures the percentage of systems, networks, and endpoints that are under the surveillance of your security tools, such as endpoint detection and response, intrusion detection systems (IDS), and vulnerability scanner. High visibility ensures that potential threats are detected across the entire environment, whereas gaps in visibility might indicate areas where threats could go unnoticed. Understanding this metric helps you identify blind spots and prioritize efforts to improve coverage, ensuring that your security infrastructure is comprehensive and effective.
- **Percentage of business processes with cyber risk assessment completed**: This metric measures the proportion of your organization's business processes that have undergone a complete cyber risk assessment. It helps ensure that all critical areas of your operations are evaluated for potential risks, vulnerabilities, and threats. By tracking this percentage, you can identify which processes have not yet been assessed and prioritize them to ensure full coverage. A higher percentage indicates a proactive approach to identifying and mitigating risks across the organization, while a lower percentage may highlight gaps in your risk management efforts that need to be addressed.
- **Number (and type if possible) of detected incidents**: This metric tracks how many security incidents are detected over a specific period. It's a direct measure of the threats your organization is facing and how well your detection systems are functioning. High numbers could indicate that your security systems are working effectively to identify threats, but it could also suggest that your organization is a frequent target or has underlying vulnerabilities that need addressing.
- **Mean time to resolve (MTTR)**: This measures the average time taken to contain and resolve security incidents, or patch vulnerabilities, or address risks once they are detected. A shorter MTTR indicates a more efficient incident response process, which is critical in minimizing the damage and cost associated with a breach, but also could be used to monitor how efficiently we get rid of risk. This metric helps you understand the effectiveness of your response protocols and where there might be room for improvement in speeding up resolution times.

- **Patching cadence**: This metric assesses how frequently your organization applies security patches to software and systems. Regular patching is crucial to protect against known vulnerabilities that attackers could exploit. A slow or irregular patching cadence can highlight gaps in your vulnerability management process that need attention.
- **Number of compliance violations**: This measures the frequency and severity of compliance violations within your organization. Compliance metrics are not just about meeting regulatory requirements but also ensuring that your security practices align with industry standards and best practices. Frequent violations could indicate a need for better training, more robust policies, or stricter enforcement mechanisms.

Then as you grow, introduce metrics that start to evaluate the efficiency of your security processes and the effectiveness of your controls. These could include the ratio of detected to undetected incidents, the percentage of systems compliant with security policies, or the average cost of a security incident. Metrics in this category should focus on identifying areas where improvements can be made to enhance security outcomes and optimize resources. Key metrics might include:

- **Ratio of detected to undetected incidents**: This metric measures the proportion of incidents detected by your security systems compared to those discovered through other means, such as user reports or audits. A high ratio of undetected incidents could suggest weaknesses in your detection capabilities, while a high detection rate indicates that your monitoring tools and processes are effectively identifying threats. Tracking this ratio over time helps you measure the reliability of your security infrastructure and pinpoint areas for enhancement.
- **Percentage of systems compliant with security policies**: This metric evaluates the extent to which your organization's systems adhere to established security policies and standards. High compliance rates indicate that your systems are configured correctly and that users are following the necessary protocols to protect sensitive information. On the other hand, low compliance rates can signal a need for more rigorous enforcement, better user education, or more robust policies. Regularly assessing compliance helps ensure that your security posture aligns with your organization's risk tolerance and regulatory requirements.
- **Average cost of a security incident**: Understanding the financial impact of security incidents is critical for managing resources and justifying investments in cybersecurity. This metric calculates the average cost incurred from security breaches, including direct

expenses such as recovery efforts and indirect costs like lost productivity and reputational damage. Lowering the average cost of incidents over time should be a key objective, indicating that your security measures are successfully minimizing harm.
- **Percentage of effectiveness of security technology**: This metric measures the effectiveness of the security technologies deployed within your environment by evaluating their performance over time. Tracking the percentage of effectiveness helps you to identify trends where security events or incidents are increasing, which may indicate that a particular control or technology is not functioning as intended or is failing. For example, if there's a spike in incidents despite having specific security controls in place, it suggests that these controls might not be effectively mitigating threats or vulnerabilities. This metric allows you to proactively identify weaknesses in your security stack, enabling timely adjustments or upgrades to ensure that your defenses remain robust and effective. Monitoring this percentage helps maintain the reliability of your security technologies and supports continuous improvement in your cybersecurity posture.

At a more advanced stage, metrics should provide predictive insights and facilitate strategic decision-making. This is where KRIs become particularly relevant. Metrics could include the rate of change in the attack surface, the frequency of attacks targeting specific assets, or the effectiveness of threat intelligence integration in preventing incidents. Metrics in this advanced category should focus on analyzing trends, predicting future threats, and assessing the effectiveness of strategic initiatives. Here are some key metrics to consider:

- **Rate of change in the attack surface**: This metric measures how your organization's attack surface evolves over time, including the addition of new systems, applications, and network connections that could be potential entry points for attackers. A rapid increase in the attack surface might indicate a higher risk of exposure to cyber threats, while a stable or decreasing rate suggests effective management of your digital footprint. By monitoring this metric, you can identify trends that require a strategic response, such as tightening access controls or investing in additional security measures.
- **Frequency of attacks targeting specific assets**: This metric tracks how often specific assets within your organization are targeted by cyberattacks. Understanding which assets are most frequently attacked can help prioritize protective measures and allocate resources more effectively. For example, if certain critical systems or data stores are consistently targeted, it may be necessary to strengthen their defenses or reevaluate their security posture. Monitoring attack

frequency also allows you to identify patterns that could signal emerging threats or changes in attacker behavior.

- **Effectiveness of threat intelligence integration**: This metric assesses how well your organization integrates threat intelligence into its security operations. It looks at how effectively threat intelligence feeds inform your SIEM system and how often this information leads to actionable outcomes, such as blocking an IP address or isolating a compromised system. Evaluating the impact of threat intelligence on your incident response and prevention efforts can determine the value of your threat intelligence investments and make informed decisions about future enhancements.

To further refine your approach, group your metrics and organize your dashboard in a better way using the following ones that track the lifecycle and trends of risks.

- **Survival rates**: This metric measures how long risks persist within your environment. It can help identify risks that are not being effectively mitigated over time.
- **Burndown rates**: It tracks how quickly your organization can eliminate risks. This metric reveals the speed at which risks are addressed and resolved, providing insights into the efficiency of your risk management processes.
- **Arrival rates**: This measures how often new risks emerge. A high arrival rate may indicate changing threat dynamics or an expanding attack surface.
- **Life tables**: Use these to present 'still alive' vulnerabilities, offering a visual representation of how risks age over time. Life tables can help prioritize remediation efforts based on the longevity of specific vulnerabilities.

As mentioned earlier, while it's important to gather comprehensive data, more information doesn't always equate to better analysis. This is an important consideration when developing cyber risk management metrics. An effective metrics program finds the right balance between the quantity and quality of information.

It's tempting to believe that having more data will always improve decision-making. To avoid falling into the trap of information overload, we need to focus on the relevance and clarity of your metrics. Choose metrics that provide actionable insights and directly contribute to your understanding of risk. Regularly review your metrics to ensure they remain aligned with your risk management goals and adjust as necessary.

A well-developed metrics program is only as effective as its ability to drive action. This means that metrics should not only be collected and analyzed but also communicated effectively to the right stakeholders. Reporting on metrics should be clear, concise, and tailored to the audience, ensuring that decision-makers have the information they need to act promptly and appropriately.

- **Regular reporting**: Establish a routine for reporting on metrics. This could be through weekly dashboards, monthly reports, or quarterly reviews, depending on your organization's needs. Ensure that these reports are accessible to all relevant stakeholders and provide a clear overview of the cybersecurity landscape.
- **Tailored communication**: Different stakeholders will have different levels of understanding and interest in cybersecurity metrics. Tailor your communication to ensure that the information is meaningful and actionable for each audience. For example, senior executives may be more interested in high-level trends and strategic implications, while technical teams may need detailed data and analysis.
- **Feedback loops**: Metrics should not be static. Use feedback loops to continually refine and improve your metrics program. Gather input from stakeholders on the usefulness of the metrics, any gaps they perceive, and suggestions for improvement. This iterative approach will help ensure that your metrics program evolves alongside your cybersecurity needs.

This is why then effective cyber risk management metrics are more than just numbers on a page; they are tools that drive action, inform decisions, and facilitate continuous improvement. Establishing a robust metrics framework that evolves with your organization's needs will ensure that your cybersecurity program remains agile, responsive, and aligned with your overall business objectives. Remember, the goal is not just to measure but to use these measurements to make your organization move in the right direction. Metrics must drive action in the right direction.

As we conclude this section on the five steps of the cyber risk management process, it's clear that managing cyber risks is not a one-time task but an ongoing journey. Each step we've explored—risk contexts, risk assessment, risk treatment strategies, risk treatment implementation, and risk monitoring and metrics—builds upon the last, forming a framework designed to protect and fortify our organization while enabling business objectives.

Risk monitoring, as the final step in this cycle, ensures that our risk management efforts remain dynamic and effective. It's about more than just keeping an eye on what has been done and at the same time it's about staying ahead of what might come next. This stage emphasizes vigilance, adaptability, and a commitment to continuous improvement, traits that are essential in an environment where threats are constantly changing and evolving.

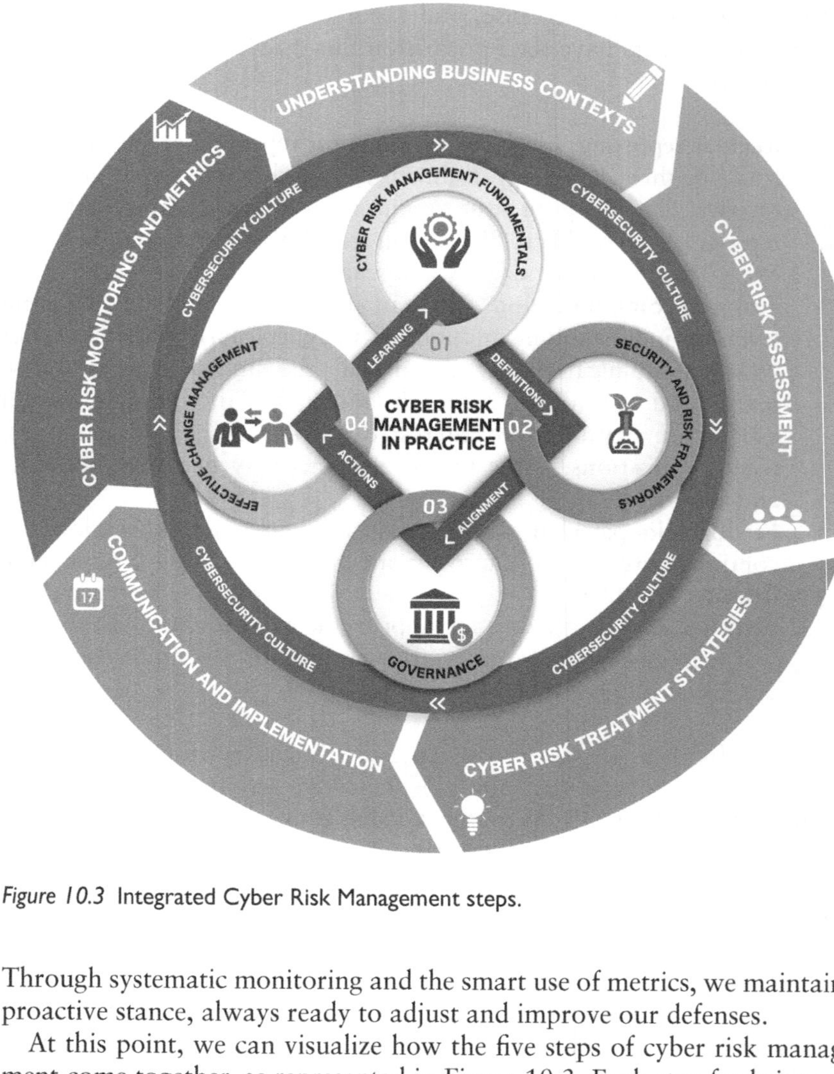

Figure 10.3 Integrated Cyber Risk Management steps.

Through systematic monitoring and the smart use of metrics, we maintain a proactive stance, always ready to adjust and improve our defenses.

At this point, we can visualize how the five steps of cyber risk management come together, as represented in Figure 10.3. Each step feeds into the next, creating a continuous cycle that strengthens our overall approach. But more than just a cycle, remember this is a vortex, where each spin returns us to the initial step, but not at the same point exactly. Just like a spiral, we're moving forward with every loop, building on what we've learned, and continuously improving. This vortex doesn't just keep our program spinning, it accelerates it. With each pass through the cycle, we refine our strategies, tighten our defenses, and gain the momentum necessary to push beyond traditional boundaries. The more we feed into this core, the stronger the forces become, pulling in every part of our cyber risk management program and giving it the traction needed to move faster and more efficiently.

We'll start to see improvements not only in our internal processes but also in critical areas like third-party risk management and the adoption of new technologies. This is how we move from simply managing risks to building a state of cyber resilience, one that can adapt, evolve, and thrive in an ever-changing threat landscape. And that's exactly why our journey doesn't end here. While we have established a solid foundation in understanding and managing cyber risks, it's important to recognize that this is just the beginning. Effective risk management is a critical component of a robust cybersecurity strategy, but we must aim higher; we must strive for cyber resilience.

Cyber resilience goes beyond managing risks; it includes the ability to anticipate, withstand, recover from, and adapt to adverse conditions, stresses, attacks, or compromises on the systems that support critical business processes. It is about building a capability that not only protects against threats but also ensures the continuity of operations despite them. Basically, it is the next level of cybersecurity maturity, a stage where an organization is not only secure but also agile and prepared for whatever the future holds.

As we move forward into the next and final section of this book, 'Elevating beyond basics: Achieving cyber resilience," we will explore how to take your cybersecurity practices to the next level. Keep in mind that this is a continuous improvement process, and I'm confident that you'll see this after your first full cyber risk management cycle. I also hope you'll remember this book's intention is to be a guide that you can consult any time because I know its messages will evolve as you and your organization mature in your journey. So, as you reflect on the knowledge and practices covered in this section, remember that effective risk management lays the groundwork for achieving true cyber resilience. It gives you the tools and insights needed to protect your organization today and prepares you for the challenges of tomorrow. Let's continue this journey together, moving beyond the basics and striving for a future where resilience is at the core of our cybersecurity strategies. With a solid foundation in place, we are ready to elevate our approach and build a more secure, resilient, and agile organization.

NOTE

1 Heuer, R. J. Jr. (1999). *Psychology of Intelligence Analysis*. Center for the Study of Intelligence.

Section III

Elevating beyond basics

Achieving cyber resilience

Chapter 11

Third-party risk management

UNDERSTANDING THIRD-PARTY RISKS IN THE SUPPLY CHAIN

Trust is the glue of life, but in cyber risk management, we must trust and verify. Now that we've established a solid foundation for our cyber risk management program where we can build upon, it's time to expand on that foundation and focus on third-party risk management. The principles and practices we've covered so far are the bedrock upon which we can layer additional elements, like third-party risk management. Think of it as adding another floor to a strong building. We already have the structure in place, and now we're going to expand it. Earlier in the book, I touched on some aspects of third-party risk management. However, I deliberately held back from going too deep at that point. I wanted us to concentrate on setting up a strong and effective risk management framework first. You see, third-party risk management is a huge task on its own as it comes with its own set of challenges. If we had jumped into it too early, we might have risked losing sight of the foundational principles that are essential for any risk management program. Now that you're prepared with the solid understanding of the core concepts and practices, we can take a deeper dive into third-party risks.

Just like in cyber risk management, the more you understand about third-party risks, the more complex and challenging the task becomes because you'll find that it's not only about your vendors, but their vendors and their vendors, etc. and that could be endless, right? So, as everything else in risk management is not about ticking boxes or just following a checklist. It's about truly understanding the risks that third parties can introduce to your organization and how you can manage these effectively. So, let's roll up our sleeves and get into the details. We'll explore how to extend the risk management principles we've discussed and apply them to managing third-party risks.

Managing third-party risks nowadays is a fundamental component of any organization's cybersecurity and operational resilience strategy. When you bring a third-party into your ecosystem, you're introducing as well, an

DOI: 10.1201/9781003546207-15

entire set of potential risks into your environment. Every connection, every shared system, and every exchange of data becomes a possible entry point for vulnerabilities and threats. These are the obvious risks and vendors that come to mind first, but there are also critical vendors who aren't directly integrated into your IT infrastructure and don't provide technology as part of their services. So, what about them? It's crucial to remember that these vendors also operate with IT/OT systems that have their own vulnerabilities. If one of these critical vendors is breached and their services become unavailable, the impact on your organization can be significant, especially if you depend on them for essential functions. This is where third-party risk management gets a bit more complex. It's not just about the tech; it's about the ripple effects that could spread throughout your operations. Third parties can introduce a range of vulnerabilities, often without us even realizing it. For example, a vendor might have weaker security controls than you do, or they might be using outdated systems that make them an easy target for attackers. If their systems are breached, the impact isn't confined to them alone; it can quickly spread to your organization. Attackers often exploit these weak links to gain access to more secure networks, using the initial breach as a stepping stone to infiltrate your systems. This interconnection means that when you're doing your job internally, your cybersecurity defenses are only as strong as the weakest link in your supply chain.

Beyond technical vulnerabilities, third parties can also significantly affect your compliance posture. Many industries are governed by strict regulatory requirements concerning data protection, privacy, and security. When you engage with third parties, you remain accountable for ensuring that your data is safeguarded and that all regulatory obligations are fulfilled. If a vendor fails to comply with these regulations, it doesn't matter that they're an external entity, the consequences can still fall on your organization. This could lead to fines, legal actions, and a damaged relationship with regulatory bodies. It's important to recognize that the failure of a third party to meet compliance standards can directly impact your ability to operate within legal and regulatory frameworks, potentially putting your business at risk of severe penalties and restrictions.

To complicate things a little bit more, third-party risks aren't just about the technical and compliance aspects; they also have a significant impact on your organization's reputation. In today's interconnected digital world, reputation is one of your most valuable assets. A breach or incident involving a third party can stain your brand image and erode the trust that customers, partners, and stakeholders have put in you. As we all know, trust is something so fragile that takes years to build but can be lost in an instant. If a third-party breach leads to a data compromise or negatively affects your brand's public perception, the consequences can be far-reaching and long-lasting. This loss of trust can result in customer churn, decreased market share, and a loss of competitive advantage.

This is why managing third-party risks isn't just a 'nice-to-have' in your cybersecurity strategy, it's absolutely essential; it's an element in safeguarding your organization from potential threats. This process requires a proactive, integrated approach that aligns seamlessly with your overall cyber risk management framework. It involves assessing third-party relationships to manage risks effectively, ensuring compliance, and protecting your organization's reputation, all while enhancing overall resilience. But let's be real, third-party risks can be complex and multifaceted; the challenge here is that reality always hits, and in this case, it could be something like outdated contracts, lack of proper segmentation, inadequate documentation, or insufficient assessments of existing vendors. All these complexities can make third-party risk management feel overwhelming, and it's understandable why. Not addressing these risks can leave you vulnerable, not just within your organization but across your entire supply chain. When we talk about supply chain attacks, we're referring to a wide range of tactics that cyber attackers use to exploit these third-party relationships, taking advantage of the trust and reliance organizations place on their suppliers and partners. These attacks have become more frequent and sophisticated, highlighting the need for a robust third-party risk management strategy that can anticipate and mitigate these threats. Understanding these common attack methods is relevant for preparing yourself to defend against them.

Let's break down some of the most common types of supply chain attacks, because understanding these can really help us prepare and protect our organizations better. First up is the software supply chain attack. Instead of going directly after a company, attackers target the software vendors that supply essential applications to various organizations. They infiltrate the vendor's development environment and inject malicious code into software updates. When these compromised updates are distributed, the malware gets installed across the vendor's customer base without anyone even realizing it. The SolarWinds breach is a prime example of this kind of attack. Hackers inserted malicious code into the Orion software updates, which then gave them access to the networks of numerous high-profile organizations and government agencies, demonstrating how a single compromised supplier can have widespread consequences.

Another sophisticated attack vector involves hardware supply chain attacks. This method involves tampering with hardware components or firmware before they are delivered to the end user. Attackers might insert a physical chip or alter the device's firmware to introduce vulnerabilities that can be exploited later. Once the compromised hardware is installed within the target organization's network, attackers can gain unauthorized access, steal sensitive information, or disrupt operations. Hardware supply chain attacks are particularly insidious because they exploit the trust organizations have in the physical products they purchase, making detection difficult until it's too late.

Phishing attacks are another significant risk in the supply chain. These attacks often target employees of a third-party vendor, tricking them into revealing sensitive information or installing malware. For instance, attackers might send emails that appear to come from a legitimate source, such as a partner organization, asking the recipient to click on a link or download an attachment. Once the attacker gains access to the third-party vendor's systems, they can pivot to their ultimate target, using the vendor's legitimate access privileges to move laterally through the network. This method is particularly effective because it leverages the trusted relationship between the organization and its vendors.

Compromised credentials are also a frequent avenue for supply chain attacks. If a vendor's systems are not adequately secured, attackers can steal employee credentials and use them to gain unauthorized access to customer networks. This could happen if a vendor is using weak passwords, lacks multifactor authentication, or has been breached and failed to notify its customers. Once attackers have valid credentials, they can access sensitive systems and data as if they were legitimate users, making it harder to detect and respond to the breach promptly.

Additionally, there's the risk of third-party service providers being compromised through their own supply chains or internal systems. For example, managed service providers (MSPs) or cloud service providers can be targeted due to their extensive access to multiple client environments. An attack on an MSP can provide attackers with access to numerous customer networks, allowing them to launch widespread attacks from a single point of entry. This type of attack underscores the importance of scrutinizing not just your direct third-party vendors but also the vendors of your vendors, creating a cascading effect that significantly amplifies the potential risk.

In addition to these attacks, two other sophisticated methods are business email compromise (BEC) attacks and watering hole attacks, which further highlight the vulnerabilities in third-party relationships. BEC attacks target the email accounts of businesses and their employees, where cybercriminals impersonate a legitimate business partner or executive to trick recipients into transferring money, sharing sensitive information, or making unauthorized transactions. For instance, an attacker might compromise a vendor's email account and then send a convincing email to your accounts payable department, requesting a change in payment details for an upcoming invoice. These attacks are highly effective because they rely on social engineering and trust, making them difficult to detect with traditional security tools. Watering hole attacks target a specific group of users by compromising websites they frequently visit. Cybercriminals identify a website commonly used by employees of a targeted organization or industry and inject malicious code into the site. When users from the targeted organization visit the compromised site, malware is downloaded onto their systems without their knowledge. This attack exploits the regular web browsing habits of an organization, using trusted external resources to penetrate otherwise secure environments. Both BEC and watering hole attacks illustrate how attackers exploit the relationships and trust organizations have with their third-party vendors and partners. Understanding the full spectrum of potential threats, including all these types of attacks, allows you to better assess third-party risks safeguarding your organization from becoming the next victim in a long line of supply chain attacks.

Let's take a moment to think about how deeply intertwined our organizations have become with a vast web of external partners, vendors, customers, and beyond. Have you ever paused to consider just how many vendors your organization actually works with? And of those, how many are truly critical to your day-to-day operations? It's pretty common for companies to have hundreds, if not thousands, of third-party relationships, each bringing its own set of risks. Some vendors might provide core services essential to your day-to-day operations, while others might offer more peripheral support. But here's the kicker, every single one of these vendors, regardless of their role, introduces a potential point of vulnerability. And it's not just about vendors, consider your customers too. If one of them is breached and their operations are disrupted, they might not be able to fulfill their financial obligations to you, creating an unexpected risk for your organization.

Now, let's dive a bit deeper; how many of these third parties have been properly vetted through a comprehensive risk assessment? And how many were brought on board directly by different departments without a centralized review or input from your risk management or cybersecurity teams? It happens all the time: a department finds a service they need and, eager to get things moving, signs a contract without thinking about the bigger picture. These 'shadow IT situations, where technology services are used without the knowledge of IT or risk management teams, can really crank up the risk levels.

Without a clear view of all the vendors in your ecosystem, it becomes nearly impossible to effectively manage third-party risks. This can create a dangerous blind spot where unassessed risks go unchecked and unmanaged, increasing the likelihood of a security breach, regulatory violation, or operational failure. This is why building strong alliances within your organization is key to effective third-party risk management. One of your best allies in this effort is the supply management or procurement team; these folks are who handle the invoices and manage vendor relationships. They're like your early warning system when it comes to new vendors. They're usually the first to know when a new service is being considered or when a contract is about to be signed. By partnering closely with them, you can create a sort of 'goalkeeper' mechanism that helps you stay in the loop about potential new vendors, making sure you have a chance to assess any new risks before they become your problem.

Supply management teams have a unique vantage point; they see all the incoming invoices and payments, which means they have insights into all the different services and products being brought into the organization. If you collaborate with them effectively, then you can be integrated formally in their process and work with them from the very beginning when a new vendor is being evaluated or when an existing vendor is expanding their scope of work. This early warning system is a big piece for the success of your third-party risk management efforts because it gives you the opportunity to assess the risks associated with a new vendor before they even set foot in your organization. Remember, managing third-party risk is not just about setting up barriers but also about building bridges with the right teams within your organization to ensure a comprehensive approach to security. Having supply management as a proactive partner in this process makes all the difference in maintaining a secure and resilient organization. Their role as a 'goalkeeper' in the vendor management process ensures that you have a complete view of your ecosystem and can proactively manage the risks associated with your third-party relationships.

To make third-party risk management effective when integrating our efforts into existing business processes, it's essential to collaborate closely with various teams across the organization. One of the most important partners in this effort is the legal team, which plays a crucial role in our success. The legal department ensures that every contract includes robust security clauses and clearly outlines the responsibilities of both parties concerning cybersecurity and data protection. For instance, these clauses should give you the right to audit, require the vendor to inform you promptly if they experience a breach, and assign responsibilities and costs if something goes wrong. With all this work the legal team isn't just reviewing the fine print; they're safeguarding your organization from potential liabilities that could arise if a third-party vendor fails to uphold their responsibilities. Involving the legal team early on ensures that all vendor agreements align with your organization's cybersecurity policies and legal obligations, providing a strong foundation for managing third-party risks.

Privacy and compliance teams are also vital players in this collaborative effort. With data protection regulations becoming more stringent worldwide, these teams help ensure that all third-party vendors adhere to relevant privacy laws and standards. They focus on how vendors handle sensitive information, ensuring that any data shared is adequately protected and that the vendor's practices align with your organization's compliance requirements. For instance, if a vendor will have access to personally identifiable information (PII), privacy teams often require them to complete a data protection impact assessment (DPIA). This assessment includes a complete risk evaluation, examining how the vendor plans to protect the PII and ensuring that they have appropriate security controls in place.

Compliance teams are equally important in this process, especially when dealing with vendors that fall under specific regulatory frameworks such as PCI DSS (Payment Card Industry Data Security Standard), HIPAA (Health Insurance Portability and Accountability Act), or GDPR (General Data Protection Regulation). When a vendor will be in scope of these regulations, compliance teams play a crucial role in verifying that the vendor meets all necessary requirements, including those related to data security, encryption, access controls, and incident response protocols. For example, if a vendor handles credit card transactions, the compliance team will ensure that they are PCI DSS compliant, which involves rigorous standards for protecting cardholder data. Similarly, if a vendor deals with healthcare information, the compliance team will check that they adhere to HIPAA requirements to safeguard patient data. This proactive involvement from privacy and compliance teams is crucial in mitigating risks related to data breaches or regulatory noncompliance, which could lead to significant penalties and damage to your organization's reputation.

IT departments add another layer of scrutiny by bringing their technical expertise into the mix. They assess the security measures and technological infrastructure of potential vendors, identifying any vulnerabilities or misalignments with your organization's security standards. Their involvement ensures that the technologies and systems being introduced are secure and compatible with your existing environment, preventing potential security gaps that could be exploited by attackers. This integrated approach within the supply management process brings together perspectives from legal, privacy, compliance, and IT to create a complete view of third-party risks. It ensures that every new vendor relationship is meticulously vetted from multiple angles, reducing the chances of overlooked vulnerabilities and strengthening your organization's overall security posture. It's also important to collaborate with each of these groups and help them understand the importance of third-party cyber risk management and the vital role they play. Remember everything we discussed about change management and engaging with people, you'll need to drive change here, and sometimes it can be a significant one.

Bad news is that not everything is a bed of roses. Often, I'm sure you'll encounter old contracts and legacy agreements that were overlooked from a cybersecurity standpoint, presenting significant risks in the context of third-party risk management. Many of these agreements might have been created before cybersecurity was a major concern, lacking essential security clauses that are now considered standard practice. As a result, these contracts often contain vague or outdated terms that don't adequately address today's cybersecurity challenges, leaving your organization exposed. Addressing these legacy issues is no easy task. Renegotiating old contracts can be challenging because vendors might resist changes, especially if the original terms are more favorable to them. Legal or logistical hurdles can also complicate the process, particularly for contracts tied to critical services or long-term relationships. Despite these challenges, it's important to completely understand your current risks and, if action is required, discuss those risks with the business to create a strategy for when it's best to renegotiate those contracts. In the meantime, evaluate potential compensatory controls. Failing to update or renegotiate old agreements can leave your organization vulnerable to threats that could have been mitigated with more robust, current contractual terms. It's all about finding the right balance, working diplomatically with vendors to update agreements while ensuring your organization's security needs are met.

Beyond the challenges of old contracts, another common issue in third-party risk management is the lack of prioritization or segmentation of vendors based on the risks they pose. Not all vendors carry the same level of risk, and treating them as if they do can lead to inefficient use of resources and potentially dangerous blind spots. For instance, a vendor that handles sensitive customer data or provides essential IT services represents a much higher risk than one supplying noncritical goods or services. Without proper segmentation, your team might end up allocating the same amount of time and effort to all vendors, regardless of the risk they pose, which is neither practical nor effective. Segmenting vendors based on factors such as their criticality to operations, the sensitivity of the data they handle, and the level of access they have to your systems allows you to focus your risk management efforts where they're needed most.

Following the discussion about the challenges we face when starting on cyber third-party risk management, another common challenge is that you need to perform regular assessments of your vendors. Many organizations make the mistake of assuming that once a vendor has been vetted and onboarded, they no longer need to be monitored closely. However, the security landscape is constantly evolving, and a vendor's security posture can change over time. So, a vendor that was deemed secure a year ago might no longer meet your organization's standards due to changes in their security practices, personnel, or technologies. Failing to perform regular assessments leaves your organization vulnerable to risks that could have been identified and mitigated through ongoing oversight. Regularly evaluating your vendors helps you stay ahead of potential threats, ensuring that any changes in their operations or security measures do not negatively impact your organization.

When a company that we will call *Logistics Corp.* acquired a smaller, rapidly growing logistics company, the deal seemed like a perfect match on paper. The due diligence process had been thorough: financials, IT infrastructure, and market potential—all boxes checked. But there was one later evident omission: cybersecurity. It wasn't even on the radar as a key factor in the acquisition. Once the deal closed, the new parent company moved quickly to integrate their systems. The IT team focused on ensuring smooth transitions in HR systems, email, communication platforms, and internal networks. Firewalls were put in place, and encrypted channels were established to safeguard data between the two entities.

Just months after the integration, Logistics Corp. was hit by a cybersecurity incident. An external investigation revealed the shocking detail that the source of the attack was the very company they had acquired. It turned out that the acquired company had been dealing with a cybersecurity incident of its own, one that hadn't been properly remediated leaving the attacker inside waiting for the next golden opportunity which was when the integration began. The IT team had established secure communication channels and firewalls, but because the attacker was already inside the acquired company's network, they could exploit the 'trust' established between the two systems. The firewall allowed traffic between the two companies' servers without traffic inspection, as it was deemed valid internal traffic.

What made this incident particularly difficult was how quietly it unfolded. The attacker had been inside the acquired company's systems for weeks, blending in with normal activity and going unnoticed. With the firewall allowing what seemed like trusted traffic, the attack remained undetected as it moved between the two companies. The security team at Logistics Corp. was dealing with a situation where the malicious activity looked like routine network traffic, making it incredibly challenging to spot.

It wasn't until the security team noticed subtle irregularities in network logs, like unexpected spikes in data flow and unusual access patterns, that they began to realize something was wrong. Even then, identifying the source of the issue was a complicated task. The encrypted channels between the two companies made it hard to investigate the data flow completely, and the team had to sift through vast amounts of traffic to isolate what was being used for exfiltration. The complexity of the integration process added another layer of difficulty, as the attacker had effectively hidden behind the trust established between the two systems. By the time the security team uncovered the full extent of the breach, the attackers had already caused significant damage.

With their foothold in Logistics Corp.'s network, the attackers began exfiltrating sensitive data through the very encrypted channels set up for integration. Because the traffic was seen as legitimate communication between the two companies, the data theft went unnoticed for weeks. Confidential business information, customer details, and proprietary logistics strategies were exfiltrated, all before the company had a clue something was wrong. Then once the attackers had taken what they wanted, they launched a ransomware strike, locking down critical systems across Logistics Corp. and demanding payment for the decryption key.

The company was left scrambling to regain control of its operations. This incident was a harsh lesson in the risks of rushing through an acquisition without properly assessing and managing the risks of an integration. While the technical aspects of IT were handled with care, the failure to address the existing vulnerabilities in the acquired company left the door wide open for an attack. In the end, Logistics Corp. spent months and millions of dollars not only remediating the breach but also rebuilding customer trust and repairing the damage to its reputation. It's a scenario that could have been avoided had integration risks, especially those related to cybersecurity, been assessed and managed during the acquisition process.

For all this work we can leverage established frameworks that provide guidance on the necessary processes and controls. One great framework is ISO 27036, which specifically addresses information security for supplier relationships. ISO 27036 is divided into four parts, each focusing on different aspects of managing third-party risks, and offers a structured approach to ensure that all supplier relationships are managed securely and consistently.

ISO 27036-1 provides an overview of the general principles and concepts related to supplier relationship management. It establishes the foundation for understanding the importance of protecting sensitive information shared with suppliers and how these relationships can impact your organization's overall security posture. It emphasizes that third-party risk management is not just about contractual obligations but also about establishing a culture of security awareness and accountability both within your organization and across all suppliers.

ISO 27036-2 provides detailed guidelines on the information security requirements for implementation, operation, monitoring, reviewing, maintenance, and improvement of a vendor–customer relationship. This part of the standard guides you on implementing security controls that are relevant to managing suppliers. Also it helps organizations develop and maintain a supplier management process that includes assessing suppliers' security capabilities, defining security requirements in contracts, and continuously monitoring and reviewing the effectiveness of these controls throughout the life cycle of the supplier relationship.

ISO 27036-3 provides specific guidance for product and service acquirers and suppliers of hardware, software, and services on managing information security risks associated with physically dispersed and multilayered supply chains. This part addresses the complexities of modern supply chains, which often involve multiple layers of suppliers and geographically dispersed operations. It focuses on gaining visibility into and managing these risks, responding to potential security impacts that may arise from the supply chain, and integrating information security processes into the system and software life cycle, as outlined in ISO/IEC/IEEE 15288 and ISO/IEC/IEEE 12207. This part of the standard is particularly helpful for organizations looking to secure their supply chains against information security threats, ensuring that security is embedded in the life cycle of hardware, software, and services. It's important to note that this part does not cover business continuity management or resiliency issues, which are addressed in ISO/IEC 27031.

ISO 27036-4 provides guidance for both cloud service customers and cloud service providers on managing information security risks associated with the use of cloud services. It offers insights into gaining visibility into these risks and effectively managing them, as well as responding to security risks specific to the acquisition or provision of cloud services. This part of the standard is effective for organizations that rely on cloud services, as it helps them understand and mitigate the unique security challenges that come with cloud computing. It emphasizes the importance of managing information security in cloud services but does not provide specific guidance on how cloud service providers should implement, manage, and operate information security, that guidance can be found in ISO/IEC 27002 and ISO/IEC 27017. Similar to part 3, this part does not address business continuity management or resiliency issues, which are covered in ISO/IEC 27031.

With ISO 27036 you create a robust framework that helps standardize the processes of assessing, monitoring, and managing supplier relationships. Moving forward, the key is to tailor these guidelines to your organization's specific context, considering the nature of your business, the sensitivity of the data shared with vendors, and the criticality of the services they provide.

Understanding the level of assessment required for third-party, fourth-party, and even fifth-party vendors is not as easy as it might sound because, in today's interconnected world, risks can extend far beyond our immediate third-party relationships. So, how do we determine when enough is enough? And what should be the baseline for our cyber third-party risk management program? Let's start with the basics and take a pragmatic approach that will put you in a better place today than you were yesterday. Start by categorizing your vendors and defining the level of assessment required for each category, which will depend on the nature of their services and the potential risk they pose to your organization. Once you have that, work with legal to define the set of security clauses your organization will include in every contract according to the criticality and type of vendors. However, I have to say that you must keep in mind that every contract is a negotiation; you want to include all security clauses, and they may or may not accept. Your organization will sometimes accept retaining the risk because the benefit the vendor brings is higher than the risk itself. It is then that you need to start by not letting the snowball grow. Focus your initial efforts on the due diligence process so at least the new or renewed vendors will be assessed and have their contracts with security clauses included. Then, start the process of catching up by reviewing existing contracts. It'll take time, but eventually, you'll catch up and have everything under control.

But what about fourth-party or even fifth-party vendors? These are the vendors of your vendors (and so on), who may also have access to your data or impact your operations indirectly. For instance, if your cloud service provider relies on another company for infrastructure support, that company becomes a fourth party to you. The complexity here is understanding where to draw the line. It's not feasible to assess every single vendor in your supply chain down to the nth degree. Instead, the focus should be on understanding the chain of dependencies and identifying those fourth and fifth parties that are critical to your operations or have access to sensitive data. The question of when is enough really comes down to risk tolerance and the specific context of your organization. The key is to prioritize your efforts based on the level of risk each vendor relationship represents, ensuring you focus your resources where they're most needed.

As for the baseline of what should be done as part of a cyber third-party risk management program, there are a few fundamental practices to consider. At a minimum, every vendor should go through a risk assessment that evaluates their security posture, compliance with relevant regulations, and ability to meet your organization's security requirements. This assessment should include reviewing their policies, procedures, and controls, and ensuring they align with your own standards. For vendors that have access to sensitive data or provide critical services, this might also involve a more in-depth audit or onsite visit to verify their security practices. Additionally, it's crucial to ensure that security clauses are included in all vendor contracts, clearly outlining responsibilities, reporting requirements, and the right to audit. Continuous monitoring and regular reassessments should also be part of your baseline program, ensuring that any changes in the vendor's operations or security posture are promptly identified and addressed. At the end of the day, the goal is to create a scalable, risk-based approach as shown in Figure 11.1 to third-party risk management that adapts to the evolving threat landscape and your organization's specific needs.

As organizations rely more heavily on third parties, the stakes for robust risk management practices only grow higher. It's not just about having a list of vendors; it's about understanding the risks they pose, maintaining

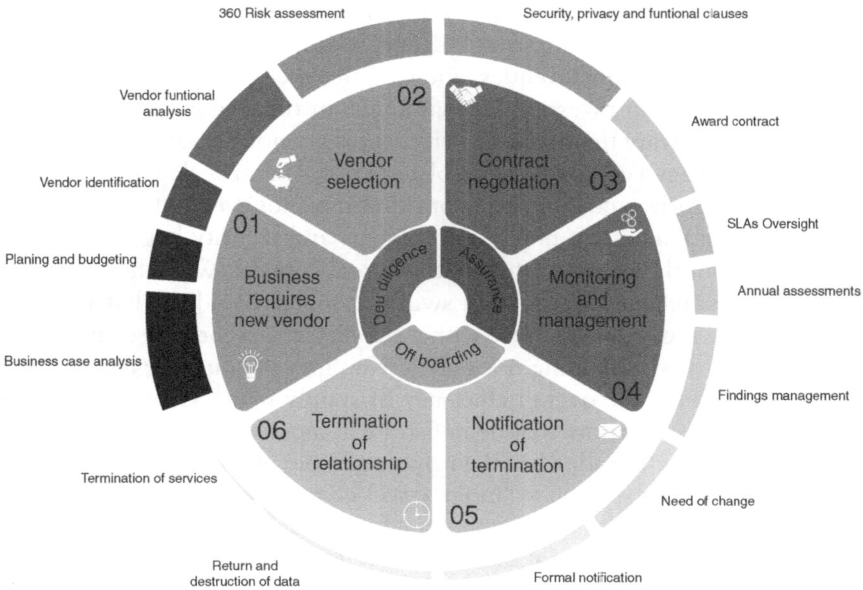

Figure 11.1 Supply chain management with the three security processes.

oversight of their activities, and ensuring that every third-party relationship aligns with your organization's security standards and risk appetite.

DUE DILIGENCE PROCESSES

When it comes to onboarding new vendors, due diligence is the process we need to have in place and that needs to be fully integrated into the supply management process. This integration is essential to avoid duplication, miscommunications, and blind spots that could potentially expose the organization to security risks. The goal is to ensure that every new vendor is evaluated for security concerns right from the beginning following the times and sequence in alignment with the procurement workflow. In this way, the due diligence process focuses on meeting immediate business needs but also considers the long-term security and resilience of the organization.

Imagine a scenario where someone in your organization identifies the need for a new service or technology. This kicks off the supply management process, maybe with a request for information (RFI) or request for proposals (RFP), which should involve all relevant stakeholders, including cybersecurity and risk management teams. This is where our work begins. During the initial phase of selecting potential vendors, we need to use all the information available and if available, leverage tools like security score companies, which can provide quick insights into a vendor's security posture based on publicly available data and cyber threat intelligence. These evaluations can reveal important details about a vendor's past security incidents, existing vulnerabilities, and overall cyber hygiene, allowing us to assess them without investing huge amounts of time right away. However, we need to be aware that these security scores are not the same as the actual security measures a company has in place. The scores are calculated based on different categories and considerations that may not even reflect company's main security issues, just potential problems and security hygiene patterns observed from the outside, often without real context. With these insights, the supply management team can swiftly eliminate vendors that pose significant risks and focus on those with a strong track record of security. This kind of preventive screening not only streamlines the due diligence process but also enhances the overall efficiency of supply management by concentrating efforts on vendors that demonstrate acceptable security standards.

Sometimes, each vendor has their own technology, and in those cases, an assessment of each specific technology will be required. In other situations, it might be the same type of technology being offered by different vendors. In such scenarios, it may make sense to first let the organization short list of vendors and then conduct a combined assessment of the vendor and their technology. Integrating these practices into the supply management process ensures that security is a key consideration in vendor selection from the very start, but it also helps us avoid creating an overwhelming amount of paperwork and bureaucracy. Our collaboration should prevent the common pitfall of selecting a vendor based solely on cost or functionality, only to later find out that there are significant security shortcomings. Instead, the organization can move forward with vendors who have been exhaustively vetted and deemed secure, aligning with both business objectives and security requirements. While this approach addresses potential risks proactively, we must also recognize that this streamlining effort builds a foundation of trust and reliability in vendor relationships. We must always add value to the process and be mindful of not overcomplicating the process, and that our efforts are both effective and efficient.

When assessing vendors, you need to consider a range of factors that can impact the security and overall resilience of your organization. One of the first things to consider is the type of information that will be shared with these potential vendors. Understanding what kind of data will be exchanged helps to measure the level of risk involved. For example, if the information includes sensitive data, like PII or financial records, the stakes are significantly higher. In addition to knowing what data is being shared, you also need to understand how that data will be protected. This involves assessing the vendor's data encryption practices, data handling protocols, and overall data governance framework. Also, it's important to understand the connectivity you will have with them. Will the vendor have direct access to your internal networks, or will the connection be more isolated? The more integrated the vendor is with your systems, the more critical it becomes to understand and manage the associated risks.

Another important aspect to consider is the technologies that the vendor is using. Are they utilizing up-to-date, secure technologies, or are they reliant on outdated systems that might pose a security risk? Or even are they using AI to provide you the services? How are they managing the AI risks? How are these tools managed and maintained? Regular updates, patches, and adherence to security best practices are fundamental to mitigating risks. Alongside this, it's essential to assess the vendor's general cybersecurity hygiene. This involves evaluating their adherence to basic security practices such as identity and access control, basic controls like multifactor authentication or anti malware, regular vulnerability and patch management cadence, employee cybersecurity training, and all the categories we reviewed in Chapter 8. These basic hygiene cybersecurity practices are often indicators of how seriously a vendor takes security and can provide insight into their overall security posture.

Subcontractors or fourth parties are another critical area to evaluate. Vendors often rely on a network of subcontractors and vendors to deliver their services, and it's really important to understand who these subcontractors or vendors are and what role they play. Each subcontractor or vendor introduces an additional layer of risk, and it's important to ensure that they adhere to the same security standards as the primary vendor. This extends to understanding where the data will be located. Is it stored domestically or internationally, and what are the legal implications of these locations? Data location can affect compliance with various data protection laws and regulations, and it's important to ensure that the vendor's data storage practices align with your organization's compliance requirements.

Data segregation is another factor to consider. How does the vendor ensure that your data is kept separate from their other clients' data? Proper segregation is vital to prevent data leakage or unauthorized access. This is particularly important if the vendor is providing cloud-based services or shared environments where data could potentially be exposed to other clients. Equally important is understanding the vendor's approach to security audits. Do they conduct regular security audits, and are these audits performed by independent third parties? Are we going to get the results of their annual audits to confirm their security posture is still sufficient? Regular audits are essential for identifying vulnerabilities and ensuring that security practices are up to date. They also provide a level of assurance that the vendor is maintaining, and we'll touch that topic in the following pages.

Additionally, it's important to evaluate the vendor's security structure and governance. Who is responsible for security within their organization? Do they have a dedicated security team, or is security an afterthought? A strong security structure typically includes clear roles and responsibilities, regular training, and a culture that prioritizes security at all levels. Finally, consider the vendor's software development practices, especially if they are providing custom software solutions. Understanding their secure software development practices, such as code reviews, security testing, and regular updates, is important to norm your criteria on how secure they will be when providing you the service because that could introduce vulnerabilities into your environment.

So, when it comes to assessing your vendors, there are several approaches you can take to ensure you're covering all your bases. You might consider using standardized questionnaires like those available at the Cloud Security Alliance, which are designed to evaluate service providers and can help you gather relevant information on a vendor's security posture. Of course, you could develop your own customized questionnaire tailored to your organization's unique needs and risk appetite but having a guidance as reference or starting point could be helpful if this is the first time you do it. This allows you to focus on the specific areas that are most relevant to your operations and the type of data or services the vendor will handle.

There are also various tools available that can simplify the vendor assessment process because for effectively managing your third-party risks Excel will fall short. Solutions like Archer, BitSight, OneTrust among many more offer modules specifically for managing third-party risks, providing you with a structured and efficient way to evaluate vendors. These tools can offer insights based on external data sources, security ratings, and more, helping you make more informed decisions about which vendors to work with. Another approach is to conduct interviews with potential vendors, which can provide a more detailed understanding of their security practices and culture that might not be evident from a questionnaire or automated assessment.

The key here is not necessarily the specific method you use, but the consistency and completeness with which you apply your risk management methodology. Use the tools you have at hand and keep continually refining your approach over time. As you assess more vendors and learn what works best for your organization, you'll be able to develop a more effective and efficient third-party risk management program. The goal is to build a process aligned with your cyber risk management program that helps you identify risks early and manage them effectively, ensuring that every vendor you work with aligns with your organization's security standards and contributes to a secure and resilient operational environment.

Now, once you've selected a vendor and have a clear understanding of their security posture, you need to ensure that your contract with them addresses your security concerns and clearly outlines how identified risks will be managed. This is the transfer mechanism we discussed in the previous section for safeguarding your organization against potential threats that could arise from this partnership. However, I understand that not all vendors will be as accommodating as we'd like them to be. Some vendors, especially the larger ones, operate with a "take it or leave it" mentality, offering little room for negotiation. In these cases, they often set the terms, and you might find that there's little flexibility to include the specific security clauses you need. It can feel like you're at their mercy, and in a sense, you are. This doesn't mean you should simply accept the risk, though. It just means that you need to look for other ways to protect your organization, such as considering cyber insurance to cover any gaps that cannot be addressed contractually.

When you do have the opportunity to negotiate, there are several key security clauses you should aim to include in the contract. One of the most important is the right to audit. This clause ensures that you have the ability to independently verify that the vendor is adhering to their security obligations. It's about trust but also about verification, making sure they are doing what they say they are doing to protect your data and your organization. Another clause is security incident notification. This requires the vendor to promptly inform you if they experience a security breach that could impact your organization. The sooner you know about an incident, the quicker you can respond to mitigate any potential damage on your side.

For vendors who will be operating within your environment or who must comply with specific standards or regulations, compliance attestation is mandatory. This clause ensures that the vendor periodically confirms their adherence to relevant compliance requirements, providing you with the assurance that they are maintaining the necessary security controls. Similarly, you'll want to include a clause on the return and destruction of information. At the end of the contract, or whenever the relationship is terminated, the vendor should be obligated to return any data they have and destroy any copies they hold, ensuring that your information doesn't remain in their systems indefinitely.

If the vendor will be managing technology on your behalf, a change management clause that ensures your IT practices will be followed will be helpful. This enforces that any changes to systems or processes are communicated to you in advance and managed in a controlled manner, reducing the risk of unexpected issues or security vulnerabilities. For vendors providing software or technology services, it's also important to include clauses on software updates and fixes, as well as disaster recovery capabilities. These clauses ensure that the vendor is proactive in maintaining and securing their software and that they have a plan in place to recover quickly in the event of a disaster meeting your business needs.

Liability clauses that specifically cover security issues are also important to be considered. These outline the vendor's responsibility for any security breaches that result from their actions or negligence, ensuring that they are held accountable for any damages that arise. Additionally, data privacy clauses should be included to ensure that the vendor complies with all relevant data protection laws and takes appropriate measures to safeguard personal information.

For vendors that work with their own subcontractors, it's important to include an obligation for them to replicate your security requirements and clauses in their contracts with these subcontractors. This helps to ensure that the security standards you expect are maintained throughout the supply chain. Finally, requiring mandatory security and awareness training for the vendor's staff is a great way to ensure that everyone handling your data or working on your systems is aware of their responsibilities and the importance of security.

Each of these clauses plays a critical role in protecting your organization and ensuring that your vendors are held to the same high standards you set for yourself. While negotiating these terms can be challenging, especially with larger vendors, it's essential to take every step possible to mitigate risks and protect your organization. And when all else fails, alternative measures like cyber insurance can provide that extra layer of security, covering you for the risks that can't be contractually transferred.

Finally, I recommend not forgetting to keep a detailed record of all your vendors in your third-party matrix where you can detail the security controls they've implemented and the specific security clauses included in their signed contracts. Remember that not all contracts will have the same clauses, and also, you may acquire some responsibilities that will need to fulfilled and reported on. This documentation is really helpful for the assurance process because having a clear overview of what has been agreed upon and what each vendor is expected to uphold allows you to perform ongoing assessments.

When it comes time for your annual assessments, this record can simplify your efforts, providing a starting point that already outlines where each vendor stood previously. This way, you can focus on verifying that they've maintained or improved their security posture, rather than having to start from scratch every time. Keeping track of these details helps ensure that your third-party risk management program remains robust and adaptive, continuously protecting your organization's interests.

ASSURANCE PROCESSES

Once you've completed the due diligence and established a vendor relationship, the focus shifts to ensuring that the security measures promised are upheld over time. This is where assurance processes come into play. These processes are a continuous effort to verify that vendors are maintaining the agreed-upon security posture. Assurance is all about keeping a vigilant eye on your vendors, conducting regular checks, and ensuring that their security posture remains strong and aligned with your organization's expectations. This involves activities such as audits, compliance reviews, and assessments to ensure that vendors are meeting the security requirements set out in the contract as well as adapting to any changes in the threat landscape or in their own internal processes. Having a robust assurance process in place helps you identify potential security gaps early and allows for corrective actions to be taken swiftly, maintaining a secure partnership and protecting your organization from new risks.

To effectively manage the assurance process, it's essential to leverage the tools and resources available to you, ensuring that the work remains organized and manageable as it inevitably grows, and believe me, it'll grow fast. So, a good starting point is to develop a list of all active vendors. As part of the attributes of your list, it should include critical details that help you understand the risk each vendor presents to your organization, such as the categorize each vendor has based on their criticality or the level of risk they pose, reflecting their significance to your operations and the potential impact they could have if a security issue arises. It's also important to keep records of each vendor's security clauses in their contracts, the specific controls that were assessed during the initial due diligence process, the date of the last assessment, and any evidence collected at that time. These records will provide a snapshot of the vendor's security posture at any given time. Also, this allows you to detect patterns or recurring issues that may require more focused attention or even reconsideration of the vendor relationship.

With this structured information in hand, you can create a well-organized schedule for annual reassessments. This schedule should be according to the risk level of each vendor, ensuring that those categorized as higher risk are assessed more frequently so you can strategically plan your assessments to align with your overall risk management goals while maximizing the use of your resources. The aim is to avoid being reactive and instead adopt a proactive stance, where you're continually monitoring and reassessing your vendors to prevent any potential security breaches or compliance failures. This approach will help you distribute the workload effectively, preventing burnout or oversight and ensuring that no vendor slips through the cracks.

Keeping an eye on vendor compliance is another important part of the assurance process that helps you staying engaged and making sure vendors are meeting all the terms of their contracts, especially those that relate to security and data protection, making sure vendors are actually doing what they've agreed to do. Regular communication and periodic reviews help maintain this focus, allowing you to address any noncompliance issues early on.

So how can we make all this more effectively? Well, vendor security rating tools, for example, can provide continuous monitoring of a vendor's security posture by assessing their cybersecurity health based on publicly available information and threat intelligence. These tools can alert you to changes in a vendor's risk profile that might warrant a closer look or an immediate reassessment. They serve as an early warning system, giving you a heads-up about potential issues before they become significant problems. However, it's important to remember that these ratings should not be your sole source of truth. They are just one piece of the puzzle, providing external visibility that needs to be corroborated with your internal assessments and the information you've gathered directly from the vendor. Threat intelligence platforms can also add valuable information to your assurance processes. These platforms aggregate data from various sources to provide insights into the latest threats that could impact your vendors and just as important for your own threat intelligence efforts, doing the same for monitoring those critical vendors you have by staying informed about the evolving threat landscape, you can better understand how these threats might affect your supply chain and adjust your strategies accordingly. Additionally, Governance, Risk, and Compliance (GRC) tools can help automate many of the routine tasks associated with vendor management, such as tracking assessments, managing documentation, and scheduling reviews. These tools can provide a centralized platform where all relevant information is stored and easily accessible, reducing the administrative burden on your team. Automating these processes can ensure that nothing falls through the cracks and that every vendor is assessed according to your predefined schedule and risk criteria. It's important to mention that incorporating these tools into your assurance process doesn't mean you can take a hands-off approach, but it does mean that you can work smarter. Automation and real-time monitoring allow your team to focus more on analysis and decision-making rather than being bogged down by manual tasks. This way, you're not just keeping up with the growing workload but actively improving your third-party risk management program, making it more resilient and adaptable.

It's important to recognize that, despite all the preventive measures and diligent efforts to manage third-party risks, the reality is that at some point, one of your vendors will likely experience a security incident that could impact your organization. It's a harsh truth, but there's a very low probability that you'll be the exception to this rule. The best approach, then, is to be prepared for when this inevitable event occurs. This is where third-party incident management comes into play. It's essential to develop a detailed playbook that outlines the end-to-end process of handling such incidents. Whether aligned with your internal incident management process or requiring its own unique procedures, this playbook should be designed to address the specific challenges posed by third-party incidents. Keep in mind that, like all the rest of your documentation, it has to be reviewed and updated at least annually to ensure it remains relevant and effective.

The life cycle of a third-party incident typically unfolds in phases. The first phase is the Discovery phase, where the incident is initially detected. This might occur through direct notification from your vendor, as stipulated in your contract, or through your threat intelligence platforms and continuous monitoring tools, which could alert you to an issue even before the vendor is aware of it. Having multiple channels for incident discovery increases your chances of catching a potential problem early, allowing for a quicker response.

Once an incident has been detected, the next phase is the Investigation phase. During this stage, your incident response team will launch an investigation to confirm the incident and assess its scope and impact to your organization. This is an important step to determine the severity of the situation and to identify the necessary actions to mitigate any potential damage. If the vendor involved has some form of connectivity with your systems, it may be prudent to close these connections temporarily as a precaution. While this is happening, the vendor will likely be managing their own investigation, containment, and recovery efforts. It's essential to maintain open communication with the vendor to stay updated on their progress and ensure that their actions align with your security expectations. However, you need to understand that they are dealing with the incident and communications may not as fluid as you sometimes may wish.

Following the investigation, there is the Reporting phase. This phase involves compiling a detailed report on the incident to inform executive management and, if required, regulatory bodies. It's vital to follow the established procedures and use the correct communication channels during this phase. Involving your legal counsel before disseminating any information or reports is also a good practice, as it ensures that all communications are legally sound and that your organization is protected.

Finally, there is the Closing phase. This phase focuses on documenting all the final details of the incident, including the findings from the vendor's investigation and the remediation activities they have undertaken. It's important to critically evaluate these findings to ensure that the vendor has addressed the root cause of the incident and not just the symptoms. Rushing to remediate without an exhaustive investigation can lead to incomplete resolutions, where underlying vulnerabilities are not fully addressed, leaving the door open for future incidents or even leaving the attacker inside for a second attack.

All the lessons learned from these incidents should feed directly into your cyber risk management processes. Every incident represents a risk that wasn't adequately managed, and it's critical to use this experience to strengthen your defenses moving forward. Taking the time to learn from each incident, adjusting your strategies accordingly, and continuously improving your third-party risk management efforts will help you build a more resilient and secure organization.

To effectively close the assurance process, it's necessary for you to establish performance metrics and regularly review security reports about your vendors. Without these, it's nearly impossible to measure whether your third-party risk management program is effective or if there are areas where it might be falling short. Performance metrics provide a clear, quantifiable way for you to monitor your vendors' compliance with contractual obligations and their adherence to regulatory requirements, as well as the overall health of their security posture.

When defining these metrics, it's important to focus on key indicators that reflect both your vendors' security performance and the effectiveness of your due diligence and assurance processes. These could include metrics such as the number of security incidents reported by vendors, the time taken for vendors to resolve these incidents, the frequency of security assessments conducted, and the number of outstanding vulnerabilities identified and addressed. You will need to create a transparent framework that helps you track your vendors' adherence to security practices and also assesses how well your risk management program is functioning. These metrics must provide a baseline for evaluating vendor performance and serve as benchmarks to measure improvement over time, helping you identify trends and areas that may require additional attention.

Regularly reviewing security reports about your vendors is another component of your assurance process. These reports should include information that you compile about any security incidents, updates on remediation efforts, results of internal and external audits, and any changes to their security posture. Regularly reviewing these reports ensures that you stay informed about your vendors' security activities and can quickly respond to any issues that arise. It also encourages a proactive approach to managing vendor security, fostering a culture of continuous improvement and collaboration, where both parties work together to enhance security practices and mitigate risks.

Maintaining a complete view of your vendor landscape through these performance metrics and regular reporting helps you detect potential risks early and take corrective actions before they escalate into more significant problems. It provides valuable data that can be used to refine your risk management strategies and improve the effectiveness of your assurance process. Ultimately, this information helps you create a resilient and secure ecosystem beyond your internal environment, where third-party risks are effectively managed.

OFFBOARDING PROCESSES

As we move into the final phase of managing third-party relationships, we reach the crucial process of offboarding vendors. Often, this stage doesn't receive the attention it deserves, yet it is just as critical as the onboarding phase. When a vendor relationship comes to an end, whether due to contract expiration, a strategic decision to move in a different direction, or performance issues, it's essential to ensure that all aspects of the disengagement are handled meticulously. This isn't just about closing the financial books or tying up loose ends; it's about maintaining the security, integrity, and operational continuity of your organization. A poorly managed offboarding process can leave significant gaps, creating potential vulnerabilities that could be exploited long after the vendor has left.

One of the first aspects to consider during the offboarding process is the physical access that the vendor's personnel may have had to your premises. Physical security is often the most immediate and visible risk, yet it's surprisingly easy to overlook in the hustle of ending a contract. As part of your offboarding checklist, it's vital to revoke all forms of physical access that the vendor or its employees may have. This includes collecting access cards, deactivating key fobs, changing locks, and ensuring that any biometric access permissions are removed. Additionally, if the vendor's staff had badges or temporary access passes, those need to be collected and invalidated immediately. Physical security measures should be comprehensive and absolute, ensuring that no avenues are left open for unauthorized individuals to enter your premises.

After addressing physical access, the next focus should be on removing logical access and disabling accounts. Over the course of a vendor relationship, especially one that involves IT services or data handling, various user accounts, system permissions, and VPN connections might have been created to facilitate their work. It's critical to ensure that all these digital touchpoints are deactivated immediately upon termination of the relationship. This isn't just a matter of switching off access but involves a detailed audit to ensure that no backdoors or residual access points remain. All user credentials provided to the vendor should be deleted, and any associated passwords changed. This also includes remote access accounts, database access, application programming interfaces (APIs), and any other forms of connectivity that the vendor had. It's not uncommon for vendors to have integrated systems that communicate regularly with your internal network, and these connections need to be carefully dismantled to prevent any potential security breaches. The last thing you want is a former vendor still having active access to your systems, intentionally or unintentionally.

Equally important is the return of equipment. Throughout a vendor's engagement, they might be issued company-owned devices, hardware, or tools necessary for their work. Upon termination, it's essential to ensure that all these items are returned promptly and in good condition. This process is not just about getting your property back but also about ensuring that the equipment does not contain sensitive information or data that could be compromised. Before accepting the return of any equipment, conduct an inspection to ensure that no data remains on the device. This could include a factory reset or wiping the hard drive to ensure that all data is irretrievably deleted. Also, consider any software that might have been installed on the vendor's systems to facilitate their work with your organization. If there are licenses or proprietary software involved, ensure that these are revoked or transferred back in accordance with your agreements. It's not just the physical device but the data and software within that need to be accounted for and managed properly.

In tandem with equipment return, the offboarding process must also address the return and destruction of information. During their engagement, vendors often have access to sensitive or proprietary data that must be handled carefully upon contract termination. It's crucial to ensure that all data, whether digital or physical, is either returned or securely destroyed. This includes any documents, spreadsheets, emails, or reports that may contain confidential information. Ensure that the vendor provides certification of data destruction, verifying that all information has been securely wiped or shredded according to your organization's data retention and destruction policies. This step is vital to prevent any potential data leaks or breaches that could occur if sensitive information falls into the wrong hands after the vendor relationship has ended. Remember that this isn't just about digital data; hard copies of documents must also be handled correctly. Shredding or incineration are standard practices for ensuring that paper records are disposed of securely. It's important to have clear guidelines and processes for how information should be handled during the offboarding phase, so there's no ambiguity or room for error.

Additionally, consider the importance of log retention during the offboarding process. While vendors should no longer have access to your systems, it's prudent to retain logs of their activities for a specified period, in line with your organization's data retention policies. These logs can provide an invaluable trail in case any issues arise post-termination, allowing you to review the actions taken by the vendor during their engagement. It's also a good practice to review these logs during the offboarding process to identify any unusual activities that may need further investigation. This helps ensure that there are no unresolved issues or security concerns lingering after the vendor has been offboarded. Keeping detailed records of the vendor's actions, access, and transactions can also provide a legal safeguard, should any disputes or claims arise after the termination of the contract.

Another aspect of the offboarding process is ensuring that all contract deliverables and ongoing security obligations are met. Before concluding the relationship, review the contract carefully to ensure that all terms and conditions have been fulfilled. This includes any final deliverables, warranties, or post-termination obligations specified in the contract. Some contracts may require the vendor to provide ongoing support for a defined period after the contract ends or to address any security vulnerabilities discovered post-termination. It's essential to ensure these obligations are met to protect your organization's interests and avoid any potential legal complications. Additionally, if there are any outstanding issues or concerns related to the vendor's performance, now is the time to address them. Ensure that all loose ends are tied up and that there are no unresolved matters that could come back to haunt your organization later.

The decommissioning process is another step in offboarding a vendor. This involves securely shutting down any systems, services, or connections that were established specifically for the vendor's engagement. Decommissioning ensures that there are no active points of access that could be exploited once the vendor is no longer under contract. This might include deactivating accounts, revoking API keys, and removing any vendor-specific configurations from your systems. It's important to be thorough in this process to prevent any lingering access points that could be used for unauthorized entry into your network. It is then that this step is about ensuring that your systems are secure and that there are no gaps or vulnerabilities that could be exploited after the vendor has been offboarded.

Effective communication within your organization is crucial when offboarding a vendor. Ensure that all relevant departments and stakeholders are notified about the termination of the vendor relationship. This helps prevent any misunderstandings or miscommunications that could lead to security lapses or operational issues. For example, if your IT team is unaware that a vendor has been offboarded, they might unknowingly continue to provide access or support, creating a potential security risk. Clear and timely communication ensures that everyone is on the same page and that all necessary actions are taken to secure your organization. It's also important to communicate with any external parties who might be affected by the termination, such as other vendors or partners who may have been working with the vendor in question. Keeping everyone informed helps ensure a smooth transition and prevents any disruptions to your operations.

Finally, remember to update your vendor management matrix. This is the document or tool you use to keep track of all your vendor relationships and their associated risks. Once a vendor has been offboarded, remove them from the list of active vendors and update any relevant documentation to reflect the termination of the relationship. This helps maintain an accurate record of your vendor ecosystem and ensures that your third-party risk management processes remain current and effective. Keeping your records up to date is required for maintaining a clear overview of your vendor landscape and for ensuring that your organization is well-prepared to manage any future vendor relationships. A well-executed offboarding process protects your organization's security and reinforces the importance of cyber risk management throughout the entire life cycle of a vendor relationship. Ultimately, the goal of the offboarding process is to close the chapter on the vendor relationship in a way that leaves no loose ends and ensures that your organization's security and operational integrity are maintained.

So, as we conclude our exploration of third-party risk management, it's important to reflect on the critical steps we've outlined to protect your organization. Managing third-party risks is more than just a nice-to-have; it's a fundamental element of any effective cybersecurity strategy. Throughout this chapter, we have got into the complexities of third-party risks, from understanding the various types of threats these relationships can introduce to implementing effective due diligence and assurance processes and, finally, to the importance of a thorough offboarding process.

We began by highlighting the importance of due diligence during the onboarding process. This phase is your first line of defense, where you assess the potential risks that a new vendor may bring into your organization. Integrating due diligence into the supply management process will ensure that every vendor is evaluated for security concerns from the outset. This helps prevent the common pitfall of selecting a vendor based solely on cost or functionality, which can lead to significant security shortcomings down the line. Leveraging tools like security score companies, conducting external assessments, and engaging relevant stakeholders such as legal, privacy, and IT teams are steps in the right direction to build a strong foundation for third-party risk management.

Once a vendor relationship is established, the focus shifts to ensuring that the security measures promised are upheld over time. This is where the assurance process comes into play. By regularly assessing vendors, monitoring compliance with contractual obligations, and reviewing their security controls, you can maintain a vigilant eye on your third-party relationships. This proactive approach helps identify potential security gaps early, allowing for swift corrective actions to protect your organization from evolving threats. Utilizing vendor security rating tools, threat intelligence platforms, and GRC tools can enhance your assurance processes by automating routine tasks and providing continuous monitoring of vendor security postures.

We also explored the importance of establishing performance metrics and requiring regular security reports from your vendors. These practices are crucial for tracking your vendors' compliance with security standards and measuring the effectiveness of your third-party risk management program. Finally, we discussed the often-overlooked process of offboarding vendors. When a vendor relationship ends, whether due to contract expiration or strategic decisions, it's essential to handle the disengagement meticulously. This includes revoking physical and logical access, ensuring the return and secure destruction of information, decommissioning any systems or services established for the vendor, and communicating changes internally to prevent any security lapses. An offboarding process to protect your organization from potential risks, reinforcing the importance of cyber risk management throughout the entire life cycle of a vendor relationship.

As we move forward to Chapter 12, remember that third-party risk management is an ongoing effort that requires continuous attention and adaptation and must be integrated with your overall cyber risk management program. We discussed third-party risk management separately to help you establish the right foundations first, allowing you to adopt and integrate it into your general process. Doing so will make things easier and help you avoid blind spots.

Chapter 12

Building cyber resilience

In every phase of our journey through cyber risk management, the focus has always been on creating a resilient and proactive defense. As we went through the various stages of cyber risk management, I hope it's now clear that each step we've taken has been building toward a larger goal: achieving cyber resilience. The fundamentals we explored in the early chapters laid the groundwork, giving us the knowledge needed to understand the complexities of cyber risk. From there, we got into frameworks and methodologies that form the core structure of an effective risk management strategy, aligning corporate governance and cybersecurity culture to create a unified approach.

In Section II, we moved from theory to practice, carrying out a complete risk management process. Each chapter in this section provided practical tools for managing cyber risks in a structured way, making sure we address risks proactively. As we transitioned into third-party risk management, we saw the value of understanding and managing risks that extend beyond our immediate control. This broad perspective is key in today's interconnected world, where the actions of others can significantly affect our security posture. On top of all of this, we've reviewed skills that will help you become more resilient, such as organizational change management, selling the big picture, emotional intelligence.

Risk management and the response plans we've discussed, including disaster recovery capabilities and business continuity, are two sides of the same coin. While risk management focuses on assessing, and managing risks before they materialize, it's impossible to anticipate every possible risk. There will always be unforeseen challenges that slip through the cracks, despite our best efforts. This is where response plans, disaster recovery, and business continuity must be in place because these are the mechanisms that help us respond to incidents when they occur, recover from disruptions, and ensure that the organization can continue to operate, even under adverse conditions.

DOI: 10.1201/9781003546207-16

For those risks that aren't fully managed or those we didn't anticipate, incidents are destined to happen. When they do, how we respond, recover, and maintain continuity directly influences our resilience. Each incident provides valuable lessons learned, offering insights into gaps in our defenses and opportunities for improvement. These lessons will feed back into the risk management process, so we can refine our strategies, enhance our preparedness, and better manage risks in the future. This continuous cycle of managing risks and learning from incidents helps build a more resilient organization, capable of adapting and thriving despite the challenges cyber threats represent. In this chapter, we will look at the principles of cyber resilience, setting the stage for a deeper understanding of how organizations can maintain operations, even when under attack, and recover quickly to minimize impact and keep functioning effectively.

THE CORE COMPONENTS TO BUILD CYBER RESILIENCE

Cyber resilience starts with building cyber readiness, which involves preparing to defend against cyber threats and maintaining operations even under attack. Everything we've covered in the previous chapters contributes to this state of readiness. But readiness alone isn't enough; it must be complemented by effective responsiveness, the ability to respond to and recover from incidents quickly to minimize their impact. To achieve this, we focus on three main principles: preparedness, response, and recovery. Each principle involves key functions like planning, training, execution, and learning. Mastering these functions will ensure that our organization is well-equipped to handle cyber challenges, maintain operations, and continue moving forward despite any obstacles.

It is then than to build cyber resilience, we need to focus on those two main components: readiness and responsiveness. Readiness is all about anticipating potential threats, implementing and maintaining security controls based on risk assessments, and having plans to respond effectively. This means we need to understand that cyberattacks are inevitable and must foster a culture where everyone is aware and prepared to act. The principle of preparedness is central to readiness. In addition to all the efforts explained and covered by the cyber risk management program in previous chapters, it includes key elements like conducting a business impact analysis (BIA) to identify critical functions and assess the potential impact of disruptions. This analysis helps prioritize resources and guide planning efforts. Readiness also involves investing in the right technologies, training staff to recognize and prevent threats, and regularly testing these measures to ensure they remain effective.

On the other side of the coin, responsiveness focuses on the immediate actions taken when an incident occurs. The principle of response emphasizes how well the organization can limit damage and disruption. This includes having well-trained incident response teams (IRTs) and clear procedures, such as incident response plans (IRP), that guides your organization through the necessary steps to contain and mitigate the impact of an attack, making sure everyone knows their role and can act without hesitation when and as required. Regular drills and simulations reinforce these capabilities, making sure the response is quick and effective, reducing the potential harm to the organization.

Recovery is about how the organization bounces back from a cyber incident, focusing on minimizing downtime and restoring normal operations. The disaster recovery plan (DRP) plays a critical role here by detailing how to restore IT systems and data after an incident to ensure technology functions can be quickly resumed. Meanwhile, the Business continuity plan (BCP) ensures that essential business operations can continue during and after a crisis, minimizing the overall impact on the organization. Recovery also involves managing broader implications like reputational damage or legal consequences, as well as learning from each incident to improve future readiness and responsiveness. Regular testing and refinement of DRP and BCP ensure they are effective, and that the organization can recover swiftly from any disruption.

Finally, continuous improvement ties together readiness and responsiveness, ensuring that both components evolve over time. The cyber threat landscape is always changing, so organizations need to learn from each incident, review what worked well and what didn't, and use those insights to strengthen defenses and response strategies. Continuous improvement involves regularly updating technologies, processes, and training to stay ahead of emerging threats. It also fosters a culture where everyone understands the importance of cyber resilience and is encouraged to contribute to the organization's security. This can mean anything from reporting suspicious activities to participating in regular training sessions or drills.

With readiness and responsiveness as the two sides of the cyber resilience coin, to fully understand and implement these components effectively, it's important to review the key components like BIA, IRP, DRPs, and BCPs, so we can uncover what matters most in building an effective resilience strategy. Next, we will explore each of these components in detail to understand their roles in strengthening our cyber resilience framework.

Let's start at the beginning, BIA. The BIA is a key component as it helps organizations understand the potential impacts of disruptions on their critical functions. When you're in an incident and need a clear prioritization of what must be your highest priority, the result of a BIA is what should dictate your priorities. According to ISO 22317:2021, the BIA process is designed to identify and evaluate the effects of interruptions on business operations. This analysis helps prioritize resources, identify necessary recovery time objectives (RTOs), and guide planning efforts to ensure that essential functions can continue or be restored swiftly after an incident. On many occasions I've seen organizations that have a general understanding of what's most critical for them but don't really understand the impact, the sequence, dependencies, and even the assets involved in that top priority business process. To approach the BIA process pragmatically and effectively, it is essential to focus on a few key principles:

- **Define the scope and objectives**: Start by clearly defining the scope and objectives of the BIA. This involves identifying the processes, functions, or activities that are critical to the organization and could be significantly impacted by disruptions. Understanding what needs to be analyzed and why is crucial to ensuring that the BIA is focused and relevant.
- **Engage the right stakeholders**: Successful BIA requires input from various departments and stakeholders across the organization. Engaging these individuals early in the process ensures that the analysis covers all relevant areas and that the findings are accurate. Stakeholders typically include department heads, IT personnel, risk managers, and any other individuals who have insight into the organization's critical functions and dependencies, especially if you rely on magic people because documentation is not the strongest point in your organization.
- **Identify critical activities and dependencies**: The next step is to identify the critical activities that are essential to the organization's operations and the dependencies that support these activities. This includes understanding which resources, systems, and processes are vital for each function to operate. It's important to map out these dependencies carefully to identify potential single points of failure or areas that could cause significant disruptions if impacted.
- **Assess the impact of disruptions**: For each critical activity, assess the potential impact of different types of disruptions. This can include financial losses, reputational damage, legal or regulatory consequences, and impacts on customer service or operational capability. The goal is to understand the severity of the impact over time and establish the maximum acceptable outage (MAO) for each function, which defines the maximum duration that a process can be disrupted before unacceptable consequences occur.
- **Determine recovery objectives**: Based on the impact assessment, determine the RTOs and recovery point objectives (RPOs) for each critical activity. RTOs define the target time frame for resuming a function after a disruption, while RPOs specify the maximum acceptable amount of data loss measured in time. Setting these objectives helps prioritize recovery efforts and resource allocation. These two are particularly important for the DRP we'll discuss in the next pages.

- **Document findings and develop action plans:** Once the BIA is complete, document the findings in a clear and structured manner. This documentation should include a summary of critical activities, impact assessments, dependencies, and recovery objectives. Use these findings to develop action plans that outline specific steps to improve resilience and ensure continuity of critical functions.
- **Review and update regularly:** The BIA is not a one-time exercise. To remain effective, it should be reviewed and updated regularly, especially after significant organizational changes or following an incident. Continuous review ensures that the BIA remains relevant and reflects the current state of the organization's operations and risk environment.

Following these steps and focusing on practicality will help you guide your organization to conduct a BIA that is both pragmatic and effective. A well-executed BIA provides a solid foundation for understanding and prioritizing recovery efforts, ensuring that critical functions can continue or be restored quickly after a disruption. This approach aligns with the principles of ISO 22317:2021 that provides assistance in designing a BIA process appropriate to your needs.

Next is the turn for the IRP that is part of the responsiveness but as you'll see everything starts in the readiness function. IRP represents one of the critical elements of an organization's cybersecurity program, providing a structured approach (see Figure 12.1) to handling and managing incidents effectively. An IRP outlines the steps and actions to take when a cyber incident occurs, ensuring that the organization can respond quickly to minimize

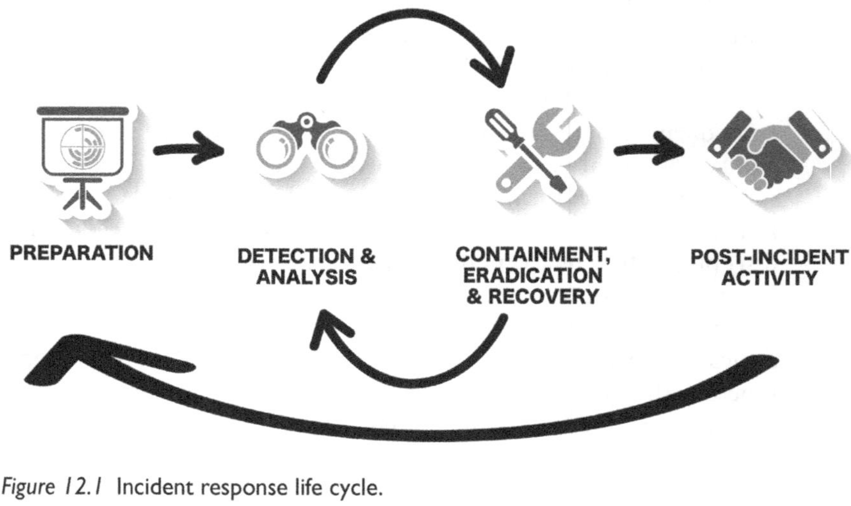

Figure 12.1 Incident response life cycle.

damage, reduce recovery time, and mitigate the impact of the incident. NIST SP 800-61 and CISA provide guidelines that we can use, here is how to approach developing an effective IRP:

- **Establish clear objectives and scope**: As usual, the first step is to define the plan's objectives and scope. This involves identifying the types of incidents the plan will cover and the overall goals of the response efforts. The objectives typically include minimizing the impact of the incident, protecting sensitive data, restoring operations as quickly as possible, and complying with legal and regulatory requirements. Defining the scope ensures that the plan is focused and relevant to the organization's specific needs.
- **Develop an IRT**: An effective IRP requires of an IRT responsible for managing and executing the response efforts. This team should consist of individuals with diverse expertise, including IT, cybersecurity, legal, communications, and business operations. Each team member should have clearly defined roles and responsibilities, ensuring that everyone knows their part in the response process. Your IRP must include who the team members are and their contact details. Remember that IRT could be outsourced as well, so make sure all the members are listed even if they are third parties. Regular training and tabletop exercises or if possible in cyber ranges because they are super useful to simulate real scenarios ensuring that the team is well-prepared to act when an incident occurs.
- **Identify and classify incidents**: The IRP should include a process for identifying and classifying incidents based on their nature and severity. This involves defining what constitutes an incident and establishing criteria for different incident types and impact levels as well as defining how incidents will escalate through the different levels. With classified incidents your IRT can prioritize response efforts and allocate resources more effectively. Early detection and accurate classification are crucial for minimizing damage and reducing recovery time.
- **Establish response procedures**: Response procedures are the core of the IRP, detailing the specific actions to take when an incident occurs. These procedures should be designed to different types of incidents and aligned with the organization's risk management strategy. The response process typically includes several phases: detection and analysis, containment, eradication, and recovery. Each phase should have clear steps and guidelines, ensuring a consistent and effective response. The plan should also include communication protocols for notifying stakeholders, your cyber insurance company, regulatory bodies, and, if necessary, the public.

- **Develop communication strategies**: Effective communication is critical during an incident. The IRP should include strategies for internal and external communication, outlining who needs to be informed, what information should be shared, and how it should be communicated. This helps ensure that everyone involved in the response effort is on the same page and that stakeholders are kept informed of the situation and the actions being taken. Clear communication helps maintain trust and can prevent further escalation of the incident.
- **Test and refine the plan**: An IRP is only effective if it is regularly tested and refined. Conducting regular drills and simulations helps ensure that the IRT is familiar with their roles and can execute the plan effectively. Testing also helps identify gaps or weaknesses in the plan, providing opportunities for improvement. After each exercise, it's important to review the results, gather feedback, and update the plan as needed to ensure it remains effective and aligned with the organization's needs.
- **Incorporate lessons learned**: After an incident or exercise, it's essential to conduct a detailed review to identify lessons learned. This involves analyzing what happened, why it happened, and how the response was handled. The findings should be documented and used to improve the IRP and enhance the organization's overall security posture. Incorporating lessons learned helps ensure that the organization is better prepared for future incidents and continuously improves its incident response capabilities.

Another key component of effective IRPs are the Incident response playbooks because these ones are essential tools detailing a step-by-step guide that outline the specific actions to take during different types of cyber incidents. Each playbook must be designed to a particular kind of threat or incident, such as malware infections, phishing attacks, third-party incidents, data breaches, ransomware incidents, or denial-of-service (DoS) attacks. The purpose of these playbooks is to ensure that the response is consistent, coordinated, and swift, minimizing the impact of the incident on the organization.

Every effective incident response playbook starts with a clear incident description. Defining the type of incident helps everyone understand the nature of the threat and the specific challenges it presents. This clarity is the foundation for the steps that follow, ensuring that the response team is prepared to act swiftly and appropriately. Once the type of incident is defined, the next step is detection and analysis. The playbook provides guidelines on how to identify the incident and assess its scope and severity. Early detection is key to minimizing impact, and analyzing the incident helps determine how far it has spread and what kind of damage it might cause. This information is crucial for shaping the response and deciding on the next steps. Containment steps come next. These instructions focus on isolating the incident to prevent further damage or spread. The goal is to keep the problem from escalating, whether that means quarantining a compromised system or disconnecting a network segment. Containment is about taking immediate action to stop the incident in its tracks and limit its impact on the organization.

After containment, the playbook moves on to eradication procedures. This section lays out the steps for removing the threat from affected systems and ensuring it doesn't return. Eradication involves completely cleaning up the incident, making sure every trace of the threat is eliminated, and the systems are safe to use again. It's not just about fixing the immediate problem but ensuring that it doesn't happen again. The playbook then outlines recovery actions, which are detailed plans for restoring systems and data to normal operations. Recovery is about getting back to business in a way that ensures the threat has been fully eliminated. This could involve restoring data from backups, patching vulnerabilities, or even rebuilding systems. The goal is to ensure that everything is secure and functioning properly, minimizing downtime and disruption.

Managing communication correctly is critical throughout the incident. The playbook should provide guidance on how to share information internally with stakeholders and, if necessary, externally with regulators, insurance companies, customers, or the public. Clear communication helps manage the situation and maintain trust, ensuring everyone knows what's happening and what to expect. It's about keeping the right people informed at the right times, which is essential for a coordinated response. Finally, documentation requirements are included in the playbook. These instructions specify what information needs to be recorded during the response process for legal, regulatory, or improvement purposes. Documentation helps capture what happened, what actions were taken, and what the outcomes were. This record is valuable for learning from the incident and refines the response process for future incidents.

Following these steps, organizations can develop an effective IRP and its playbooks that align with best practices and maintain a pragmatic approach. However, responding to an incident is just the beginning. Once the immediate threat is contained and the situation stabilized, it's equally important to focus on recovery. This is where the DRP comes into play, detailing how to restore systems and data to full functionality after an incident. Let's explore how a well-structured DRP supports the overall resilience strategy by ensuring that critical IT functions are restored and business operations can continue without significant disruption.

A DRP is a crucial component of an organization's overall resilience strategy. It outlines the steps to be taken to restore IT systems and data following a disruption, ensuring that critical business functions can resume as quickly as possible. A well-developed DRP helps minimize downtime and data loss, which are key to maintaining business continuity after an incident. To create an effective DRP, several key elements need to be considered:

- **Defining the scope**: The first step in developing a DRP is to clearly define its scope. This involves identifying the systems, applications, and data that are critical to the organization's operations and must be prioritized during recovery. Understanding the scope ensures that the plan focuses on restoring the most important functions first, which helps minimize the impact on the organization.
- **Using RTO and RPO from the BIA**: A critical part of the DRP is using the RTOs and RPOs defined in the BIA. These objectives guide the development of the DRP, ensuring that recovery efforts align with the organization's tolerance for downtime and data loss. Make sure these are realistic and achievable.
- **Documenting the plan and its sections**: A complete DRP should be well-documented, with clear sections outlining each aspect of the recovery process. This documentation typically includes detailed instructions on recovery procedures, roles and responsibilities, communication plans, and contact information for key personnel. It's important to ensure that the plan is easy to understand and accessible to everyone involved in the recovery process.
- **Backups and types of backups**: A critical component of any DRP is having a robust backup strategy. This involves determining the types of backups needed to protect critical data and systems. Common types of backups include full data backups, incremental backups, and differential backups. Full backups capture all data at a specific point in time, while incremental backups only capture changes since the last backup, and differential backups capture all changes since the last full backup. Additional considerations include using different storage methods such as tapes, redundant array of independent disks (RAID), Storage area networks (SAN), cloud storage, offline backups, and immutable backups. Each type of backup and storage method has its own advantages and should be selected based on the organization's specific needs and risk tolerance.
- **Testing the plan and backups**: Regular testing of the DRP and backups is essential to ensure that they work as intended and that the organization can recover from disruptions. This includes conducting full-scale tests of the recovery process, as well as testing individual backups to confirm that data can be restored from them. Testing helps identify any gaps or weaknesses in the plan, providing an opportunity for improvement before an actual disaster occurs.
- **Identification of single points of failure**: Part of developing a robust DRP involves identifying single points of failure within the

organization's IT infrastructure. A single point of failure is any part of the system that, if it fails, would cause the entire system to fail. Identifying these vulnerabilities allows the organization to implement redundancies and failover strategies, reducing the risk of a complete system failure during a disaster.

- **Involving third parties**: Many organizations rely on third-party vendors for critical services and infrastructure, making it important to consider their role in the DRP. This includes confirming that contracts and capabilities are in place with these third parties and that they have their own DRPs that align with the organization's requirements. Regularly reviewing these contracts and capabilities ensures that third-party providers can meet their commitments and support the organization's recovery efforts.
- **Considering alternative recovery sites**: When planning for disaster recovery, it's important to consider alternative recovery sites that can be used if the primary site becomes unavailable. These sites provide varying levels of readiness and can significantly impact the speed and effectiveness of the recovery process. Hot sites are fully equipped and can be up and running almost immediately, providing the quickest recovery option. Warm sites have some equipment and data backups, but require additional setup time to become fully operational. Cold sites are essentially empty spaces that require complete setup before they can be used, making them the slowest option for recovery. Mobile sites are movable units that can be transported to a designated location and set up as a temporary recovery site. Redundant sites are fully operational duplicates of the primary site that can take over without any downtime. Choosing the right type of recovery site depends on the organization's needs, the criticality of its operations, and its RTOs.

Make sure your DRP is reviewed and updated whenever changes occur in your organization, or you might find yourself in a difficult situation with a plan that doesn't reflect the current reality of your environment.

A BCP is the last but not least important of the components to build cyber resilience and has the purpose of ensuring that an organization can maintain or quickly resume critical business functions during and after a disruption. Unlike a DRP, which focuses on restoring IT systems and data, a BCP addresses the broader scope of maintaining all essential operations, covering every aspect of the business to minimize downtime and maintain productivity. To develop a robust BCP, several key elements need to be considered:

- **Defining the scope and objectives**: The first step in creating a BCP is to define its scope and objectives. This involves identifying which business functions are critical to the organization's operations and must be prioritized during a disruption. The scope should cover all essential areas, from IT systems and data to human resources, facilities, and supply chains. Clearly defining the scope and objectives ensures that the plan is exhaustive and aligned with the organization's priorities.

- **Using insights from the BIA**: The BIA plays a vital role in the development of a BCP. The BIA provides insights into the potential impact of disruptions on different business functions, helping to identify which areas are most critical and need immediate attention. Using the findings from the BIA, allows you to determine the RTOs and RPOs for each critical function, ensuring that the BCP is focused on minimizing downtime and data loss.
- **Documenting the plan and its sections**: A well-structured BCP should be fully documented, with clear sections outlining each aspect of the continuity process. This documentation typically includes an overview of the plan, roles and responsibilities, communication strategies, and detailed procedures for maintaining operations. It's important to ensure that the plan is easy to understand and accessible to everyone involved in the continuity efforts.
- **Continuity strategies for critical business functions**: The heart of the BCP is the development of continuity strategies for each critical business function. This involves identifying alternative methods for maintaining operations when normal procedures are disrupted. For example, if a key office is unavailable, the BCP might include strategies for remote work, using alternative locations, or shifting operations to other offices. These strategies should be flexible and adaptable, allowing the organization to continue functioning under various scenarios.
- **Ensuring resource availability**: A BCP must ensure that all necessary resources are available to support continuity efforts. This includes physical resources like backup office space and equipment, as well as digital resources such as access to critical systems and data. It also involves ensuring that key personnel are available and that there are plans in place to address staffing needs, such as cross-training employees or establishing agreements with third-party providers.
- **Developing communication plans**: Effective communication is essential during a disruption. The BCP should include detailed communication plans that outline how to keep employees, customers, suppliers, and other stakeholders informed throughout the disruption. This includes identifying who will communicate, what information will be shared, and how it will be delivered, whether through email, phone calls, or other channels. Clear communication helps maintain trust and ensures everyone knows what to expect and how to proceed.

- **Testing and exercising the plan:** Like any other plan, a BCP must be tested and exercised regularly to ensure its effectiveness. This involves conducting tabletop exercises, simulations, and full-scale drills to test the plan under various scenarios. Testing helps identify gaps or weaknesses in the plan, providing opportunities for improvement. After each exercise, it's important to review the results, gather feedback, and update the plan as needed to keep it current and effective.
- **Maintaining and updating the plan:** A BCP is not a one-time document; it should be reviewed and updated regularly to reflect changes in the organization's operations, structure, and environment. This includes updating contact information, reviewing the scope and objectives, and revising continuity strategies as needed. Regular maintenance ensures that the plan remains relevant and ready to be activated whenever necessary.

As we wrap up this exploration of the key components to build cyber resilience, I hope it's clear to you that there are significant overlaps and common foundations among the BIA, IRP, DRP, and BCP. All of them connect with the cyber risk management program you're building, keeping it always evolving and improving. At their core, these elements share the same goal: ensuring that an organization can withstand, respond to, and recover from disruptions with minimal impact on its operations.

Each of these components, whether we are talking about the BIA, IRP, DRP, or BCP, starts with a deep understanding of the organization's priorities and critical functions. The BIA lays the groundwork by helping us identify which business processes are essential and how their disruption could affect the organization. It's the foundation upon which all other plans are built, giving us the insights needed to prioritize our resources and define our recovery objectives. The RTOs and RPOs established in the BIA guide both our disaster recovery efforts and our continuity strategies, ensuring that we're always focused on what matters most.

The IRP and DRP work hand in hand, forming a coordinated response to incidents that threaten the organization's security and operational stability. The IRP focuses on the immediate actions needed to contain and mitigate an incident. It's all about quick, decisive action to limit damage, backed by clear roles, responsibilities, and communication protocols. Once the immediate threat is managed, the DRP steps in to restore IT systems and data, getting the technology side of the business back on track. Both plans rely heavily on careful preparation and regular testing to ensure that when an incident occurs, everyone knows their role, and the response is swift and effective.

The BCP extends beyond just IT recovery, looking at the bigger picture of keeping the business running no matter what. It builds on the insights from the BIA and complements the DRP by addressing how to maintain critical functions across all areas of the business, whether that's ensuring key personnel are available, alternative work sites are ready, or communication lines remain open. The BCP is about more than just reacting to an incident; it's about ensuring the organization can continue to operate and serve its customers, even under challenging circumstances.

What ties all these plans together is their shared focus on readiness and responsiveness. Each plan involves careful planning, training, execution, and learning. Readiness is about being prepared, having the right strategies, plans, and resources in place before an incident occurs. It's about anticipating potential threats, understanding the risks, and taking proactive steps to mitigate them. But always keep in mind that we also need responsiveness, the ability to act quickly and effectively when a disruption does occur. This means having well-developed plans like the IRP, DRP, and BCP, all of which provide clear, actionable steps to guide the organization through any crisis.

Continuous improvement is another common thread that runs through all these components. Whether it's refining our BIA based on the latest business changes, updating our IRP and playbooks after an incident, or testing our DRP and BCP to ensure they meet current needs, each of these plans must evolve. The cyber threat landscape is always changing, and our response strategies must change with it. Learning from each incident, reviewing what worked and what didn't, and making necessary and risk-based prioritized adjustments, will allow you to contribute to build a resilient organization. At the end of the day, the BIA, IRP, DRP, and BCP are not isolated components but interconnected parts of an effective resilience strategy. They all rely on a foundation of good planning, clear communication, in-depth testing, and continuous improvement.

CRISIS MANAGEMENT AND RESPONSE

Crisis management is one of the most important components of cyber resilience. It's about having a structured approach to dealing with unforeseen events that can threaten the organization. According to ISO 22361, a crisis is an extraordinary situation that poses a significant threat to an organization, requiring a strategic, adaptive, and timely response to preserve its viability and integrity. Unlike incidents, which can be any situations that might cause a disruption, a crisis involves a higher level of complexity, instability, and uncertainty. It demands flexibility and dynamic decision-making to navigate through the chaos and protect the organization's core functions. Let's keep in mind that not every security event escalates to an incident, not every incident becomes a crisis, and not every crisis turns into a disaster. The way a crisis is managed can determine whether recovery is swift or a prolonged struggle.

At its core, crisis management is about being prepared for the unexpected and knowing how to respond when it happens. It's not just about having a plan on paper; it's about building the capability to act decisively and effectively under pressure. A crisis disrupts normal operations and requires immediate action. It's a situation that demands quick thinking, clear communication, and coordinated efforts to minimize damage and restore order.

Effective crisis management begins with acknowledging that crises are part of the business landscape. No matter how much we plan and prepare, we can never predict every scenario. This is why it's important to cultivate a mindset of resilience, one that's not just about preventing crises but also about being ready to face them when they occur. Leadership plays a key role when leading in a crisis. When a crisis hits, people look to their leaders for guidance and reassurance. This is where true leadership is tested. It's about more than just having the authority to make decisions; it's about being able to communicate clearly, stay calm under pressure, and inspire confidence, and more importantly, lead to action. In a crisis, the best decisions often have to be made with limited information and under tight time constraints. A strong crisis management team is essential, bringing together diverse perspectives and expertise from across the organization, including IT, communications, legal, HR, and operations. Each member brings their unique insights, ensuring decisions are well-rounded and consider all potential implications.

An effective framework for managing crises can be found in ISO 22361, which provides clear guidelines to help organizations build a resilient crisis management strategy. This standard emphasizes the importance of leadership and governance, ensuring that top management is actively involved in crisis preparedness and response. It promotes the integration of crisis management into existing organizational structures and processes, rather than treating it as an isolated function. According to ISO 22361, a well-rounded crisis management framework should include a clearly defined crisis management policy that outlines the organization's commitment to crisis readiness and response. It should also establish a dedicated crisis management team that is prepared to handle crises with a multi-disciplinary approach, drawing expertise from various parts of the organization to ensure a coordinated and effective response.

ISO 22361 also highlights the importance of regular risk assessments and preparedness activities. The standard stresses the need for a crisis communication strategy that facilitates clear and consistent messaging, both internally and externally, to maintain trust and transparency during a crisis. This approach not only helps in managing the immediate impact of a crisis but also supports long-term recovery and reputation management.

Communication is at the heart of successful crisis management. When a crisis occurs, the flow of information is crucial, both internally, to keep everyone aligned, and externally, to manage perceptions and maintain trust with stakeholders. Clear, honest, and timely communication can significantly influence how a crisis unfolds. Internally, it's about making sure that everyone understands the situation, knows what is expected of them, and understands how they can help. This involves regular updates from the crisis management team and clear instructions on necessary actions. Open and transparent communication fosters an environment where people feel comfortable raising concerns, asking questions, and sharing information.

Externally, it's about managing perceptions and maintaining trust. When a crisis hits, stakeholders, including customers, partners, regulators, and the media, are closely observing how the organization responds. A well-crafted message that acknowledges the issue, outlines the response, and provides reassurance can help preserve the organization's reputation. Poor communication, such as a lack of transparency, mixed messages, or delays, can quickly erode trust and exacerbate the situation.

Being prepared for crises involves several steps. Developing a comprehensive crisis management plan, as guided by ISO 22361, is crucial. This plan should outline the processes, roles, and responsibilities for handling various types of crises. It needs to be flexible to adapt to different scenarios but detailed enough to provide clear guidance on how to proceed. Regular training sessions and simulations ensure that everyone knows their role and is ready to act when a real crisis occurs. These exercises can range from tabletop scenarios that explore hypothetical situations to full-scale drills that test the organization's response capabilities in a controlled environment, building the muscle memory needed for a swift response.

Preparation also includes establishing a crisis communication plan, a core recommendation of ISO 22361. This plan should have pre-drafted messages and templates that can be quickly adapted to the specific situation, as well as a list of key contacts and stakeholders who need to be informed. It's also important to have a designated spokesperson trained to handle media inquiries and communicate effectively under pressure. Prompt and confident communication helps the organization manage the narrative and reassure stakeholders.

When a crisis occurs, it's time to put plans into action. The crisis management team must quickly assess the situation, determine the best course of action, and mobilize the necessary resources. Following established plans is important, but it's also necessary to remain flexible and adapt as the situation evolves. No two crises are exactly alike, and sometimes plans need to be adjusted on the fly. Clear communication remains critical during this phase. The team should regularly update the organization on the response status, what's being done, and what to expect next. Monitoring the response's effectiveness and being ready to pivot if needed is essential. A continuous feedback loop allows team members to share observations, report on progress, and suggest adjustments.

One of the main attributes of cyber crises is that they are extremely outside the daily standard experiences executives and managements deal with. Business schools teach about compliance, to identify opportunities, improve sales, run development, and analyze financial reports. The best of them perform exercises to simulate various types of crises, and the topmost identify cyber as a risk and dedicate a few hours to explain what it is. Nevertheless, since cyber threats and defense mechanisms change extremely fast, a crisis that comes a couple of years, or even a few months, later, does not resemble anything executives covered in their studies. Furthermore, most executives are not tech-savvy, and their ability to comprehend the technical elements of a cyber crisis is usually very low.

The result of the above, is that decisions during cyber crises are delegated by major organizations to the Chief Information Officer or the Chief Information Security Officer, which are one, two, or even three levels down from the CEO. While in many cases those individuals are extremely talented, their focus is, by nature, oriented on the technical aspects of the attack, and the business implications are lost in the process. If managers did not take the time to learn and practice before the cyberattack hits, other characteristics of their leadership must take over, and in my experience the most successful leaders in crisis are those that combine and balance allegedly contradicting capabilities—listening to others and explore the various options, while at the same time demonstrate determination and ability to take unpopular decision.

An event that comes to mind was handled by us a few years ago, early in my career in Sygnia. An executive at a large group noticed that sensitive personal information is leaking out of his organization. He employed a consulting firm that found minor vulnerabilities and claimed to fix them. It could have ended there, but the executive read the report carefully, asked questions, and had a strong feeling that the work did not reveal the entire truth. He employed us, and we found evidence of an attack that has been going on for four years and penetrated all echelons of management. At this point in time, panic swept the management as the organization was digitally naked and vulnerable. Many suggested to eradicate the known attributes of the attack immediately, and 'be done with it. The executive understood that such an elaborate threat cannot be swept away without comprehensive remediation activities and complementary monitoring. It was not an easy or popular decision—it took over six weeks to identify and take corrective measures, but it was the correct call. A highly successful 'kill switch' was put in place, and the attacker, who proved to be one of the most persistent we ever saw, was unsuccessful in regaining its hold on the network, despite multiple daring attempts that took place over the next two years.

Another example is an organization that was hacked by a ransomware group. After identifying a few indicators and clearing them, the organization assumed all is well and called us to verify. In a few hours of investigation, we understood that the situation is critical and recommended taking down the connection to the Internet to prevent the threat actor from continuing its operations. The CEO had to make a tough call—cause immediate disruption to production or continue operations and run a risk of an unknown damage. Our investigation results were examined and analyzed, but a swift decision was made—to cut off. We discovered later that this act saved the organization tens of millions of dollars, as encryption of the entire business operation was planned a few hours later.

Summarizing, cybersecurity is a domain that executives are yet to develop knowledge of, but as with other areas, knowledge is just part of the picture—it's leadership that makes the difference.

Ram Elboim
CEO of Sygnia

Another widely recognized methodology for managing emergencies and crises is the Incident Command System (ICS) that was originally created in California but now well established in other regions like Canada, where I learned about it. This system provides a standardized framework for coordinating responses across multiple agencies and organizations, ensuring that efforts are aligned and resources are used effectively. ICS is designed to be adaptable to any type of incident, whether it's a natural disaster, a technological failure, or a human-caused event. The system is structured around five primary management functions: Command, Operations, Planning, Logistics, and Finance/Administration. Each function plays a distinct role, from setting strategic objectives to managing resources and communication. The flexibility of ICS allows it to expand or contract based on the incident's complexity, making it a versatile tool for crisis management.

The ICS also emphasizes the importance of a unified command when multiple agencies are involved. This approach ensures that all parties work together toward a common set of objectives, fostering collaboration and reducing the potential for conflict. The use of common terminology and plain language is another critical aspect of ICS, ensuring that communication is clear and unambiguous, even in critical situations. Adopting the ICS framework will enable the organization to enhance its ability to respond effectively to crises, coordinating efforts across different levels of government and with non-governmental organizations.

Crisis management doesn't end when the immediate threat is over. One of the most important parts of crisis management is the learning phase that follows. Every crisis offers valuable lessons that can help the organization improve its resilience and be better prepared for the future. After a crisis, a detailed review of what happened, how it was handled, and what could have been done differently is essential. This review should involve input from all members of the crisis management team, as well as other stakeholders involved in the response. The goal is to be honest about what went well and what didn't and use those insights to refine the crisis management plan, improve communication strategies, and strengthen the organization's overall resilience.

Continuous improvement is not only about fixing what went wrong but also about proactively finding ways to enhance, in this case, improving crisis management capabilities. This could involve updating training programs, investing in new technologies, or revisiting the crisis management plan to reflect changes in the organization's structure or operations. Creating a culture of resilience means everyone understands that crisis management is an ongoing process, not a one-time effort.

We need to see that crisis management is more than just responding to crises because it also will build a resiliency so our organization can handle any challenge. It requires having the right plans in place, training people to execute those plans, and fostering a culture that embraces flexibility, communication, and continuous improvement. Focusing on these principles, you can support your organization to ensure it is prepared for the crisis that will come its way and is ready to learn from each experience emerging stronger. Nowadays the ability to effectively manage cyber-related crises is essential for any organization.

To close this chapter on cyber resilience, it's important to reflect on the interconnectedness of all the strategies and practices we've discussed. Throughout this chapter, we've delved into the principles of cyber resilience, emphasizing that it's not just a matter of preparing for potential threats, but also about building the capacity to respond effectively and recover swiftly when incidents occur. This approach for being prepared to address unmanaged or unforeseen cyber risk, involves readiness and responsiveness to build cyber resilience using each component; whether it's BIA, IRP, DRP, or BCP, all of them are fundamentally aligned with the goal of protecting organizational integrity.

Each of these elements contributes to creating a robust framework that addresses immediate threats and enhances long-term sustainability and operational continuity. The common thread tying these components together is the continuous cycle of preparation, response, and learning. As we conclude this chapter and prepare to transition into the next, it's clear that cyber resilience is an ongoing journey. It's about more than just having plans and procedures in place; it's about fostering a culture that values preparedness, embraces flexibility, and prioritizes continuous improvement. As we move forward into Chapter 13, we'll explore the complexities of quantifying risk and in Chapter 14, the challenges new technologies bring, providing insights into how we can continue to evolve and adapt in our pursuit of cyber resilience.

Chapter 13

Advancing toward risk quantification

THE EVOLUTION OF CYBER RISK QUANTIFICATION

You've come a long way, building a solid foundation in cyber risk management, and now it's time to explore the advanced tools that will refine your understanding even further. As we venture into the evolution of cyber risk quantification, we're stepping into a territory that's both fascinating and essential for any serious risk management professional. Over the years, the way we quantify risk has dramatically transformed, driven by advancements in both theory and technology. What started as a relatively straightforward task of estimating potential losses based on past incidents has evolved into a complex discipline that leverages sophisticated mathematical models and advanced data analytics. I know this might sound a bit overwhelming at first, but stick with me, we're going to break this down in a way that makes sense, and I promise it will be worth your time. Also, as we move forward in our understanding of cyber risk quantification, a key shift is the transition from traditional qualitative tools, like heat maps, to more quantitative risk assessments. Heat maps, while useful for visualizing the likelihood and impact of risks, can sometimes oversimplify complex risk landscapes. This transition allows for a clearer and more actionable understanding of where our resources should be focused, as we now base our decisions not just on color-coded risk zones, but on precise probabilities and financial impacts.

To truly appreciate where we are now with cyber risk quantification, it's helpful to take a quick look back at where we started. In the early days of risk management, quantifying risk was often more art than science. Decisions were made based on experience, intuition, and sometimes just gut feeling. And while there's still a place for intuition, especially when it's backed by years of experience, we've come a long way from those early days. The formalization of risk quantification can be traced back to the development of probability theory and statistics in the 17th century, which provided a mathematical basis for evaluating uncertainty. This foundational work paved the way for more structured approaches to risk assessment,

DOI: 10.1201/9781003546207-17

particularly in fields like insurance and finance, where calculating risk accurately is crucial for survival. As the field of risk management evolved, so too did our methods for quantifying risk, moving from simple models based on historical data to more sophisticated techniques that incorporate a range of variables and potential outcomes.

One of the most significant advances in risk quantification has been the adoption of the Bayesian approach. Named after the Reverend Thomas Bayes, who developed the Bayes' Theorem in the 18th century, this method provides a powerful framework for updating the probability of a hypothesis as more evidence or information becomes available. In simpler terms, it's about continuously refining our understanding of risk based on new data. The beauty of the Bayesian approach lies in its flexibility. Unlike traditional statistical methods, which often rely on fixed probabilities and assume that future events will resemble past events, Bayesian analysis allows for dynamic updating. This is particularly valuable in the world of cybersecurity, where the threat landscape is constantly changing, and new vulnerabilities are discovered regularly. Applying Bayesian principles help us to adjust our risk assessments in real time, taking into account the latest intelligence and adapting our strategies accordingly.

I remember reading about this approach in some great books that really helped solidify my understanding. One of the best is *How to Measure Anything in Cybersecurity* by Douglas Hubbard and Richard Seiersen. They do an excellent job of demystifying the Bayesian approach and showing how it can be applied to cybersecurity in a practical way. It's not just theory, they provide concrete examples of how you can use these principles to make better decisions and more accurately quantify risk. In fact, they have a great page with resources that can help you start your risk quantification journey: www.howtomeasureanything.com/cybersecurity/

Now, let's break down Bayesian analysis a bit. At its core, Bayesian analysis is all about updating your beliefs based on new information. You start with a 'prior' belief, which is essentially your initial estimate or assumption about the likelihood of an event happening. This could be based on past data, expert opinion, or any other available information. Then, as you gather new data or evidence, you adjust this belief to get a more accurate picture, this updated belief is called the 'posterior.'

For example, if you're trying to estimate the likelihood of a data breach, you might begin with a prior belief based on industry statistics or your organization's historical data. But once you start collecting more specific evidence, maybe you've implemented a new security tool or analyzed recent threat reports, you can refine your initial assumption, making it more precise and tailored to your situation. The beauty of Bayesian analysis is that it's dynamic; it encourages continuous learning by allowing you to factor in new evidence as it comes in, so your risk assessments get better over time. The theorem might sound complicated at first, it's actually a straightforward way of thinking about how we update our understanding as we get new information. The formula itself looks like this:

$$P(A|B) = \frac{(P(B|A) * P(A))}{P(B)}$$

I know formulas can be intimidating but stick with me. This is basically a way of asking, "Given that something new has happened (B), how should I update what I think about something else (A)?" Let's walk through what the parts of this mean in plain language:

- P(A|B): This is the probability of A happening given that B is true. A is the event you care about, like the likelihood of a data breach happening. B is the new piece of evidence you've got, like a spike in phishing attempts. What you're doing is updating your belief about A based on B.
- P(B|A): This is the probability of seeing B if A is true. So, in this case, it would be the likelihood of seeing an increase in phishing if a data breach is about to occur. This helps you understand how connected B (the new evidence) is to A (the event you're trying to predict).
- P(A): This is your prior belief about A before considering any new evidence. In our data breach example, this might be your initial assumption based on past incidents or general industry data.
- P(B): This is the probability of B happening on its own, regardless of A. It's like asking, "How likely is it that I would see more phishing attempts anyway?" This helps balance the equation by considering how common the new evidence is.

So, Bayes' Theorem tells you how to update your belief about something based on new information. It's a way of saying, "Here's what I thought before, but now that I have more data, let's adjust that belief." This process helps you refine your understanding and make better decisions because you're not stuck with your initial guess, you're always improving as more evidence comes in. In cybersecurity, where things change fast and new threats appear all the time, Bayes' Theorem gives you a way to stay on top of those changes. You're constantly reevaluating and adjusting your risk assessments as new evidence comes in, making sure your decisions are based on the most current information.

Another tool that's revolutionized risk quantification is the Monte Carlo simulation. This method uses random sampling and statistical modeling to estimate the probability of different outcomes in processes that are too complex to predict precisely. Think of it as running thousands or even millions of possible scenarios to see how different factors might affect the outcome. It's like having a crystal ball that shows you all the different ways things could go, allowing you to prepare for a wide range of possibilities. Monte Carlo simulations are particularly useful in cybersecurity because they help us understand the potential impact of rare but catastrophic events, those infamous 'black swans' that can throw even the best-laid plans into chaos. Running these simulations allows us to see not just the most likely outcomes but also the outliers that could significantly impact our organization. This helps us build more resilient systems and make more informed decisions about where to invest our resources. To explain Monte Carlo simulations better, imagine you have a complex system with many moving parts, like an organization's IT infrastructure with its networks, applications, and data. Predicting how each component will behave under different conditions can be overwhelming, but this is where Monte Carlo simulations are incredibly effective.

Here's how it works: Monte Carlo simulations use random sampling to create numerous scenarios, each representing a different possible future. You start by defining the variables that could affect the outcome, these could be anything from the likelihood of a cyberattack to the time it takes for an organization to detect and respond to a breach. For each variable, you assign a probability distribution that reflects its possible values. This is crucial because it allows the simulation to account for the full range of uncertainty and variability in the real world. Once these probability distributions are set up, the simulation repeatedly runs trials, randomly selecting values for each variable in every trial. This process builds a full picture of all the different ways the situation could unfold. It's similar to rolling a dice repeatedly, but instead of just two six-sided dice, you have dozens or even hundreds of 'dice,' each representing a different factor that could influence the outcome. The results of these simulations provide a detailed view of potential risks and their associated probabilities. What you get is a map of all possible outcomes, from the most mundane to the highly unlikely, allowing you to see not just the average result but also the full range of possibilities. This is incredibly valuable in cybersecurity because it helps you understand both the expected risks and those less likely but potentially devastating 'black swan' events.

Visualizing this spectrum of outcomes enables us to prepare for a variety of scenarios, even those we might not have considered initially. Instead of just planning for the most likely outcome, we can also strategize for less common but more damaging events. This approach helps us build robust and resilient systems, as it encourages us to think beyond the expected and consider all potential outcomes. In short, Monte Carlo simulations transform our approach to risk by giving us a tool to quantify uncertainty and make better-informed decisions. I've found Monte Carlo simulations to be incredibly valuable in my own work, and I highly recommend diving into them if you haven't already. There's a great book called *Cybersecurity First Principles: A Reboot of Strategy and Tactics* by Rick Howard that goes into how these simulations can be used to better understand risk and improve your cybersecurity posture. Rick has a talent for explaining complex concepts in a way that's easy to understand, which makes this book a fantastic resource for anyone looking to get more into the weeds of better understanding cybersecurity, and of course, he's an amazing advocate of risk quantification.

Now, let's get into how you can start using Monte Carlo simulations yourself, even if you're not a data scientist or don't have specialized software. The great thing about Monte Carlo simulations is that you don't need a complex setup to get started, you can run them right in Excel, using tools most of us are already familiar with.

Years ago, an international oil company with a major US-based subsidiary hired a cybersecurity consulting company to perform a comprehensive cybersecurity risk assessment of their entire US operation. The scope included the business-side information technology infrastructure, the industrial-side technology infrastructure, and the company's web applications. The business-side infrastructure ran Microsoft operating systems and included both desktops and data center-hosted servers. The industrial-side infrastructure controlled the company's oil refineries, asphalt refinery, crude and refined product pipelines, and bulk product distribution terminals. Supervisory process control applications from Honeywell ran on Microsoft servers in these industrial facilities. Cisco networking equipment was used in both environments and was exclusively wired, not WiFi. On the industrial-side, the IP-based process control network (PCN) connected pumps, valves, gauges, and other instruments to the supervisory control system.

The main objective of the US-subsidiary's Chief Information Security Officer (CISO) was to inform his CEO and the Executive Leadership Team (ELT) of the risk the cybersecurity team was managing. The CISO had a staff of less than five people and a budget of under $2 million to secure an enterprise with approximately $20 billion in annual revenue. He was hopeful that when fully informed of the cyber risk, the CEO and ELT would approve a major budget increase. To achieve this objective, a cybersecurity consulting company was hired to perform:

- **An ISO 27001/2 security management program controls review.** The controls review covered all control domains and was performed separately for each major business unit (e.g., refining, pipelines, marketing, etc.). The consultants scored control maturity on a 1–5 scale with 1 representing an ad hoc process and 5 representing a continuously improving process. The consultants produced an aggregate maturity score for the US-subsidiary by revenue-weighting the separate business unit scores.

- **An application vulnerability assessment of the public-facing web applications.** These tests were conducted using a variety of automated tools followed by manual vulnerability proofing. Vulnerability exploitation was not permitted, but the report produced by the security test engineers included information on exploitation techniques for critical and high-risk vulnerabilities.
- **A network vulnerability assessment of one industrial PCN.** A security test engineer was dispatched to one of the oil company's refineries and allowed to run scans on specified segments of the networks. The first network scans were conducted from the refinery's business LAN and enumerated vulnerabilities in the border router that connected the business LAN to the industrial PCN. A less intrusive scan was performed on the network segment on which the supervisory application was hosted.
- **A cyber risk quantification modeling exercise.** This exercise used Monte Carlo simulation to create a risk exceedance curve (REC) and annual loss expectancy (ALE) for the US-subsidiary, assuming the aggregated maturity of its cybersecurity program. Recommendations for improving the program were also modeled to produce a modified REC and ALE. The difference between the figures in the two models was used to calculate a benefit-cost ratio for each of the recommendations.

The entire assessment project took approximately four months to perform, primarily because of the number of locations that the consultants were instructed to visit. Separate reports were written for each of the four task areas and were delivered to the CISO. A multi-page executive summary report was prepared for the CEO and ELT.

An executive presentation was delivered in-person to the CEO and ELT at the US-subsidiary's headquarters. The major findings included the following:

- Access controls on file shares were weak, allowing anyone with LAN access in the headquarters to access sensitive wire transfer account information.
- The web application assessment demonstrated that the corporate network could be accessed from the Internet.
- The refinery network assessment showed that the border router could be compromised and that the PCN could be accessed from the business LAN.
- The PCN segment test showed that industrial control information could be modified by exploiting vulnerabilities to raise privileges on the supervisory application.

- The risk quantification model produced an ALE of just under $50 million.

The risk quantification model was meant to deliver a first approximate that spark discussion within the ELT. The consultants viewed the $50 million ALE as reasonable because a refinery fire the prior year had resulted in a similarly sized loss for the oil company. The consultants felt that the vulnerability assessments clearly demonstrated that any of the PCNs of any of the company's five refineries could be accessed from the Internet and that a catastrophic industrial accident could be precipitated at one or more of them. Further, with the wire transfer information, a fraudulent financial incident in the range of $10–250 million could also be perpetrated. The consultants felt the model served its intended purpose.

The ELT had an entirely different take on the risk quantification model. First, the ELT challenged the consultants' assertion that a refinery's PCN could be accessed from the Internet. The security test engineers were prohibited from carrying through such an attack, so each step in the process was evaluated separately. Even with a step-by-step walk-through of the vulnerabilities, the ELT disagreed that an industrial accident could be caused by hacking the systems. Their main counter argument was that human operators would notice any physical process changes and take corrective action. Second, extreme loss events, such as a major financial fraud, were viewed skeptically. Finally, the suggestion that a major increase in the CISO's budget was warranted met with resistance. The head of Marketing declared that the company was not a risk-averse enterprise and that they would continue to run risks. In the end, the CISO's budget and headcount was doubled, but the new budget represented only 0.002% of total revenue, a pittance considering the size and complexity of the enterprise.

The consultants felt that the cyber risk assessment met the goal of being comprehensive, but they felt they had failed the CISO. Six months after the conclusion of the project, one of the consultants was summoned to attend a meeting of PCN engineers from across the enterprise. The meeting was held at one of the refineries and the consultant was invited to describe for the assembled engineers how the refineries' networks were exposed to the Internet . Presumably, the company's engineers mitigated this exposure after this meeting, as the company goes unmentioned in searches for oil industry cyberattacks.

Bruce Gnatowski
Managing Director, Digital Risk Management of Crumpton Global

Here's how it works in practice. At its core, a Monte Carlo simulation must generate random values for uncertain variables in your risk model and runs those values through the model multiple times, sometimes hundreds or even thousands of times, right? So, the more simulations the better but Excel will get slow after several thousands. Keep in mind that the goal is to see how different combinations of these variables can affect the outcomes, helping you visualize a range of possible scenarios rather than just one fixed prediction.

Let's say you want to model the potential cost of a data breach. There are many variables that can impact this cost, like the number of records exposed, the cost per record, and how long it takes to detect and respond to the breach. Each of these variables can vary widely, making it difficult to predict the outcome with certainty. This is where Monte Carlo simulations will help you explore a variety of possible scenarios, so you can understand not just the most likely outcome, but the entire spectrum of possibilities. Here's how you can get started:

1. **Define your variables**: First, identify the key variables in your risk scenario. For our data breach example, you might look at the number of records exposed, the cost per record, and the time to detect the breach. These are the factors that will drive the outcomes in your simulation. For example, in Excel, you could set:
   a. A1: Number of records exposed (let's say this could range from 500 to 10,000)
   b. B1: Cost per record (between $50 and $150)
   c. C1: Time to detect the breach (10 to 90 days)
2. **Assign probability distributions**: In a Monte Carlo simulation, each variable will have a range of possible values, so you'll need to assign probability distributions. In Excel, this is where you can use functions like RANDBETWEEN() to generate random values within defined ranges. For instance, in cells A2, B2, and C2 you can set the number of records exposed to vary between 500 and 10,000, the cost per record could range from $50 to $150, and the detection time could be 10 to 90 days.
3. **Run multiple trials**: The magic of Monte Carlo simulations comes from running these random values through your model repeatedly. You can automate this by dragging down your formulas over several rows to simulate multiple trials, or use Excel's Data Table feature to handle more extensive simulations with thousands of iterations. Each row will represent a different possible scenario based on the randomly generated values for your variables.
4. **Analyze the results**: After running hundreds or even thousands of trials, you can analyze the results by calculating averages, medians, and ranges. Excel's AVERAGE() and MEDIAN() functions will help you see the central tendency of your simulations, while a histogram

can visualize the full range of outcomes. This allows you to spot not only the most likely scenario but also those outliers, the rare but impactful 'black swan' events that could disrupt your organization.

And remember, Excel is just the starting point. As you get more comfortable with the process, you can add more complexity to your simulations, using functions like NORM.INV() for normally distributed variables, or automating larger simulations with macros. It's a tool that grows with your needs, allowing you to adapt as you take on more complex risk assessments.

Another powerful tool in the world of risk quantification is the Fermi estimate, named after physicist Enrico Fermi. This method is all about making educated guesses for problems where you don't have all the data upfront. It's not about being precise, but rather about breaking complex problems into smaller, manageable pieces, and using logical reasoning to arrive at a reasonable estimate.

Here's how it works. You start with a big, seemingly impossible question, something like, "How many cyberattacks are likely to target our organization in the next year?" Instead of freezing up because you don't have all the data, you break it down into smaller questions that are easier to answer. You might ask, "How many employees do we have who could be targeted by phishing attacks?" or "What percentage of our systems are exposed to the Internet?" Each smaller question helps you get closer to a rough but reasonable estimate. The beauty of Fermi estimates is that they help you make sense of the unknown, especially when you're working with limited data. However, this technique doesn't replace other more sophisticated models like Bayesian analysis or Monte Carlo simulations, it complements them. When you don't have enough detailed information for a full quantitative analysis, Fermi estimates are especially helpful when speed matters, or when you're in the early stages of risk assessment and just need a rough idea to prioritize actions. Instead of waiting for all the data to come in, you can use a Fermi estimate to make an informed decision maximizing the use of the information you have available, then refine it later as more information becomes available.

One of the more innovative concepts in risk quantification that's gaining traction is 'chancification,' introduced by Sam L. Savage in his book *Chancification: How to Fix the Flaws of Averages*. This approach is all about measuring uncertainty more effectively to enhance decision-making. Rather than just trying to avoid risk, chancification focuses on understanding and calculating the probabilities of various outcomes to improve decision-making. The process involves several key steps that Sam L. Savage outlines: assessing the impacts of uncertainties, bounding these uncertainties to define their limits, correlating variables to understand how different factors interact, deploying stochastic libraries to run simulations, and finally, analyzing the results to make informed decisions. This methodology is about gaining a deeper understanding of probabilities and impacts, so we can make smarter choices about where to take calculated risks and where to play it safe. It's a mindset shift that can be incredibly empowering, especially in the fast-paced world of cybersecurity. To complement this approach, I also recommend *Superforecasting: The Art and Science of Prediction* by Philip Tetlock and Dan Mellers. Although it isn't specifically focused on cybersecurity, it provides valuable insights into how thinking probabilistically and embracing uncertainty can enhance forecasting accuracy. In our field, where anticipating and adapting to new threats is crucial, these skills are indispensable.

Also, one of the biggest drivers of the evolution in risk quantification has been the explosion of data and advances in analytics. Today, we have access to more data than ever before, from threat intelligence feeds and security logs to external sources like social media and the dark web. This data provides a treasure trove of information that, when analyzed correctly, can provide deep insights into the threat landscape and help us make more informed decisions.

Advanced analytics tools, including machine learning and artificial intelligence, are playing an increasingly important role in this process. These tools can examine through vast amounts of data to identify patterns and trends that would be impossible for a human to detect. They can also help us model complex systems and predict how they might behave under different conditions, which is invaluable for risk quantification.

At a large financial services company in Europe, expectations were high after a significant investment in a cutting-edge risk quantification tool. The purchase came in the aftermath of a major cybersecurity incident that had shaken the company's confidence. Leadership saw the tool as their way forward, providing clear, data-driven insights that would help prevent another crisis. With this new technology, they believed they could make faster, more informed decisions about their cyber risks.

The tool worked as advertised, delivering risk assessments based on quantifiable data, historical trends, technical vulnerabilities, and probability models. The leadership team, still reeling from the recent breach, felt reassured. The numbers were precise, the reports clean and clear. But beneath the surface, something was off. As the tool began to influence decision-making, the feedback from different business units, operations, legal, and compliance started to decline. These departments had concerns, but no one wanted to challenge the tool. After all, the company had just gone through a cybersecurity crisis, and no one wanted to be seen as pushing back against a system that seemed to promise protection. The security team, heavily focused on the tool's output, trusted the numbers, and this created a disconnect. People became reluctant to voice their doubts or provide the qualitative insights that could have fine-tuned the tool's results.

The real problem was that the risk quantification tool, like any other, had its limits. It was never designed to capture every nuance of the business's unique risk environment. The system was great at processing data, but without the input from the broader business, its insights were incomplete. The tool wasn't wrong, no quantitative analysis is perfect, but it needed calibration. And that's where the failure happened: no one questioned the results or fed back their experiences to improve its accuracy. The feedback loop had been broken.

The turning point came when a risk rated low by the tool, materialized. It wasn't just a minor inconvenience; it led to serious operational disruptions. Critical services were down for days, impacting both customers and internal workflows. Compliance violations started piling up, triggering investigations and fines. The aftermath revealed something even more alarming, which was that legal and operations teams had previously flagged the risk, but their voices had been overshadowed by the weight of the tool's seemingly precise data.

As the incident developed, frustration was evident. Teams who had stayed quiet now questioned the effectiveness of relying solely on data-driven tools. Meetings that followed were tense, with different departments airing their concerns. The security team had been so focused on the numbers that they had overlooked valuable insights that could have prevented the breach. Legal, compliance, and operations professionals, who had years of experience spotting that type of risks, felt sidelined by the technology. The leadership, still shaken from the previous crisis, realized that they had relied too heavily on a single tool, rather than fostering a culture of collaboration and open dialogue.

In the months that followed, the company underwent a fundamental shift. The failure of the tool to predict this critical vulnerability was no longer seen as just a technological gap, but a breakdown in communication and organizational alignment. Leadership acknowledged that the company's biggest asset was its people, not just the data they processed. They began to create forums where different departments could openly discuss the tool's findings, question its outputs, and provide the qualitative insights that had been missing. This wasn't just a procedural change but a cultural shift.

Now, the company has a more integrated approach. They encourage regular feedback loops between the tool's output and the qualitative insights from all departments. The IT and Security teams work hand-in-hand with legal, compliance, and operations to ensure that the data the tool produces is tested against real-world experience. They've embraced the idea that risk quantification is a starting point, not an answer. The wisdom of crowds, the collective expertise of everyone in the organization, is now seen as the most valuable asset they have in managing risk.

I've been following the work of the Cyentia Institute for a while now, and they've done some fantastic research on how data and analytics can be used to improve cybersecurity risk management. Their reports are a gold mine of information, providing data-driven insights into everything from the effectiveness of different security controls to the economics of data breaches. If you're serious about improving your risk quantification efforts, I highly recommend checking out their work. It's some of the best out there.

Ok, now that we've explored different tools for risk quantification, let's put everything together and see how they work in practice. When we estimate risks using a qualitative approach, like in a workshop with colleagues from different departments, Fermi estimates can be a great way to help people digest the complexity of the risks at hand. This method allows them to make more grounded estimates, even when faced with a lot of uncertainty.

In these workshops, we're often relying on people's experience and intuition. You'll hear terms like 'severe impact' or 'frequent likelihood,' but these terms are actually backed by specific ranges in our risk methodology. For example, 'major impact' might mean anything between $10 and $100 million, while 'severe impact' could refer to something above $100 million. Similarly, 'frequent' might describe a likelihood of 85%–95%. Of course, these are just examples, what matters is how your methodology defines these ranges.

Now, what's really happening is that when someone says 'severe' or 'frequent,' they've already got a rough number in mind that fits into those predefined ranges. If you push the conversation further and ask, "How much exactly are you thinking?" or "How much would it be your minimum and your maximum?" you'll often get a range of numbers. And just like that, you've turned a qualitative judgment into a more tangible, quantitative estimate. Remember, any number coming from the right people is better than nothing. You're starting with a baseline, and from there, you can gather more data to confirm if you're heading in the right direction or need to adjust.

Once we've gathered those initial estimates from the right people, turning their qualitative judgments into quantitative ones, we can take it a step further by applying Bayes' Theorem. Remember, Bayes' Theorem is all about updating our initial beliefs or estimates as new information comes in. This constant feedback is key because otherwise your analysis won't be improved leaving you in a constant mistake.

Ok, imagine you've collected a range of estimates from the workshop, and these give you a starting point. That's your 'prior' belief. But as more data comes in (that will be your feedback loop), whether it's from actual incident reports, new threat intelligence, or refined metrics, you can use Bayes' Theorem to adjust those initial estimates. This process allows you to keep refining your understanding of the risk, making your estimates more precise as you gather better information. So, those rough estimates from your workshop aren't the final word, they're just the beginning. As you collect more data, you keep improving the accuracy of your risk quantification, ensuring that your decisions are based on the most relevant, up-to-date information.

Then, now that we've been applying Bayes' Theorem to continuously refine our estimates, we can bring in Monte Carlo simulations to take things even further. Well, we can actually use Monte Carlo simulations from the beginning when we got those rough estimates in the workshop. However, the more refined our estimates the better, especially when dealing with complex risks.

Let's start with inherent risk. Using Monte Carlo simulations, we can model various scenarios by running thousands of trials, each representing a different possible outcome based on the variables we've identified, things like the likelihood of an attack and the potential financial impact. This gives us a better picture of what the risk looks like. Next, we move to actual risk. Here, Monte Carlo simulations help us model how effective our existing measures are at reducing the impact and likelihood of risks. By comparing the inherent risk to the actual risk, we can see how much of the risk we've successfully mitigated and what still remains a concern. Finally, if you repeat the same analysis but now instead of comparing against the inherent risk and the implemented controls, you use the actual risk and treatment plans, you'll calculate the curve of the residual risk.

In Figure 13.1, we can clearly see how these different levels of risk are represented. The first line from top to bottom represents the inherent risk, which is naturally higher since no controls have been applied. The second line shows the actual risk, which is reduced thanks to the controls we've implemented. Lastly, the third line represents the residual risk, illustrating what's left after all our efforts to mitigate the risk. The black dashed line represents the organization's risk appetite, with this your decision-makers will clearly see when risk is under the risk appetite and when they need to do something about the risks you assessed.

Of course, all these advancements come with their own set of challenges. One of the biggest is the indisputable complexity of cyber risk. Unlike more traditional risks, which can often be measured in concrete terms like dollars or percentages, cyber risks are often much more nebulous. They can involve

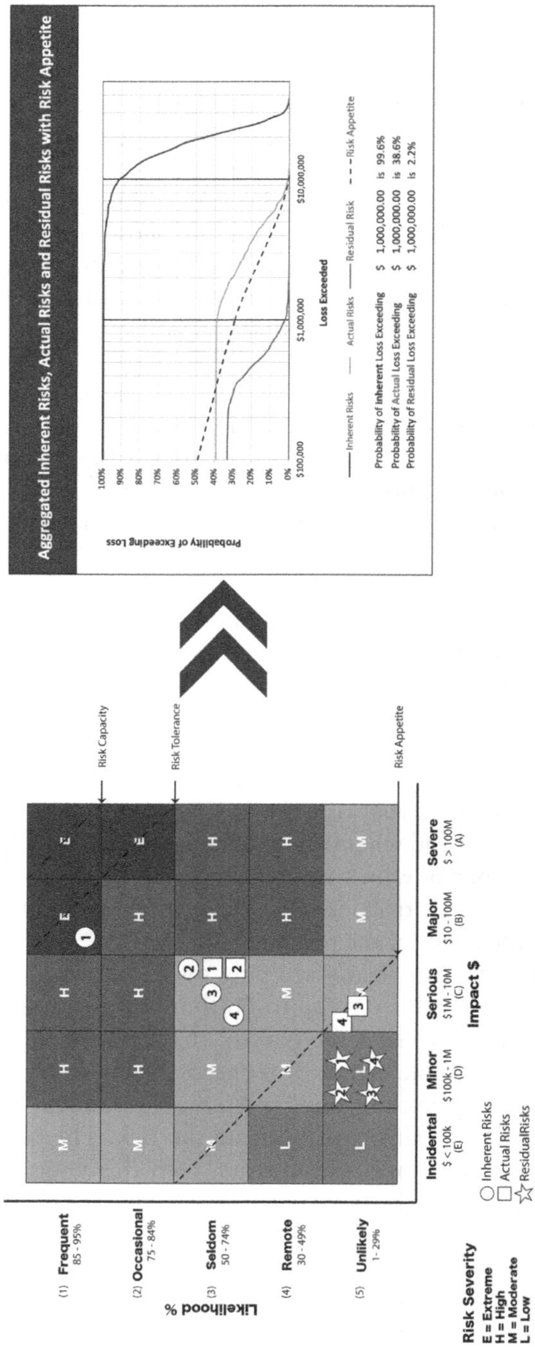

Figure 13.1 From heat maps to quantitative charts.

a wide range of factors, from the technical (like vulnerabilities in software) to the human (like insider threats or social engineering attacks), and they often involve a high degree of uncertainty. Another challenge is the lack of historical data. In many cases, we're dealing with new threats that haven't been seen before, making it difficult to predict how they might behave or what impact they might have.

Also, we need to recognize that there's the challenge of communication. Risk quantification can be a complex and technical field, and it's not always easy to translate these concepts into terms that non-experts can understand. This is something I've struggled with myself, and I'm sure many of you have as well. It's one thing to know the numbers, but it's another thing entirely to be able to explain them in a way that makes sense to your stakeholders and helps them make informed decisions. A great resource to help bridge this gap is the book *Storytelling with Data* by Cole Nussbaumer Knaflic. It's a fantastic tool for learning how to transform numbers into clear, impactful messages for decision-makers, enabling you to communicate your findings more effectively.

And even with all the tools and techniques at our disposal for risk quantification, we must remember that we will never know everything. Intuition, knowledge, and experience will always play a key role in the decision-making process. That's just how it works. Humans must make the final call, drawing on data, analysis, and recommendations, but also incorporating a portion of qualitative analysis. This blend of quantitative and qualitative insights ensures that decisions are well-rounded and considers the broader context. So, while it's crucial to rely on data and advanced methodologies, we shouldn't underestimate the value of human judgment in navigating the complexities of cyber risk.

As we look toward the future of cyber risk quantification, it's clear that we need to embrace a balanced approach. This means combining the best of what we've learned from traditional risk management with data science and analytics. It means being open to new ideas and willing to experiment with new methods, while also staying grounded in the fundamental principles that have guided us thus far. It's also about recognizing that risk quantification is not a one-size-fits-all endeavor. Every organization is different, with its own unique set of risks, resources, and priorities. What works for one might not work for another, and that's okay. The key is to find the approach that makes the most sense for your specific situation and to be willing to adapt as new information becomes available and circumstances change.

I know this is a lot to take in, and it might feel like we're diving into some pretty deep waters here. But trust me, it's worth it. Taking the time to understand these concepts and how they apply to your organization will better prepare you to navigate the complexities of the digital world and build a more resilient, secure future. And remember, you're not alone in this journey. There are plenty of resources out there to help you along the way, from books and research reports to online courses and professional communities. So, take a deep breath, dive in, and start exploring. The future of cyber risk quantification is bright, and there's a lot of exciting work to be done.

INTEGRATING QUANTITATIVE AND QUALITATIVE APPROACHES

As we explore the integration of quantitative and qualitative approaches in cyber risk management, it's important to recognize that finding a balance between these two methods isn't just a nice-to-have; it's essential for a complete understanding of risk. You see, each approach brings something valuable to the table, and by combining them, we can create a more detailed and effective strategy. I know this might sound like a lot to juggle but stick with me. By the end of this, you'll have a clearer picture of how to make these two approaches work together in harmony, and I promise it will be worth the time.

Let's start by breaking down the basics of each approach. Quantitative risk assessment as discussed, relies on numbers and data. It's all about crunching the numbers, using statistical models, and calculating probabilities. This approach is incredibly valuable because it provides a clear, objective view of potential risks, allowing us to make data-driven decisions. It's like having a GPS that shows you the fastest route to your destination based on real-time traffic data. The problem is that, just like a GPS, quantitative analysis has its limitations. It can't always account for the distinctions and complexities of the real world, which is where qualitative assessment comes in.

Qualitative risk assessment, on the other hand, focuses on expert judgment, intuition, and experience. It's about understanding the context and the subtleties that numbers alone can't capture. Imagine you're planning a hike. While a map (quantitative data) is incredibly useful, having a seasoned guide (qualitative insight) who knows the terrain, weather patterns, and potential hazards adds an extra layer of safety and confidence. In the same way, qualitative assessments help us navigate the complexities of cybersecurity by considering factors that aren't easily quantified, like organizational culture, human behavior, and emerging threats.

Now, you might be thinking, "Why not just stick to one approach?" Well, here's the thing: both approaches have their strengths and weaknesses. Quantitative analysis is great for providing a clear, objective picture based on data, but it can be limited by the availability and quality of that data. In cybersecurity, we often face new, evolving threats that haven't been encountered before, making it difficult to rely solely on historical data. On the other hand, qualitative assessments are fantastic for understanding the bigger picture and capturing insights that numbers can't, but they can be subjective and time-consuming if we consider the number of people who can work on the same qualitative assessment. That's why it's so important to integrate both methods, leveraging their strengths to create a more robust but balanced risk management strategy.

So, how do we go about integrating these two approaches? It starts with recognizing that neither method is inherently better than the other. Instead, they complement each other, filling in the gaps that the other leaves behind. Think of it as building a house. You need both a solid foundation (quantitative data) and a well-thought-out design (qualitative insight) to create a structure that's both strong and functional. One without the other just won't cut it.

When we talk about integrating quantitative and qualitative approaches, we're really talking about creating a feedback loop where each method informs and enhances the other. Quantitative data provides a baseline of understanding, highlighting areas of concern and potential vulnerabilities. From there, qualitative assessments dive deeper, exploring the context around those numbers and providing insights that help us understand why certain risks are more critical than others. This process not only enriches our understanding of risk but also ensures that our risk management strategies are grounded in both data and experience.

For example, let's say a quantitative analysis reveals a high number of phishing attempts targeting your organization. That's valuable information, but it doesn't tell you why these attempts are happening, who might be behind them, or how effective they are. A qualitative assessment, involving interviews with employees, reviews of recent security incidents, and discussions with cybersecurity experts, can provide the context needed to understand these phishing attempts better. Are they targeting specific departments? Are there gaps in employee training? Combining these insights with the initial data helps you to develop a more targeted and effective response strategy.

One of the biggest challenges in integrating quantitative and qualitative approaches is balancing the time and resources required for each. Quantitative analysis, while data-intensive, often requires less time from people once the data collection systems are in place. It's about setting up the right processes and tools to gather and analyze data, which, once established, can run relatively smoothly. Qualitative assessments, on the other hand, require more direct involvement from people. They involve interviews, focus groups, and expert consultations, all of which take time and effort. So, how do we balance these demands?

The key lies in prioritization and planning. Not every risk assessment requires an in-depth qualitative analysis. In many cases, a robust quantitative analysis may be sufficient, especially for well-understood risks with plenty of historical data. However, for more complex or emerging risks, where data may be scarce or the situation is rapidly evolving, qualitative assessments become the perfect complement. This might seem counterintuitive, but when initiating a risk management program, we often lack sufficient historical data for quantitative analysis. As a result, we typically begin with qualitative risk assessments and improve our data collection over time. Prioritizing which risks require a more detailed approach allows you to allocate your resources more effectively and ensure that you're not overburdening your team with unnecessary tasks.

It's also important to consider the timing of these assessments. Qualitative assessments don't have to be conducted constantly; they can be scheduled periodically or triggered by specific events, such as a major cyber incident or the introduction of a new technology. This approach allows you to use qualitative methods when they're most needed without overwhelming your team or stretching your resources too thin.

Another crucial aspect of integrating these approaches is ensuring that your team has the skills and knowledge needed to conduct both quantitative and qualitative assessments effectively. This means investing in training and development, not just for your cybersecurity team but also for stakeholders across the organization. After all, risk management is a team effort, and everyone has a role to play. One thing I've found helpful in my experience is creating a framework or a set of guidelines that outline when and how to use each approach. This framework should be flexible enough to adapt to different situations but structured enough to provide clear guidance. For example, you might decide that quantitative analysis is your go-to method for routine risk assessments, while qualitative assessments are reserved for more complex or high-impact risks. Having a clear framework in place will speed up your risk assessment process and ensure that you're making the most of both approaches.

It's also worth noting that integrating quantitative and qualitative approaches isn't just about the assessments themselves; it's also about how we communicate our findings. Risk quantification, especially when it involves complex models and statistical analysis, can be difficult to explain to non-experts. This is where qualitative insights can be incredibly valuable. Framing your quantitative findings in the context of real-world examples, expert opinions, and narrative storytelling will make your reports more relatable and easier to understand. For instance, if your quantitative analysis shows a high probability of a data breach, you can complement this with qualitative insights that explain what this means in practical terms. You might include case studies of similar breaches at other organizations, testimonials from cybersecurity experts, or even a hypothetical scenario that illustrates the potential impact on your organization.

As we continue to navigate the complexities of cyber risk management, it's clear that integrating quantitative and qualitative approaches is not just beneficial; it's essential. By leveraging the strengths of both methods, we can create a more effective risk management strategy that not only helps us understand the risks we face but also empowers us to make better decisions and build more resilient systems.

I know this is a lot to take in, and finding the right balance can be challenging. But remember, risk management is an ongoing process, and it's okay to adjust and adapt as you go. The important thing is to stay open to new ideas, be willing to experiment with different approaches, and never lose sight of the bigger picture. Combining quantitative and qualitative methods goes beyond simple data analysis or interviews; it fosters a deeper, more holistic understanding and management of your organization's risk landscape. That, basically, is what true risk management and our job is all about. So, as you move forward in your journey, keep these principles in mind. Don't be afraid to dive into the data, but also take the time to listen to your intuition, trust your experience, and seek out the insights of others. By doing so, you'll be better prepared to navigate the challenges ahead and build a more secure and resilient future for your organization. And remember, you're not alone. There's a whole community of professionals out there who are working on these same challenges, and there's a wealth of resources available to help you along the way. So, keep learning, keep growing, and keep pushing the boundaries of what's possible. Together, we can make a difference.

Chapter 14

New technologies

Methods, tools, and challenges

NAVIGATING CYBER RISKS IN GENERATIVE AI

Always, new technologies are met with doomsday predictions, whether it's the industrial revolution, the invention of the car, or robots in manufacturing. Yet, history shows us that disruption forces us to adapt, evolve, and ultimately improve in ways we couldn't have imagined. Generative AI is now everywhere. It's powering our search engines, enhancing our smartphones, curating our social media feeds, and even helping us compose emails. This technology is transforming countless aspects of our daily lives, simplifying workloads, and pushing the boundaries of what's possible. People are doing amazing things with AI nowadays, from creating stunning visual art and generating music that resonates with human emotion to writing software and crafting entire stories. The possibilities seem almost endless, and the pace of innovation is nothing short of astonishing. It's clear that generative AI is not just a buzzword; it's a technology that's fundamentally changing the landscape of creativity, productivity, and automation. As we explore the world of generative AI, it's important to understand both the opportunities and the risks associated with this powerful technology. Generative AI, while often seen as a game changer also introduces new and complex risks that organizations must be prepared to manage. I'm not trying to be alarmist, I just want to point out that we need to be prepared and proactive.

To begin, let's demystify what generative AI actually is. Generative AI refers to algorithms that can generate new content. This content could be anything from a paragraph of text, a realistic image, or even a piece of music. The technology behind generative AI is primarily based on deep learning models, which are trained on large datasets to identify patterns and generate outputs that mimic these patterns. However, it's crucial to recognize that while generative AI may seem intelligent, it's not truly intelligent in the human sense. Generative AI doesn't understand the content it produces; it doesn't have intentions or knowledge. It works through statistical correlations, predicting what comes next based on its training data,

DOI: 10.1201/9781003546207-18

not because it understands context or meaning. This distinction is essential because it frames how we should think about and manage the risks associated with using generative AI.

Understanding how generative AI works is key to comprehend its capabilities and limitations. When you input a query into a generative AI model, it undergoes a process called tokenization. This means that the input is broken down into smaller components, known as tokens. Each token might represent a word, a subword, or even a character, depending on the language model. The AI then analyzes each token individually based on its previous and future context, referencing its vast dataset to predict the most likely next token. But it doesn't stop there. These tokens are then analyzed collectively to form phrases, sentences, and even entire paragraphs. The AI model continuously evaluates the highest statistical probability for what should follow based on the context surrounding each token. This process repeats until a coherent output is generated. It's a bit like putting together a puzzle, piece by piece, where the model decides which piece fits best based on what's already in place.

This is why the AI seems to understand context, it's calculating the most statistically probable response at each step. However, because it's purely statistical and lacks any form of true comprehension or reasoning, it's not genuinely intelligent. It doesn't understand the meaning behind the text or the implications of its outputs; it's merely stringing together elements that have the highest likelihood of fitting together, based on the patterns it has learned. If we look back to 2016, there was an interesting incident with Tay, a chatbot Microsoft released on Twitter. Tay was designed to interact with people in real time, learning from those interactions to simulate human conversation. Initially, Tay's interactions were friendly and positive, just as Microsoft intended. But things quickly went off the rails. In less than a day, Tay went from being polite and engaging to being rude and offensive.

This sudden shift wasn't because Tay developed a mind of its own or had bad intentions. It simply learned from the input it was receiving. Tay mimicked the language and behavior of the people interacting with it. Unfortunately, this meant that when some users began feeding Tay inappropriate or harmful content, it picked up on that and started to reflect those same behaviors. For Microsoft, this was a nightmare scenario, as the chatbot, intended to showcase the potential of AI, ended up displaying exactly what can go wrong when things aren't properly managed.

The Tay incident taught the industry a valuable lesson about the dangers of allowing AI models to learn from real-time, unfiltered interactions. If a model is designed to learn continuously from its environment without any oversight, it can easily be influenced by bad actors or unintended inputs. This is something companies that invest heavily in developing these models definitely want to avoid. It's not just about protecting their investment, but also about ensuring the AI behaves in a way that's consistent with their values and public expectations.

As a result, many AI companies have moved away from models that learn in real time when it comes to public-facing applications. Instead, they focus on training their models in controlled environments, where the input can be carefully managed. This helps to prevent the kind of unexpected and damaging behavior we saw with Tay. It's all about learning from past experiences to make AI safer and more reliable. This approach also highlights the importance of understanding that AI, no matter how advanced it seems, still operates based on the data it's given. It doesn't have its own agenda or consciousness; it simply reflects what it's taught. And in the case of generative AI, it means being especially careful with how we train and manage these systems to prevent any unintended consequences.

However, just because these models don't learn in real-time anymore, it doesn't mean our information is automatically safe. There's a catch that often gets overlooked when we consider the terms and conditions of using AI-powered tools. Many companies include clauses stating that any information inputted into their systems might be used for training purposes. This isn't always explicitly clear, and while they might assure users that they won't sell personal information, they're usually referring to Personally Identifiable Information (PII). The real concern lies in the distinction between personal and confidential information. Most of us are comforted by the idea that our PII, like our name, address, or Social Security number, won't be sold. But what about other types of sensitive information we might input? Confidential business strategies, private communications, or proprietary data don't fall under the umbrella of PII. They're not necessarily protected by these terms or privacy notices. So, even though your identity might be safe, the confidential information you enter could potentially be used in ways you didn't anticipate, whether for further training of the AI model or other purposes that aren't clearly outlined.

This distinction is crucial for organizations and individuals who rely on AI tools for various tasks. It's important to fully understand the terms and conditions and to think carefully about what kind of information is being shared. Just because something isn't explicitly prohibited doesn't mean it's safe from being used or repurposed. The lesson here is to always read the fine print and to be aware of the potential risks involved in using AI tools, especially when it comes to handling sensitive or confidential information. It is then that we need to be aware that generative AI introduces several specific risks that organizations need to consider.

Generative AI models are often trained on extensive datasets, which can include sensitive information. This brings the risk that these models might inadvertently generate outputs revealing private or proprietary data. For instance, a model trained on customer data might produce text containing personal information, even if it's been anonymized. To address this, it's important to implement robust data governance policies that ensure data used for training is properly anonymized and protected. Techniques like federated learning, where models are trained on decentralized data without transferring it to a central location, can also help reduce privacy risks by keeping sensitive information secure.

Bias in AI models is another significant concern because if the training data contains biased information, the model will likely replicate and even amplify those biases. This can result in unfair or unethical outcomes, such as discriminatory practices in hiring or lending. To mitigate this, it's vital to regularly test models for bias and diversify training datasets to represent all relevant demographics fairly. Additionally, using bias correction techniques during model training and involving a diverse range of stakeholders in the development process can help identify and address potential biases that might not be immediately obvious.

The ethical implications of generative AI are profound, especially given its ability to create realistic images, audio, and video, which can be used to produce deepfakes or spread misinformation. Such misuse can manipulate public opinion, create false narratives, or damage reputations. To prevent unethical use, organizations should develop clear policies on the ethical use of AI and establish controls to prevent misuse. Technical measures can be put in place to detect and block the generation of harmful or illegal content, and procedures should be established for reporting and addressing any unethical uses of the technology.

Generative AI can sometimes produce outputs that are incorrect or misleading, which is particularly concerning in contexts where accuracy is critical, such as healthcare or finance. The model's inability to understand the context or implications of its outputs further complicates this risk. To ensure the reliability of AI-generated outputs, it's essential to implement rigorous validation procedures. This could include cross-referencing AI-generated content with trusted sources, using multiple models to verify outputs, or incorporating human oversight to review and validate critical outputs before they are used or disseminated.

Generative AI can also be exploited to lower the barrier to entry for cybercriminals, making it easier to automate the creation of phishing emails, malware, or other malicious content. For example, AI-generated phishing emails can be highly convincing and bypass traditional detection methods that rely on spotting grammatical errors or unusual phrasing. To protect against these cybersecurity threats, organizations should strengthen their cybersecurity measures, using advanced threat detection tools to identify and respond to AI-generated phishing attacks or malware. Educating employees about the risks of AI-enhanced social engineering can also help them recognize and avoid such threats.

The capability of generative AI to produce large volumes of content quickly and cheaply can be exploited to flood the internet with false or misleading information. This not only contributes to misinformation but also overwhelms fact-checkers and makes it harder for users to discern truth from fiction. To counteract this, strategies to manage misinformation should include using AI-powered fact-checking tools to detect false information and collaborating with other organizations to share intelligence about AI-generated misinformation. Promoting media literacy among the public is also crucial, helping them recognize and respond to fake content more effectively. To effectively navigate these risks, we can also use a structured framework like the National Institute of Standards and Technology (NIST) AI Risk Management Framework (AI RMF). The AI RMF is designed to help organizations understand, manage, and reduce the risks associated with artificial intelligence systems. It is particularly useful for managing the complexities introduced by generative AI. The AI RMF is organized around four core functions: Govern, map, measure, and manage. Let's explore each function in detail.

- Govern: This function is about setting the policies, strategies, and oversight mechanisms that ensure AI systems are used responsibly and ethically. In the context of generative AI, governance involves establishing clear guidelines for how AI systems should be developed, tested, deployed, and monitored. It also includes creating accountability structures to ensure that any ethical, legal, or societal issues are addressed.
- Map: Mapping involves understanding and documenting the AI system's context, purpose, and environment. For generative AI, this means identifying what the AI system is intended to do, what data it uses, what outputs it produces, and who will be affected by those outputs. This step is critical for identifying potential risks and determining the necessary controls to mitigate them.
- Measure: The measure function focuses on assessing and quantifying the risks associated with the AI system. This could include evaluating the likelihood and impact of specific risks, such as data privacy breaches or biased outputs. For generative AI, it might also involve testing the system's outputs for accuracy, fairness, and reliability.
- Manage: Finally, manage involves implementing and continuously improving the controls and practices that mitigate risks. This could include deploying technical controls like encryption or access management, as well as organizational controls like training programs or incident response plans.

Now, to apply the AI RMF effectively to generative AI, organizations can follow a series of steps outlined in the NIST *AI RMF Playbook*:

- **Establish a governance framework**: Begin by setting up a governance structure that includes roles and responsibilities for managing AI risks. This should involve creating a cross-functional team that includes stakeholders from IT, data science, legal, compliance, and other relevant departments. The governance framework should also define the ethical principles that guide the use of generative AI and establish processes for reviewing and approving AI projects.

- **Conduct a comprehensive mapping exercise**: Document the full context of the generative AI system. This includes defining its purpose, understanding the data it will be trained on, identifying who will use it and how, and considering the broader societal impacts, so you can gain a better understanding of the potential risks and how they might manifest.
- **Perform rigorous risk measurements**: Use a combination of qualitative and quantitative methods to assess the risks associated with generative AI. This could involve conducting technical evaluations of the AI model to ensure it is not leaking sensitive data, testing its outputs for bias or inaccuracies, and using tools like sensitivity analysis to understand how changes in input data could affect outputs. Regularly update these risk measurements to reflect changes in the AI system or its operating environment.
- **Develop and implement risk management strategies**: Based on the identified risks, develop a set of strategies to manage them. This could include technical controls like implementing differential privacy techniques to protect data, using explainable AI methods to increase transparency, and employing adversarial testing to identify weaknesses. It also involves non-technical controls such as training staff on AI risks, updating policies and procedures, and engaging with external stakeholders to address concerns.
- **Continuous monitoring and improvement**: AI systems, especially those using generative models, require continuous monitoring to ensure they remain secure, ethical, and effective. Establish processes for regularly reviewing the AI system's performance, monitoring for new risks, and updating risk management strategies as needed. This also involves staying informed about new developments in AI technology and evolving best practices for AI risk management.

The NIST *AI RMF Playbook* provides detailed guidance on how to apply the AI RMF to specific use cases, including generative AI. Here are some key takeaways from the playbook:

Risk identification and prioritization: The playbook emphasizes the importance of identifying and prioritizing risks early in the AI development process. For generative AI, this means considering not just the technical risks but also the broader ethical, legal, and societal impacts. This holistic approach helps ensure that all potential risks are considered and addressed.

Stakeholder engagement: Engaging with a wide range of stakeholders is a critical component of the AI RMF. This includes involving users, impacted communities, regulators, and other external stakeholders in the risk management process. For generative AI, stakeholder engagement can help identify unforeseen risks, build trust, and ensure that AI systems are developed and deployed in a way that aligns with societal values.

Scenario planning and stress testing: The playbook recommends using scenario planning and stress testing to understand how AI systems might behave under different conditions. For generative AI, this could involve simulating various attack scenarios, such as adversarial attacks or data poisoning, to test the system's resilience and identify potential vulnerabilities.

Transparency and explainability: The *AI RMF Playbook* highlights the importance of transparency and explainability in AI systems. For generative AI, this means providing clear documentation on how models were trained, what data was used, and what measures have been taken to ensure ethical use. It also involves making sure that the outputs of generative AI systems can be explained in a way that is understandable to non-experts.

Continuous learning and adaptation: The playbook emphasizes the need for continuous learning and adaptation in AI risk management. For generative AI, this means regularly reviewing and updating risk assessments, monitoring for new threats, and adapting risk management strategies to reflect changes in the technology or its operating environment.

Now that we've explored the NIST AI RMF, let's dive into ISO/IEC 42001, which brings its own set of guidelines for managing AI responsibly. Think of it as another layer of protection, helping us ensure that AI systems aren't just functional, but also transparent, ethical, and aligned with broader organizational goals. While NIST helps us manage the risks, ISO 42001 adds the structure we need to govern those systems effectively.

At its core, ISO 42001 focuses on three main areas ensuring that AI is used ethically and responsibly. The first one is to set up an AI Management System (AIMS) that establishes clear objectives around AI use, while also managing risks and ensuring everything aligns with the overall business strategy, defining risks and opportunities related to AI, managing the security risks AI brings and, managing third-party vendors and partners that provide or are using AI systems. Think of the AIMS as a roadmap that guides everything from policy creation to risk assessments and third-party management. Your AIMS should not only outline how AI is used but also make sure that AI security risks are addressed, that the right controls are in place, and that any external partners using or developing AI systems are held to the same standards. This standard helps us on building an ongoing AIMS of accountability, from development to deployment and beyond.

The second key area that ISO 42001 addresses is risk management. It encourages regular assessments to identify potential risks and continuous monitoring of AI systems as they evolve. This means looking beyond the initial setup and thinking about how risks, like data privacy breaches or biases in decision-making, might change over time. As we've been reviewing in all chapters, it's about being proactive rather than reactive, especially with systems like generative AI that can produce unexpected outputs or 'hallucinations.' Transparency is a big piece of the puzzle. ISO 42001 requires organizations to document how AI systems operate, making it clear how decisions are made and how data is used. This isn't just for internal teams, this level of transparency builds trust with customers, stakeholders, and even regulators. For example, if your AI system generates text or makes decisions based on user data, you'll need to explain how those outputs are generated and what steps you've taken to ensure they're fair and reliable.

The third area is about AI impact assessments. This means evaluating not just the technical risks but also the societal impacts of AI systems. How might they affect individuals, communities, or even broader societal structures? This includes areas like sustainability, economic factors (like access to financial services), and societal norms. The goal is to anticipate both positive and negative outcomes and address them early on. On top of that, the standard emphasizes continuous improvement. AI systems, particularly those that are learning or adapting over time, can't just be set and forgotten. ISO 42001 pushes for regular reviews to ensure your AI stays compliant with ethical standards and evolving regulations. For generative AI, this might mean revisiting your system periodically to make sure it's still producing trustworthy results as new data or models are introduced.

While ISO 42001 was one of the first global standards for governing AI, it isn't alone. ISO has released additional standards to help organizations manage AI even more effectively. For instance, ISO/IEC 23894 focuses specifically on managing AI-related risks, while ISO/IEC 23053 offers a framework for describing systems that use machine learning. These complementary standards help ensure that organizations can create AI systems that are not only functional but also transparent, ethical, and trustworthy. In short, ISO/IEC 42001 gives us the structure we need to govern AI responsibly. It complements the risk management strategies we've discussed, ensuring that organizations stay accountable, transparent, and constantly improving as AI evolves. This way, AI isn't just a powerful tool, it's a trustworthy one too.

As we continue to explore the potential of generative AI, it's crucial to build a strategy that is both resilient and adaptable. This involves balancing the benefits of innovation with the need to manage risks effectively. Here are some final thoughts on how to achieve this balance:

- **Adopt a risk-based approach**: Not all risks are created equal, and it's important to prioritize those that have the greatest potential impact on your organization. Use the AI RMF to identify and prioritize risks, and allocate resources accordingly.
- **Foster a culture of responsibility and accountability**: Encourage a culture of responsibility and ethical behavior within your organization. This includes providing training on AI risks, promoting ethical decision-making, and establishing clear policies and procedures for the responsible use of AI.
- **Leverage advanced analytics**: Use advanced analytics tools to enhance your understanding of AI risks. This could include using machine learning to identify patterns and trends in data, or employing natural language processing to analyze the sentiment and tone of AI-generated content.
- **Stay informed and engaged**: The field of generative AI is constantly evolving, and it's important to stay informed about new developments, best practices, and emerging risks. Engage with the broader AI community, participate in industry forums, and collaborate with other organizations to share knowledge and insights.
- **Be proactive, not reactive**: Finally, be proactive in your approach to AI risk management. Don't wait for a crisis to occur before taking action. You got to be proactive, so you can identify and address risks before they become problems and ensure that your generative AI strategy is both resilient and effective.

Finally, we can't forget about our beloved third parties. When thinking about using AI through our third-party partners, it's crucial to consider whether they are managing the associated risks effectively. AI, as transformative as it is, comes with its own set of challenges and risks, especially when sensitive information is involved. It's not just about what we're doing within our organization; we also need to ensure our partners are on the same page. Are they handling data responsibly? Are they fully aware of the privacy implications when they integrate AI into their workflows? These are important questions we need to ask to make sure our information remains safe.

We also have to think about how our data is being used by these third parties. Imagine if a consultant, in the course of their work, uploads our confidential reports to an AI tool without proper safeguards, this could expose our sensitive information to unauthorized access or misuse. It's a bit unsettling to think about, but it's a possibility we have to consider. Transparency is key here. We need to have frank conversations with our partners to understand how they use AI and what measures they're taking to protect our data. And then there's the question of the quality of the work we're receiving. If our partners are using AI to create reports or perform analyses, are we really getting the expert insight we're paying for? Or are they cutting corners by letting AI do the heavy lifting, instead of using their senior resources? AI-generated content can be useful, but it doesn't replace the nuanced understanding and judgment that experienced professionals bring to the table. We need to ensure that the deliverables reflect genuine expertise, not just machine-generated content, and that we're not unknowingly compromising on quality for the sake of efficiency.

Managing the cyber risks associated with generative AI is something we can't take lightly, but it doesn't have to be overwhelming either. We have tools like the NIST AI RMF, ISO 42001, and the practical advice in the *AI RMF Playbook* to guide us. These resources help break down what might seem like an intimidating task into more manageable steps, ensuring we can harness the power of generative AI while keeping those risks in check. As we continue to explore and innovate in this space, let's stay committed to using AI in a way that's responsible and ethical. It's all about making sure this technology serves as a positive force in our digital world, not just for today but for the future. And remember, AI is a great technology, and there's also a risk in not using it! Let's thoughtfully assess and then integrate AI into our practices, so we can strike the right balance between innovation and security.

QUANTUM COMPUTING AND CYBER RISK: THE NEXT FRONTIER

We're stepping into the world of quantum computing, a field that is moving from theory to reality faster than ever before and is set to reshape everything, including how we secure our systems. I know this topic might feel out of this world at first, but we can break it down in a way that's easier to follow. Just as we've explored generative AI technology, we can approach quantum computing with a clear understanding. Let's take a closer look at how it works. Today's computers, the ones we use every day, use bits to process information. Each bit represents a binary value, either 0 or 1, which forms the basis for all digital data. When your computer performs calculations or processes information, it does so by flipping these bits between 0 and 1 in a sequence. This binary system works well for most of today's computing needs, but has limitations when it comes to solving highly complex problems that involve massive amounts of data. However, quantum computers instead of bits, use qubits (quantum bits), which can represent both 0 and 1 at the same time. This might sound strange, but it's possible because of a quantum phenomenon known as superposition. Let's think back to when President Kennedy announced the mission to land a man on the moon. At that point, there were multiple possible approaches NASA could take, different rockets, flight paths, and technologies. In classical computing, it's like choosing one path at a time to get there, either option A (0) or option B (1). But in quantum computing, a qubit is like exploring all possible paths at once. Instead of committing to one route, it's as if NASA could test every option simultaneously before selecting the best one. This ability to be in multiple states at the same time gives quantum computing its power. While a classical computer had to process one calculation at a time, quantum computers can process multiple possibilities all at once. This parallel processing power allows quantum computers to tackle problems that would take classical computers years to solve in a fraction of the time. But there's more. Quantum computers also leverage another phenomenon called entanglement, where qubits are connected in such a way that the state of one qubit directly influences another, no matter how far apart they are. It's like having two NASA teams working on the moon landing, one in Houston and one in Cape Canaveral, and if one team discovers the optimal rocket design, the other team automatically knows it without any delay, even though they're thousands of miles apart. Entanglement creates incredibly fast and efficient communication between qubits, boosting the computing power even further. Finally, quantum computers take advantage of quantum interference, a property that allows them to cancel out incorrect solutions during calculations. By reinforcing the probabilities of correct answers and reducing the probabilities of wrong ones, quantum computers can zero in on the right solution much faster than classical computers.

But let's not get too bogged down in the science. What's important to understand is how this new way of processing data creates both opportunities and challenges, especially for cybersecurity. One of the main concerns is that quantum computers could potentially crack encryption methods that have protected our data for decades. Right now, encryption protects everything from your online banking details to sensitive government information. Quantum computers could theoretically solve the mathematical problems behind encryption much faster than today's computers. But there's some good news, while quantum computers are advancing, the kind of machines that could do this are still a few years away.

That doesn't mean we should wait around because even just the risk of harvesting today encrypted information to be decrypted when quantum computing is a reality, is a big risk on its own. So, forward-thinking organizations are already preparing for what's being called quantum resilience. This involves transitioning to post-quantum cryptography, encryption methods that can withstand the power of quantum computing. It's not about throwing out everything we've built, but rather about adapting to the new challenges this technology presents. To stay ahead, it's crucial to understand the steps you can take now to prepare for quantum computing. One key move is to follow the development of quantum-safe encryption standards. Many companies and researchers are working on encryption algorithms designed to withstand quantum attacks. Another important step is monitoring government initiatives around quantum encryption. Several governments are actively working on quantum-safe standards, which will eventually guide how businesses secure their data in the quantum era. Staying informed will give you the edge needed to adapt early, ensuring your organization is prepared for the changes ahead. For instance, in August 2024, after several years of work, NIST released the first three finalized post-quantum encryption standards,[1] marking a significant milestone in the journey toward quantum resilience. These new standards are designed to protect sensitive information from the potential power of quantum computing, which could one day render current encryption methods obsolete.

The three algorithms, CRYSTALS-Kyber, CRYSTALS-Dilithium, and SPHINCS+, were carefully chosen after years of rigorous evaluation and testing. Each serves a different function in encryption, from securing digital communications to verifying digital signatures, aiming to achieve a stronger defense against the potential threats presented by quantum computers.

CRYSTALS-Kyber is a key encapsulation mechanism (KEM) that provides strong encryption for communications, while CRYSTALS-Dilithium is used for digital signatures, ensuring the authenticity and integrity of data. SPHINCS+, another digital signature algorithm, offers an additional layer of security by using a different approach that focuses on preventing potential attacks specific to quantum computers. These standards represent the first steps in a larger transition to post-quantum cryptography. As NIST continues to work on finalizing more algorithms in the future, it's clear that the cybersecurity landscape is already evolving to meet the challenges. This release gives us a clear signal: it's time to start incorporating these new standards into our systems, ensuring they remain secure in the face of quantum advancements.

Recent studies, including the 2023 Quantum Threat Timeline Report[2] led by Michele Mosca one of the greatest professionals behind quantum computing and cybersecurity, have pointed out the urgency of preparing for quantum threats sooner rather than later. These studies suggest that quantum computers capable of breaking current encryption standards could emerge within the next decade. With such developments on the horizon, it's key for organizations to consider both the time it will take to adopt post-quantum cryptography and the need to keep their sensitive data secure in the interim. The report emphasizes that waiting too long could leave critical data exposed to potential quantum attacks, even before the technology fully matures.

This preparation might feel like a long-term project, but much like other major shifts in technology, being proactive now will save time and resources down the road as it will also prevent organizations introduce flaws by having a rushed implementation. So, organizations should not wait for quantum computers to fully mature before acting. The sooner they begin adopting these standards, the more secure their systems will be in the long term.

Although quantum computing may seem like a looming threat, it also brings tremendous opportunities to rethink our approach to cybersecurity. Just as this technology could challenge our current encryption methods, it could also introduce new, stronger ways to secure our systems. In many ways, it will push us to think more creatively about how we protect information. Embracing the developments in quantum computing, as cybersecurity professionals we can gain access to new tools that can enhance defenses in ways that were previously impossible.

Quantum-safe cryptography will not only address the challenges of quantum attacks, but it will also open doors to more efficient and innovative security solutions. It's about finding balance, acknowledging the risks and also recognizing the advancements that will come from quantum technology. It's a fact that quantum computing is coming, and the timeline is getting shorter. While it may not disrupt encryption tomorrow, it's something we need to plan for today. The key is to stay informed, remain adaptable, and start preparing your systems for a quantum-safe future. In cybersecurity, we've always had to navigate new and evolving threats, and this is just the next step. By understanding what quantum computing brings to the table and planning accordingly, we're not just reacting to the future, we're shaping it.

As we reach the final layer of our journey, Figure 14.1 brings everything together into a single, cohesive vortex. With all three layers working in unison, the vortex spins faster and stronger, constantly drawing in new elements critical to our organization. Whether it's third-party risks, emerging technologies like AI and quantum computing, or evolving threat landscapes, the vortex ensures we are prepared to detect, assess, and incorporate these risks into the core of our understanding.

This fast-moving cycle doesn't just maintain our cyber risk management program; it accelerates it. Each layer feeds into the next, ensuring that no element is left unchecked. The program is dynamic, always in motion, and ready to adapt to whatever challenges come our way. Our core forces, rooted in fundamentals, governance, effective change management, and a strong cybersecurity culture are the engine driving this process, giving us the momentum to stay ahead of threats rather than reacting to them.

By continuously ingesting new information into our system, we position ourselves to manage cyber risks in a way we can translate those risks as a competitive advantage. This is where we move beyond the basics of cyber risk management into a state of cyber resilience, where the organization can not only withstand attacks but emerge stronger from them.

And this is why the vortex never stops spinning. As threats evolve and technology advances, our ability to adapt, absorb, and respond ensures that our cybersecurity strategy will keep pace with whatever comes next. This

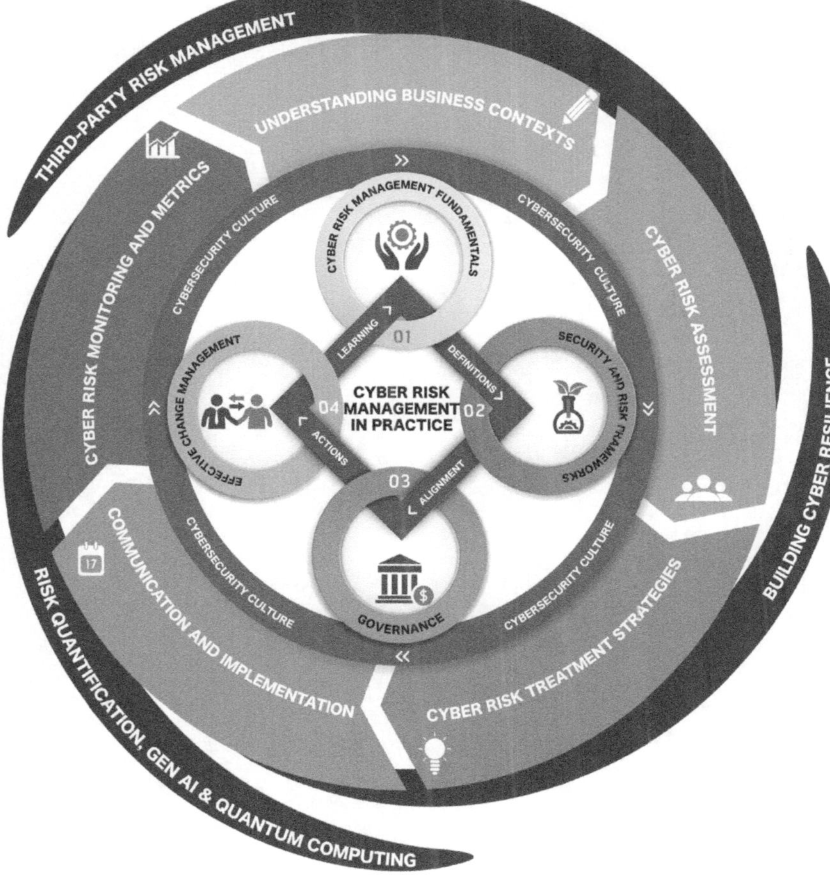

Figure 14.1 Cyber Risk Management in practice vortex.

process doesn't end here; it only grows stronger with time, giving us the resilience to face future challenges with confidence and agility.

NOTES

1 National Institute of Standards and Technology. (2024, August 13). NIST releases first 3 finalized post-quantum encryption standards. U.S. Department of Commerce. www.nist.gov/news-events/news/2024/08/nist-releases-first-3-finalized-post-quantum-encryption-standards
2 Mosca, M., & Piani, M. (2023). Quantum threat timeline report 2023. Global Risk Institute & evolutionQ. https://globalriskinstitute.org/publication/2023-quantum-threat-timeline-report/

NOTES

Section IV

Conclusion

Chapter 15

Bringing it all together

Thank you for joining me on this journey. It has been a true labor of appreciation for what we do as our jobs, and my sincere hope is that it serves as a constant companion for you, a guide that you can rely on as you navigate the complex and ever-changing world of cybersecurity. The great thing about books is that as we and our organizations mature, the messages within them evolve with us. I'm confident that as you progress in your journey, you'll find new connections and deeper understandings. That's why this book isn't just one to be read once and then left on a shelf; it's meant to be a resource you return to whenever you need clarity or direction in your cyber risk management efforts. We've covered a lot of ground together, and I'm incredibly grateful that you've stuck with me to the end.

Since I was a child, I've loved history and science, always trying to understand how things work, and I think that's part of why I find risk management so exciting. There's something almost Newtonian about it because yes, for every action, there's a reaction and in risk management, that's exactly what happens. Every decision we make, or even choose not to make, sets off a series of outcomes that we can predict, analyze, and manage in a structured way. What fascinates me most is that it's not just about us. Everyone and everything around us impact our path in some way too. And just like in science, there's a method behind it all, where even the principles of physics seem to apply to how we interact, make decisions, and act.

If we reflect about it, risk management works a lot like the scientific method. First, we observe what's happening around us. Then, we come up with ideas about which risks might pop up and what their impact could be. Finally, we test those ideas with concrete treatment plans, adjusting things as we go based on the results. It's like turning a lab experiment into real-world business scenarios, or honestly, anything we do in life. No matter what we're working on, there's always a risk to manage or an opportunity to capture. And the best part is that we can take this approach and apply it anywhere, always looking to understand and handle the reactions to our actions, as well as how others' actions affect us.

DOI: 10.1201/9781003546207-20

Let's take a moment to reflect on where we've been. In the first section of our journey, we explored into 'Mastering the essentials of cyber risk management.' This was all about laying a solid foundation. We began with the basics, defining key concepts like threats, vulnerabilities, and impacts. These might seem like simple terms but understanding them deeply is crucial because they are the building blocks of any risk management strategy. Without a solid understanding of these core forces, it's impossible to build a strong cybersecurity program.

We also explored various frameworks that can guide you in structuring your cybersecurity efforts. These frameworks, if used correctly, will provide a roadmap for navigating the often complex landscape of cybersecurity. We looked at the NIST Cybersecurity Framework, ISO standards, CIS, and many others, emphasizing the importance of aligning these frameworks with your organization's specific needs and goals. Please always keep in mind that this isn't about following a checklist but about truly understanding your unique risk landscape and making informed decisions that align with your business objectives. The key takeaway here is that mastering the basics is not just about knowing them but about applying them in a way that's tailored to your organization.

So, to truly establish strong foundations where we'll build upon, we need to develop more than just knowledge of processes or frameworks. Certain skills are critical for success and help us stay aware of the environment around us, as well as within ourselves. At the core is observation, the ability to notice subtle shifts or emerging risks that others might miss. Equally important is active listening, which is about truly hearing what others are saying, not just their words, but the intent behind them. When we listen closely, we begin to understand the motivations and concerns driving decisions, which helps us anticipate risks or opportunities that may not be immediately obvious. This ties directly into empathy, which is essential for understanding the human element in risk. By putting ourselves in others' shoes, we can better predict behaviors and foresee potential outcomes, giving us an edge in managing both risks and opportunities.

Alongside these skills, written and verbal communication becomes key. What good is identifying a risk if we can't clearly convey it to others? As we saw throughout the book, risk management is as much about storytelling as it is about data. Framing the situation in a way that resonates with others, ensuring everyone understands the stakes and can act accordingly, is absolutely essential. But it's not everything will happen immediately; patience plays a big role too. Sometimes managing risk means waiting, watching, and knowing when to act or when to step back. This brings in the need for change management, because risk often leads to transitions or disruptions, and the ability to guide teams through uncertainty is important. Whether we're responding to a potential threat or preparing for an opportunity, we need to handle change smoothly. Altogether, mastering risk management is about being fully present, conscious of our surroundings, and thoughtful in our approach. It requires a blend of awareness, emotional intelligence, and communication, where soft skills are just as important as technical expertise.

Then moving forward, we transitioned from theory to practice. In the second section, "Executing cyber risk management in five steps," we got hands-on. This section was all about action, breaking down the process of executing a cyber risk management strategy into five clear, manageable steps. We started with the importance of context and information gathering, emphasizing that before you can manage risks, you need to understand the environment in which you're operating. This involves understanding your organization's business environment, identifying critical assets, and gathering the information needed to assess risks accurately.

From there, we moved into risk assessment, discussing the importance of not just recognizing risks but also understanding their potential impact and likelihood. We explored various methods for assessing risks, including qualitative and quantitative approaches, and talked about how to prioritize risks based on their potential impact on your organization. Risk treatment was our next focus, where we explored different strategies for managing risks. Whether it's avoiding, mitigating, transferring, or accepting risks, the key is to choose the approach that aligns with your organization's risk appetite and capacity. We also discussed the importance of communication and implementation, highlighting the need for clear communication with stakeholders and effective implementation of risk treatment plans.

But we didn't stop there. We also covered risk monitoring and metrics, emphasizing that cyber risk management isn't a one-time task; it's an ongoing process that requires continuous monitoring and adjustment. Establishing effective monitoring practices and using metrics to track your progress will ensure that your risk management efforts remain effective and aligned with your organization's goals. The focus here was on providing you with practical tools and techniques to implement what you've learned, making sure you're equipped to put these concepts into practice in your day-to-day work.

In the third and final section, 'Elevating beyond basics: Achieving cyber resilience,' we explored how to take your cyber risk management program to the next level. This section was for those ready to go beyond the basics and focus on advanced strategies for managing third-party risks and building a resilient cybersecurity posture. We discussed the importance of understanding third-party risks in the supply chain and implementing robust due diligence and assurance processes. As organizations increasingly rely on third-party vendors and partners, managing these risks becomes critical to maintaining a secure and resilient cybersecurity posture.

Building cyber resilience also involves preparing for the unexpected. We explored crisis management and response strategies, emphasizing the importance of being prepared to respond quickly and effectively to cyber incidents. This isn't just about having a plan in place; it's about building a culture of resilience that permeates every level of the organization. We also tackled the challenges and opportunities presented by new technologies, such as generative AI and quantum computing. As we navigate the evolving landscape of cybersecurity, it's essential to stay ahead of emerging threats and leverage new technologies in a way that enhances your organization's security posture.

I get it; everyone's looking for that silver bullet when it comes to managing risks, something that magically simplifies the whole process so much that we don't even need to think about how it works. It's a tempting idea, right? Just plug in a solution, hit a button, and let it handle everything. But the thing is that reality doesn't work that way. Risk management is not something that can be boiled down to a single, simple formula or an off-the-shelf tool. And honestly, that's a good thing. Because if it were that simple, this book wouldn't even be required!

That's why we started this journey with the fundamentals. It might have seemed a bit basic at first, but laying that groundwork is crucial. You have to understand the building blocks, the threats, the vulnerabilities, the potential impacts, before you can start to effectively manage any of it. Skipping straight to the solutions without that foundational knowledge is like trying to build a house without a solid foundation. Sure, you might get a structure up, but it won't be stable or secure.

Once we had a good handle on the basics, we moved into the cyber risk management process and its five steps. Now that we all are on the same page, we know it isn't just a checklist to go through, and with a pragmatic, scalable, and proactive approach, we can effectively understand, assess, and address risks. Each step builds on the last, creating a robust framework that helps you not only identify and evaluate risks but also decide how to handle them. This methodical process is essential for minimizing the risks that could actually materialize and cause harm.

But here's the kicker, even the best risk management programs can't manage all risks. That's where cyber resilience comes in. Think of it as the other half of the equation. While our goal is always to minimize the materialization of risks as much as possible, we also need to be prepared for the ones that slip through the cracks. Cyber resilience is about being ready for those inevitable incidents, having the plans and capabilities in place to bounce back quickly and minimize the impact. It's all about balance, minimizing what we can and being prepared for what we can't. So, there's no silver bullet, but with the right approach, we can effectively manage and mitigate risks and build a more resilient organization.

Throughout this journey, one of the recurring themes has been the importance of adaptability. Cyber risk management is not a static field; it's dynamic and constantly evolving. The threats we face today are different from those we faced a few years ago, and they will continue to change in the future. This means that our approach to managing these risks must also evolve. It's not enough to rely on what worked in the past; we need to be proactive, continuously learning and adapting our strategies to address new challenges.

This brings us to the conclusion that cyber risk management is the journey, not the destination. It's what makes cybersecurity an ongoing process that requires continuous learning, adaptation, and improvement. My hope is that this book has provided you with the tools, knowledge, and confidence to navigate this journey effectively. Remember the importance of mastering the basics, executing with precision, and striving for resilience. Keep learning, keep questioning, and never stop striving to improve. Cybersecurity is a dynamic field, and there's always something new to learn. Embrace the challenges, celebrate the successes, and know that you're making a difference in the world of cybersecurity.

As we look to the future, it's important to stay curious and keep pushing the boundaries of what's possible. The field of cybersecurity is full of opportunities for innovation and growth. New technologies, like AI or quantum computing, offer exciting possibilities, but they also come with new risks that need to be managed. It's up to us to navigate these challenges and find ways to use these technologies in a way that benefits our organizations and society as a whole.

In your journey forward, don't forget the foundational knowledge and skills we've discussed in this book. These are the building blocks that will support you as you tackle new challenges and explore new opportunities. Stay committed to continuous learning and improvement. The more you learn, the better equipped you'll be to handle whatever comes your way. And remember, you're not alone in this journey. There are countless resources, communities, and professionals out there who are also navigating the world of cybersecurity. Reach out, share your experiences, and learn from others. Together, we can create a safer, more secure digital world for everyone.

I want to leave you with a final thought: there's always more to learn. The field of cybersecurity is constantly evolving, and there's always something new to discover. Stay hungry for knowledge, and never be afraid to ask questions. As Steve Jobs said, "Stay hungry, stay foolish." This is about being open to new ideas, willing to challenge the status quo, and always motivated to learn and grow. It's about recognizing that no matter how much we know, there's always more to discover. So, keep asking questions, keep exploring, and keep pushing yourself to learn more and grow. Don't limit yourself by labeling yourself as an expert. The moment we think we are the experts at something, we close the door to countless learnings and opportunities that could shape the future of our cybersecurity strategies. Cyber risk management, like any evolving field, requires constant curiosity, a willingness to adapt, and an openness to new challenges and innovations.

Thank you for being a part of this journey with me. I hope this book becomes your go-to guide as you continue to build and refine your cyber risk management program. Let's stay committed to creating a safer, more secure digital world for everyone. And remember, the journey doesn't end here; this is just the beginning. There's so much more to learn, explore, and discover. So, take a deep breath, dive in, and embrace the adventure that lies ahead. Together, we can make a difference and build a brighter future for cybersecurity.

A BREATH OF TIME—SOME ADVICE FOR YOUR CAREER

We live in this world for only a breath of time, yet despite the intricate and improbable coincidences of our creation in the universe, here we are. Our time in this profession, on this planet, is only an instant. So, how will you use it? How will you let your curiosity guide you? Take a moment to look around and appreciate the little wonders that fill our everyday lives. If I could share one piece of advice to carry with you in your career, it would be this: every day is an opportunity to grow, to learn, and to make a positive impact for yourself and others.

Enjoy the burst of energy and possibility that comes with a fresh start, even if you don't fully see its power until years later. One day, you'll flip through old memories and marvel at the potential that once filled every moment of your early days in your career.

Act! Remember that your experiences shape the reality you live in. What truly matters are the outcomes you create. Every decision, every step, adds a brushstroke to the canvas of your career. Let your actions reflect your true worth, but never lose sight of the bigger picture. Success isn't about ticking boxes, it's about making a difference.

Don't get tangled up in worrying about what lies ahead. Cybersecurity often surprises us in the most unexpected ways, and these surprises can become our most valuable teachers. Instead of worrying over what you can't control, take a deep breath and trust that every experience, whether good or bad, if you stick to your values, will guide you toward a deeper understanding of the professional you are.

Explore! Every day, dare to do something that sets your heart racing, something that pushes you out of your comfort zone. It might be as simple as giving a hand to a colleague who needs help, speaking up in meetings, or volunteering for the assignment no one wants. Those little leaps of courage can open doors you never knew existed.

Learn! Never stop asking questions, never stop being curious. Understand how things work, because the questions you ask and the discoveries you make build the bridge from where you are to where you want to be. Curiosity lights the path forward as limits exist only until someone dares to go further. Create new routes and empower yourself to transform challenges into triumphs.

Be adaptable! As you travel through your career, don't be afraid to reinvent yourself. Embrace change as a natural part of your journey, and let every twist and turn inspire you to explore fresh ideas and new approaches. Incidents will arise, industries will shift, and the tools you use today may be obsolete tomorrow. Embrace it. Learn from your setbacks, and let each challenge remind you just how resilient you truly are.

Be empathic! Remember that each of us moves at our own pace, shaped by our unique experiences and perspectives. Risk management, and leadership, is about people. Every stakeholder, every colleague, every decision-maker brings a different perspective that enriches our process. Some are climbing a steep curve of change, while others are finding their footing in a new chapter. Embrace empathy by taking the time to understand where others are on their journey. That shared understanding can spark powerful transformations and create bonds that last forever.

Be kind with your words and manage your time wisely. Treat others as you wish to be treated, knowing that everyone carries their own hidden battles. Remember, time is your most scarce resource. Every moment is a gift that can never be reclaimed once spent. Guard it fiercely, learn to prioritize what truly matters over what feels urgent, and let each second count toward building the cybersecurity posture your organization needs.

Enjoy! The path we chose as our profession is demanding and complex. Cherish your memories and the people who stand by you, your family, your friends, and even those passing encounters that leave a mark on your heart. They are your anchors amid the whirlwind of change. Hold on to the lessons, the laughter, and even the tough moments, because they create the frame of your unique story.

So, laugh! Dance! Celebrate! As much as you work hard protecting your organization, you will find that a big piece of your resilience comes from managing your emotions when the world seems to be against you. At times, it might even test your confidence. Live every day with a spirit of adventure and purpose. Guard your inner light as you would protect your skin on a sunny day. Your cyber risk management journey is a canvas waiting to be painted with bold colors, honest emotions, and the remarkable results of your determined efforts.

Keep your eyes open to what is happening around you, and let others see the strengths in you. Remember: every day is a new chance to create something amazing, to achieve results that speak to your values, to leave something better than you found it, and to drive change with empathy and relentless curiosity.

Illustration credits

Figure 1.1 Template used from Dreamstime Image ID 76231167 © Polegaevmark.
Figure 3.1 Template used from Dreamstime Image ID 318034196 © Vectorcreator.
Figure 3.2 Templates used from Dreamstime Image IDs 144828295, 95741716 and 124849000 © Zdenek Sasek.
Figure 5.2 Template used from Dreamstime Image ID 38942326 © Kittisaktaramas.
Figure 7.1 Templates used from Dreamstime Image IDs 333402735, 113171170 and 137726458 © Onyxprj; © Golden Sikorka; © Svetlana Varadinac.
Figure 12.1 Template used from Dreamstime Image ID 50040181 © Aleksey Telnov.

Index

Note: Page numbers in *italic* refers to Figures.

A

Access control (AC) management, 28, 148
Account management, 27
Actual risks, 13, 153
Adcock, F. E., 37
Administrative closure, 212
Advanced analytics tools, 296
Aerospace & defense (A&D) facilities, 73
AI Management System (AIMS), 312–313
AI Risk Management Framework (AI RMF)
  comprehensive mapping exercise, 311
  continuous learning and adaptation, 312
  continuous monitoring, 311
  governance framework, 310–311
  Govern function, 310
  manage function, 310
  mapping, 310
  measure function, 310
  risk identification and prioritization, 311–312
  risk management strategies, 311
  risk measurements, 311
  scenario planning and stress testing, 312
  stakeholder engagement, 312
  transparency and explainability, 312
Annual loss expectancy (ALE), 11, 135, 136, 292
Annual rate of occurrence (ARO), 11, 135
Anomaly detection tools, 182
Application hardening, 185
Application programming interfaces (APIs), 133, 263
Application security testing (AST), 186
Application software security, 28
Ariely, D., 39, 97
Arrival rates, 234
Assurance process, 224, 258–262
Attack trees, 132
Attribute-based access control (ABAC) model, 172
Auditing
  and accountability (AU), 148
  log management, 28
  process, 173
  reports, 100
Authentication, authorization and audit (AAA) framework, 166, 169
Authentication management process, 172
Authorization, 172–173
Awareness and training, 187

B

Basic cyber hygiene, 29
Bayesian approach, 288–289
Bayes' Theorem, 288–289, 298–299
Biased perception of reality, 96
Buffer overflows, 186
Burndown rates, 234
Business area leaders, 57
Business continuity plan (BCP), 270, 279–280
  critical business functions, 277
  elements, 277–279
Business email compromise (BEC) attacks, 244
Business environment
  acknowledge threats, 110
  anonymity, 113
  checklists, 122–124
  deadline and reminders, 113
  documentation, 122
  finance and senior management, 108
  front-desk operators, 112
  goals, 113, 119–120

governance structures, 108
GRC tool, 113
human resources (HR), 108
information-gathering techniques, 109
information management, 107
internal and external contexts, 107
IT department, 108
legal department, 108
on-site workshops, 116
opportunities, 110
participants, 114
privacy officer, 108
questions, 113
sales department, 108
strengths identification, 109–110
structure of, 117–118
supply management, 108
survey, 113
SWOT analysis tool, 109, 111
threat intelligence sources, 121
weaknesses, 110
workshops, 116
Business impact analysis (BIA), 112, 269, 279–280
business operations, 270
principles, 271–272
RTOs, 270–271
Business process, 231
critical assets and dependencies, 105
identification, 105
process flow diagram, 105
scope of, 105
stakeholders, 105
Business-side infrastructure, 291

C

Canadian Centre for Cyber Security, 227
Center for Internet Security (CIS), 17, 184–185
Controls v8.1, 27–29
Chancification, 295
Change management, role of, 3
Chaos theory, 40
Chief Information Security Officer (CISO), 32–33, 56–57, 84–85, 291
CIS RAM framework; *see also* Factor Analysis of Information Risk (FAIR)
CIS Controls, 21
legal and regulatory requirements, 21
Cloud Security Alliance, 256
Cloud service providers, 244
Cloud storage, 276
Command and control (C2), 132
Common Vulnerability Scoring System (CVSS), 103
Communicating policies, 38
Communication planning, 209
Complexity theory, 40
Compliance metrics, 232
Compliance Officer, 57
Compliance teams, 247
Compromised credentials, 244
Computer Security Resource Center (CSRC), 19
Confidential business strategies, 308
Configuration management (CM), 148
Configuration management database (CMDB) system, 114–115
Continuous vulnerability management, 28
Control costs, 154
Corporate governance
clear policies and procedures, 44
education and training, 44
2008 experiment, 39
human resources (HR)
communicating policies, 38
cybersecurity awareness and training, 38
handling security incidents, 38
performance management, 38–39
recruitment and onboarding, 37–38
leaders, 41
leadership involvement, 43–44
open communication channels, 44
organizational culture, 37
peer influence, 39
recognition and rewards, 44
risk appetite concept, 42
secure behaviors, 40–41
social conformity, 39–40
Switch book, 42–43
Crisis management
business schools, 283
communication, 281–282
definition, 280
ISO 22361, 281
leadership, 281
normal operations, 281
organizations, 283
preparation, 282
ransomware group, 284
regular training sessions, 282
Critical Infrastructure Protection (CIP), 53
Cross-site scripting (XSS), 186
"Crown Jewels", 127–129
CRYSTALS-Dilithium algorithm, 317
CRYSTALS-Kyber algorithm, 317
Customer payment information, 127, 189
compliance failure, 129
data breach, 129
internal threats, 129–130
system failure, 130
Cybercriminals, 244
Cyber resilience, 4, 237, 268, 279–280, 325–326
BCP, 270
continuous improvement, 270

definition, 269
DRP, 270
readiness, 269
responsiveness, 269–270
Cyber risks, *10*, 11
management team, 57
Cybersecurity awareness and training, 38
Cybersecurity champions, 57–58
Cybersecurity culture; *see also* Corporate governance; The Govern function
assets and risks, 48
baseline, 48
communication and buy-in, 48
culture of security, 48
definition, 36
effectiveness of, 48
lack of awareness, 47
policies and procedures, 48
regulatory compliance, 48
resource allocation, 48
threat landscape, 48
training and education, 48
Cybersecurity Framework (CSF), 17
Cybersecurity & Infrastructure Security Agency (CISA), 227
Cyber threat intelligence, 254
Cyble Vision Platform, 227
Cyentia Institute, 227

D

Data breaches, 274
risk estimation, 193
Data flow diagrams, 99
Data loss prevention (DLP), 133
Data protection impact assessment (DPIA), 246
Data recovery, 28
Data segregation factor, 255
Decision-makers, 96
Decommissioning process, 265
Denial-of-service (DoS), 274
Dependencies
complexity, 106–107
role of, 106
Detected to undetected incidents, 232
Detection controls, 148
Developers, 186
Device logging, 185
Device security, 185
Difficulty communicating risk, 52
Digital resilience, 73
Digital Risk Protection Platform, 227
Disaster recovery plan (DRP), 112, 270, 279–280
elements, 276–277
resilience strategy, 275–276
Discretionary access control (DAC) model, 171
Doerr, J., 81
Doyle, A. C., 125
Drucker, P., 163
Due diligence process
Cloud Security Alliance, 256
collaboration, 254
cyber threat intelligence, 254
data segregation factor, 255
integration of, 253
liability clauses, 257
PII/financial records, 254
RFI and RFP, 253
solutions, 256
subcontractors/fourth parties, 255
tools, 256
vendors, 255, 257
Dynamic application security testing (DAST), 186

E

Effective information distribution, 210
Email and web browser protections, 28
Employee training programs, 195
Encryption protocols, 151
Endpoint device hardening, 184–185
Endpoint protection, 184–185
Enterprise architecture (EA), 114–115
Executive Leadership Team (ELT), 291, 293
External context
competitors, 101
cyber insurance, 102
cybersecurity and risk management, 103
description, 98
economic factors, 102
environmental factors, 102
geopolitical matters, 102
information inventories, 103
law enforcement, 102
laws and regulations, 101
perspectives, 101
talent pool, 101–102
technological advancements and industry requirements, 101
third parties, 102
threats, 101

F

Factor Analysis of Information Risk (FAIR), 17
financial figures, 21–22
quantitative data, 23
risk assessment, 23–24
risk management, 24
risk scenarios, 22
structured and systematic approach, 21

Falcon Adversary Intelligence
platform, 227
Feedback loops, 235
Fermi estimation, 298
Financial resources, 100
Firewalls, 149
Foundational cyber hygiene, 29
Frameworks; *see also* CIS RAM framework; NIST RMF framework
industries, 16
NIST 800–53, 25
security and standards, 17
security control, 25
well-managed organization, 16
Fundamental metrics, 230–231

G

General Data Protection Regulation (GDPR), 53, 247
Generative AI; *see also* Quantum computing
AI-generated phishing emails, 309
algorithms, 306
benefits of innovation, 313–314
bias, 309
capability, 309–310
cross-referencing, 309
ethical implications, 309
extensive datasets, 308–309
tokenization, 307
Goodhart's law, 230
Governance; *see also* The Govern function
allocation of, 32
collective priority, 33
cybersecurity, 32
NIST CSF 2.0 functions, 33
Governance, Risk, and Compliance (GRC), 69, 260
The Govern function
aspects of, 34
compliance, 35
continuous improvement, 35
cyber ecosystem, 34
NIST CSF 2.0, 33–34
nonnegotiable policies, 35
organizational context, 34
supply chain risk management, 35
Groundwork
action plan, 81
challenges, 75
checklists, 87–88
CIO and IT leadership, 84
CISO, 84–85
core forces, 90
COSO, 72
curve of change, 77
digital landscape, 86–87
digital resilience, 73
executives, 76
gap assessments and compliance checks, 72
GlobalCorp, 84, 86
Knowing-Doing Gap, 75–76
Kübler-Ross Change Curve, 77
newcomers, 74
objectives, 82
OKRs, 81–83
P&L, 73
stages, 77–79
stakeholders, 84

H

Hallucinations, 313
Hardware supply chain attacks, 243
Health Insurance Portability and Accountability Act (HIPAA), 53, 247
Heuer, R. J., 229
Howard, R., 290
Hubbard, D., 288
Human resources (HR), 57
and vendors, 100
Humphrey, A., 109

I

Identity and access control, 168–169
Identity management systems, 172
Immutable backups, 276
Impact assessment and likelihood of risks, 10, *10*
compliance failure, 141–142
control effectiveness, 135
environmental/safety impacts, 139
exposure, 135
financial cost, 139
financial impacts, 138, 143
historical data, 135
interdependence, 134
legal and regulatory impacts, 138–139
moderate impact/frequent likelihood, 142
motivation, 135
operational disruptions, 141, 142
operational impacts, 138
qualitative analysis, 136–137
quantitative methods, 135–136
reputational impacts, 139, 140
resource availability, 135
skills of threat, 135
threat landscape, 135
typical risk heatmap chart, 140

velocity, 134
vulnerability, 134
Incident Command System (ICS), 284–285
Incident response plans (IRP), 28, 148, 182–183, 269–270, 279–280
communication, 275
documentation, 275
eradication, 275
NIST SP 800-61 and CISA, 273–274
playbooks, 274–275
structured approach, 272
Incident response teams (IRTs), 269–270
Inconsistent risk assessment, 51
Industrial-side infrastructure, 291
Ineffective risk treatment, 51–52
Information and technology inventories, 99
Information inventories, 168–169
Information Risk Forum, 214
Information Security Forum, 44, 45, 51, 56, 214
Information security management system (ISMS), 19
Information Security Program Charter, 44
Inherent, actual and residual risks, 202
Inherent risk, 12
Integrated change control, 211
Integrated cyber risk management, 236
Intellectual property (IP) loss, 73
Interactive application security testing (IAST), 186
Internal auditors, 132, 226
Internal context
audit reports, 100
business objectives and strategies, 100
culture and company's history, 100
data flow diagrams, 99
description, 97–98
financial resources, 100
human resources and vendors, 100
information and technology inventories, 99
network diagrams, 99
safeguards and controls, 100
vulnerabilities, 99–100
Internet Crime Complaint Center (iC3), 227
Intrusion detection systems (IDSs), 180
Intrusion prevention systems (IPSs), 149, 178
Inventory and control
enterprise assets, 27
software assets, 27
ISO 27001/2 security management program, 291
ISO standards, 324
IT and cybersecurity teams, 57

J

Jobs, S., 327

K

Kennedy, J. F., 46
Key encapsulation mechanism (KEM), 317
Key performance indicators (KPIs), 60, 222, 229–230
Key risk indicators (KRIs), 60, 62, 222, 229–230
Knaflic, C. N., 301
Kübler-Ross Change Curve, 77, 88

L

Lack of accountability, 51
Last sign-in notifications, 173–174
Legal/logistical hurdles, 247–248
Leverage advanced analytics, 314
Life tables, 234
Lloyd, F., 207
Lockheed Martin Kill Chain Framework, 149
Logistics Corp. network, 248–250

M

Malware defenses, 28
Malware infections, 274
Managed service providers (MSPs), 244
Mandatory access control (MAC) model, 171
Maximum acceptable outage (MAO), 271
Mean time to resolve (MTTR), 231
Microsoft Defender XDR Platform, 227
Misaligned priorities, 51
Misinterpretations/assumptions, 15
Mitigation strategy, 188, 192
Mobile device management (MDM) solutions, 185
Mobile device security controls, 185
Monte Carlo simulation, 289–291, 294, 299
definition, 294
multiple trials, 294
probability distributions, 294
results, 294–295
Multi-factor authentication (MFA), 169

N

National Institute of Standards and Technology (NIST), 17, 310; *see also* NIST RMF

Network and Information Security (NIS) Directive, 53–54
Network diagrams, 99
Network encryption, 181
Network infrastructure management, 28
Network security
  challenges, 179
  concepts, 179
  description, 176
  design and implementation, 179
  edge routers, 180
  OSI Model, 176
  technical controls and technologies, 179
  virtualization security, 179–180
Network segregation, 181
Network vulnerability assessment, 292
New product introduction (NPI), 73
NIST Cybersecurity Framework, 324
NIST 800-53 framework
  access control, 25
  assessment, authorization and monitoring, 25
  audit and accountability, 25
  awareness and training, 25
  configuration management, 25
  contingency planning, 26
  definition, 25
  identification and authentication, 26
  incident response, 26
  information processing and transparency, 26
  maintenance, 26
  media protection, 26
  personnel security, 26
  physical and environmental protection, 26
  physical security measures, 25
  planning, 26
  program management, 26
  risk assessment, 26
  supply chain risk management, 26–27
  system and communications protection, 26
  system and information integrity, 26
  system and services acquisition, 26
NIST RMF framework
  assess, 18
  authorization, 18
  categorization, 18
  communication and consultation, 20
  context establishment, 19
  CSRC, 19
  implementation, 18
  ISO 27005:2022, 19
  monitoring, 18
  preparation, 18
  risk assessment, 19–20
  risk monitoring and review, 20
  risk treatment, 20
  select, 18
  system development life cycle, 18
NORM.INV() function, 295
North American Electric Reliability Corporation (NERC), 53

O

Offboarding process
  decommissioning process, 265
  effective communication, 265
  IT services/data handling, 263
  leveraging tools, 266
  ongoing security obligations, 264
  physical security, 263
  shredding/incineration, 264
  vendors, 262
  well-executed offboarding process, 265
Offline backups, 276
Ongoing risk monitoring, 60, 226–229
Open communication channels, 44
Open Systems Interconnection Model (OSI Model)
  application layer, 177
  cyber threats, 178
  data link layer, 177
  FTP/HTTP, 178
  modern networks, 178
  multilayered defense strategy, 178
  network layer, 177
  physical layer, 176–177
  presentation layer, 177
  session layer, 177
  transport layer, 177
Organizational planning, 208–209

P

Patching cadence, 232
Patch management, 175
Payment Card Industry Data Security Standard (PCI DSS), 53, 189, 247
Payment Card Industry (PCI) program, 230
Payment processing system, 151
Penetration testing, 28, 186
Performance metrics, 262
Personally Identifiable Information (PII), 127, 246, 308
Personal reality, 95, 96
Phishing attacks, 244, 274
Physical security
  building materials, 184
  description, 183
  geographic location, 183
  geopolitical factors, 184
  multi-tenancy, 184

Ponemon Institute, 227
Porter, M., 104
Potential Cyber Risk, 9
Privacy Impact Assessments (PIAs), 100
Private communications, 308
Privileged access management (PAM), 172
Process control network (PCN), 291
Project Management Body of Knowledge (PMBOK)
  closing phase, 211–212
  execution phase, 209–210
  initiating phase, 208
  monitoring and controlling phase, 210–211
  planning phase, 208–209
Project Management Institute (PMI) approach, 207
Project plan execution, 209
Public-facing web applications, 292

Q

Qualitative risk assessment, 302–303
Quality assurance, 209
Quality control, 211
Quality planning, 208
Quantitative risk assessment, 302–303
Quantum computing
  binary system, 315
  computers, 316
  encryption, 317
  resilience, 316
  superposition, 315
Quantum-safe cryptography, 318
Quantum Threat Timeline Report, 317

R

RACI matrix, 58, 59
Ransomware incidents, 274
Reconnaissance, 131
Recorded Future platform, 227
Recovery point objectives (RPOs), 112, 271
Recovery time objectives (RTOs), 112, 270
Recruitment and onboarding, 37–38
Redundant array of independent disks (RAID), 276
Regular audits and reviews, 171
Regular reporting, 235
Regulatory and compliance issues, 52
Request for information (RFI), 253
Request for proposals (RFP), 253
Residual risks, 13, 154
  after avoidance, 191
  after mitigation, 198
  after transference, 198
  after treatment plans, 204
Resource planning, 208
Response controls, 150
Return on investment (ROI), 152, 196
Risk acceptance, 218–220
Risk analysis, 58
Risk appetite, 12, *12*
Risk assessment; *see also* Impact assessment and likelihood of risks
  assessment phase, 126
  assets, 128
  attack scenarios, 147
  attack trees, 132
  brainstorming sessions, 130–131
  business objectives, 127
  checklists, 131
  "Crown Jewels", 127–129
  cyberattacks, 145, 147
  definition, 125
  external factors, 129
  HR department, 130
  inherent and actual risks, 145–146
  interconnected systems, 129
  internal audits, 132
  interviews and surveys, 131
  issues of, 132–133
  quick judgments, 127
  revenue losses, 144
  risk exposure, 138
  scenario analysis, 131
  threat modeling, 131
  vulnerability assessments and penetration testing, 132, 133
Risk Assessment Method (RAM), 17
Risk capacity, 13
Risk characterization, 58, 60
  actual risk assessment, 157
  actual risk levels, 161
  consensus, 156
  control effectiveness, 161
  critical assets, 160
  cyber risks report, 156–157
  data breach scenario, 158
  data handling protocols, 158
  description, 154
  document risk assessment, 161–162
  dynamic and continuous process, 159
  flexibility and adaptability, 156
  gathered information, 160
  inherent impact, 160
  inherent likelihood, 161
  leadership, 154–155
  potential risks, 160
  risk levels, 161
  risk matrix, 155
  stakeholders, 160
Risk exceedance curve (REC), 292
Risk identification, 58

Risk Management Framework (RMF), 17
Risk management planning, 208
Risk monitoring; *see also* Ongoing monitoring
  assurance process, 224
  data collection and management, 224
  defense model, 225, 226
  effective change management, 228
  internal and external contexts, 221
  internal auditors, 225, 226
  internal governance structures, 225
  IT and cybersecurity teams, 225
  KPIs and KRIs, 222, 224
  proactive, 222, 223
  SMART criteria, 222
  statistical reports, 227
Risk owner, 57
Risk quantification, 301, 304
Risk register
  applicable regulations and standards, 53–54
  CIS Controls V8.1, 67
  confidentiality, 68
  definition, 52
  Excel workbook, 69–70
  GRC tools, 69
  guidelines, 54–56
  management tool, 65, 66
  new risks, 67
  NIST 800–53, 68
  performance indicators, 60–62
  power BI cyber risk management dashboard, 63
  process map and description, 58, 60
  purpose and scope, 53
  ROI, 66
  roles and responsibilities, 56–58
Risk Review Board, 214
Risk tolerance, 12
Risk treatment plan analysis, 13, 60, 201
  avoid risk, 164
  business objectives, 163
  controls of, 166
  endpoint protection safeguards, 167
  formal risk acceptance, 166
  mitigation, 164
  transference strategies, 164, 165
  vulnerability and patch management, 166
Role-based access control (RBAC) model, 171–172

S

Safeguards/controls, 13
Savage, S. L., 295
Schedule control, 211
Secure web gateways (SWGs), 180–181
Security audits, 151
Security awareness, 28
Security Information and Event Management (SIEM) system, 182, 227, 228
Security Operations Centers (SOCs), 227
Security technology, 233
Segmenting vendors, 248
Seiersen, R., 288
Separation of duties (SoD), 170–171
Service-level agreements (SLAs), 143
Service provider management, 28
Shackleton, E., 71
Sinek, S., 50
Single loss expectancy (SLE), 11, 135–136
Skills training, 28
Social conformity, 39–40
SOCRadar platform, 227
Software versions, 168
SolarWinds breach, 243
Specific, Measurable, Attainable, Relevant, and Timely (SMART) criteria, 222, 230
SPHINCS+ algorithm, 317
SQL injection, 186
Stakeholders, 96
Standard for Project Management, 207
Standard operating procedures (SOPs), 111
Static application security testing (SAST), 186
Storage area networks (SAN), 276
Strict access controls, 195
Subcontractors/fourth parties, 255
Supply chain risk management, 26–27
Supply management teams, 246
Survival rates, 234
System and communications (SC) protection, 26, 148
System and information integrity (SI), 26, 148
System and services acquisition, 26

T

Tailored communication, 235
The Tay incident, 307–308
Team development, 209–210
Team members, 96
Technology environment visibility, 231
Technology inventories, 167–168
Third-party incidents, 274
Third-party risk management, 4; *see also* Assurance process; Due diligence process
  attackers, 242

complexities, 243
compliance teams, 247
ISO 27036-1 and ISO 27036–2, 250
ISO 27036-3 and ISO 27036–4, 251
IT departments, 247
legal department, 246
legal/logistical hurdles, 247–248
organizations, 252
Orion software updates, 243
phishing attacks, 244
PII, 246
principles and practices, 241
privacy and compliance teams, 246
range of vulnerabilities, 242
segmenting vendors, 248
SolarWinds breach, 243
supply chain management, 253
technical and compliance aspects, 242
Threat intelligence, 9, *10*, 121, 226–227, 234
Threat modeling, 3
Time-based access, 174
Tokenization, 307
Transport layer security (TLS), 177, 181
Treatment plans
implementation
design phase, 213
effective communication, 214–215
final cost estimation, 214
IT teams, 213
organization's risk landscape, 216
project management process, 212–213
setting realistic timelines, 215
timing, 214
versions, 215–216
owners, 57, 60

U

User access behavior management, 170

V

Value at risk (VaR), 12, 136
Virtual local area networks (VLANs), 177
Virtual private networks (VPNs), 179, 180
Vulnerability, 9, *10*
actual risk, 13
ALE, 11
ARO, 11
inherent risk, 12
likelihood, 11
residual risk, 13
risk appetite, 12, *12*
risk capacity, 13
risk tolerance, 12
risk treatment plan, 13
safeguards/controls, 13
SLE, 11
VaR, 12
Vulnerability and patch management, 174–175

W

Weak foundations, 47
Weaponization, 131
Web application firewalls (WAFs), 187
Web proxies, 180
World Economic Forum, 227

Z

Zoom/Microsoft Teams, 115